T0192554

LEVEL DESIGN

PROCESSES AND EXPERIENCES

LEVEL DESIGN

PROCESSES AND EXPERIENCES

CHRISTOPHER W. TOTTEN

CRC Press
Taylor & Francis Group
Boca Raton London New York

CRC Press is an imprint of the
Taylor & Francis Group, an **informa** business

AN A K PETERS BOOK

CRC Press
Taylor & Francis Group
6000 Broken Sound Parkway NW, Suite 300
Boca Raton, FL 33487-2742

© 2017 by Taylor & Francis Group, LLC
CRC Press is an imprint of Taylor & Francis Group, an Informa business

No claim to original U.S. Government works

Printed on acid-free paper
Version Date: 20161109

International Standard Book Number-13: 978-1-1386-2880-9 (Hardback); 978-1-0322-7671-7 (Paperback)

Library of Congress Cataloging-in-Publication Data

Names: Totten, Christopher W., editor.
Title: Level design : processes and experiences / edited by Christopher W. Totten.
Description: Boca Raton, FL : CRC Press, [2016] | Includes bibliographical references and index.
Identifiers: LCCN 2016028360 | ISBN 9781498745055 (pbk. : acid-free paper) | ISBN 9781315313412 (ebook)
Subjects: LCSH: Level design (Computer science) | Computer games--Testing.
Classification: LCC QA76.76.C672 L478 2016 | DDC 794.8--dc23
LC record available at https://lccn.loc.gov/2016028360

Visit the Taylor & Francis Web site at
http://www.taylorandfrancis.com

and the CRC Press Web site at
http://www.crcpress.com

To my parents for teaching me that nothing comes easily

Contents

SECTION IV **Testing Levels**

Acknowledgments

THIS BOOK WOULD NOT EXIST WITHOUT CHRISTOPHER BUSHMAN. It is from our discussions of level design, film theory, and game-building processes at Game Developers Conference (GDC) that this book came about. There are a great many others who have assisted in this book's production that I will attempt to acknowledge here (sorry if I miss anyone).

I would like to thank the staff at AK Peters/CRC Press for allowing me to develop this project for publication, especially Rick Adams and Jessica Vega. Likewise, I would like to thank my wonderful reviewers Jeff Howard, Matthew Kramer, Tom Dowd, and Sarah Hope Scoggins.

Probably the biggest thanks goes to my wonderful contributors, Gavin Greene, Daniel Johnson, Huaxin Wei, Chaoguang Wang, Heidi McDonald, Scott Rogers, Fares Kayali, Josef Ortner, Chanel Summers, Gillian Smith, Brian Upton, João Raza, Benjamin Carter, Dr. Mark R. Johnson, Joel Burgess, Dr. Alessandro Canossa, Jonathan Moriarty, and Hadar Silverman. This book is primarily their words and it has been an honor to have them in this volume.

Thanks also to the organizers of the GDC for putting on an event that allows game developers, writers, teachers, and students to meet and make valuable networking connections, some of which made this book possible. Thanks also to the GDC Conference Associate program for being such a wonderful part of my life and allowing me to get to GDC in the first place.

Many thanks go to my supportive colleagues at the American University Game Lab: Joshua McCoy, Mike Treanor, Anne Sullivan, Benjamin Stokes, Lindsay Grace, and Bob Hone. I'd also like to thank the DC and Baltimore game development communities and chapters of the International Game Developers Association (IGDA) for being such great collaborators. Thanks to the dev team for my current project for allowing me the time to put this book together.

Lastly, I must thank my parents, who this book is dedicated to, for teaching me the hard work and perseverance that has gotten me into the game industry. Finally, I want to thank my amazing wife Clara, who makes me a better professional, person, and father.

Editor

Christopher W. Totten is the game artist in residence at American University in Washington, DC. He is the founder of Pie for Breakfast Studios, a DC-area independent game studio, and founder of the Smithsonian American Art Museum Indie Arcade. Totten is an active writer in the game industry, with articles featured in industry journals, chapters in several academic publications, and two books: *Game Character Creation in Blender and Unity* (Wiley 2012) and *An Architectural Approach to Level Design* (CRC 2014). He has also spoken at GDC China, Foundations of Digital Games (FDG), East Coast Game Conference, Digital Games Research Association (DiGRA) conference, and Games for Change, and displayed his games at MAGFest, The Smithsonian Innovation in Art event, and Baltimore Artscape. He earned a master's degree in architecture from The Catholic University of America in Washington, DC.

Contributors

Joel Burgess is a game developer specializing in open-world and level design, and is currently a world director at Ubisoft Toronto. He spent 11 years at Bethesda Game Studios, where he cofounded the level design group that helped create *Fallout 4*, *The Elder Scrolls V: Skyrim*, *Fallout 3*, and *The Elder Scrolls IV: Oblivion*. He previously worked for the now-defunct Terminal Reality in Dallas, Texas, where he contributed to *Bloodrayne 2*, *Aeon Flux*, and *Demonik*. Joel helps organize and present the Level Designer's Workshop at both GDC San Francisco and GDC China in Shanghai. He earned a BA in digital media from the University of Central Florida and owns too many dogs.

Alessandro Canossa is associate professor at Northeastern University. He has worked both in the game industry and in academia. In the industry he covered roles such as level designer, game designer, and game analytics consultant for a wide variety of games, from titles focused at children (*LEGO*, *HUGO*) to franchises intended for more mature audiences (*Hitman*, *Tomb Raider*). As a researcher he focuses on user-centric design and evaluation methods, employing psychological theories of personality, motivation, and emotion to investigate individual differences in behavior among users of digital entertainment. He coauthored the first book on game analytics, a milestone publication in a burgeoning field that is being used to evaluate user experience and behavior in a variety of game environments.

Benjamin Carter earned a BA in philosophy from George Washington University. He has a published paper in philosophy and is a regular commentator and critic of video games.

Gavin Greene travels in the freelance realms of both game production and gaming industry press. From 2012 to 2014, he acted as associate producer with independent developer-publisher Phoenix Online Studios, helping to bring titles like *Cognition: An Erica Reed Thriller* and the 20th anniversary edition of Jane Jensen's *Gabriel Knight: Sins of the Father* to life. His coverage on the industry has been published in a variety of online outlets, including *Gay Gamer*, *Elder Geek*, and *GamesBeat*. He has acted as a judge for several series game showcases and spoken on the topics of community management and game writing at events sponsored by the International Game Developers Association and Game Developers Conference.

Daniel Johnson is an enthusiast game writer and the author of *Game Design Companion: A Critical Analysis of Wario Land 4*. Through his writing and collaborative work, Daniel advocates for a more constructive discourse around video games. He believes that through sharing a common vocabulary and grounding our arguments with clear examples, we are able to stay on the same page and better make sense of the complex, interdisciplinary medium that is video games. Daniel's writing draws on his experience as a language teacher, a profession he feels enlightens his understanding of the functional and pedagogical aspects of game design.

Mark R. Johnson is a postdoctoral fellow in game studies in the Science & Technology Studies Unit at the University of York. The main focus of his work is currently on eSports and professional gaming, and he has published papers on these topics, game aesthetics, gambling and gaming, hacking and modding culture, arcade gaming, strategy games, games and cinema/literature, and the media politics of games. He is currently working on his first monograph, *The Unpredictability of Gameplay*, to be published by Bloomsbury Academic. In addition to his scholarly work, he is a retired professional poker player, a multiple arcade game world record holder, a freelance game writer, the cohost of the *Roguelike Radio* gaming podcast, and an independent game developer and designer of the experimental roguelike game *Ultima Ratio Regum*, inspired by the literary works of Umberto Eco, Jorge Borges, and Wu Ming. More information on his academic work, game development, and gameplay can be found at www.ultimaratioregum.co.uk.

Fares Kayali is a game designer and researcher living and working in Vienna, Austria, and earned a PhD in computer science. Fares has headed the design of several digital games that were finalists at IndieCade and the Independent Games Festival and has presented his work at renowned international conferences including Games for Change, GDC, Games, Learning, & Society (GLS), Games for Health, and DiGRA. He works as a postdoctoral researcher at the Vienna University of Technology and the University of Applied Arts Vienna, and he is cofounder of the Positive Impact Games Lab. Fares lectures in game design at several Austrian universities and is principal investigator of the game-based learning project Sparkling Games and the art-based research project Breaking the Wall—Playful Interfaces for Music Audience Participation. His research interests include game design, music and interactivity, serious and positive-impact games, media, and game art as well as topics around human-computer interaction (HCI) at the intersection of health care and technology.

Heidi McDonald (Deathbow) is a writer, composer, and game designer whose award-winning work with Schell Games includes *PlayForward: Elm City Stories* (an HIV prevention game created for Yale University School of Medicine), *The World of Lexica* (a literacy game for grades 6–8, created with Amplify Education), and *Orion Trail* (2016 IGF Honorable Mention for Excellence in Narrative). Winner of Women in Games' Rising Star Award in 2013, McDonald's independent research about romance in single-player role-playing games (RPGs) has resulted in multiple academic publications and highly rated lectures around the world, including at four GDCs. Currently, McDonald serves as the creative director for iThrive Games, an organization that supports developers who make games promoting positive psychology concepts in adolescents. She is also pursuing releases of independent IPs under her LLC, Deathbow Productions. A bawdy piratess and unrepentant wearer of magnificent hats, McDonald seeks to fill the world with more ABBA, more cupcakes, and more games that do good and positive things for the human race.

Jonathan Moriarty is a freelance game developer living and working in Baltimore, Maryland. In addition to working with local game companies, he is the founder of Ganglyfish, a small independent game team working on releasing original intellectual property (IP) games for PC and consoles. He is an active participant in the local game development community, serving as chair of the Baltimore chapter of the IGDA. He showcases many of his games at events in the Baltimore-Washington area, including Gamescape at Baltimore's Artscape, the Smithsonian American Art

Museum Indie Arcade, and the MAGFest Indie Videogame Showcase. His areas of interest include game jams, design, code design, and the development and analysis of interesting game mechanics. He earned a BS in computer science and a BA in visual arts from The University of Maryland, Baltimore County.

Josef Ortner is an independent game designer and game researcher from Vienna. He creates applications and games for the iPhone and designed augmented reality (AR) and location-based games at the Vienna University of Technology and the University of Applied Arts Vienna. He also teaches game design and game programming at the Danube University Krems.

João Raza has been working in the game industry for more than six years in a variety of roles. Currently he is a program manager at Microsoft where he oversees various game system development kit (SDK) scenarios. He has published papers on the Game Programming Gems and GPU Pro series. His games have been selected for Seattle Independent Expo and Seattle's iFest. He holds a bachelor's degree in computer science from Universidade Federal de São Carlos.

Scott Rogers is a game designer and creative director of more than 50 AAA games for Disney, Sony, Capcom, Namco, and THQ on titles such as *God of War*, *Pac-Man World*, *Darksiders*, *Maximo*, and *Drawn to Life*. His games have sold over 50 million copies worldwide and are greatest hits. As an Imagineer, Scott helped create interactive games for Disney's theme parks. He currently lectures and teaches video game level design at the University of Southern California's prestigious school of Interactive Media and the New York Film Academy. His first tabletop game *Rayguns and Rocketships* is being published by IDW Games in 2017. Scott authored two books on game design, *Level Up! The Guide to Great Video Game Design* and *Swipe This! The Guide to Touchscreen Game Design*. Both books are top sellers and are used as the foundation of video game design curriculums at universities all over the world. He earned a BA in fine arts and a BA in screenwriting from California State University at Long Beach. He currently lives in Los Angeles with his family and many, many games.

Hadar Silverman is an independent game developer with Earthborn Interactive, which he founded in 2012. With a bachelor of architecture from Pratt Institute, he has over 10 years of architectural experience, 7 years of which were in the transportation industry. This experience, combined with a focus in computer graphics, has led to a continued study in the development of virtual reality content, game design, and experimentation with linking virtual worlds and real worlds. He has presented his work at several festivals and venues including the Smithsonian American Art Museum, NACE Conferences, Baltimore's Gamescape, and several tech festivals local to the Baltimore/Washington region.

Gillian Smith is an assistant professor at Northeastern University in game design and computer science. Her research focuses on procedural content generation, computational crafts, and gender issues in games. Her work has been published in *IEEE Transactions on Computational Intelligence and AI in Games*, ACM CHI, the Foundations of Digital Games conference, and the International Conference on Computational Creativity, among other venues. Her games have shown in festivals including the Smithsonian American Art Museum Indie Arcade, ACM CHI Interactivity, and Different Games conference. She has also been an invited speaker at the AI Summit at the Game Developers Conference. Gillian earned her PhD in computer science from the Center for Games and Playable Media at UC Santa Cruz in 2012. She lives outside Boston, Massachusetts, with her husband, son, and goofy rescue pit bull.

Chanel Summers is cofounder of Syndicate 17 and director of the USC School of Cinematic Arts Experimental Audio Design Lab. A pioneer in the field of interactive audio, Chanel has been a highly regarded game producer and designer, Microsoft's first audio technical evangelist, and a member of the original Xbox team, helping to design and support the audio system for that groundbreaking console and creating the first ever support team for content creators. A highly regarded touring drummer, Chanel now owns and runs her own audio production and design company, Syndicate 17, lectures and educates around the world on subjects as diverse as the aesthetics of video game audio, world building, and secondary-level Science, Technology, Engineering, and Mathematics (STEM) education for young women, and consults for a variety of innovative technology companies. Chanel serves as a lecturer and director of the Experimental Audio Design Lab at the USC School of Cinematic Arts, artistic director at Forest Ridge School of the Sacred Heart, external examiner at the Dublin Institute of Technology, and technology advisor to acclaimed virtual reality company VRstudios, Inc. Chanel can be reached at www.syndicate17.com.

Brian Upton is a senior game designer at Sony's Santa Monica Studio where he has collaborated with third-party teams on titles such as *Fat Princess, Warhawk, Sorcery, Escape Plan,* and *Everybody Has Gone to the Rapture.* Prior to joining Sony in 2002, he was the creative director at Red Storm Entertainment where he pioneered the tactical shooter genre as the lead designer of *Rainbow Six* and *Ghost Recon.* He is a member of the advisory boards of the NYU Game Center and the UC Santa Cruz Games and Playable Media program. He is also the author of *The Aesthetic of Play,* a book about the relationship between play, narrative, and meaning, which was published by MIT Press in the spring of 2015.

Chaoguang Wang is a PhD candidate in the School of Design at the Hong Kong Polytechnic University. His research interests focus on user studies enriched with physiological measurement, player experience, and game design. Previously he worked as a game designer and researcher for more than six years at NetEase Inc., China, where he helped to develop the major massively multiplayer online role-playing game (MMORPG) title, *Fairy Tale,* from concept through delivery and live operation.

Huaxin Wei is an assistant professor in the School of Design at the Hong Kong Polytechnic University, where she teaches game design and interaction design. Her research interests include interactive storytelling, game design and analysis, and human-computer interaction. Her research on game narrative has resulted in a descriptive framework for systematic analysis of video games using a variety of structural perspectives, demonstrated by various case analyses in several published works. Huaxin earned a PhD in interactive arts and technology from Simon Fraser University, Canada, and an MSc in computing science from University of Alberta, Canada.

Introduction

IN BOTH THE COMMERCIAL VIDEO GAME INDUSTRY AND ACADEMIC GAME DESIGN PROGRAMS, we are paying closer attention to the goals of gameplay design and defining the aesthetics of well-designed interactive works. Each year at venues like the Game Developer's Conference (GDC), postmortem analyses of famous games by their developers, design tutorials, and the Experimental Gameplay Workshop are among the most popular events on the schedule for developers hoping to expand their knowledge. After nearly two decades of consistent design writing, developers have many choices to help them find the next killer game mechanic, tell a great interactive story, or apply their game design knowledge to solve real-world problems. Great game designers are revered in the industry like great Hollywood directors—visionary auteurs whose ideas drive innovation—and many new designers are clamoring to get in on this creative action.

Game design is more than just the games themselves, however. In a panel on the place of games in museum collections at the Music and Gaming Festival (MAGFest) in 2016, I was on a panel with Brock Rough, a doctoral candidate exploring the question of whether games are art. His main argument, to poorly paraphrase, is that games themselves are not art, but rather the combination of a myriad of artistic works that combine to create an interactive experience. Whether one agrees with this answer to a very contentious question or not, there is truth in it from a production standpoint. Games are more than the sum of the many works that go into creating them. Events like MAGFest and other fan-focused conventions are great at pointing this out: the music from games is covered by bands in different styles, the artwork from games is recreated and remixed into strong visual work, and game stories are fondly remembered and retold. As an industry, however, we are still focused on studying games as wholes. The cracks in this approach show when new designers try to dive deeper into the fields that collaborate to form a whole game—art, user experience design, sound design, and others—and cannot find much beyond manuals for development software. Level design, the thoughtful execution of gameplay into gamespace for players to dwell in* and traditionally seen as a subset of game design, falls into this trap.

At industry events, I've spoken with a lot of level designers and collegiate-level design instructors about this issue. Many express frustration at the lack of specific level-design writing available beyond tutorials for game-engine-level editors. Students often comment that level design is something they would like to see additional specialized instruction in beyond the few lessons in their general game design courses. What they see is that their game design knowledge has taught them to create great mechanics and stories, but they need to learn how level designers arrange these elements into a satisfying experience: controlling things like gameplay instruction, pacing, and distribution of rewards.

As we dig deeper into game design we are realizing that level design and other aspects of game making are fields in their own right that need their own deep inquiry.

WHAT IS THIS BOOK ABOUT?

The idea for this book began one evening during the yearly GDC when I was talking with a colleague of mine about level design writing. He commented that it would be great to see a volume exploring the thought processes of level designers as they work and wondered if I'd considered writing something like that. As only one designer, I was intimidated by such a task: most level designers have different approaches based on the specific game they are working on and methods can vary from designer to designer. Likewise, the industry is not devoid of people sharing level design knowledge. At GDC there is a yearly tutorial series called "Level Design in a Day" that features industry veterans discussing their approaches to creating gamespace. Likewise, websites like World of Level Design (worldofleveldesign.com), level-design.org, Gamasutra (gamasutra.com), and others offer tutorials and short articles on design concepts. I thought, therefore, that a good approach would be to create a resource that gathered sources like these into one place.

That is why this book about level design is not written by just one author, but is instead a collection of 16 writings organized into four sections on topics relevant to level design.

---

* Totten, Christopher W. An *Architectural Approach to Level Design*. Boca Raton, FL: CRC Press. 2014.

Beyond just the words of game developers, this collection features writers approaching game levels from the perspectives game players, journalists, academics, industry veterans, commercial developers, indie developers, and so on. They have formed their own processes for designing high-quality game worlds based on experiences playing games or working for studios. This book offers knowledge from 16 such professionals representing a cross section of voices like those mentioned above. In this book you will find practical-but-evergreen (i.e., not software-dependent) advice on building game levels, educational theories on introducing new mechanics to players, advice on using popular games as inspiration for your own work, and a myriad of other things to put you on the path to finding your own way as a designer of meaningful gameplay experiences.

WHAT THIS BOOK WILL TEACH YOU

Each chapter is written with an eye toward providing takeaways relevant to current level design practices. The utilized approach groups chapters based on whether they primarily approach level design from the perspective of a player, designer, constructor, or tester. The chapters in this book will teach you about the following.

Analyzing as you play

Just as an important part of being a filmmaker is understanding movies, an important part of being a game designer is playing games. Throughout several chapters, the authors demonstrate ways in which playing games has informed their own design work. Among others, you will find a writer observing how popular games make better gameplay by not laying out gamespaces like real spaces and a producer who gains inspiration from how Japanese open-world games manage 3D art assets. Likewise, you will also find academic frameworks that help better understand the design of many games and how they communicate with players.

Design approaches

In addition to documenting successful elements of existing levels, many chapters provide overviews of a designer's methods or general design philosophies. A diverse array of writers has led to a diverse set of perspectives on considerations to use as design goals. Examples include indie developers creating strongly mechanic-centric levels, an audio designer who makes sound design an integral part of her process, and historical analyses of level types. Many chapters provide insight into what a designer finds important as they plan their own game worlds.

Construction methodologies

Beyond analyzing and planning game worlds, the chapter authors also share their approaches to constructing levels that fit their design goals or that create emotional experiences. Examples include how pacing action with stillness creates effective horror sequences and how open-world designers can properly distribute points of interest. Construction-based portions of this book provide practical theory and examples of how levels may be assembled to create interesting experiences for players with contemporary engines and tools.

Playtesting methodologies and considerations

Lastly, this book will offer insight into the process of testing your levels with players to create optimal experiences. Iteration is a vital part of the level design process, and getting feedback from testers is an important part of ensuring each iteration of your level is moving toward your original vision. Inside are chapters from indie developers describing their approach to showing games in public, data-driven approaches to identifying player personas, and considerations for testing virtual reality games. These topics will provide ideas for designers responding to player feedback on their work.

WHAT THIS BOOK WILL NOT TEACH YOU

While this book offers a range of topics relevant to level designers, there are other topics that are beyond its scope. This section exists to alleviate any confusion over the content of this book.

Game Engines

Game engines are software packages that contain premade frameworks for making games run. These packages include software that controls how games are rendered on screen, how they handle physics, and how inputs are handled, among other things. These packages also often contain level editors that many new designers are eager to master.

While this book features a lot of practical information that can be implemented in contemporary game engines like Unity, Unreal, Lumberyard, Construct, and Game Maker, it does not contain tutorials for these software packages or level editors. This is done so that the book can focus on evergreen design topics that will be relevant long after current game engines are obsolete. Information on learning game engine software can be found either in an array of quality books or in online tutorials.

Environment Art and Art Software

Likewise, this book does not provide information on how to operate software used to create environmental art or be an environmental artist. Environmental art is comprised of the objects, props, and architectural pieces littered throughout game environments that form a level's geometry. Software used to create these pieces include 3D Studio Max, Maya, and Blender for 3D models and Adobe Photoshop, the GMU Image Manipulation Program (GIMP), Quixel, or Substance Painter for textures and materials.

This book treats environment art as a distinctly different discipline from level design, as it mainly deals with the creation of art assets used to create levels, while level design is about creating gameplay experiences for players through the arrangement of art assets, interactive objects, and scripted game events. This distinction is important both to keep the book focused and to allow the chapters of the book to comment on how environment art can be used by level designers to communicate with players effectively.

Production Management

Production management refers to how software development teams schedule deadlines and meetings to optimize their creative output. There are different management frameworks like Scrum, Waterfall, and Agile that lead to efficient development timelines in the industry.

While several chapters refer to the need for effective development production management in the level design process, this book does not offer in-depth instruction in any of these methods. Many of the methods contained in this book may be integrated into these frameworks and interested designers are encouraged to do so. Like the software packages described above, there are publications and online materials available that describe these methods.

WHO SHOULD READ THIS BOOK

This book is a series of essays written by practicing game analysts, reviewers, developers, and academics about level design. While it does not have tutorials on how to operate game engine or environment art creating software, it does provide practical industry-relevant insights on methods and approaches used across the game industry. If you are reading this in a bookstore or browsing online deciding if you would like to purchase this book, you may want to see if you fall into one of these groups.

Practicing Game and Level Designers

One of the primary goals of this book is sharing level design methods between sectors of the industry. In this way, game developers can greatly benefit from its content. Contained within are workflows, developer testimonies, and analyses that can be beneficial to many game development teams. Many new level designers find that information on level design theories or processes beyond software tutorials are rare, so this book introduces evergreen methods from industry veterans to help fill that void.

Academics/Instructors

As with professional game developers, this book looks to provide both practical information and design philosophies from qualified and noteworthy authors. In this way, the methods within can be utilized both as useful precedents for practical courses on game development and as citations for game design research. Chapters are written to maximize takeaways for readers, so they are appropriate for instructional courses in level design.

Students

As with instructors, students can benefit from the material within as both a supplement to practical instruction in level design software and as a source of citations for assignments. For someone spending a lot of time learning the software tools of level design and environment art, this book provides testimonies from industry veterans that can help new developers start making their own game levels with some expert guidance.

WHAT'S INSIDE THIS BOOK

As stated previously, this book's goal is to approach level design from four distinct perspectives while offering multiple voices in each topic area. Level design benefits from general spatial concepts, such as how humans react to height, but workflow-centric information can differ from game to game and designer to designer. The writers of these chapters come from varied backgrounds—teachers, writers, industry veterans, architects, and others—and take diverse approaches to how they view game worlds.

Experiencing Levels

Section I, "Experiencing Levels," features essays on playing game worlds and how these worlds influence the player outside of the game itself. The section begins with "Kamuro Nights: A Personal Retrospective of the *Yakuza* Series" by game journalist and writer Gavin Greene. Through his explorations of Kamurocho, the fictionalized Tokyo red-light district from Sega's *Yakuza* series, Greene discusses how his interactions with the games' consistent environmental setting has influenced him at different points of his career, from player to producer.

Next, teacher and writer Daniel Johnson's "Cracking the *Resident Evil* Puzzle Box" explores how classic *Resident Evil* levels control the pacing of information introduction to players so they can form mental models that guide them through the game. Featured in this chapter are a number of progression models that level designers, particularly ones interested in puzzle design, may find useful. "From Construction to Perception: Three Views of Level Design for Story-Driven Games" by assistant professor Huaxin Wei and PhD candidate Chaoguang Wang presents a framework for playing games and analyzing levels as storytelling spaces. By combining spatial and narrative analysis, this chapter treats levels as instruments for delivering narrative. Finally, game writer and designer Heidi McDonald's "Everything I Learned about Level Design at an Orlesian Ball" describes the valuable lessons one designer learned from playing *Dragon Age: Inquisition*. Like other chapters in this section, the designers' own personal gaming history becomes the precedents for their own design work, and shows how continued gameplaying introduces new inspirations. This mix of gameplay with game design also serves as a bridge into the next section on planning levels.

Designing Levels

This section deals with processes and methods for planning levels. It begins with veteran game designer of the *Maximo* and *Pac-Man World* series Scott Rogers's "Hell, Hyboria, and Disneyland: The Origins and Inspirations of Themed Video Game Level Design," a history of themed level design. This chapter is a designer's notebook of themes and historical precedents to help level designers create interesting combinations of popular environment types. Designing with historical precedents is again seen in "Level Design Practices for Independent Games" by indie developers Fares Kayali and Josef Ortner. These designers present methods for developing strong mechanically driven levels that are tested with several iterations through case studies of their work and those of other designers.

"Making the Most of Audio in Characterization, Narrative Structure, and Level Design" by Syndicate 17 founder and sound designer Chanel Summers outlines audio-centric considerations for level designers. In this chapter, methods for setting emotional tone with audio, pacing the sounds of your level, and mapping your level's audio are outlined so that designers may incorporate quality sound into their game from the beginning of development. Lastly, *Threadsteading** designer and artificial intelligence (AI) researcher Gillian Smith's "Procedural Content Generation: An Overview" offers a typology of methods for generating game levels with artificial intelligence systems. It not only covers technical aspects, but also highlights the different ways that players interact with procedurally generated content. This mix of practical advice and design-driven methods sets up the next section on building levels.

Constructing Levels

In the industry, there is a divide between the theoretical elements of game design and the practical elements of developing and building games. This section presents practical methodologies from industry veterans used in popular game productions. Sony Santa Monica Senior Game Designer Brian Upton begins the section with "*P.T.* and the Play of Stillness," which analyzes the horror game *P.T.* and outlines a process for building player experience through moments of inactivity, choice, and consequence. Here Upton lays the groundwork for a method he calls situational game design, which builds experiences with an awareness of moment-to-moment interactions. Next is "The Illusion of Choice: How to Hide the Linearity of Levels from Players" by Microsoft Program Manager João Raza and video game critic Benjamin Carter. This chapter outlines progression patterns that game designers can use to hide the perception of linearity in levels. Their method includes practical tips for incorporating art and sound assets as well as narrative segments to expand a player's perception of freedom in game worlds.

Procedural level generation gets a second look in *Ultima Ratio Regum* designer Dr. Mark R. Johnson's "Integrating Procedural and Handmade Level Design," which demonstrates how traditional level design may be used in games along with procedural generated (computer-assembled)

---

* An experimental game played on a sewing machine, codeveloped with Disney Research Pittsburgh.

levels. This chapter weighs the benefits and challenges of each method and finds a way for both to coexist to create interesting game worlds. This section ends with UbiSoft World Director Joel Burgess's "Level Design Planning for Open-World Games," where he shares world planning techniques used in the *Elder Scrolls* and *Fallout* series. Burgess covers documentation of game world features and how to visualize the distribution of points of interest in game worlds before working in-engine.

After exploring these practical elements of level design, the book moves on to an often overlooked aspect of level design: testing.

Testing Levels

Many experienced level designers will tell you that they did not create their best work out of thin air. Great level design comes from iterating, testing multiple times, and making changes after each test. This section features writers documenting their own processes for testing levels with players.

Alessandro Canossa, an associate professor and game industry consultant, begins the section with "Play-Personas: Mental Tools for Player-Centered Level Design," which outlines processes identifying common player behaviors into personas that designers can plan around. This chapter is presented with case-studies from popular games. In indie developer Jonathan Moriarty's "Evaluating Level Design Using Public Events," the author outlines his typical setup for testing games at public events such as game conventions or art festivals. He then discusses his latest game, *Lost Cave*, and how several of its levels have changed based on feedback given at these events.

Architect and game designer Hadar Silverman's "The Rule of 27s: A Comparative Analysis of 2D Screenspace and Virtual Reality Environment Design" presents spatial and design considerations for developers creating virtual reality (VR) games. This chapter compares traditional concepts of scale, navigation, and other elements of games and discusses how they can be implemented in VR based on his own extensive tests with the hardware. Lastly, my own chapter, "Expression versus Experience: Balancing Art and Usability Needs in Level Design" describes my process for creating a game based on a famous piece of art and the challenges balancing the expressive elements of the artwork with the needs of a game design.

SUMMARY

Level Design: Processes and Experiences gathers an exciting collection of writings on a traditionally underserved element of game design writing and scholarship. Beyond discussing level design theory, this book considers the perspective of players, designers, developers, and analysts in multiple applications of gamespaces. Contained within are chapters describing how existing levels can be precedents for new design ideas, how designers plan their spaces, the multiple methods for building these spaces, and advice on presenting these spaces to players. Included are stories of learning to make games, level theme typologies, discussions of procedural generation, methods for mapping out large worlds, and other things to benefit level designers from novice to expert.

I

Experiencing Levels

CHAPTER 1

Kamuro Nights

A Personal Retrospective of the Yakuza *Series*

Gavin Greene

CONTENTS

FOR ABOUT ONE HUNDRED and fifty hours of my life, I have been a Japanese gangster.

On three different occasions over the past eight years, I have smuggled myself into the Tojo clan and acted on execution orders with varying degrees of brutality. I have wooed dozens of women over karaoke and tonkatsu, lost millions at mahjong, and beat a street thug to death with a ten-speed bicycle. I have been Kazuma Kiryu, a man who—despite his best efforts—cannot escape the criminal underworld of Kamurocho.

Sega has published entries in their *Yakuza* open-world crime drama series (known natively as Ryū ga Gotoku, or "Like a Dragon") since late 2005. The franchise has been roughly on a yearly release schedule since, with seven main entries, five spin-offs, and multiple remakes. Franchise director Toshihiro Nagoshi and the *Yakuza* design team within Sega settled on a core formula almost from the get-go: inviting players to live out the life of a Japanese mob enforcer through hundreds of street fights, elaborate cut-scenes, and a massive world of sin and distraction.

Despite the franchise persisting for over a decade, the team has deviated little from this core aesthetic. Whether each new game takes place in a vision of current-era downtown Tokyo or an idyllic interpretation of the Edo period, players make use of the same fundamental skill sets and fall into largely unaltered routines. The designers' collective ability to stave off tedium despite demanding hundreds of player hours in the same location is the crowning achievement of the *Yakuza* franchise.

Kamurocho, a fictionalized red-light district of Tokyo, has remained the central fixture of the Sega design team's interactive urban planning across an entire in-game generation of continuity. *Yakuza*'s core neighborhood has thrived over the years (both real and in-game) thanks to a keen eye for constant, steady aesthetic refinement and iterative design. Most impressively, Sega's *Yakuza* team has demonstrated a remarkable understanding of the emergent behavior seen in tangible cities through the relationships and behavior exhibited by Kamurocho's nonplayable denizens. And as a result of it all, provided an excellent example of an effective, flexible cityscape primed for virtual tourism.

Each time I have returned to Sega's gangland series has been—by happenstance—during a major turning point in my career. As my appreciation and understanding for game design has grown, the flexible bedrock of *Yakuza*'s Kamurocho district has invited and substantiated multiple layers of sophisticated and involving design work.

VISITING: PLAYING KAMUROCHO AS A GAMER (*YAKUZA*, 2007)

Before we begin this dissection of memory in earnest, I must acknowledge the unique lens through which I will be analyzing this series. As a gamer living within the Western market, the *Yakuza* series has not been released as a yearly franchise. Most *Yakuza* spin-offs have never been localized, and English translation of main series entries has often taken years. This delay between experiences puts me in a much different position than native players, as does interacting with the majority of the series through a subtitled language track.

The plot of the first *Yakuza*, and indeed most of the series, revolves around a one-time *Yakuza* enforcer by the name of Kazuma Kiryu. Kiryu has just returned to Tokyo after enduring a 10-year prison sentence, having taken the heat for a crime committed by a friend. The Tojo Clan, a crime organization of which Kiryu is a member, is robbed of 10 billion yen (or one hundred million dollars). Kazuma is swept up in the underworld's search for the lost money, and along the way befriends a young girl with possible connections to the theft.

My first visit to Kamurocho was at the very start of what became an erratic but persisting career in both game culture and development. I had only returned to games the year before, following a period of several years between earnest childhood console play and a world-weary dry spell during high school. But even in my halcyon days with controllers and memory cards, I was limited to parents with a budget and an inclination to encourage more proactive activities. By the time I first stepped into the slick shoes of Kazuma Kiryu, I had only been "core" for about a year.

Up until this point, my knowledge of game design and criticism was limited only to a barrage of second-hand terminology and discussion topics picked up from the first generation of YouTube-based industry coverage. I knew enough at this entry-level point of my career to dominate any conversation in a video game retailer, but functionally not much else. My introduction to Kamurocho was a purely experiential one, guided by whatever side or main story quest activity that caught my interest at any particular moment.

Truth in Advertising

Kamurocho, although fictional, is strongly based on the Kabukicho neighborhood in Tokyo's commercial Shinjuku ward. *Yakuza*'s more interactive take on the district shares—not outright pilfers—its most noticeable street layouts and landmarks from this real-life equivalent, including the series' de facto emblem: a red-framed, lighted entry sign welcoming visitors to the main thoroughfare of Tenkaichi Street. The real and fictional districts also share reputations. Kabukicho also operates as a red-light district, colloquially referred to as the "sleepless town."

What first sold me on Kamurocho and *Yakuza* were, coincidentally enough, the signs and people trying to sell items and admissions to in-game events. Street-side barkers hawking discount admissions to their nightclubs, scantily dressed women passing out café flyers, all of it was reminiscent of a big city Main Street one might reasonably come across in any country. Convenience stores sold products pulled from real life, appearing in separate inset screens when selected with market-accurate labels viewable at all angles.

In-game advertising has been a long-running point of contention between players and producers. But here—perhaps due to my not being constantly exposed to these native Japanese brands—products were placed well enough (and offered in a diverse enough variety) to fold into Kamurocho's overtly capitalistic aesthetic and effectively function diegetically.

These weren't just a few licensing deals made by the publisher and tossed in as the game went gold. If there was a stipulation in any of the marketing contracts to smear logos and trademarks carte blanche across all in-game surfaces, it was pleasantly ignored. Instead, these real-life products acted as a sort of novelty catalog, on display with appropriate shelving under reasonably authentic banner advertisements. They looked to be lit, animated, and rendered in the same fashion as the labels of the fake, in-game brands.

Most examples of product placement deemed egregious by critics and players revolve around scaling up brands beyond any reasonable reach the product would have in the real marketplace: Second-tier cola brands with animated logos in sports stadiums, or popular candies having print ads plastered across a subway station. Kamurocho is drowning in advertisements, but most appear to be accurately placed in terms of market share and intended demographics. Energy drinks are in convenience stores, Sega's name is plastered on an arcade marquee, and useless trinkets pop up out of a chute when a quarter is put in a prize machine.

And Kamurocho's commercial enterprises come across as oddly endearing for it all. The visual product assault, be it for tangible or fictional goods, is equal in density and range to what players unconsciously expect from major commercial districts. Nothing sells the idea of a healthy, trade-rich city district than being assaulted with ads with every step.

This act of selling something to a player proved an apt excuse for the *Yakuza* team to showcase a strong sense of pride in their unreal neighborhood. Both real-life and fictional products come with lengthy descriptions about their flavor and composition. A connoisseur of any one pastime will likely find their depth of pedantic knowledge about their hobby reflected in its digital equivalent within Kamurocho. Anyone with an affinity for alcohol, for example, will recognize the kind of lofty pitches about aging processes and regional distinctions given for one of the many—sadly virtual—scotches in each game.

Being absorbed by the advertisements naturally drew my eyes to the buildings the ads were placed on. Shops, offices, and living spaces were scrunched together in tight clumps. These dense clusters gave Kamurocho an immediately personal connection, being reminiscent of some of my favorite districts of my own nearby metropolis of San Francisco. The lack of available ground space had forced the buildings of Kamurocho into creative uses of vertical space, giving signage and marquees a steep quality that helped distinguish each of Kamurocho's boroughs.

The core layout of *Yakuza*'s fictional red-light district city has barely changed over the course of the franchise and is spread across multiple neighborhoods. The player is most frequently brought into town through the south entrance at West Showa and Tenkaichi streets beneath the aforementioned landmark sign. The next few blocks operate as an intense chokehold of gameplay tutorials and narrative activity, as the nightclubs Serenity and Stardust play a seismic role in the series. These two establishments would continue to hold significance as the series scaled up to include multiple stories and even building rooftops.

Bordering this thoroughfare are the Nakamichi Alleys, the thrift store and burger chain sister neighborhood to Tenkaichi's nightclubs and cafes. Further east is the isolated, poor Champion District, sitting beneath the West Park area that dominates the Northeast section of Kamurocho.

The district's largest buildings are collected in the upper Northwest portion of the map. Both the Hotel District and Theater Square divvies out space between hotels, sports clubs, and arcades. Lastly, central to both the district and the plot of several *Yakuza* adventures is Millennium Tower, a massive business-commercial complex with a view of the entire neighborhood.

These neighborhoods become second nature to players over the course of each *Yakuza* playthrough, in function if not in name. The vast majority of your time with Kazuma Kiryu is running between objectives, cutting across side streets and alleys to save time while failing to avoid getting into scraps with the local riffraff.

Kazuma and the player would be drafted into the whims of one clan leader or another and set to various named buildings in the district. There, a person would need to either be talked to or beaten to near-death (sometimes both) before the plot could progress. Mission variety could vary at certain points of the game—and progressively more mechanically diverse objectives would be added as the series continued—but for this initial outing, life in Kamurocho was one that revolved around tongue wagging and fisticuffs.

In terms of basic gameplay structure, the *Yakuza* franchise is one of the dozens of intellectual property (IP) to arise in the wake of *Grand Theft Auto III*'s successful formula. A main plot thread is played out in portions of the map purposefully distant from each other, with a multitude of minigames teased at every step between story cut-scenes. The series also owes at least a portion of its distinctly Japanese aesthetic to the *Shenmue* franchise, an earlier open-world Sega series equally concerned with towns filled with side activities.

Fast travel is eventually introduced in each game, but the distance between objectives or side missions is never so great that players can't justify simply running to a map marker to avoid the more severe loading screens. The constant back and forth between objectives involve the player in a multitude of minute crowd interactions, from bumping into a few people every time you rush through some loiterers to being chased by all of the thugs you managed to avoid immediately triggering a fight with.

The Playground of the Real

But the driving force that kept my playthrough of this installment largely unconcerned with plot (aside from an incongruous English vocal track) was the universe of side activities and distractions constantly vying for attention and playtime. At any one point in *Yakuza*, one could conceivably go to the batting cages, an arcade, karaoke bars, a bowling alley, ramen shops, convenience stores, thrift stores, bars, and restaurants. This embarrassment of riches approach to microobjectives quickly became a defining feature of the brand, later entries expanding the side activity catalog to include (among others) mahjong, ping pong, massages, photo booths, dance competitions, rock-paper-scissors, and multiple variations of driving.

Here again the player could feel a tangible sense of civic pride from the design staff. The design team's dedication to engaging pastime approximations permeated each block of Kamurocho. It is apparent in each micro-objective that serious design time and resources were spent to ensure all virtual activities held as much potential for amusement as their tangible counterparts. Practically all side activities required their own control schemes, adapting the range of motion and input layout to the event at hand. Most modified controls borrowed from or otherwise emulated other gamified interpretations of an activity. While in the batting cages,

Kazuma and the player moved in a restricted, lateral range along the batter's box, aesthetically identical to the batting controls and camera angle seen in the majority of modern baseball games.

In terms of gameplay justifications, engaging in most of these activities fed either directly or indirectly into Kazuma's combat statistics and/or inventory. Eating pork ramen gave back some health, convenience stores sold items that granted attack boosts, and most everything else either yielded money, a new weapon, or a new defensive item. But my own reason for engaging in dozens of hours of narratively irrelevant minigame fluff can be summarized in another, more unique side activity: hostess clubs.

A Day in the Life

The business model of a hostess club is to simulate social interaction with a woman that a man can pay into through admission, ordering off drink and food menus, and buying gifts for their hostess. Most interaction between customer and hostess is through small talk and idle flirtation. In *Yakuza*, this relationship is gamified through an attraction meter that rises and falls based on the player's response to certain dialog options sprinkled throughout each conversation.

If I could attribute the *Yakuza* franchise's cult success in the West to one thing, it would be a kind of cultural voyeurism. This is not something commonly attributed to the game by fans or even the publisher itself, Sega of America opting to not include hostess clubs in the Western release of *Yakuza 3*. But Japan has held an almost mystical allure for many in the West, particularly pervasive in gaming communities given the country's place of prominence in game and hardware development. Games like *Yakuza* permit entry into a sort of removed performance of everyday life in Japan, with the safety of having complete control over most action inputs.

Within the pretense of an open-world action game, I could experience a proxy of eating foreign food and engaging in regionally distinctive activities. The approximated realism of Kamurocho's map helped reinforce a functioning sense of place, providing a level of authenticity to these activities. The player's control and preference over which activities were engaged in, as well as the progression of each activity, continues to give *Yakuza* a visceral edge over static representations of the same cultural institutions from the likes of travel shows or documentary programs.

But Kamurocho's effectiveness as a cultural window is most mechanically interesting when examined in the context of the transition of control and camera placement between basic exploration and minigames. Despite the elements in the heads up display (HUD) becoming more intrusive in side activities, the player is brought into a greater degree of intimacy with the world as play shifts to microobjectives.

When outside, our perspective hovers several feet above Kiryu in the air, with full camera and movement control afforded to the player. We retain that control when Kazuma enters the game's more open indoor environments, mainly office spaces and thrift stores, or anywhere with a walking area sufficient to conceivably transition to a fight scene.

But in most of the available minigames, the control scheme and camera placement shift dramatically. Some universal minigames, like the batting cages or bowling alley, will have an activity-appropriate control layout, the camera transitioning in a utilitarian rhythm to best showcase the cause-and-effect of the player's swing or ball roll. Contrast that with the more dramatic treatment of social behavior that is seen most frequently when ordering food or speaking with a hostess.

Through most of the game, prompts occupy the lower third of the screen, usually only requiring input from the player to progress or close a dialog or expository blurb of text. When Kazuma sits down to order food or chat with a hostess, not only is our control over the character restricted to cycling through and responding to text prompts, the user interface occupies a dramatically larger portion of screen real estate. Our perspective is still removed from Kazuma's, but at a much closer distance, the camera adopting either an eye-line or security-camera-style angle.

Prompts now operate on a scrolling menu, our selections frequently displaying a visual representation of a food item we have ordered, a prize we have won, or the level of a hostess' affection. The hostess clubs in particular are a sort of hybrid of the game's filmic cut-scenes and distant third-person camera. Conversations are cut into a three-camera setup (shot, reverse-shot, establishing) popularized in situation comedies, the interplay between Kiryu and his hostess of choice playing out like a television show.

This further splinters *Yakuza*'s often alluded-to Adventure-Battle-Event (or open-world roaming, combat, and cut-scene, respectively) gameplay dynamic. These minigames didn't offer me the same functional experience as exploring the environment, fighting thugs, or watching a cut-scene. Instead, minigames felt like microstage plays, little capsules of cultural approximation. A picture-in-picture displayed over the broader exploration of the district, made temporarily full-screen.

My avatar had a name, face, and relationships in the world, but for the vast majority of my time, I projected myself as a virtual tourist of Tokyo life through the face of Kazuma Kiryu. I am still functionally illiterate in Japanese and could no more pass off my in-game experiences here as any sort of meritorious component on an immigration form. But in playing *Yakuza*, I was introduced to elements of Japanese culture previously unknown in an identifiable and socially translatable way. The world became no less complicated by any stretch, but it did feel smaller.

RENTING: PLAYING KAMUROCHO AS CRITIC (*YAKUZA 3*, 2010)

In 2010, with *Yakuza 3*, Kamurocho became a full-fledged character. Kazuma Kiryu has effectively retired from the red-light district, opting to adopt a calmer lifestyle in an island town in (equally fictionalized) Okinawa. But fate conspires against Kiryu, an eminent domain conflict with the landowner of his orphanage and the shooting of the Tojo Clan chairman forcing the extremely reticent Kazuma back to Tokyo. This wouldn't be the last time land played an important role in a *Yakuza* narrative.

We spend the first several hours of the game away from Kamurocho in *Yakuza 3*, taking on missions and running around the smaller but equally dense Ryukyu Islands. Every subsequent main entry in the franchise adopted a similar policy of small environmental asides, with *Yakuza 4* adding multiple locations, including a full-fledged prison, to the wider *Yakuza* world before or in between the player's return to Kamurocho.

Within a production pipeline, these minor locations could be turned around faster than a brand-new map the size of Kamurocho. The environmental diversity also cleanses the player's palette before returning to spend the bulk of the game in a familiar borough. More importantly in this third installment, this new motif also served to characterize Kamurocho itself, casting the lighted sign over Tenkaichi Street as the figurative threshold of monomyth, one Kiryu is forced to cross again, once the main thrust of the narrative sets in.

My writing career in games had progressed into published criticism in the interim three years since my first *Yakuza* adventure. The studies and play hours related to my reviews immersed me enough in common design practices to recognize and appreciate the successful implementations thereof. Now that I knew where and how to look for them, the progressive narrative design of Kamurocho, the minute ins and outs of which were lost to me as a player some years earlier, were now readily apparent.

Planned Spontaneity

Most of the unspoken narratives in Kamurocho are a natural by-product of the designers' translation of true-to-life urban planning, even when the team is not directly referencing real-life equivalences in Kabukicho. A real-life city's layout will, if allowed to persist long enough, evolve organically with population trends to the point where it could effectively speak to its own past nonverbally. One could assess much of New York's life span by tracing population and demographic movements within a bureau at any given time. Similarly, Kamurocho's success in environmental narrative is its ability to have an apparent history despite never truly existing.

Yakuza 3 was the franchise's first main series entry on the seventh generation of hardware consoles (after the Japan-only spin-off Ryū ga Gotoku Kenzan! made the first console leap for the series a year earlier). The technological advancement was most heavily advertised through the team's improvements in character facial animation, largely present in the title's many lengthy cut-scenes. But the most tangible manifestation of the hardware upgrade was in the size and density of crowds shopping around the district throughout the game.

My rediscovery of Kamurocho as a living city came about with the recognition of the district's facsimile of spontaneous order particularly evident in crowd movement. Purposefully designing something intended to have a convincing appearance of not being designed is an uphill challenge in most production respects. Kamurocho's small map size—compared to other open-world game productions—would also mean any pockets of nonplayable character (NPC) behavior would be operating in close proximity to others within the environment, the player easily able to navigate between them quickly.

Admittedly, this is not one of *Yakuza 3*'s most successful design implementations. But given the available hardware capability of the time, the design team managed to construct enough interesting movement and grouping patterns to draw the attention of a wet-nosed games reporter. Crowd patterns and density indicated the profitability and popularity of nearby businesses. The pathfinding of individual NPCs within crowds may not have accurately mirrored the hike of an actual person through an actual town, but the intermingling walking areas and idle animations of NPC groups did give a decent representation of crowds hanging out at their favorite spots.

An NPC's preferred stomping grounds in Kamurocho was also reflected in their style of dress. Wealthy visitors and citizens congregated in the more upscale northern portion of the map, most visible in the Hotel District or Theater Square. Their range of postures, background conversations, and reactions to being jostled by the player were noticeably different from the crowds congregating around nightclubs. A business class that was equal parts stiff and formal, stressed and lecherous. Compare that to the loitering hostess club patrons, relaxed and casual, or rushed and annoyed.

Another subtle but key design element of Kamurocho's virtual citizenry is its attention to more realistic interpretations of racial identity. *Yakuza* is a rare series in that the designers endeavored to design its characters with more authentic Asian features rather than the more stylized, anime-influenced art aesthetics employed in a majority of localized games developed in (and depicting) Japan. The design team's casting of both its main and nonplayable cast as racially congruous to the region emulated within the game only furthered a distinctive sense of place that has since permeated Kamurocho across the entire franchise.

Space as Social Indicators

Combined with the design team's use of space, we can find a play on both poverty and social values being expressed in the environment of Kamurocho. Those enterprises on the intersection of popularity and social acceptability occupy the cleanest, most spacious districts of the map. The bowling alley, batting cages, and Millennium Tower offices all operate in the wide-open complexes and clean streets of the Hotel District and Tower Square.

As we approach the seedier districts of Kamurocho, where businesses are profitable but lack the benefit of a safe and family-friendly atmosphere, the occupied space becomes denser. These areas house the more audacious nightclubs and hostess clubs alongside the cheaper and less healthy restaurants. The same-size block that held half of a sprawling arcade now houses four separate offices on the second story, with a nightclub and a couple of shops sharing the ground floor. Tenkaichi Street and Nakamichi Alley have more people moving in tighter spaces, exponentially increasing a feeling of claustrophobia at street corners and other chokeholds.

Worst off in this environmental play of poverty is the Champion district, a comparative hovel of dirty, ramshackle housing projects with only the nearby bar as a balm. More, smaller housing units occupy each floor of the surrounding buildings, all of which face inward into a sectioned-off courtyard. There are only two entry/exit points for the Champion district, giving the impression of an animal curving itself inward into a ball for warmth.

Although the design staff's interpretation of Okinawa was the most prominent map extension, Kamurocho itself wasn't entirely left out of *Yakuza 3*'s overall environmental expansion. A new underground fighting arena—a host of gambling dens and shops dotting the single road leading up to it—was built into the area beneath Kamurocho Hills, an in-progress housing project occupying the area formerly known as West Park or Purgatory. Known as the Underground Coliseum, Kiryu can participate in a variety of less-than-legal mixed martial arts tournaments for story progression or stat-boosting.

This expansion is another production calculation in the vein of the Ryukyu Islands, another gameplay aside to season the average interest curve with visual and gameplay diversity. But the Underground Coliseum plugs into the urban metaphor of Kamurocho as well, both above and below ground. The Kamurocho Hills housing development can be seen as an act of gentrification. Middle-class ready living, blocks away from the most destitute projects in the district. And just below the surface, the criminal class is pushed into more flagrant and expansive illegality, the truer side of Kamurocho beneath the increasingly safe façade.

Yakuza 3 broadened my experience of Kamurocho from a mechanical playground to one steeped in environmental narrative. Its adherence to real-world city emulation brought with it—intentionally or not—an emotional resonance not dissimilar to the apparent histories visible in tangible cities and towns. The plot-irrelevant residents of Kamurocho didn't bare any individual resemblance to authentic citizens, but their placement en masse against the game's shifting socioeconomic backdrops did function somewhat akin to actual human traffic flow.

LIVING: PLAYING KAMUROCHO
AS PRODUCER (*YAKUZA 4*, 2011)

Yakuza 4 is the game that took Kazuma Kiryu out of the solo protagonist slot and further expanded the character of Kamurocho for me from a living city to a design inspiration. The addition of three playable leads expanded the game's story to an ensemble play revolving around the murder of a local gang leader, apparently by a woman named Lily.

By 2011, my design knowledge was passing into practical application. In starting to help design and build games (at this point for noncommercial release), I was growing increasingly aware of the design formulas that went into the creation of each usable production asset. Finally being able to recognize the *Yakuza* design team's clever environmental iteration, both exclusively in the fourth installment and across the series as a whole, was a watershed moment in my understanding of budgeted game design.

Urban Planning

In my prior ventures into Kamurocho, I had effectively been missing the design forest for the trees. Across the main entries of the franchise, the skyline of the fictional red-light district had been shifting, and in no uncertain terms. The aforementioned Underground Coliseum was held beneath a construction site that transitioned the game's largest park into a housing project, visible as three distinct environments (park, construction site, houses) across multiple games. Millennium Tower itself was blown up and rebuilt, its plot of land hosting cranes or completed buildings depending on the specific game.

As our playable character base expanded, so did our playable areas within and without the core district map. Kamurocho proper still exists as the chief ground level map of play, structurally and functionally identical to previous main series entries. The *Yakuza* design team added to that base a series of rooftops connected to certain neighborhoods, a parking garage, city sewers, and a subterranean strip mall. Some backstreets to Kamurocho were also playable, acting more as a separate-but-related extension similar to the Underground Coliseum of *Yakuza 3*.

Iterative Urbanism

This production style of adding assets on top of a flexible base structure has become a defining design philosophy of mine, beginning with the successive iteration on display in *Yakuza 4*. This latest version of Kamurocho in particular offered several templates for iterative design through asset reallocation and manipulation, all of which were scalable to a product's budget and scope.

On the grandest scale, we can return to the idea of new locations as gameplay asides, as discussed earlier. Like the Ryukyu Islands and the Underground Coliseum before it, one of the more expansive sets added onto Kamurocho in *Yakuza 4* directly reflected on the game's core location while simultaneously broadening its scope.

The rooftops of the red-light district offer views of the city at a new angle, both visually within the environment and metaphorically throughout the story. Long-standing Kamurocho buildings and signage within the district—formerly far above the character's (and often the camera's) head—are now frequently seen at eye level or from above. Altering the angle of an existing three-dimensional environment is not the most time-sensitive tactic, but it does have the effect of casting familiar iconography from a new perspective. The ability to run behind a familiar marquee and see its underside only furthered my appreciation for Kamurocho as an environment and the verisimilitude the developers were able to inspire.

From a production standpoint, adhering to a generic visual aesthetic of downtown rooftop design may have greatly reduced the expected asset turnaround. The final in-game rooftops are evocative of a function-over-fashion aesthetic designed to reflect the usability of various railings, roof-to-roof bridges, and scaffolding by workers. There is also the additional benefit of expressing a dynamic contrast between Kamurocho's lavish lights below and the dull pipe-work above.

Kamurocho's underground strip mall also proved a proof-of-concept for environmental connectivity through shared assets. Seeing the same ground textures in the floor and entering stores with space and stock laid out similarly to those above ground was—to my new designer eyes—a proof of concept for intelligent asset recycling. An example I still utilize in design documents to this day.

THE NEXT LEVEL

We are in the second generation of the Age of the Perpetual Level.

The growing relevance of the games-as-service model in mobile, e-sports, and high-budget AAA game development communities has shifted the production focus of many of the most profitable design teams. A focus on reusability dots more production pipelines now than ever before. With expected player hours rising on all fronts, the levels and maps that get priority are frequently those that can most conceivably stand up strongest against hundreds if not thousands of play sessions per user.

Visual diversity is still highly valuable across all game design types. But when you are designing for a prospective player base that will be engaging with your game on a daily basis, sometimes for considerable lengths of time, intricate maps with branching pathways that account for multiple gameplay styles are the ones that find the most success. And the more your production budget is a concern, the more a smaller environmental selection with greater complexity is going to be at a premium.

Kamurocho's carry-over nature is most likely a child of these kinds of budget and time demands. Yet from that crushing design albatross came a breathing and thriving perpetual environmental with a unique tangibility. This fictional district of Tokyo was made real to me in the same way that new, physical locations grew on me, by laying the groundwork for a constant state of discovery.

I effectively piloted Kazuma Kiryu through the same in-game acreage at three points in my life, but rarely as the same person. As my expertise on the intricacies and execution of game design grew, the bedrock of Kamurocho held up to new scrutiny and offered different but equally complex insights. I first came to town a virtual tourist, then as an environmental detective, and finally as a greenhorn developer. And through it all, the affection held for the district by the *Yakuza* design team was both exposed and made self-evident through play.

A surprisingly well-appointed bar, nestled in a hard-to-reach corner in Kamurocho, has a couple of exclusive drink items on the menu. Among them is a cocktail by the name of Kamuro Nights. The drink is licorice-flavored, served in a martini glass, on the rocks. What makes it unique is that each ice cube is a different flavor of frozen fruit juice, representing the lights of the city against the night sky.

It tastes awful in real life. But to read how the bartender describes it is to see one man—albeit digital—express his love for the neighborhood.

CHAPTER 2

Cracking the *Resident Evil* Puzzle Box

Daniel Johnson

CONTENTS

I N LATE 1994, CAPCOM USA started putting together marketing plans for *Biohazard*, an upcoming survival horror game for the Playstation. The publisher would not be able to use the game's original Japanese title for the Western release due to copyright issues, prompting the head of marketing to hold a company-wide competition for the best new name. Ideas were put forth and votes were tallied, with the team settling on *Resident Evil*.

Resident Evil. The two words do not quite sit right together and yet time has eased the pair into collocation. The title has a strange dichotomy of interpretation to it. I remember when I first heard the name as a kid. I inferred it in a grisly, *Lord of the Flies*-esque way as the sort of barbaric evil that manifests inside ordinary citizens, those who live among us, but which is imprisoned by social order. My twelve-year-old self, upon seeing those two words in magazines, would feel heavied by the title's brooding undertones. Yet for all my adolescent pondering, the name is premised on a pun: the evil has taken residence in the mansion; it is a "resident evil." One interpretation is serious and abstract, while the other is silly and literal. It is a dichotomy, I would argue, that is fundamental to understanding classic *Resident Evil* (the first three games and *Code Veronica*; herein collectively referred to as *Resident Evil*).

Outwardly, the games exhibit a thick layer of B-movie cheese. Like the pun of the series' title, the poor script writing and stilted voice acting make it difficult to take the games seriously. These elements of context constitute the silly and literal side of *Resident Evil*. They are immediate and apparent and we understand them well. Video games are often mistakenly regarded as products of low culture on such grounds of context. This is unfortunate because, as *Resident Evil*'s dichotomy demonstrates, the artistry of the video game medium tends to lie deeper. What engages the players of *Resident Evil* is the puzzle box environment and the mental models, planning, and execution required to solve it. This system of design constitutes the serious and abstract side of *Resident Evil*. It is the part of the series we appreciate, but also the part of the series we have difficulty talking about.

With the release and sales success of *Resident Evil HD Remaster*, recent at the time of this writing, there appears to be a renewed appreciation of the original puzzle-environment design. Consider the announcements of further remakes and talk of *Resident Evil 7* being a return to series roots, and one might go as far to say that classic *Resident Evil* is due for a renaissance. It is under this not-so-prerendered backdrop that this chapter will attempt to unravel the mystery of classic *Resident Evil* puzzle box design. We will begin by looking at the mechanisms of the classic *Resident Evil* puzzle box. Afterward, we will apply this understanding in an extended analysis of *Resident Evil: Code Veronica*. This analysis is presented in such a way that it is accessible regardless of one's level of familiarity with the *Resident Evil* series.

DEFINING THE *RESIDENT EVIL* KNOWLEDGE GAME

This chapter will explore the knowledge game that underpins classic Resident Evil (*Resident Evil, Resident Evil 2, Resident Evil 3: Nemesis,* and *Resident Evil: Code Veronica*; herein referred to as *Resident Evil*). In real-time action games such as *Resident Evil*, knowledge of the game world and the dexterity, reflex, and timing needed to defend oneself against enemies are both essential sets of skills, and different players will strike a different balance between the two. For the purpose of this chapter, though, we are focusing almost exclusively on the mental challenges that take place in the player's mind.

One of the comments often made about *Resident Evil* is that the series is puzzle-like in nature. The games do indeed contain puzzles quite separate from the main course of gameplay (the bookshelf puzzle in *Resident Evil 2* or the oil level puzzle in *Code Veronica*, for instance), but I think this comment speaks to something more deeply embedded in the games' fabric.

Lock and Key Progression

A helpful starting point when articulating core gameplay is to identify the barriers put in the player's path (locks) and what must be done to overcome them (keys). In action games like *God of War, Ninja Gaiden,* and *Devil May Cry,* the player is usually confined to small enemy-filled arenas by gates and other artificial barriers. Defeating the enemies brings down the gate mechanism. The relationship between the key (player actions used to defeat the enemies) and the lock (barriers) allows the designers to establish the core gameplay, in this case combat. This simple example gets us thinking in the right direction, which is particularly helpful for games with a more diverse gameplay palette, such as *Resident Evil*.

In *Resident Evil,* two forms of locks engineer player progression: *item locks* and *boss battles*. An item lock—whether that be a control panel with a missing lever, a statue in need of two gemstones, or, quite simply, a locked door—can be opened with an *item key*. Boss battles are set piece peaks in the game's pacing, usually isolated confrontations with a large enemy with sophisticated movement and attack patterns. *Resident Evil*'s moment-to-moment gameplay tends to be dictated by item locks and keys more so than boss battles, which are few in number.

In this sense, we can see how *Resident Evil* evolved out of the progression format established in point-and-click adventure games, which are entirely about putting item keys to item locks. An important distinction, however, is the ease of *Resident Evil*'s problem solving. Deducing that the blue key opens the blue door hardly qualifies as a test of knowledge skills—neither are putting the square-handled crank in a square-shaped hole or using an ice pick to clear a keyhole blockage.

In point-and-click adventure games, the obscure relationship between locks and keys is the backbone of the gameplay. It is the thin wedge that sustains the challenge of skill and defines these titles as games and not other forms of interactive experiences. *Resident Evil* dilutes most of the challenge out of the key-lock process and uses it simply as a function of having the player crisscross (i.e., explore) the game world. The same template serves *Super Metroid*, *Castlevania: Symphony of the Night*, and the legion of Metroidvania Kickstarter projects in their wake. These games, like *Resident Evil*, are about exploring an interconnected space through a series of locks and keys that prompt movement through the game world.

Defining Survival Gameplay

If item keys and item locks, which move the player back and forth across the game world, are the mechanisms of progression, then what exactly is involved in this process, the core gameplay, beyond simply deducing which key fits which lock? The survival dimension of survival horror, the subgenre convention Capcom coined with the release of the first *Resident Evil*, answers this question. Games that emphasize survival do so by limiting resources and increasing the threat to players (i.e., the threat of entering the fail state). In *Resident Evil*, survival translates to a limited supply of ammunition and healing items, few inventory slots, enemies that are as powerful as the player, and claustrophobic environments that restrict freedom of movement. Even ink ribbons (the items used to save your progress) are a scarce commodity. In order to complete a *Resident Evil* game, one needs to play so as to minimize risk. Successful players avoid rooms with enemies, but flush them out of critical junctures. They account for space in their inventory when entering a new area and plan their save room pit stops to avoid backtracking for supplies. Those who know which rooms hold locks, which rooms hold resources, which rooms hold enemies, and which routes are possible and therefore the safest and shortest to their destination are at an advantage. *Resident Evil* is a game of mental frameworks, where success hinges on the player's ability to build a working model of the game world in their head. The more developed a player's mental model, the more able they are to make informed choices. Those who fly blind have a higher likelihood of wallowing in the quagmire of trial and error.

Mental Models

When faced with limited resources, a high threat of failure, and the interconnection of locks and keys spread across the environment, there exists a strong impetus to put whatever relevant information one can obtain from the game world to use. The first step in developing such a survival plan involves perceiving and encoding information. According to Miller's law,[1] human beings are only able to remember 7 ± 2 bits of information in their working memory, about as much important data a player would encounter in their first 10 minutes of play (rooms, relative positions of rooms, routes, keys, locks, ammo, enemies, save rooms, etc.). So in order to make progress, the player must develop some kind of system that organizes and therefore simplifies the influx of information. This way, details of the game world can easily be encoded into and retrieved out from one's long-term memory. I call this schema the player's mental model.

Whether or not we do it consciously, each player will have a way of managing the mental load. How they do it very much depends on the individual. Below I talk about my experience with creating mental models in the *Resident Evil* games.

Rooms, as the smallest integer of a game world, are the foundation of my mental model. As I play, I store each room in my mind as a snapshot of the backdrop. The realistic settings of *Resident Evil* maps, where each room and the contents within are defined by utility, makes it easy to attach keys, locks, resources, and enemies to each image. There is no map in my model; rather, the individual images sit in relative proximity to one another. I interpret this as a consequence of the fixed perspective used in each room, which does not convey a great sense of shape or space. The relative positioning of rooms (i.e., how I organize the information) is probably the biggest structural weakness in my model. When I recall a particular room, I have no higher-order way of accessing the information other than visualizing the avatar moving between slides of prerendered stills. Over time the stills coalesce into routes and the model evolves into a network of options and possibilities. Reliance on certain rooms and routes adds depth to the model as favor and hierarchy pull certain images to the front of my mind while pushing others into the corners. At this stage, despite some holes, my mental model is to the point where I can move reasonably assertively through the environment.

One of the tensions that the *Resident Evil* games thrive on is that few players are able to retain enough information or recall the right information to make informed choices all the time. At some point they will be caught short and forced to walk blindly into the unknown. In this sense, the player is not surviving against zombies and bioweapons (read: monsters) as much as the constant decay of stored knowledge.

Types of Knowledge-Based Gameplay

The notion of *Resident Evil*'s puzzle-like nature can now be addressed. If we define a puzzle, quite simply, as a test of one's knowledge skills, then we can conclude that the following processes constitute the puzzle flavor that permeates through classic *Resident Evil* design:

Identifying clues and foreshadowing

Encoding, retaining, and recalling details of the game world

Fitting details of the game world into a schema

Reorganizing and updating the mental model when new information becomes available

Predicting what sort of key will fit a certain lock

Deducing which keys belong to which locks

Using the mental model to make informed decisions about how to move about the game world, where to go, what to take with you, and what to leave behind

Conducting moment-to-moment risk assessments (i.e., determining when to retreat and when to plow ahead)

This list demonstrates the range from low-level actions such as recalling and retaining information to more high-level actions such as deduction, logic, and problem solving.

All games, no matter the genre, depend on the player's ability to perceive and encode information about the game system and play environment. What the discussion so far has demonstrated, though, is that the survival elements of *Resident Evil* increase the significance of decision making and thereby increase the potency of knowledge as a dynamic force that underpins player actions. When choices have weight, knowledge is everything. When knowledge is everything, every action is important because it feeds back into the knowledge loop. I believe that it is this aspect of *Resident Evil*—player choice and its relation to the knowledge game—that makes the original games engrossing experiences.

Player Choices

All player choices ripple forward in time and affect subsequent decisions. Choices come in three flavors—resource-based, enemy-based, and knowledge-based—and are possible because of the way resources, enemies, and knowledge are consistent through all moments of play unless removed by the player. Resource-based choices pertain to decisions that develop or diminish the player's health and supply of ammunition and healing items. For example, wasting ammo on an unexpected enemy dips into the resource pool, which in turn shapes the player's offensive options in the future.

Enemy-based choices pertain to decisions that determine the composition of enemies (i.e., when, where, and whether to fight or flee). Knowledge-based choices determine the player's exposure to the environment. When, what, and where the player perceives something in the game world shapes how they encode and fit that information into their mental model.

The categorization separates the variables affecting player choices, but does not paint an accurate picture of decision making in *Resident Evil*. Given the relationship between resources, enemies, and knowledge, most of the player's decisions involve more than one set of variables, if not all of them. For example, deciding to clear a hallway of a group of powerful monsters shrinks the resource pool, alters the composition of enemies, and reassigns the room as a safe zone in the mental model. The complex constellation of variables, their interrelatedness, and the depth of potential outcomes makes it difficult for the player to foresee the impacts of their decisions. Since consequence cannot easily be measured, solutions can't be optimized, and so when presented with choice, no one course of action appears better than the others: there are only options. We might think of these options as meaningful choices in comparison to propositions such as "Will you help save the kingdom?" or "Do you want the strong armor or the slightly less-strong armor?", which are redundant. The former question is simply a prompt and the latter is no choice at all: of course you want the strong armor!

In contrast to dialog trees, which pause the gameplay so that the game designer can ask the player a question, *Resident Evil* is an ongoing conversation of meaningful choices between player and game designer that is initiated by the player on their own terms by simply playing the game. The player has a fine degree of agency in the decision-making process (certainly more than three or four selections). Choices are also grounded in the language of the game world as player actions, unlike multiple choice, text responses in conversation sequences, which tend to be abstract (happy response, witty response, angry response, etc.) and quite apart from the core gameplay. Given the weight of each decision, the frequency at which players encounter them, and the way choices ripple forward in time to affect subsequent choices, players are able to mold their own unique survival horror experience out of *Resident Evil*'s gameplay.

Environmental Storytelling

The process of creating a mental model feeds into and reinforces the environmental storytelling, creating a strong cohesion between narrative as communicated through gameplay and narrative as communicated through environment. *Resident Evil*'s environmental storytelling operates in various forms. At its simplest level, the appearance of the world conveys narrative visually. Backgrounds embed details of a previous life, bloodied walls speak of death, and destruction gives context to the aftermath. Interactions within the environment convey narrative through function. Inserting the MO Disk into the passcode terminals in the original *Resident Evil* offers insight into Umbrella's digital security system, for example. Sometimes these interactions allude to a deeper reading of the narrative conveyed through cut-scenes. In *Code Veronica*, the player removes the wings of a silver model of a dragonfly to form a key. Later, they attach four wings to a gold dragonfly body. Disassembling and reassembling these two keys is symbolic of Alfred and Alexia's insect fetish, which itself can be read as a metaphor for their treatment of their father Alexander. Enemies, whether or not considered part of the environment, also lend meaning to the narrative. A zombie's clothes tell their gender and occupation, while their location speaks to how they became caught up in the outbreak. The environmental storytelling is not merely window dressing, though. As we know, mental models are built on linkages between individual pieces of knowledge: the more connected the information, the stronger the memory network. The narrative details shared through the environment provide the player with context that helps them organize their schema and elaborate information into their long-term memory. That is, we intuitively use the narrative clues provided to us to craft our own stories (mnemonics) that aid in the memorization process. For example, imagining Alfred entertaining rich aristocrats affiliated with the Ashford family with drinks and live piano music overlooking the Palace entrance is a much easier image to recall a piano (lock) than simply the piano being in the room to the left of the stairs in the Palace. Building the mental model therefore unifies the separate strands of narrative to provide a holistic story of the environment. By the end of a *Resident Evil* game, the player is likely to feel a strong connection with the game world because they have come to internalize it as part of their play experience.

I have chosen to use the terms puzzle box and mental model to describe the sequential and interconnected nature of *Resident Evil*'s lock-and-key system and the player's mental response to it. The terms may imply a conformity of level design throughout the series, but each game varies greatly in their application of these concepts. The original *Resident Evil* probably fits the image one has of a puzzle box most accurately. The game is a gradual unfolding of a single interconnected space. *Resident Evil 2* is a series of self-contained chapters completed one at a time, with some backtracking to previous areas. *Resident Evil 3* is similar to 2, but with the Nemesis enemy signposting explicit branches in progression. *Code Veronica* returns to the format of the original game, but is separated into two areas that are explored from two different perspectives. *Resident Evil 0*'s level design is characterized by the dynamics of separating, joining, and managing items between Billy and Rebecca. The evolution of *Resident Evil*'s level design is a topic far beyond the scope of this chapter. However, the case study of *Code Veronica* should equip you with all the tools you need to tackle these games for yourself. I would certainly encourage you to do so.

PROGRESSION, PEDAGOGY, AND THE PLAYER'S MENTAL MODEL IN *CODE VERONICA*

So far we have discussed the *Resident Evil* puzzle box in general terms, but as the previous paragraph suggested, each game offers its own take on the concept that is worth analyzing in more detail. For this second half of the chapter, we are going to explore the intersection between level design,

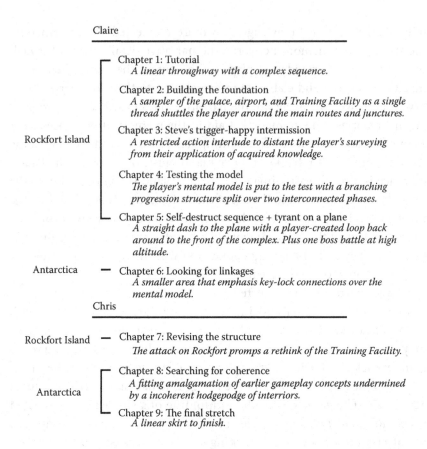

FIGURE 2.1   Resident Evil: Code Veronica progression sequence.

teaching design, and progression systems as we examine the mental model concept in action in *Resident Evil: Code Veronica*. We will track how the game designers scaffold the player's awareness of the game world, challenge them to draw connections, and upset their familiarity in unexpected ways. The idea is that we want to get inside the player's head by observing the forces that are acted upon them.

Figure 2.1 is our roadmap. It frames *Code Veronica* as a sequence of evolutions in the player's understanding of the game world. As you will note, each chapter advances the chapter prior, so in order to explore the end, we have to start at the beginning.*

---

* For those of you playing along at home, Evil Resource is a fantastic reference: http://www.evilresource .com/resident-evil-code-veronica/maps.

Chapter 1: Tutorial
(Prison – Claire)

Rockfort Island Prison functions as a tutorial in preparation for the larger, more elaborate areas ahead. A giant, steel door that can only be opened by a Hawk Emblem keeps the player within the penitentiary grounds. Its hulking size and position at the first juncture telegraphs the player's initial goal. Although the rooms are variable in shape, size, and relative position, movement through the complex follows a single linear pathway (Figure 2.2). The Barracks, a wood cabin holding supplies and an equal number of zombies, is the only tangible deviation that the player can take to customize their experience.

The player acquires the Hawk Emblem at the end of the linear path, but does so after passing through a corridor with metal detectors at either entrance. Returning to the large door is therefore not as simple as one might have expected as the emblem sets off the metal detectors, prompting shutter doors to come down and block the path. The metal detector problem is dependent on a separate sequence of actions as presented in Figure 2.3. Fortunately, the game up to this point has been preteaching the undoing of the Hawk Emblem knot. As the player follows the breadcrumb trail through the Prison, the keys and locks of the metal detector sequence are foreshadowed:

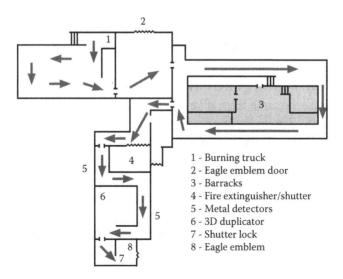

1 - Burning truck
2 - Eagle emblem door
3 - Barracks
4 - Fire extinguisher/shutter
5 - Metal detectors
6 - 3D duplicator
7 - Shutter lock
8 - Eagle emblem

FIGURE 2.2   Movement paths around the prison complex.

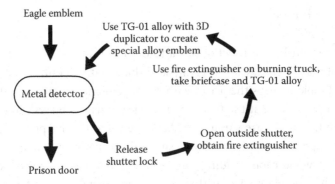

FIGURE 2.3   Prison complex lock.

The briefcase is in the fire of the burning truck (cut-scene)

The shutter lock needs to be released so the shutter door can be opened (environmental, description)

How to use the 3D duplicator (3D Duplicator User Manual file)

The briefcase contains the TG-01 alloy (Facility Entrance Fax file)

The shutter lock is next to the computer (environmental, cut-scene)

The items are presented out of order, so it is up to the player to recall these clues and fit them into the proper sequence. A complete narrative is not required, simply enough framework to keep an active lead.

The Barracks, as an optional aside, creates distance between when the player sees a key or a lock and when they need to act on that information. The extra resources come at the expense of being distracted from the main thread of progression and having to retain important information for a longer period of time. Along the same lines, if key clues are overlooked or forgotten, players have the freedom to backtrack and fill any holes. This backtracking is not necessarily a waste of time as all observation feeds into the underlying knowledge game and strengthens the model. Today's backtracker may be rewarded the knowledge to make them tomorrow's assertive player. These two points, the Barracks and the backtracker, may seem inconsequential, but they demonstrate the subtle ways in which the player's decisions determine the flow of information and thereby shape their mental model. Later on, when the environment opens up and player agency blossoms exponentially, it will not be feasible to make such observations, and so, for the ease of simplicity, I thought it would be better to discuss them now.

The locks and keys see the player traverse the length of the Prison four times before they leave (prison cell to shutter lock, shutter lock to shutter to burning truck, burning truck to 3D duplicator, 3D duplicator to Eagle Emblem door). The backtracking teaches players that enemies and resources have permanence and do not disappear or respawn once the player leaves the room.

Chapter 2: Building the Foundation
(Palace, Airport, and Military Training Facility – Claire)

The Prison tutorial can be thought of as a miniaturization of Claire's main adventures on Rockfort. The initial information-gathering period (the linear walk) and the subsequent pursuit of active leads (the complex lock)—the tutorial's two halves—correspond to this chapter, "Building the Foundation," and the subsequent chapter, "Testing the Model." "Building the Foundation" has players sweep the Palace, Airport, and Training Facility, familiarizing themselves with the main routes and junctures of each area before moving on to the next. As they progress, the player slowly develops the foundation of their model, which will not be put to use until after the intermission that divides "Building the Foundation" and "Testing the Model."

Although the single thread of locks and keys orients players toward the main path (the Steering Wheel in the Palace grants access to the Airport and the Biohazard Card in the Airport unlocks the main throughway in the Training Facility), the great expansion of available environments allows the player to deviate more freely. Variability exists at both a macro and micro level. At a macro level, the player can ignore (or overlook!) the key-lock sequence and explore the three areas out of order (i.e., go to the Training Facility before the Palace or return to the Palace after exploring the Airport). At a micro level, they can explore the wealth of optional resource rooms within each of the environments, much like the Barracks in the Prison. Figures 2.4 and 2.5, which contrast the optional rooms (dark gray) against the mandatory key-lock route (light gray), give a sense of the available micro-level options and overall bump in game world size.

With more freedom, the game designers hand over more responsibility to the player to manage their bearings in the new environment and keep an active checklist of potential leads. Although "freedom" is a word imbued with positive connotation, in a pedagogical sense it can be a poison. The freedom to explore by oneself is also the freedom to wander aimlessly.

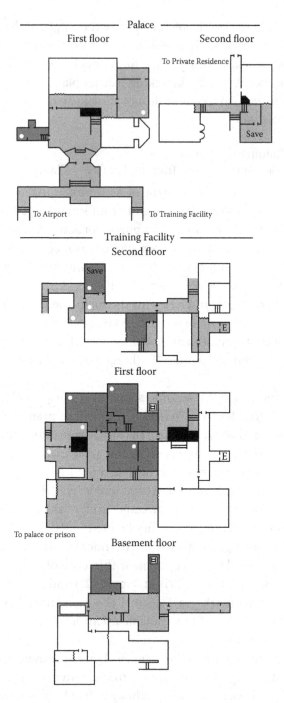

FIGURE 2.4   Mandatory rooms (light gray), optional rooms (dark gray), discardable rooms (dots).

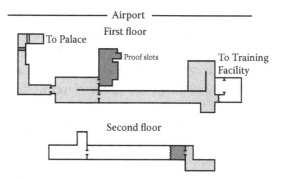

FIGURE 2.5　Mandatory rooms (light gray), optional rooms (dark gray).

The player is not walking on eggshells, though. Rather, freedom is carefully controlled to increase autonomy while minimizing wandering. The Palace, Airport, and Training Facility are distinct environments with each room holding some functional purpose within the game's fiction. The player is also not yet asked to travel back and forth between the main areas either, which helps to distinguish the three categories in one's mind. Organizing the model and encoding details into one's long-term memory is therefore an easier process than if the environments were a contextual jumble and the main thread of progression were less straightforward. With a bit of deduction, it should not be too difficult to recall most of the locations encountered so far.

Where the player chooses to explore and which rooms they choose to explore first will shape their mental model. For the player who investigates the Training Facility first is likely to sweep the lock- and keyless rooms at the back of the building and therefore render this section out of their mental model earlier, leading to a smoother transition through to the Back Courtyard on return. Alternatively, the player who overlooks the (optional) Bathroom in the Palace will have it lingering about in their headspace until it is returned to later on.

By the end of the chapter, the player can render two of the Palace's six available rooms and eight of the Training Facility's 19 available rooms out of their mental model (as marked with dots in Figure 2.4), assuming they explore all of the optional rooms. The discardable rooms either contain no locks, keys, or other clues or are inaccessible post-"Building the Foundation" (i.e., Albert's "special playground"). Trimming this excess from the model lightens the overall mental load. And so the system implicitly rewards players who are comprehensive in their exploration and show initiative in maintaining their knowledge base.

The thread of locks and keys strings the player through the main hubs, junctures, and save points of the Palace, Training Facility, and Airport. As such, few revelations or rabbit holes await the player in the next substantial chapter ("Testing the Model"). Rather, each unlockable area, including the larger excursions to the Private Residence and Prison Clinic, are self-contained branches that build onto the existing map. *Resident Evil Remake* follows a similar design, but several of its locks hide sprawling digressions. By having the player pass through the save rooms and move between floors and between the front and back sides of the Palace and Training Facility, the game is not just familiarizing the player with the building blocks of the new environments, but they are modeling the paths and pit stops that they will be using when putting keys to lock in the "Testing the Model" chapter. Each step of the player's learning is carried forward to the next step.

As a consequence of the increased size of the game world, the compartmentalized design of the three isolated areas, and the presence of hubs, junctures, and discardable rooms, hierarchy is likely to develop within the player's mental model. Frequently visited rooms harden into long-term memory, less visited rooms are pushed into the background, and resource rooms mined of their worth are removed.

By the end of the "Building the Foundation" chapter, the player will have formed a list of active leads. At most, it will contain all of the following:

Golden Lugers (key)

Golden Lugers slot (lock)

Unexplored east side of Training Facility

Hemostatic (optional key)

Rodrigo in need of Hemostatic (optional lock)

Biohazard Card

Indigo card slots (lock)

Control panel without lever (lock)

Storage key (optional key)

Locked cabinet in Front Office (optional lock)

K-402 airport door (lock)

Gold crest door (lock)

Silver crest door (lock)

Three proof slots (lock)

Navy Proof (key)

Duralumin case (optional lock)

Door with missing knob (lock)

Passcode for the Biohazard Containment Room (lock)

The 18 possible clues, their locations, and the makeup of the game world exceed the 7 ± 2 limitation imposed on our memory. The player is over-loaded with potentially useful information and so the game world and all its contents become like a soup as key details flow in and out of the player's conscious thought. This is where the decay of retention and the associated tension creep into the gameplay.

Chapter 4: Testing the Model
(Palace, Military Training Facility, Private Residence, and Prison – Claire)

As the singular thread of progression unwinds into multiple directions across the four areas of the map, the player is left to find their own path forward. Their mental model, a culmination of their individual decisions, observations, and encoded information, is the compass that guides progression. In this chapter, the player must use their mental model to guide them through the freer environment.

One of the great mental pleasures of *Resident Evil*'s puzzle box comes from the tension between the timing and sequence that the player acquires certain knowledge and the timing and sequence that the lock and keys tease out this knowledge. The player's decisions shape their knowledge base into a particular form that the game designers then have them reshape to fit the gradual unfolding of the game world. When the player encounters locks and keys as part of the "Testing the Model" branches of progression (Figure 2.6), the relevant part of their mental model must be found, uprooted, attached to the new piece of information, and put back into place. Old information is reactivated from a new perspective and then reencoded.

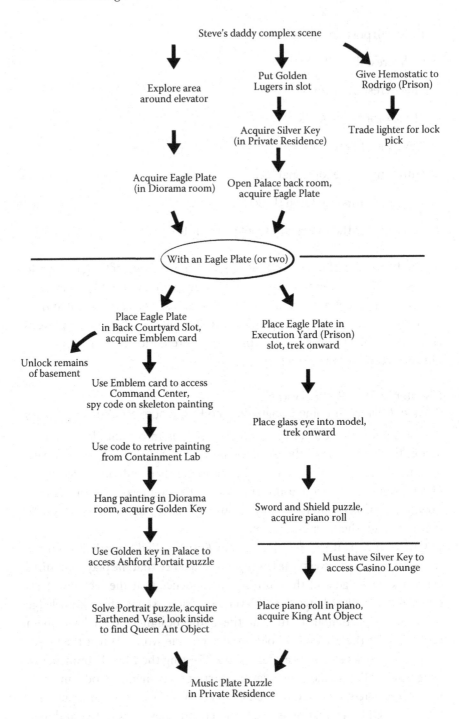

FIGURE 2.6 Testing the Model's branching progression struture.

Since the player is fed each bit of information (key, lock, or other clue) in "Building the Foundation" at different intervals, the process of mentally mapping across details has an inconsistency, a texture. Each connection that the player makes feels unique because of the time, place, and nature they encountered each lock and key. The player's experience breathes meaning into each mental frame, brick, lick of cement, and sheet of glass that goes into their internal representation of the game world.* In "Revising the Structure," that texture is of a finer grain, being a richer representation of the player's mental relationship with details of the game world.

An anxiety underpins the player's mental renovation work. Since the player is overloaded with important information, some details sit more firmly in their model than others. Following the breadcrumb trail of locks and keys therefore involves simultaneously recalling and modifying certain details while keeping other details in active memory. It is a bit like spinning plates.

As is immediately evident in Figure 2.6, the single threads of progression that have restricted gameplay thus far have been replaced by a sprawling network of branches. The freedom provided by the structure places further responsibility on the player to manage their progress. The game takes a number of steps to ease the player into their new responsibilities, though. The two mandatory threads have immediate initial prompts that help set the player on their way. The Silver Key (Figure 2.6) and the priming of the Eagle Plate slots (lock) scaffold a suggested sequence (taking the bottom-left thread before the bottom-right). The player's mastery of their mental model is not at the stage where they can tackle such a complex branching structure on their own, and so, for now at least, these aids are necessary.

Chapter 5: Self-Destruct Sequence + Tyrant on a Plane
(Private Residence, Airport, Military Training Facility, and Plane – Claire)

The freedom and decision making of the previous chapter is juxtaposed against this restrictive and straightforward escape sequence and boss battle pair. Once Claire and Steve pilot the plane, they realize that the bridge needs to be raised, delaying the all-too-convenient escape in a much clichéd fashion. To complicate matters further, raising the bridge cuts off the player's direct route back to the plane. By solving one problem, another is

---

* This is to say nothing of the player's own encoding processes.

created: my favorite kind of lock.* An elevator leads back around to the Training Facility, which sets up a short confrontation with the Tyrant to be continued on the plane ride to the Antarctic.

Chapter 6: Looking for Linkages
(Antarctic Transport Terminal – Claire)

The Antarctic is not only a fresh change of scenery, but also a fresh twist on the mental model concept. A handful of satellite rooms holding ammo and healing items make this portion of the Transport Terminal feel bigger than it actually is. A conveyor belt puzzle anchored around the Sorting Room, four adjacent rooms, and two of the satellites is the single linear thread that composes this chapter. Once the player has swept the terminal for clues, it is all a matter of piecing together keys and locks in a logical through line. The contained space of around 10 rooms, compared to the 50 or so pertinent to the branching behemoth in "Testing the Model," allows for a rapid turnaround in key-lock connections. As such, deducing connections between locks and keys is emphasized, while the route planning, mental model testing, and branching structures of "Testing the Model" is put to one side.

"Looking for Linkages" is a highly compressed version of the game thus far (sans tutorial)—an opportunity for the player to consolidate their learning with a mini puzzle box. The complete autonomy and lack of familiarity with the transport terminal encourage the player to systematically sweep the environment for clues—something that was useful earlier, but is more or less a requirement from here on out.

Chapter 7: Revising the Structure
(Military Training Facility and Airport – Chris)

The Training Facility's layout has been overhauled ready for Chris's arrival, forcing the player to rewire their neural networks to accommodate the designers' reinterpretation of the building.

Despite initial appearances, this is not a true return to Rockfort Island. Chris is limited to the Training Facility and Airport, the latter of which remains identical to how the player last left it, albeit with a fresh smattering of undead workmen. The Training Facility, the centerpiece for this

---

* Oh, but it gets better. When Chris returns to the Airport (through the Training Facility's cargo elevator), he must lower the bridge again to claim the three proofs. And so by solving one problem, two more are created—one immediate problem and one delayed problem.

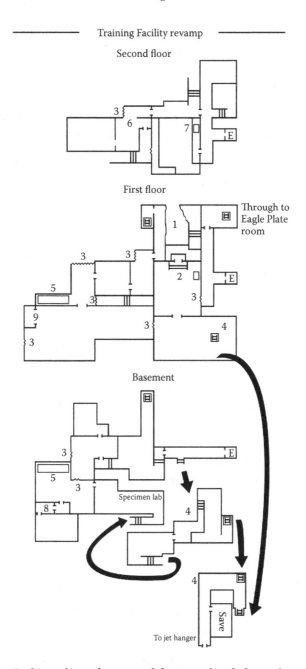

FIGURE 2.7   Each number refers to modifications detailed on subsequent page.

chapter, has seen no small number of changes as a result of the bombing raid following Claire and Steve's departure. As mapped in Figure 2.7:

1. The Back Courtyard is split through the middle

2. Chris enters the island through an underground passage carved out of a cliff and takes a secret elevator to the Garage

3. A handful of previously accessible doors are blocked, which in some cases removes whole portions of the map

4. New underground passages reconfigure the nature of movement through the facility

5. The turntable elevator facilitates east–west travel through the basement (as it is no longer possible to take the front Exercise Yard or the Back Courtyard on the first floor)

6. A wall is destroyed, creating a new throughway

7. The construction lift functions as a substitute elevator

8. The Chemical Storage Room door has been opened

9. The cargo elevator to the Airport is still accessible

An interesting aside, before we explore the implications these examples have on the player's mental model, is that many of the changes were foreshadowed in the series of cut-scenes* leading into Claire and Steve's escape:

- Alfred opens the Tyrant's capsule, which foreshadows the Specimen Lab (marked in Figure 2.7).

- The explosion behind Alfred as he runs toward the tank splits open the Back Courtyard (#1).

- Alfred pushes the button behind the tank to move it forward, revealing a secret passage (first floor, #4).

- Alfred uses a golden halberd to access the jet hanger. This gives context and purpose to Chris's exploits on the island. He is not simply trying to open a random door, but rather the door that leads to his escape.

---

* Evacuation Cutscenes https://youtu.be/1zMqgvzqZE4?t=41m18s.

The return to the Training Facility and the variety of changes that come with it force the player to once again reevaluate their mental model. This time, though, their conception of the facility is further entrenched in their long-term memory and the process of reconciling the differences is much more complicated. These two characteristics define the knowledge game in "Revising the Structure."

The former is a result of the deeper levels of mental processing when the player recalled locks, keys, and routes from "Building the Foundation" and connected them with new information in "Testing the Model." The dilemma is similar to the bridge lock in the Airport. The game designers facilitate a situation where to succeed, the player has to process the Training Facility more deeply, and yet this deeper level of processing makes this encore chapter all the more challenging. Once something has been committed to long-term memory, it becomes harder to rewire the original associations and memory networks that were used to encode the information.

The latter is an evolution in the application of the mental model concept. In "Testing the Model," the upheaval of the player's model was relatively straightforward: recall and employ a piece of information in the decision-making process (i.e., X hub will lead me to the room with the Y lock that can be opened with the Z key, so I will take the XYZ route) or recall old information and attach new information to it (i.e., now that I have the Emblem Card, I can open the indigo card gate in the Boiler Room). In "Revising the Structure," all the changes, as listed above, pertain to the structure of the building and therefore the player's ability to move through it. Although "Testing the Model" contained some structural evolutions,* the environment's body pretty much remained untouched and every new area was simply an extension to the foundation established in previous chapters. What differentiates keys and locks and structure within the mental model construct is that individual keys and locks are only bound to one another. The structure of the game world, though, is the node that links all individual pieces of knowledge together. It is the medium itself in which all other bits of information reside. Therefore, the difference between "Testing the Model" and "Revising the Structure" is that "Testing the Model" deals with recalling and reencoding individual pieces

---

* There are two exceptions. The first is when the player unlocks the door between the Command Center and Back Courtyard (just above #7 in Figure 2.7), which allows them to move across the facility and between floors more easily. The second is the Emblem Card example mentioned earlier, which adds a new entry point into the basement.

of information, while "Revising the Structure" deals with recalling and reencoding entire memory networks. Where "Testing the Model" is transformational in being additive to the player's mental model, "Revising the Structure" is transformational in reinterpreting the model.

In practice, the changes amount to the following:

- West–East travel now occurs exclusively through the basement instead of through the front or back of the first floor of the facility.

- The front of the facility is now a conduit to the Airport.

- The Iron Walkway (#4 in the basement, no save room) has assumed its place as the main juncture of player traffic. It links the two basement throughways that lead to the main keys for this chapter (the clements and proofs), the sole save room and inventory box, and the locked door at the end of the chapter.

- The presence of the turntable elevator (#5) diminishes the role of the eastern elevator.

- The Back Courtyard is also diminished now that it is split through the middle.

As with "Testing the Model," the new details are teased out as the player encounters them. It is a slow overhaul as players reacquaint themselves with the new environment, works out the mental kinks into their model, and discovers new opportunities in the process. By controlling the flow of information, the game designers can create intrigue and anticipation.

Players' reinterpretation of the Training Facility is supported by the unused locks and keys from their previous escapades on Rockfort as Claire. Together these threads form a lattice of precontextualized information that eases key-to-lock deductions. The player's ability to piece together the keys and locks into a certain sequence, a process emphasized in "Looking for Linkages," is downplayed as the player enters "Revisiting the Structure" with the jigsaw already partially assembled. Along the same lines, the end goal of the chapter, and by extension the branching structure, is telegraphed ahead of time. Unlike in "Testing the Model," the player has a clearer idea of what they are working toward and can therefore play more assertively.

"Revising the Structure" is divided into two halves: a linear sequence that functions as an introduction and a branching segment that gradually

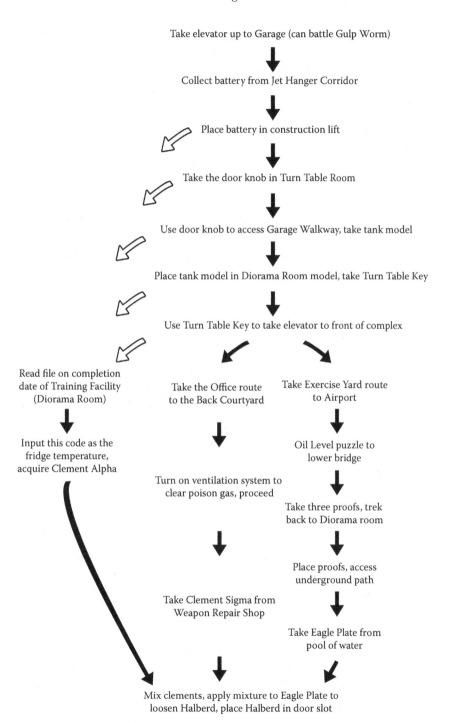

FIGURE 2.8   Revising the Structure's branching progression structure.

reinterprets the player's mental model. Parallels can be drawn with the slow increase in player freedom over the "Tutorial," "Building the Foundation," and "Testing the Model" chapters, but it is not quite that simple, as the player is able to splinter off from the linear path a few clicks into the proceedings (Figure 2.8, white arrows). Up to this point, progression has only diverged at a single node, so two potential branching points is a development of the progression system.

The linear sequence completes Rodrigo's story arc, resources Chris with a small kit of supplies, directs the player to the save room, and introduces them to the previously inaccessible southern side of the basement. By restricting player freedom, this initial preparation is quick and seamless.

Each branch leads the player to a distinct section of the map. The Clement Alpha and Sigma are held in the north and south halves of the Training Facility basement. The Eagle Plate sends the player out to the Airport and then back around to the top-right corner of the Training Facility. The smaller areas and few crossing paths makes the available options easier to read.

The scaffolding of the lattice of dangling threads, the telegraphing of the player's goals, the initial preparation, and the readable player choices focus "Revisiting the Structure" on players adapting their mental models to the structural changes of the Training Facility, while pushing earlier themes (complex locks, world building, unguided branching structures, key-lock connections) into the background.

Chapter 8: Searching for Coherence
(Antarctic Transport Terminal – Chris)

From the pedagogical perspective of this analysis, a good video game finale combines the assortment of gameplay concepts into one last megachallenge befitting of the skills and knowledge the player has gained on their quest to mastery. "Searching for Coherence" is such an amalgamation. It brings together model-building and model-testing phases, branching paths, key-lock deductions in a condensed space, dangling threads split between Claire and Chris, and additive and transformative changes to the mental model into the one package. Yet its environments lack the visual and spatial coherence that has made the model building in the rest of the game rather seamless, leading to a somewhat confounding and potentially bitter conclusion.

When excavating a path out of the Transport Terminal, Steve flooded the second basement floor with water, which has since frozen over and left Chris with a rejuvenated environment to explore. The Sorting Room and three of the four adjacent rooms, which together formed the center-piece of Claire's run, are inaccessible. Of the remaining rooms, only the Office (save room), the Machine Room (where Steve was caught staring at Claire's butt), the second floor of the Sorting Room (broken walkway), and potentially the Weapons Room (if Claire requires the serum) carry over to the key-lock sequences of Chris's campaign (Figure 2.9). The optional supply rooms remain and have seen some changes that invite a return engagement. For example, the cage housing the duralumin case in the Tool Storeroom has been split open. The frozen water discards a large chunk of the environment and opens up access to the untouched lower levels of the terminal, largely sidestepping Claire's earlier run.

Where the structural changes in the Training Facility reinterpreted the space, disrupted the player's mental model, and thereby reworked the underlying knowledge game, the structural changes in Antarctica create little interplay between the player's prior and current knowledge. Claire's

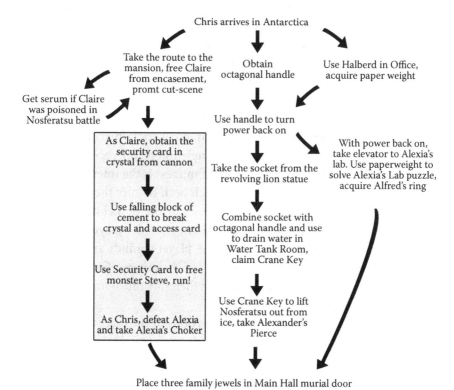

FIGURE 2.9 Searching for Coherence's branching progression structure.

earlier run informs which rooms ought to be rendered out of the model. The unused locks and keys facilitate smoother key-lock connections and lead to some extra supplies. Yet despite these few extras, most of the player's prior knowledge can be discarded with little consequence.

The lone thread of progression that has preceded every branching structure in the game so far is dropped. Once Chris reaches Antarctica, the player is free to dive into any of the three available strings (Figure 2.9). You will notice that once again we are dealing with three part-keys that open a single door, but with three unexpected quirks.

The first point of interest is the serum thread. If Claire was poisoned in the battle with Nosferatu, Alexander Ashford's monstrous form bookending "Looking for Linkages," then Chris will have to venture out to the Weapon Room to grab the serum that can heal her. If Claire was never poisoned, then the serum will not exist and the full motion video prompting the switch over to Claire will directly follow the initial cut-scene. The Queen Ant Report file in the room opposite Alexia's Lab foreshadows the position of the serum, assuming the player comes across it beforehand. As with the other *Resident Evil* games, *Code Veronica* employs a hands-off approach to player choice, allowing decision making to function as a component of gameplay. A subbranch initiated unknowingly by player action is therefore something of an anomaly but a variation on the branching progression design nonetheless.

The second point of interest is the gray box in Alexia's thread. For these four links in the chain, the player is locked into a contained environment and must see the sequence through to completion before reengaging with the other two branches. The third point of interest is the interdependency of the Albert and Alexander threads, which both require the power to be reconnected. These latter two developments in the branching structure design subvert two established assumptions: that the player can freely move between strings (active leads in the player's mind) and that each sequence of keys and locks is independent of the others.* Getting a sense for the underlying progression structure is therefore much more challenging than in any of the earlier chapters.

The three threads fit within distinct portions of the map, with reasonably minimal overlap between them. Yet chances are players won't color

---

* The dependence of the King Ant thread on the Golden Luger thread (i.e., the Silver Key) in "Testing the Model" is the exception. However, the scaffolding dissuaded the player from taking such a sequence.

inside the lines, because the terminal's layout persuades them not to. The key-lock system that underpins the player's progression operates on player knowledge of the game world. The more one knows about their environment (i.e., the richer their mental model), the more quickly and safely they can unlock the barriers in their path. It is for this reason that it is difficult to walk past an unexplored arm of a juncture several times while pursuing other keys. After all, there might be an all-too-important clue right around the corner.

The fifth floor of the Transport Terminal's basement contains one such junction. Imagine, if you will, an upside-down T. The horizontal arm of the T corresponds to the Alexander and Alfred branches, while the vertical stem leads out to a mansion holding Claire in a mucousy encasement, the first prompt of Alexia's thread. If the player ignores the junction's northern route, they can theoretically complete each string in a tidy sequence with no overlap. They're more likely, however, to take the northern arm at some point during their sweep of the map. If they then free Claire, assuming she's not poisoned, they'll be locked into the Detention Center for Alexia's thread (Figure 2.9, gray box). That is, the development of their mental model will likely be interrupted for a period of time. The player must leave an unfinished model and go on to piece together a separate model before they can return to the original. The time gap is similar to "Steve's Trigger-Happy Intermission" and "Looking for Linkages" in that it creates a tension by sidelining the player from the main task for a duration of time. Yet where the previous two interludes sat between two distinct sections of gameplay, the interval in "Searching for Coherence" disrupts the one yet-unfinished section of gameplay. The timing of the interruption, or even whether or not it occurs, is also player-determined.

As discussed in the introduction, the visual presentation of the environment provides a context that helps the player organize and encode the game world into a schema. The Antarctic Transport Terminal's lower floors, as a hodgepodge of random backdrops, damage this relationship. Here's a sample:

Mansion Courtyard: Painted to look like the façade of a mansion, includes a blue sky and water canals despite being five stories underground

Icy Corridor: Resembles a meat freezer, one of the few rooms authentic to the outside climate

High Voltage Room: A generic storeroom with a power generator

Art Room: Split into two sections, a concrete blue room and a tiled red hallway, the Art Room attempts to duplicate the same room from the original game

Main Hall: A reproduction of the Spencer Mansion entrance

Ant Farm: Half of a circular walkway that arcs around a giant cylinder surrounded by ants and insects—has a future industrial look

Alexia's Study: A dimly lit wood cabin

The visual images are distinct and easy enough to remember. However, when the context from room to room varies so wildly, the thread of coherence tying the game world together is frayed and the job of organizing the rooms into a schema becomes much more difficult. And without a sturdy mental model, it is easier to lose one's bearings and play less assertively.

The other dimension to this issue is the skewed representation of floors. The elevator that connects the corridor with the scanners and the Mansion Courtyard (i.e., the left-hand entrance of the upside-down T) drops the player four stories, from B1 to B5. This is the only time in the game where an elevator moves more than one floor without informing the player. Sure, the time spent taking the elevator is longer than usual, but I don't think that this in and of itself is a sufficient tell, especially when you consider the random handful of doors that have longer-than-usual opening animations. If the player works within the assumptions presented, a number of contradictions reveal themselves. But even if we disregard the poor communication of the elevator, it's not hard to be confounded by the logic of the underground environments. The Ant Farm exists five floors underground and yet has a floor and ceiling that extend out into the distance; the Upper Ant Farm, still underground, appears to exist at the edge of a precipice; and the Mansion Courtyard walls are painted blue to resemble a sky. The wallpapers create the illusion of indoor environments being set outdoors and thereby needlessly warp the player's sense of spatial coherence. Remember, the mental model exists in the medium of space and so when the game presents a skewed form of space, the model too is distorted and therefore less reliable. The results? A compromised knowledge base, fewer informed decisions, and more aimless wandering.

A theme that has underlined the chapter-by-chapter analysis is the reduction of scaffolding as the player's ability develops and challenge increases.

In "Searching for Coherence," scaffolding is reduced to three examples. The first is the player's prior knowledge of the transport terminal. The second is the Alfred's Diary file that comes packaged with the paperweight. Like the Alloy Report in "Revising the Structure," it outlines the branching structure. The third comes from observing the family portrait where the three gems are placed—which, like the file, sets a context for the branching structure. Outside of these aids, the player is on their own.

The minimal scaffolding in "Searching for Coherence" would be suffice if it were not for the previously discussed issues. The mishmash of visual settings, unclear division of floors, and exterior-looking interiors diminish the player's ability to comprehend the environment. The knowledge game that sits at the heart of *Code Veronica*'s gameplay is therefore compromised. The new variations for this chapter (a branching structure with an isolated thread and interdependency between the remaining two branches, and a tricky juncture that is likely to divide the player's mental model building) are solid developments, but when coupled with the environmental issues, the problems are only compounded.

CONCLUSION

Through this tour of *Code Veronica*'s use of scaffolding and mental model construction, we have given form to the knowledge game that occurs in the player's head and the invisible dialog between game designer (teacher) and player (student). But what does the weight of details say about *Code Veronica*?

Code Veronica employs a restricted-to-freer practice template for its teaching design. In the early goings, accessible rooms are few and the order in which the player can explore them are fewer. The limitations quiet the player and focus their attention on learning the game's mechanics and systems. At this stage, the spectrum of mental model permutations is relatively narrow. As the game opens up, freedom is delivered in two forms: space and sequence. The player is given access to large portions of the game world and the single thread of progression unravels into a system of branching paths. The scaffolding moves to accommodate the evolving theme. Clear prompts leading into each branch offer the player entry points and options, while a suggested sequence guides their progress, obfuscating much of the structural complexity. With more freedom comes more choice, and therefore more opportunities to shape the play experience. The lift of freedom, however, is counterbalanced with the weight of responsibility. The player must manage their own learning, which places more of an emphasis on using their knowledge base (i.e., their mental model) to make smart decisions. Being able to apply the skills and knowledge gained so far in freer contexts allows players to take ownership over their learning.

Larger game worlds and branched structures cannot sustain a fruitful development of macro-level gameplay concepts, and so scale is exchanged for sophistication as the gameplay shifts to focus on environmental upheaval and complex branching structures (variable branch points and independent and dependent branches). The player's prior knowledge of Rockfort Island and the Antarctic Transport Terminal scaffolds the key-lock connection process and cut-scenes and textual information provided by files foreshadow the shape of the branching structure, supporting the macro-level gameplay shift. The gradual transition from restricted to freer practice changes the nature of the teaching design. Direct pedagogic devices (e.g., controlling the sequence in which the player can explore the game world) become less direct (e.g., revisiting environments, where the player can use their prior experience in the area as a scaffold) and are eventually replaced with subtle guides (e.g., contextual suggestion through cut-scenes and text files). The game designer's guiding hand is always present, but it shifts and transforms to meet the evolving needs of the gameplay.

The player's decisions ripple forward in time as knowledge, resources, and enemies are suspended across moments of play. *Code Veronica* does not just facilitate this organic form of player-driven gameplay, though, it manipulates and layers the player's experiences.* The player encounters Rockfort Island three times ("Tutorial" + "Building the Foundation" + "Steve's Trigger-Happy Intermission," "Testing the Model" and "Revising the Structure") and the Antarctic Transport Terminal twice ("Looking for Linkages" and "Searching for Coherence"). In each of these encounters, the player develops a model of the game world or is required to reevaluate an existing model. The mental model can be thought of as the mental artifact of the player's journey as a learner. It is the higher-order schema, the metaphoric filing cabinet that holds their learned knowledge. By having the player explore altered environments with their old mental floor plans, the game brings prior learning and new learning into contrast. *Code*

---

* The suspension of knowledge is the central point of this argument. Resources and some enemies suspend across chapters (assuming the player has not activated a certain prompt to change the composition of a room's enemies), but their effect is not as significant as the suspension of knowledge.

Veronica, in this sense, is an exploration of the dynamics of learning, knowledge, and adaption. Each moment of learning informs our understanding of the world and through this understanding we shape our reality. I think, therefore I am. Yet if we trust our reality and our reality only, then we can become blinded by our own presumptions. In *Code Veronica*, the player's reality is their mental model and the gameplay experience is the medium through which the strengths and weaknesses of their learning and the need to reconsider one's reality are realized.

Everything is interconnected. Each layer of gameplay foreshadows and substantiates the next. The Prison instils the skills and knowledge that the player will use throughout the rest of the game. The new rooms and environmental details that emerge in "Testing the Model" are attached to the foundation of Rockfort Island that the player develops in the "Tutorial" and "Building the Foundation" chapters. The deeper level of processing makes reconciling the player's renewed model of Rockfort with the image presented to them in "Revising the Structure" all the more challenging. The unique gimmick and challenge of a single chapter is sustained by the player's earlier actions. The Rockfort Island strand is intertwined with the Antarctica substrand that abides by a similar design minus the tutorial. The intersections between these two threads, as well as Steve's intermission, create distance between the main links in the branches, which sustains the challenge of recall.

Through this chapter, I have laid out the design of the *Resident Evil* puzzle box. In the process, I introduced the concept of the player's mental model of the game world as a way of understanding how the player engages with the series' underlying knowledge game. By using the mental model as a lens for analyzing *Resident Evil: Code Veronica*, the thematic evolutions in the knowledge game as well as the scaffolding, restricted-to-freer practice, and contextual clues used to support these functions have been brought into focus. Like a small, wooden puzzle box, *Resident Evil*'s artistry lies hidden in plain sight.

REFERENCE

1. Miller, G. A. (1956). The magical number seven, plus or minus two: Some limits on our capacity for processing information. *Psychological Review* 63(2): 81–97.

CHAPTER 3

From Construction to Perception

Three Views of Level Design for Story-Driven Games

Huaxin Wei and Chaoguang Wang

CONTENTS

ESIDES THE DIVISION OF game narrative into embedded narrative and emergent narrative,* or individual story-related design concepts, such as theme, character, goal, conflict, linearity, and so on,† what more do we need to know about how to create a game that offers a satisfying narrative experience? In particular, when playing through and analyzing a narrative-enriched game level, what design considerations and principles can we see and learn? While engaged in the escalation of gameplay difficulty and character status during level traversing, a player's first impression and continuous perception of the gamespace is crucial to her or his understanding of the happenings and ability to perform actions.

This chapter looks into the gamespace in an attempt to demonstrate how the construction of game levels can shape players' perception of the game world and consequently the game plot that unfolds via gameplay. We introduce three different ways of looking at the gamespace and suggest accordingly three different areas of principles and considerations in the analysis of game levels.‡ In the first view, we examine the topographical structure of the gamespace that consists of key spatial references of the game world. In the second view, we treat the gamespace as a space-time complex where both the game and the game plot are progressing through the operation of the game. In the third view, we look at the gamespace as a representation of the storyworld, in which player's perception is shaped by visual, auditory, and mechanics design.

---

* The term "embedded narrative" was claimed to be first used by game designer and educator Marc LeBlanc, as opposed to the term "emergent narrative," in his talk at the Game Developer Conference in 2000. The two terms were then frequently used in the discussion of game narrative design, such as in Henry Jenkins, "Game Design as Narrative Architecture," in *First Person: New Media as Story, Performance, and Game*, eds. Noah Waridrip-Fruin and Pat Harrigan (Cambridge, MA: MIT Press, 2004), Katie Salen and Eric Zimmerman, *Rules of Play* (Cambridge, MA: MIT Press, 2004), and Ernest Adams, *Fundamentals of Game Design* (Berkeley, CA: New Riders, [2010] 2014).

† These concepts are frequently covered in game story sections in such game design books as Jesse Schell, *The Art of Game Design: A Book of Lenses* (Boca Raton, FL: CRC Press, [2008]2014), and Tracey Fullerton, *Game Design Workshop: A Playcentric Approach to Creating Innovative Games* (Boca Raton, FL: CRC Press, 2014).

‡ The analytical framework and some examples used in this chapter are based on parts of the first author's doctoral dissertation. An earlier version of the three-view framework was introduced in Huaxin Wei, Jim Bizzocchi, and Tom Calvert, "Time and Space in Digital Game Storytelling," *International Journal of Computer Games Technology* (2010), Article ID 897217, 23 pages. doi:10.1155/2010/897217.

A NARRATIVE PERSPECTIVE ON LEVEL DESIGN

For contemporary story-driven video games, the game world can be regarded as an accessible storyworld with audiovisual representations where players can navigate and interact with characters and objects through the game interface. When playing such a game, the game and its plot events unfold not only in time, but also in space. To design a game world, therefore, is to design the gamespace not just as a virtual space projected onto the screen, but as a ground for materializing the narrative space. How the narrative space is presented with relevant spatial elements and information is crucial for players to mentally construct the storyworld in which characters exist and events take place in a logical way. Thus, in today's 3D games, the structure of the space, visual representation of spatial information and the design of spatial characteristics are especially critical to gameplay and narrative experiences. Approaching level design from a narrative perspective helps us better understand the relation and connection between level structure and narrative structure, as well as gameplay activities and plot events.

Three Views: Topographical, Operational, and Presentational

The first and foremost thing for a level designer to create is the gamespace.* Thanks to its interactivity, gamespace is a highly multidimensional area of design. In order to detect and describe the large set of spatial characteristics and principles during the critical play of a game level, it is essential to apply a systematic approach to both individual analysis and comparative analysis. Due to a lack of mature models that can fulfill such a purpose, in a previous article cowritten by this chapter's first author,[1] a three-view descriptive framework was developed for analyzing story-driven games by drawing inspirations from professor of Hebrew and comparative literature Gabriel Zoran's comprehensive theory of narrative space[2] and professor of digital media Michael Nitsche's three perspectives on video gamespaces: structure, presentation, and functionality.[3] Using the three views contained in the framework, this chapter examines in detail the narrativized gamespace and lists out a common yet important set of level design considerations. The three views treat gamespace from three

---

* Phil Co, *Level Design for Games* (Berkeley, CA: New Riders, 2006); Rudolf Kremers, *Level Design: Concept, Theory, and Practice* (Natick, MA: A K Peters, 2009); Ernest Adams, *Fundamentals of Game Design* (Berkeley, CA: New Riders, [2010]2014).

different ontological modes that derive from Zoran's three levels of structuring of space in textual narratives.

In the first mode, the topographical view, space is considered by its original, physical nature as a static entity. Hence, the topographical structure of the gamespace is self-existent and independent of gameplay dynamics and audiovisual representations. It consists of underlying, fixed spatial references and information of the storyworld. Oftentimes the structure can be conceived as a game map, either by designers or players, which shows the spatial relations between geographical locations and entities.

In the second mode, the operational view, we examine space as a dynamic entity that is changing according to events and movements that come with game progression. The gamespace can be treated as a space-time complex where the game plot is enacted by players and the storyworld is being revealed through players' operation of the gamespace. In this view, the game plot unfolds over time with events taking place at one location after another.

In the third mode, the presentational view, space is the result of dynamic presentation of the storyworld, using patterned visual, auditory, and haptic materials and cues. The patterning itself is an application of the language of game as a medium. The presentational structure of the gamespace deals with many representational and player-game interface issues. As the foremost layer directly faced by players, the structure effectively influences, if not totally determines, players' perception of the game world.

How to Use the Three-View Analytical Framework

The three views introduced above are constructed for the purpose of analytical clarity. In the actual working of the gamespace, some spatial characteristics cast under different views function together to create certain effects. For one example that will be described later in the chapter, following the principle of spatial opposition in the operational view, the visual representation style—a characteristic cast under the presentational view—can be used as the key factor to create two visually distinct areas for contrasting effects for two opposing spaces. In a word, it takes the combination of all three modes of space to create a game world, which is always perceived by players as a whole.

The three-view analytical framework will help readers to better understand and evaluate a video game's level design. We believe that the design of a game level is not only about the visuals, the layout, and the paths, but also about the level functioning to guide players and embed narrative content. In the analysis of a game level, what is more important than visual effects is how the content is presented to players in different ways and accordingly how players interact with the level. In the actual game design process, it is important to communicate with artists and programmers to get their attention on the functionality of a game level, which is realized in both the operational and the presentational structures. In the rest of the chapter, we will discuss in detail how to use the three views to analyze game level design.

TOPOGRAPHICAL VIEW

As mentioned earlier, the topographical structure of a game world can be conceived as a map—actual or conceptual—that defines spatial relations between locations and entities. Even with an actual map, one can never have all the spatial information; hence, she or he needs to fill in the blanks with imagination or logics in order to reconstruct the storyworld in her or his mind. On the one hand, designers can add certain qualities to spatial entities when organizing a space; on the other hand, players can draw their own mental maps in different ways and for different purposes—be it way finding or gameplay performance enhancement. In this light, landmarks and regions as memory reference points are often used to mark important geographical locations or areas.* Among many considerations for the construction of landmarks, regions, and general locations, we describe three design aspects—spatial layout, game map design, and spatial opposition—and their associated principles.

Spatial Layout

The layout of the gamespace is one of the first design decisions to make by level designers since navigation is considered one basic form of player interaction with the game world. The spatial layout serves as the underlying structure of player movement and game progression; therefore, it is one of the fundamental characteristics of a game level. A common way to characterize the level layout is to look at its linearity. For instance, while Rudolf Kremers lists linear, semilinear (i.e., a foldback structure), and nonlinear level structures, Phil Co only distinguishes between linear and

---

* Jesse Schell comments on the importance of landmark design: "Any good gamespace has built-in landmarks, which help the players find where they are going, and also make the space interesting to look at. Landmarks are what players remember and what they talk about, for they are what make a space memorable," in *The Art of Game Design: A Book of Lenses* (Boston: Elsevier/Morgan Kaufmann, 2008), 334.

nonlinear layouts.* Among various typologies of spatial layouts, Ernest Adams's list of seven patterns is more detailed and practical to follow. These patterns are open layout, linear layout, parallel layout, ring layout, network layout, hub-and-spoke layout, and combinations of layout.[4]

Different layouts enable different dynamics for player navigation. The open layout is often used for action-adventure games that simulate a real-world space, oftentimes a city such as Florence in *Assassin's Creed II*[5] and Liberty City (modeled after New York City) in *Grand Theft Auto*,[6] or outdoor landscape such as Amazon in *Uncharted*.[7] Many massively multiplayer online (MMO) games also feature an open layout; however, the layout generally has a round boundary to help the online players avoid straying into some deep, pointy ends on the outer edge of the game map, feeling lost or wasting their time. In contrast to the open layout, the hub-and-spoke layout gives players a familiar spatial reference—the hub—to reorient themselves whenever they finish exploring an area in a spoke. *BioShock's*[8] level Medical Pavilion, as Steve Gaynor analyzes, is a good example of such a layout (Figure 3.1).[9]

When it comes to the high-level layout of the gamespace, not all subspaces or regions need to be physically connected. In other words, the gamespace does not have to be continuously presented on the screen and in this case, the player could use other means to move from one subspace to another, which will be discussed in detail in the section "Spatial Segmentation and Transition" in the third view. This flexibility during presentation allows those games with a large game world to adopt a combination of different layouts. For example, *Fable II's*[10] main locations are partially in a hub-and-spoke layout and partially in discrete subspaces. The game takes place in the fictional world of Albion, which is a coastal land with changeable geographic features including mountains, lakes, swamps, and caves. On the topographical layout, as illustrated in Figure 3.2, the coastline sees such main locations as Oakfield, Bowerstone, Westcliff, and Bloodstone from north to south. On the inland lie such locations as Bower Lake and Brightwood, among others. Across the coastline and in the middle of the sea, we see the rising Tattered Spire, a giant tower that is being built by Lucien, the game's villain, in order to concentrate all the Will Power to control the world. In this layout, as the most critical location in the game world, the Spire can be seen from afar at several locations, such as Bowerstone and Westcliff. It appears to be distant, mysterious, and ominous and its position manifests its central

---

* Phil Co, *Level Design for Games* (Berkeley, CA: New Riders, 2006); Rudolf Kremers, *Level Design: Concept, Theory, and Practice* (Natick, MA: A K Peters, 2009).

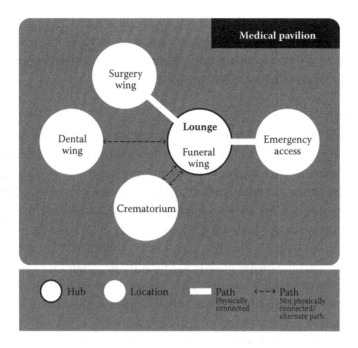

FIGURE 3.1 The level of Medical Pavilion in *BioShock* based on a hub-and-spoke layout.

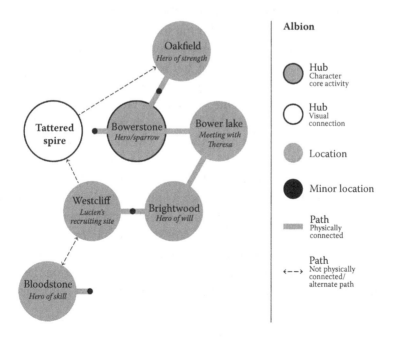

FIGURE 3.2 The spatial layout of main locations in *Fable II*.

yet hard-to-reach status. On the shore, Bowerstone and its conjunct Bower Lake serve as the origin of Albion's coordinates or the hub. It is the point of departure of the protagonist player character and the meeting point with the mentor Theresa after each major quest.

Map Design

Many AAA titles* tend to feature a huge game world that can be abstracted into one map, or more game maps when the game world contains multiple spaces. Game maps are used as a communication tool between level designers, artists, and game programmers, and sometimes offered to players as in-game maps. It is not easy to decide on how to balance the design and development resources between different aspects or areas of the map. For instance, level designers can choose to focus on building halls or churches that truly reflect the medieval style to intensify the atmosphere, which is a visual design problem, or calculating how long it should take for players to walk across the entire city in order to have a great impression of the game world, which is a scale problem. When design priority is not well managed, the game world could end up with plenty of grand buildings but empty of players or nonplayable characters (NPCs). In *EVE Online*,[11] for example, players have to spend a week or even longer just to drive their spacecraft across a game map. This type of game world may represent the universe space with high realism, but they can be boring since so much time is devoted to traveling without many game plot events going on, which is meaningless to many players. As another example, in the early version of *The World II*, a widely popular Chinese massively multiplayer online role-playing game (MMORPG),[12] players are presented with a vast virtual world with numerous beautiful architectures and palaces drawn in realistic ancient Chinese style. Most places on the game map, however, have never been visited by any players; moreover, it is very easy to get lost in that huge space. To rectify this situation, the designers had to remake the entire game map before its later official launch—a two-year hiatus since its public beta release. The lesson learned there is that the game map is not an isolated component but a part of the bigger game system and design teams should be better coordinated in order to coconstruct the overall gaming experience.

Aside from visual realism and map scale, quest and mission design is also an important consideration during map design. As a topographical

---

* In the game industry, those games with the highest budgets are usually considered to be AAA titles and expected to be high quality or best selling.

structure, the game map works as an organized container of game content and a guiding device for gameplay. Level designers can embed plot events and related missions into game maps in a way that suits the target player's playing style. This principle should be well emphasized especially in the tutorial map for new players, which should ensure every plot event, quest, route, and action are laid out in the right sequence and can be performed smoothly. Let us take *World of Warcraft*[13] as an example. In the game, a new player of the human race will be born in Northshire Abbey and instructed to finish a number of different quests one after another based on the main plotline. The map of Northshire Abbey is small, simple, and free of complicated entities like towers, basements, caves, cliffs, or rivers, which would instead appear and scatter in nearly every advanced map of *World of Warcraft*. In addition, a wall and a gate with guards are also created in the map of Northshire Abbey to protect new players from being contacted by hostile veteran players. In this tutorial map, therefore, new players can finish their training, learn the story of the game, and get familiar with gameplay methods in a safe and relaxing manner. However, this safety can still be broken, as there is no warning or restriction in this map that helps prevent a new player from leaving this warm cradle too early. She or he can break into the nearby Elwynn Forest and reach the map of Westfall when still at a very low level, and then possibly be attacked by monsters and die very easily. By way of contrast and under a more protective rule, new players of another Chinese MMORPG, *Fantasy Westward Journey*,[14] are not allowed to leave the tutorial map of their birthplace Jianye before level 10 in order not to get into trouble too early in advanced maps.

A further consideration for game map design, especially for MMO games, is how to facilitate the interaction and communication among players through design of regions and landmarks. Many MMO games provide some major or capital cities as places for players to gather and meet up with strangers. These cities as social regions are filled with landmarks for players to easily recognize. It is from these regions that players accept new quests, level up their skills, buy or sell virtual items, or simply socialize with others.

Spatial Oppositions

In the process of designing the spatial layout and the more detailed game map, the game level can be constructed to cope with different play styles and create desirable narrative and gameplay experiences using spatial oppositions as a powerful design principle. In a storyworld, we can see spatial oppositions that are typically physical, such as "inside and outside, far and near, center and periphery, city and village, etc.," listed by Zoran.* Similarly, in a narrativized gamespace, its map can be based on a series of oppositions that can follow, create, or play with gameplay conventions, in addition to endowing the space with meanings, mood, and varied experiences.

Perhaps the most obvious spatial oppositions we can observe are from those games featuring distinct level designs, very typical to platformers like *Little Big Planet*,[15] where each level has a very distinct visual, thematic, and structural design with varied gameplay mechanics. In a more story-driven game world, oppositions between spaces can be realized through not only lighting, color, and tone, as well as thematic design, but also emotional design. Ample examples of this can be seen in the level design of *World of Warcraft*. For instance, in Elwynn Forest, the first map for any newborn character of the human race, the environment is a bright green forest where the main emotion players experience is joy. The quests for players in this level seem relaxing and easier, such as picking a grape and driving away wolves or wild boars. By way of contrast, in the next map of Westfall, players find themselves in a dull, yellow area of barren mountains and deserted farmlands, inevitably feeling depressed or even desperate. The quests designed for this level are mainly to kill the infected monsters in order to save the farm, as well as destroy the bases of the bandits. Next to Westfall goes the even worse level of Duskwood, where the color here is a fearful black in the shadows of huge trees and plants. The map of this level is occupied by ghosts, ghouls, and zombies. Not surprisingly, most quests for players to take on here are to raid tombs and kill those horrible monsters. As a result of this map design and types of quests, the emotion provoked in Duskwood is anxiety and fear.

While distinct designs can be applied between levels to create oppositions, within the same level the principle of spatial opposition can still play a significant role. Consider the vertical structure in some of the indoor levels in *Batman: Arkham Asylum*,[16] where spatial oppositions are used in the level design for the player character, Batman, to better exert his physical skills. In these levels, as illustrated in Figure 3.3, the player finds herself or himself following a corridor or passing through a ventilation system first and then landing in a large room, which is constructed with two or more vertical levels. The ground level is oftentimes full of enemies or danger (e.g., poisonous gas) and the upper level (e.g., ledges, beams, platforms) is usually safer and out of enemies' reach or sight. As Batman possesses the

---

* See Ref. 2, p. 316.

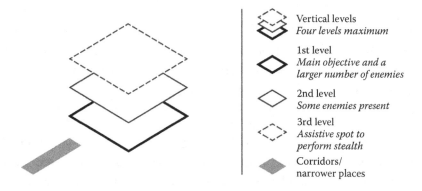

FIGURE 3.3 Vertical structure of *Batman: Arkham Asylum*'s gamespace.

ability to grapple to a higher spot, the player can make use of this opposition-based feature to make a top-down strike (e.g., a Glide Kick) tactically and stealthily. In another instance used in a larger scale, *Assassin's Creed*[17] also applies a two-level vertical structure, consisting of the ground and the rooftop, to create opposition-based gameplay (see Figure 3.4). Both games assign different gameplay mechanics and allocate different NPCs according to the vertical level, where the same convention can be observed: the ground level is for straightforward play with lots of combats whereas the upper level is for strategic, stealthy play.

While spatial oppositions can be integrated into gameplay mechanics, they can also be used to group game world content and make it more comprehensible for players. Early on we mentioned that some locations in MMO games are designated as a gathering place and other places might be

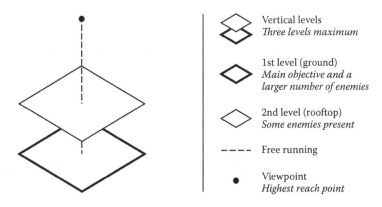

FIGURE 3.4 Vertical structure of *Assassin's Creed*'s gamespace.

designated for other purposes; therefore, different quests or plot content can be arranged accordingly. Such oppositions can be seen in many non-MMO games with a large, open game world. To reduce players' cognitive load when navigating a vast gamespace, locations are designed with clearly opposing characteristics that can be easily remembered and recognized by players. In *Fable II*, within towns are shops, pubs, inns, houses, and so on, with guards patrolling all the time, while in between towns are rural landscapes with main roads linking towns, which are active zones for bandits, just like how it was in the real world in the old days. As a result, most combats take place outside towns, either on the road or in some cave, whereas most of the errands, such as information collection or meeting with people, are done in towns. With opposition such as between inside and outside towns, designers can organically arrange plot events and action sequences. Players, on the other hand, will start to be aware of the convention and consequently adjust their alert levels and expectations of what to do accordingly.

OPERATIONAL VIEW

In the operational view of the gamespace, we see the storyworld reveal as well as the game plot unfold through movements and actions dynamically over time. The story constructed by a player is based on both the game's predefined narrative structure, which is static, and the way she or he navigates and interacts with characters and objects in the game world, which is dynamic. The operational structure of a level concerns the design of the dynamics and regulating and patterning movements in relation to the game progression. In the operational view of a reconstructed storyworld, Zoran suggests that "one should distinguish between synchronic and diachronic relationships";* the former ones are examined at a given time point by looking at what objects are at rest and what are in motion, whereas the latter ones are examined over a given time frame by looking at the direction of movements within the space. Inspired by this we discuss design considerations that help shape players' operation of the gamespace under two areas: mobility of NPCs and paths and axes.

Mobility of NPCs

Among all the entities in a game, NPCs are probably the most dynamic objects in the gamespace. Based on their mobility, NPCs can be divided

---

* See Ref. 2, p. 318.

into two groups: those attached to a specific location in the game level and those that move around. The latter group can be further divided according to their range of movement (i.e., whether they can traverse levels). Hence, we can roughly characterize their mobility as immobile, locally mobile, and globally mobile, respectively. When not interacting with players, immobile and locally mobile NPCs are more or less part of the background and hence can be regarded as environmental objects. In this case, they can be treated as a mere backdrop or as landmarks to attract players to come to their region—a strategy often used by multiplayer online game designers. In *Zhengtu*,[18] another popular Chinese MMORPG, designers go so far as to put nearly all NPCs in a very small area of the capital city and leave most other spaces empty in order to attract as many players as possible to this area for both player-to-NPC and player-to-player social interaction and communication.

Generally speaking, how mobile a character is often signifies its importance to both gameplay and plot development. Globally mobile characters tend to be key characters that grow with the player character who is usually the protagonist. A good example is Princess Farah from *Prince of Persia: The Sands of Time*,[19] who follows the player character, the Prince, all along and functions as an important narrative device for being the listener, or the narratee, of the Prince's storytelling. Similarly, Teresa in *Fable II* is another globally mobile NPC that functions as the narrator of the game story as well as the mentor of the player character. More interestingly, in the *World of Warcraft*, the boss of a quest chain is often designed to be very mobile; instead of staying in the same spot, it patrols along a specific route. One example is the NPC Mor'Ladim that patrols along a road in Duskwood. In completing the quest chain, the player has to search in the forest and locate his position before she or he can attack and kill him.

In principle, the more mobile NPCs there are, the more complex the gameplay and game plot are. Take *Assassin's Creed*'s first two installments as examples; in the original *Assassin's Creed*, the player character, Altair, rarely has company to follow him around in the storyworld, except for vigilantes and scholars, who are both only locally mobile. In *Assassin's Creed II*, which received significantly better reviews and was said to be a "sequel that triumphs over the original in every possible way,"[20] the player character, Ezio, is accompanied by the globally mobile NPC, Mario, who will move between cities and help him fight with enemies. Moreover, the game world includes many more locally mobile NPCs, such as courtesans, thieves, and mercenaries, for Ezio to hire to distract enemies. As a result, not only does the story of the second game feel richer than that of the first game, the gameplay is also much more dynamic.

Paths and Axes

Having a level layout or game map is not enough to regulate the movements inside the level. Among the means of forming desirable movement patterns, paths and axes are effective structures to regulate players' runtime behaviors. In the topographical view, paths in a game world are a collective potential of movements; in the operational view, paths are assigned with directions so that they can be unidirectional or bidirectional. In the context of this chapter, axes are primary paths where major events and actions take place; therefore, they are an important device in the creation of critical plot points as part of a predefined narrative structure that are enacted during the game operation. In role-playing games, for example, players oftentimes move along axes when pursuing main quests. On the other hand, when they want to explore the space or make social interactions by taking up a side quest, they will follow those paths that branch off from the axes.

Aside from organizing narrative and gameplay content, axes can also be endowed with certain qualities so that, in a different ontological mode, the operational space is structured with a different network of axes. In the *Assassin's Creed* games, removing opposing parties' flags can help in reducing their influence over a district. Thus, as a side goal to maximize their achievements, players can refer to the in-game map where locations of the flags are marked and specifically follow the network of related axes to remove the flags. Similarly, such qualities as treasure boxes, puzzle pieces, and other collectibles can be assigned to locations to form different networks of axes.

It is worth mentioning that the player character's movement pattern can change the seeming balance or symmetry of a spatial layout during runtime operation of a game. The spatial design of *Assassin's Creed* clearly demonstrates this problem. Its top-level map consists of three cities—Damascus, Acre, and Jerusalem—and a town, Masyaf, with the open area of the Kingdom in the middle as the geographical hub (upper diagram in Figure 3.5). The hub-and-spoke layout looks quite balanced until we start counting the frequency of travel in between locations. The lower diagram of Figure 3.5 reveals the minimum number of trips the player character, Altair, needs to make to complete the game. Because Masyaf is the

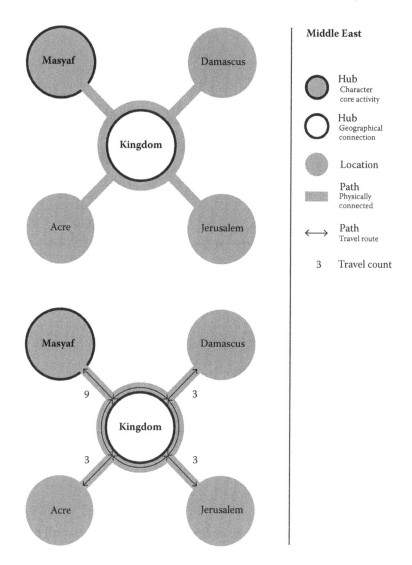

FIGURE 3.5   High-level topographical view of *Assassin's Creed*'s space and corresponding operational view with travel paths and counts.

assassin's base fortress, which Altair needs to receive missions from and report back to, the path between Masyaf and the Kingdom is used much more frequently than other paths and functions almost like an axis. Yet, because no event is created for along this seeming axis, the trips become more and more tedious and meaningless. Intentional or not, the spatial design of *Assassin's Creed II* avoids this situation successfully by balancing out the trips to and from central locations. As seen in Figure 3.6,

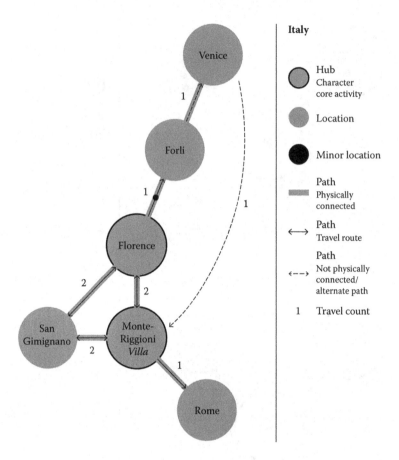

FIGURE 3.6 High-level operational view of *Assassin's Creed II*'s space with travel paths and counts.

Monteriggioni is Ezio's primary headquarters and Florence is full of core activities. These two locations are not exactly in the center of the topographical map that corresponds to real-world geographical locations; however, the operational structure is more balanced in terms of travel counts thanks to the design of paths, which are added with some unidirectional ones, and alternative travel means (e.g., fast travel between any two of the Fast Travel Booths scattered around different regions of Italy or directly going back to Monteriggioni from Venice during a flashback).

The alternative travel means as shown in the case of *Assassin's Creed II* in fact are a very common movement pattern in games with a world too large to be represented within one screen. During the procedural presentation of the game and game world, the connectivity between locations in players' perceived gamespace bears many more degrees than simply being physically connected or not. This flexibility of connectivity can be a result of the predefined plot structure, such as a cut to a different location in a flashback as mentioned above, or an option provided for players to suit their preferred play style. An example of such an option is the car travel in *L.A. Noire*[21]: the player can choose to let the player character, Cole Phelps, drive the car by himself or let his partner drive. The former case takes a while as the car will be driven from one location to another by navigating the city; the latter case, in contrast, is identical to fast travel as the car ride will be cut soon after starting and the next scene at the new location will be presented. In a visually represented game world, alternative travel means such as the examples above cannot be offered without using presentational techniques; hence, we will come back to this with more discussion in the section "Spatial Segmentation and Transition" in the discussion of presentational view.

PRESENTATIONAL VIEW

While the topographical and operational views concern the construction of spatial references and movements in the game world, the presentational view focuses more on how players perceive the gamespace through other characteristics that are not natural or native to the gamespace itself, but brought out by the ways of spatial presentation. In other words, the presentational structure concerns how to use and pattern visual, auditory, textual, haptic, and other cues to present the game world and game plot dynamically while responding to player choices and actions. Thus, in this view, the design is focused first on the means and materials of the presentation and second on how to incorporate player actions in the shaping of player perception of the game world. Since most story-driven games are visual narratives just like film, level design under the first focus can apply many film conventions in the level construction process, of which we will mainly discuss perspective and on-screen versus offscreen spaces. Under the second focus, on the other hand, we will cover some operation-related considerations including spatial segmentation and transition and cut-scenes placement.

Perspective

The perspective, or point of view, that a player takes on during gameplay is defined by both the avatar's positioning in the represented gamespace and the enacted player character's attitudes, values, and emotions. We call the former optical, or visual, point of view and the latter psychological point of view. More often than not in a story-driven game, it is expected that players assume the visual point of view together with the psychological one of the player character. Occasionally the narrative designer decides to play with the storytelling style and separate the two perspectives—oftentimes through voice-over narration—to create certain effects. Examples can be seen in *Prince of Persia: The Sands of Time* and *Max Payne*,[22] where the player-controlled protagonist would occasionally break the fourth wall and talk to the player, commenting on what has happened and turning the story experience from originally subjective and immersive to somewhat objective and withdrawn from the character.

Compared with first-person games, where the player's visual perspective simply assumes the position of the avatar's eyes at all times, third-person games tend to have a more flexible camera model giving players various degrees of view control. Third-person perspective prevails in many 3D action-adventures and action games that offer players nearly full control of their camera view, typically allowing camera pan and a switch to first-person view. While these perspectives are constructed simply using the principles of a film camera, other perspectives can be realized through a virtual, or computational, camera model. For instance, some special vision can be integrated into the gameplay to aid the player. Both *Assassin's Creed* and *Batman: Arkham Asylum* games provide players a filtered vision that differentiates the identity of characters in the view, called eagle vision and detective mode, respectively, highlighting targets in particular. For a detective-story-based game like *L.A. Noire*, an extra zooming-in option is provided for the player to inspect evidence closely. In yet another instance, games that require a lot of aiming and shooting, like *Tomb Raider*,[23] often provide a weapon zoom control that helps players to get a closer view of the target.

When not yielding to manual control, the virtual camera of a third-person game can adjust and optimize the view automatically, especially during combat scenes where the player is deeply engaged in fast actions or maneuvering a weapon. The case of action-adventure *God of War* is a classic example of automatic camera adjustment.[24] In noncombat scenes, the camera follows the avatar from a short distance in a slightly higher angle; during combat scenes, on the other hand, the camera position automatically goes higher and looks down so that the player can see more surroundings. In addition to adjustment, the virtual camera can also guide players' attention via a short cut-scene sequence of zooming in onto an object to hint at the next step or flying through an in-game area to give players a preview of the space, both techniques used in action adventures like *Assassin's Creed II*.

Besides aiding and guiding players, changing up the perspective can be further utilized as a stylistic design tool to break the conventional pattern and vary the gameplay experience or method from time to time. In *World of Warcraft*, players are usually limited to a third-person view and seldom have a chance to enjoy the game world from another perspective. In some quests, however, players need to control a cannon to shoot the enemy and can scan the gamespace from a first-person point of view through the cannon scope, which can be a surprising experience for players: at the same time they are using a cannon to sink the battleships in a quest in Tol Barad Peninsula, they can enjoy the beautiful scenery of the sea for a different view. Another example where perspective shifting happens in the game is the Flight Path, a transportation link between different maps. Along such a path players can fly across the game world in a system-generated visual sequence, appreciating the varied landscape of forests, lakes, and mountaintops from a fixed, top-down perspective.

On-Screen and Offscreen Spaces

Conventionally video games project the gamespace onto a screen. In most cases, the gamespace is too large to be all mapped onto the space of one screen. Hence, during the play, spatial information of the game world needs to be selected and structured first before being revealed and presented on the screen. The game screen displays moving images like the film screen does. For games that limit or disallow players to change the camera view (consider those highly edited cinematic games like *Heavy Rain*[25] or games with a fixed-camera like *God of War*), the on-screen space represents a relatively independent game area and how it is connected to the offscreen space is not always delineated. This is especially true for those combat scenes that take back players' camera control like in *Assassin's Creed* games, where the on-screen space is perceived to be cut off from offscreen space so that players' attention is focused on the combat itself. In this case, as well as in many cut-scenes, the on-screen space is close to the shot space of a film, where many screen composition conventions from film can be applied, such as an establishing shot at the beginning of a new scene followed by one that zooms in on the action, or shot/reverse shot for two-person conversational scenes.

For most free-roaming story-driven games with a large continuous 3D game world, the on-screen space can be operated quite differently from the shot space. Since a game's virtual camera is computational and dynamic, its functionality extends far beyond that of a film camera, which is bound by the laws of optics and physics. One such extended use of camera is fly-through. Used for architecture and virtual reality rendering as an animated preview technique, fly-through is typically applied in game design to allow players to scan an area ahead of time from a predefined viewpoint, where the camera is flying or circling around following a deliberately revealing path. This virtual camera technique breaks the screen boundaries and delivers spatial information in motion. It facilitates player perception of the gamespace in two ways. First, it eases players' navigation and spatial puzzle solving; good examples of this can be found in *Prince of Persia: The Sands of Time* and *Assassin's Creed II*, both using this technique extensively to cue their players. Second, when the camera flies and zooms in onto an object or a character, either automatically or by pressing a button (as in *Fable II*), it effectively guides players' attention and signifies the next move for players.

When the on-screen and offscreen spaces are not topographically continuous, how the game transitions from one on-screen space to another becomes a design issue, which will be discussed next.

Spatial Segmentation and Transition

As discussed earlier, in the operational view, the gamespace is constructed and presented onto the screen in a temporal continuum. The world of a 3D story-driven game tends to be too large to be projected onto one screen; therefore, the game world is often divided into distinct subspaces for both presentational and operational purposes, each with distinct spatial characteristics or even gameplay mechanics. For today's complicated 3D game levels, how to segment the space is an important design decision that affects the game balance, the fluidity of navigation across subspaces, the cost of game development and runtime performance.

When two subspaces are connected topographically, players can simply walk into one subspace from another. When they are disconnected, on the other hand, there are several design techniques to help the player move from one subspace to another. Three such common techniques are fast or automatic travel, caption, and filmic editing. Previously mentioned fast travel examples including a car ride in *L.A. Noire* and Flight Path in *World of Warcraft*, as well as Fast Travel to a map location set via the pause menu in *Fable II*, are all variations of this transition technique. Among all the variations, one popular method is to use teleportation to move the player character; Fast Travel Booths in *Assassin's Creed II* and Cullis Gates, the magical portals in *Fable II*, are both examples of this.

The second technique, caption, is to use on-screen text to tell the player about the location of the next scene, usually followed by a direct cut. This is an economical way of moving the player from one subspace to another. *Fable II* employs quite a lot of screen captions so that although its gamespace is not entirely continuous (see Figure 3.2), it is perceived so. Before the travel, the caption usually mentions the duration needed for the trip; after the player gets the new location, the caption reminds her or him that a new map has been added and thus new quests are added from the menu.

Filmic editing, the third technique, borrows the conventions of film narration and uses various types of film transitions to move the plot along, such as direct cut, dissolve, and fade in/out. The decision of when to transition is dependent not solely on the space transition, but sometimes on plot segmentation as well. Nevertheless, the more editing a game uses, the more discrete and smaller its subspaces tend to be, as smaller subspaces are easier to be set up with a preferred shot composition. Quantic Dream's highly cinematic *Heavy Rain* and *Beyond: Two Souls*[26] are two of the best examples.

Placement of Cut-Scenes

The narrative content of a game is presented with different media materials partially organized in a predefined structure and partially constructed on the fly during gameplay. Along the temporal continuum of a game, how to weave together narrative content of varied forms is critical to players' narrative and gameplay experiences. Dialogs and on-screen texts are very commonly interspersed in the game to describe the happenings and foreshadowing future events. These forms of narrative content, however, are not always welcomed by those players who just want to finish their quests and gain rewards as soon as possible. They tend to ignore the content because listening to the dialogs with NPCs and reading those texts telling the background story can feel like a chore. Cut-scenes can be used as a lighter (in terms of cognitive load) form to present the game narrative. In the meantime, they can also regulate the pacing of a game since they somewhat force players to shift their attention from actions to the game narrative. Even though cut-scenes have been widely acknowledged as an important means to deliver narrative content, they should not disrupt or stop the flow of a unitary gameplay segment. A common practice, therefore, is to present a cut-scene introducing major characters and relevant background stories at the beginning or end of a gameplay segment or the beginning or end of the entire game. Regardless of how deeply players are engaged in achieving various goals through going on endless quests, killing monsters and collecting items, they have to stop and spend some minutes to watch the cut-scenes and immerse themselves in the game story.

If we use color-coding to illustrate the placement of cut-scenes in *L.A. Noire* and *Uncharted 2: Among Thieves*,[27] we can observe the patterns of cut-scene placement along the timeline in Figures 3.7 and 3.8, respectively. Comparing the two diagrams of the two games, we can see two roles cut-scenes can play in addition to narrative content delivery. First, as previously mentioned, they break up gameplay sequences and create a temporal pattern, and in doing so they help regulate the pacing of the game and storytelling.

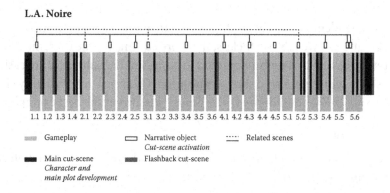

FIGURE 3.7 Temporal distribution of cut-scenes in *L.A. Noire*.

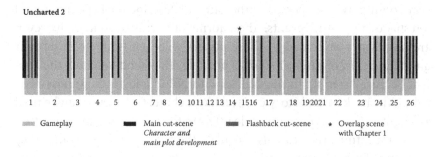

FIGURE 3.8 Temporal distribution of cut-scenes in *Uncharted 2: Among Thieves*.

Second, the longer and denser the cut-scenes are placed, the more narrative exposition and thus narrative arc they help create. This explains why both games tend to have more cut-scenes in the beginning, climax, and end. The patterns of the two games also show two different styles of storytelling. Notice that while in *L.A. Noire* the cut-scenes are placed at the beginning of a chapter in most cases, in *Uncharted 2* many cut-scenes are placed in the middle of a chapter. We can reason that these patterns reflect the functions of their cut-scenes: *L.A. Noire* uses cut-scenes mainly as a framing tool or chapter separators whereas *Uncharted 2* uses cut-scenes more for advancing the plot.

For space-driven or multispace adventure games, if mapping the cut-scenes onto a weighted location map, we can observe the pattern of cut-scene placement across the gamespace. In Figure 3.9 drawn for *Uncharted 2: Among Thieves*, we can see the game plot starts its climatic actions in Himalayas and ends in Shambhala, which is embedded with

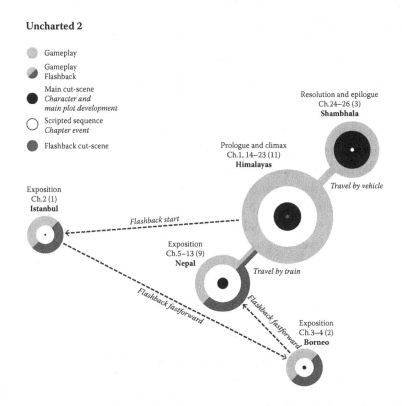

FIGURE 3.9 Spatial distribution of cut-scenes, weighted (with the circle size) for each location in a map view of *Uncharted 2: Among Thieves*.

the most cut-scenes to help shape the narrative arc, or as the game's colead game designer Richard Lemarchand said, "to help raise the emotional stakes as we race toward the game's climax."[28] A map view of cut-scenes can potentially help level designers blend the narrative and gameplay, as well as coordinate their work with writers, artists, and programmers; together the team can make sensible allocations of production efforts.

SUMMARY

For story-driven games, a successfully designed game world is not just a setting of events but an interactive narrative space for players. This chapter introduces three views that reveal the topographical, operational, and presentational structures of game levels. The topographical structure lays out the key references of the gamespace and serves as the basis for the operation and presentation of the game. The operational structure defines movement patterns and temporal progression of the game plot within the level. The presentational structure determines ways of presenting the gamespace dynamically using a variety of media techniques and materials. Within this analytical framework, we lay out some important spatial principles and characteristics that contribute to players' perception and experience of not only the game world but also the game story. The three-view approach provides a set of analytical lenses attempted to direct an analyst's attention to the structure and techniques of weaving narrative and gameplay together. Viewing game levels in the three lights, this chapter can be used as a guide for game designers and enthusiasts to analyze different story-driven games, make comparisons, and develop design strategies in their own design practice.

In summary, with the analytical framework introduced in this chapter, an in-depth level design analysis can potentially answer the following questions:

1. What spatial layout does the game or game level use?

2. What are the characteristics of the game map?

3. Is there any spatial opposition in the gamespace? If yes, what is the implication for narrative and/or gameplay?

4. How are the NPCs related to the space? Are there any NPCs with mobility? If yes, how do they influence the narrative and gameplay?

5. Are there any axes in the gamespace? How do the paths and/or axes affect the pattern of navigation and the order of events players go through?

6. What types of perspective and camera angle does the game use?

7. If the topographical space is continuous, is it (re)presented as a continuous space? If yes, what are the options of camera control for players? If not, how is the player's view limited? What roles does the virtual camera perform? Is there any stylistic use?

8. How is the gamespace segmented? How does the player or the game scene move from one subspace to another?

9. How are cut-scenes placed over the game in relation to the game timeline and space?

ACKNOWLEDGMENT

Special thanks to Betty Durango for her help in meticulously creating the diagrams for this chapter. The visualization work behind the diagrams was supported by the Inject Grant offered by the Hong Kong Polytechnic University and School of Design (project number 1-ZE3P).

REFERENCES

1. Huaxin Wei, Jim Bizzocchi, and Tom Calvert, "Time and Space in Digital Game Storytelling," *International Journal of Computer Games Technology* (2010), Article ID 897217, 23 pages. doi:10.1155/2010/897217.
2. Gabriel Zoran, "Towards a Theory of Space in Narrative," *Poetics Today* 5, No. 2 (1984): 309–335.
3. Michael Nitsche, *Video Gamespaces: Image, Play, and Structure in 3D Game Worlds* (Cambridge, MA: MIT Press, 2008).
4. Ernest Adams, *Fundamentals of Game Design* (Berkeley, CA: New Riders, [2010]2014).
5. Ubisoft, *Assassin's Creed II*, multi-platform game, Ubisoft, 2009.
6. Rackstar North, *Grand Theft Auto*, multi-platform game, Rockstar Games, 1997.
7. Naughty Dog, *Uncharted: Drake's Fortune*, PlayStation (3/4) game, Sony Computer Entertainment, 2007/2015.
8. 2K Games, *BioShock*, multi-platform game, 2K Games, 2007.
9. Steve Gaynor, "Reorienteering: Spatial organization in *BioShock*," last modified April 19, 2009, http://fullbright.blogspot.com/2009/04/reorienteering -spatial-organization-in.html.
10. Lionhead Studios, *Fable II*, Xbox 360 game, Microsoft Game Studios, 2008.
11. CCP Games, *EVE Online*, MMORPG, CCP Games, 2003–2015.

12. NetEase, *The World II (Tianxia 2)*, MMORPG, NetEase, 2009–2012.
13. Blizzard Entertainment, *World of Warcraft*, MMORPG, Blizzard Entertainment, 2004–2015.
14. NetEase, *Fantasy Westward Journey*, MMORPG, NetEase, 2004–2015.
15. Media Molecule et al., *LittleBigPlanet*, PlayStation (3/Portable) game, Sony Computer Entertainment, 2008/2009.
16. Rocksteady Studios, *Batman: Arkham Asylum*, multi-platform game, Edios Interactive & Warner Bros. Interactive Entertainment, 2009.
17. Ubisoft, *Assassin's Creed*, multi-platform game, Ubisoft, 2007.
18. Zhengtu Network, *Zhengtu*, MMORPG, Zhengtu Network, 2006–2016.
19. Ubisoft, *Prince of Persia: The Sands of Time*, multi-platform game, Ubisoft, 2003.
20. Ubisoft, *Assassin's Creed II*, multi-platform game, Ubisoft, 2009; David Clayman, "*Assassin's Creed II* Review: A Sequel that Triumphs Over the Original in Every Possible Way," IGN.com, last modified March 12, 2010, http://www.ign.com/articles/2010/03/12/assassins-creed-ii-review.
21. Team Bondi, *L.A. Noire*, multi-platform game, Rockstar Games, 2011.
22. Remedy Entertainment, *Max Payne*, multi-platform game, Gathering of Developers (Windows) and Rockstar Games (Playstation 2, Xbox), 2001.
23. Crystal Dynamics, *Tomb Raider*, multi-platform game, Square Enix, 2013.
24. SCE Santa Monica Studio, *God of War*, PlayStation (2/3/Vita) game, Sony Computer Entertainment & Capcom, 2005.
25. Quantic Dream, *Heavy Rain*, PlayStation (3/4) game, Sony Computer Entertainment, 2010/2016.
26. Quantic Dream, *Beyond: Two Souls*, PlayStation (3/4) game, Sony Computer Entertainment, 2013.
27. Naughty Dog, *Uncharted 2: Among Thieves*, PlayStation (3/4) game, Sony Computer Entertainment, 2009/2015.
28. Drew Davidson and Richard Lemarchand, "Uncharted 2: Among Thieves—How to Become a Hero," in *Games, Learning, and Society: Learning and Meaning in the Digital Age*, eds. Constance Steinkuehler, Kurt Squire, and Sasha Barab (Cambridge University Press, 2012), 98.

CHAPTER 4

Everything I Learned about Level Design at an Orlesian Ball

Heidi McDonald

CONTENTS

WELCOME TO MY INFORMAL and kinda silly chapter on how playing game levels has informed my own design work!

I'm not going to go straight into the whole level design thing. In order to understand where my initial understanding of level design came from and what it was, it is best to explain some things about my history with games, how they fit into my life, and how games one plays (or does not play) affects their design vocabulary. I'll also discuss how I ended up breaking into the game industry at 41 and learned level design on the fly, based only on an initially limited set of influences.

I'll then explain how I had that understanding completely blown apart when I played *Dragon Age: Inquisition* in 2014, and how that changed everything I knew about level design and inspired my level design work on a project during my time at Schell Games. Thanks for bearing with me. I will try to make this fun since I cannot play you ABBA or make you cupcakes or e-mail you my favorite GIF of corgis on a treadmill.*

MY HISTORY WITH GAMES

My initial understanding of level design came from the first video games I played: *Pac-Man, Centipede, PONG*. I used my entire $3.25 weekly allowance for 13 plays on the machines that stood by the cashier's area of our local grocery store in the Pittsburgh suburbs. *PONG* happened only because my sister and I opened what we thought was an ATARI-2600 on Christmas morning in 1979 only to find *PONG* in its place.†

There weren't levels in *PONG*. You just played until somebody won and somebody lost, or until you as a solo player messed up. Perhaps that's why we found it so boring. In *Pac-Man*, the maze did not change, but you knew the difference between levels based on the motion patterns and speed of the monsters, and by the type of bonus fruit that would appear. If you were lucky to have survived enough levels, you were rewarded with an animation. In *Centipede*, the difference between levels involved color changes in the creatures and mushrooms, and in the speed and frequency of the monsters.‡

We were poor, so we did not have a computer at home. My experience with games began with arcade games and *PONG* and playing Atari at my friends' houses. My friends and I actually played the crap out of that legendarily bad *E.T.* game.§ After I graduated from high school in 1988, I ditched a full scholarship to journalism school to move out West and be a musician. I was doing fine on the Scottsdale, Arizona resort circuit. I had my own place and learned more about life at 19 than most of my counterparts did. I spent three years as a musician out there, had my equipment stolen and had to move back East, then worked in and around Pittsburgh until I had enough money to buy my equipment back, while putting myself most of the way through community college. Then, life threw me a curve ball: in 1994, I got pregnant and had my daughter. I hung up my musical career and got a Practical Job in communications.

---

* I swear I would do those things for you for reading my chapter.
† That was a sad, sad day. We had to play with the *PONG* to make our parents feel good, while our Dad was all, "Isn't this *COOL*, kids?" Ugggghhhhh.
‡ Yes, I realize these examples show my age. But I can still kick your ass at any of these games, okay?
§ My friends and I all thought that E.T. looked like a poop, and it was completely hilarious to us that there was this little computerized poop waddling around.

Being a starving musician from 1988 through 1994, and then spending the rest of the 1990s as a new mom with toddlers, I fell out of touch with games because I didn't have the money or the time to play and I didn't own a computer. I missed Sega Genesis. I missed the NES. All the platformers with Mario and Sonic where levels were actually becoming A Thing, with mazes and obstacles that changed from level to level, would not find their way into my game design vocabulary.

In 1999, when I began dating my second husband, he turned me on to this thing called *EverQuest*. I LOVED IT, other than that whole having to go find your body thing. The only noticeably distinct levels in that game were earned with experience points you got based on things you did. The spatial level of the game didn't appear to change, but your personal level changed based on your negotiation of the world, and you could explore different places in the game world further based on what level you were.

I went from *EverQuest* to PC adventure games like *Syberia* and games like *Black and White*, and simulation games like *Zoo Tycoon* and *The Sims* (screw you, Tragic Clown*!). When *Dark Age of Camelot* came out, that was my first time really going hardcore. (I was an alliance master, but only because I decided that the Elitist Jerks guild needed to be taught a lesson, so I organized all the rest of the guilds on the server specifically to kick their asses.) I dropped *Dark Age of Camelot* for *World of Warcraft* (*WoW*) in 2005, and then discovered BioWare's games, and remain an unrepentant fangirl of them to this day.

Knights of the Old Republic (*KOTOR*) was the first time I ever realized that a game could make me FEEL THINGS: talk about a brainsplode, people. I had been captured in a way I had never thought possible. I cared about these worlds and these characters much, much more than I ever had before. I never understood that there were distinct levels in BioWare games like *KOTOR* and *Dragon Age: Origins*, because for me, they took me from place to place fluidly. As primarily a writer, I was blown away by the stories in these games and found myself wanting to write them, too. For the first time ever, I started dabbling in fiction.

In 2008, the recession hit. At the time, I was a stay-at-home mom with two school-aged kids and a baby. I stayed home with the baby during the day but kept busy: I served as a municipal elected official, I did freelance

---

* An annoying character in *The Sims* that appears when certain characters are depressed and makes them even more depressed.

writing, I made consignment quilts for people,* and I played games like *WoW, The Sims, Chicken Invaders,* the *Neverwinter* series, and *Dungeon Siege.* My husband was one of 5,000 people let go by IBM. Suddenly, we were both scrambling to find jobs.

Before I'd been a stay-at-home mom, I had a decent career in communications with experience in marketing, promotions, events, and freelance writing. I had a great portfolio with awards and paid work from places like the *Pittsburgh Post-Gazette, BRAVO-TV, Elle Magazine, Yahoo! Movies,* and others; I just did not have a degree. In at least three cases, I came in second place for a position to a person who had a lesser portfolio, but a degree. We were lucky. My husband did find another job, and all was well. But this whole thing made me angry, and made me realize I never wanted to be a financial liability to my family again. When my youngest started Kindergarten in 2009, I went back to school.

Back in 1988 when the Pennsylvania Newspaper Association's scholarship winner quit school to be a musician, her parents freaked out. My reasoning was, "I'm only going to be 19 once, and I don't want to be in my 40s wondering what would have happened had I pursued music. Also, school has been there for 150 or so years, it will still be there when I'm ready to go back, and if I was smart enough to get a scholarship once, I'll be able to get another one." My parents were disappointed and did not believe me, but, they should have believed me. After completing my AA at Allegheny County Community College in 2009, I found myself the recipient of a generous scholarship to Chatham University (a women's college in Pittsburgh which since 2015 has been coed), where the plan was to study pre-law. I was not so excited about my major, but, I knew I would make good money choosing a major that was so very practical.

It was really weird to be 39 years old, showing up on a college campus with students literally half my age. I felt for those young women, most of whom were there because their parents had insisted they be there, and they were going through the motions. I had lived an entire lifetime and waited until I was ready and eager to be at school, so I was the annoying old lady raising my hand too often. They rolled their eyes at me, and it kind of hurt, but I understood. Now, I've been known to be a bit of an overachiever; but I reasoned in this case that if I had to ride three school-aged children about their grades, then mine had best be perfect. And they were.

---

* Jewel-toned batik versions of traditional quilt blocks, kinda like your Grandma's quilts, electrocuted.

My majoring in pre-law didn't last long. My mom—the wisest woman I have ever known—said, "you need to go for what makes you happy, not what you think will be the safe bet." I thought a lot about this, and changed my major to a double one. I chose communications with a concentration in professional writing, to legitimize the portfolio I already had. I chose film and digital media, not just because I am a movie buff, but also because I wanted to learn some cool new multimedia tricks that would balance out the communications experience and make me more valuable. Little did I know that this would eventually land me in video games.

My media literacy professor invited everyone to a creative careers seminar at Carnegie Mellon University. I was the only person in the class to sign up, and I had chosen a talk on film and broadcast media. As the professor and I arrived at the seminar, he asked me what talk I was going to, and when I explained, he said, "Oh. I'm going to the video game one." I was like, "SHUT. UP. There's a video game one?" I stuck my talk ticket in my pocket and crashed the video game talk. Zigging when I was supposed to zag that day changed my life. To this day I still have the unused ticket from that other talk, kept to remind me that sometimes listening to your gut will change your life in the best way.

On this panel was a woman named Sabrina Haskell who was a video game designer. In that moment, my mind was completely blown. I guess I had known on some level that video games were made by people, but I had never really thought much about the people who made them. Maybe they were a bunch of goofy guys who looked like the comic book store guy on *The Simpsons*, congregating in some basement, and pounding out code? I had no idea! In this one moment I learned:

- There are people whose job it is to make video games.

- Some of these people ARE ACTUALLY WOMEN.

- There is a company in Pittsburgh that makes video games!

This blew my life apart. Video games were not anything I had ever thought of as a career path. I had played *KOTOR* and thought about how great it would be to write stories like this, and that game had made me start writing fiction. I had played the *Neverwinter* series and mucked around with their mod tools, but never completed my own mod. I begged my professor to invite Sabrina to our class so I could hear more about her job. He did, and she came, and I was the annoying one in the front peppering her with questions. She and I exchanged contact information and kept in touch. When I screwed up the nerve to ask about internships, Schell Games was just starting preproduction on a content-heavy game called *PlayForward: Elm City Stories*, for Yale University School of Medicine, to teach HIV prevention to 11- to 14-year-old children.

Right place, right time: I was the oldest intern Jesse Schell ever hired, and I will always be wildly grateful to him for taking a chance on an unlikely candidate. I was hired on full-time the day after my college graduation. *I was in video games. At 41.* Nobody told me how unusual, how rare this was until I had already done it. I took a chance, paid attention to what I loved, and had the right people believe in me. And I have tried to run with that opportunity, never looking back. More important, I try to pay it forward more, the longer I am around in this industry. It is fun and wacky but also not always stable, and nobody gets ahead without help.

Thank goodness I had a lot of help available to me when I first started. I was about to need it. My new job as a game designer soon required this of me, the moment I was asked to do some level design.

MY NEW CAREER IN GAMES AND MY FIRST LEVELS

So, after the happy shock of getting hired full-time at a video game company set in, and the rosy glasses came off a bit, I realized that making games is hard, people. HARD. I had no idea the detail and the amount of work that went into it. I did spend a lot of my time writing character descriptions and dialogue, but I also spent entire days with 4200-row Excel spreadsheets used in our XML, scouring for the one out-of-place comma that was breaking the game.

Culturally, I had to get up to speed not just on tools like Unity, but also had to start watching *Dr. Who* and playing *Magic: The Gathering* a bit in order to have stuff in common with my coworkers (something which had never been quite as important before). I'm not complaining about that, by the way. *Because David Tennant.* But, I digress.

For the first 18 months of my time working at Schell Games, I worked on *PlayForward: Elm City Stories*, doing narrative design and writing. I then wrote the combat dialogue for *Tunnel Tail*, and did narrative design and writing on *Lionel Battle Train*. To that point, I had only been a writer, but my title was technically Game Designer. When I was put on a new project and was responsible to do fast prototyping, this was my first real exposure to any kind of game design, and in particular, level design.

My first prototype that involved actual levels was intended to teach people about minerals and their hardnesses. It was a drill game where the player had to use a drill to find minerals in a grid of ground. Part *DigDug* and part *Battleship*, the idea was to uncover all the minerals in that space of ground without your drill breaking or without hitting something like a pocket of explosive gas or a power line. Players must swap out drill heads to dig deeper and extract minerals with higher hardness. The idea was that you had to fail a few times to understand where things were and how to solve the puzzle, but I tried to make the failure fun. "Great!" they said. "Can you show us two more levels?" Hooboy. Welp…let's try this out!

The next two levels, I thought about it in terms of what I knew about level design, which again, to my way of thinking at that point, was *Pac-Man* and *Centipede*:

- Same space (so I used the same grid configuration but just rearranged where everything was placed)

- More peril (so I put in more power lines and explosive gas)

- Better rewards (so I put in better, more valuable minerals and a few random helpful things the player could randomly find)

They seemed pleased with my work, and people did think the game was fun, but ultimately, this game was not chosen as one of the final minigames in the project. In retrospect, I could have done so much more with level design!

- I could have changed up the space and made the grid a different size and shape each time, forcing the player to think more about their negotiation of the puzzle.

- I could have added things like speed or time pressures.

- I could have considered more tools and benefits to help the player at the outset, and given the player a choice of which to use.

The next project I went to was *The World of Lexica*, which I was on for the next two years. This was a game that Schell Games did for Amplify Education, with the idea of increasing literacy and language arts performance in students in grades 6 through 8. It was an episodic AAA-quality

RPG, made for the iPad, in which you play as a creature called a Curioso (the physical manifestation of your curiosity), and you're dropped into a magical library in peril. With the help of the library's caretakers and famous characters from throughout literature, you would go on adventures and quests in order to help save the library. There were TONS of features in this game, including:

- Side quests

- Minigames that help with language skills

- A digital collectable literary card game called "Story Cards" that had a tournament with NPCs throughout the zones and episodes

- An e-reader containing 567 books with comprehension questions

- Bookshelves containing books found in the e-reader and also containing surprise items

- Inspiration orbs you could collect, which displayed literary quotes

- A Book Oracle you could visit for:

  - Book recommendations

  - Turning in your inspiration orbs to get gear for your character

  - Rewards based on the number of e-reader questions you answered, categorized by theme

- A story creation tool called "Scriptus," in which you could build scenes and write interactive stories. (This thing is so, SO cool, you guys. I could have played with it forever. Seriously.)

My job on the project was:

- *To be the real librarian for all the virtual books.* I was in charge of tracking all 567 books, knowing where they were both chronologically and positionally in the game and making sure they all appeared. I had to place and stock the bookshelves and place special items on the bookshelves. I was also the person tasked with all the book research (i.e., if someone needed a certain type of item we could say was pulled from a specific book, I had to find a list of referenced items from our books). I had to find literary quotes by theme and do character and plot research. This made me into something of a literary badass in terms of books in the public domain, and that's something I will use throughout my career.

- *Character dialogue and quest creation.* This was really fun for me, because I got to write as characters like the Cheshire Cat, Tom Sawyer, and Baba Yaga.

- *The Story Cards tournament.*

- *Putting character gear elements into the game.*

- *The Book Oracle feature.*

So, yeah, there was a lot I did that ended up requiring a decent amount of knowledge about Unity and SVN and Articy Draft, industry-standard tools that are really good to know and helpful for level designers. But honestly, my favorite, favorite thing about working on *The World of Lexica* was the time I spent outside of work using our Scriptus story creator, physically building stories and writing the text and dialogue that went with them. The Scriptuses, as the final stories were called, were basically story modules that could be accessed through the Scriptus tool. We could create and share stories with others, and we needed to provide a certain number of premade modules as examples for players to play. Schell Games had an internal contest in order to end up with several example modules that would ship with the game.

I decided to enter the contest and make a story module. Several of the books on our e-reader list were by Jane Austen, one of my favorite authors. I wanted to make a story module where you as the player are inserted into a fancy ball where there is social intrigue going on that you must unravel. In doing so, I'd expose players to the world that Jane Austen wrote about, the types of situations in her books, and the inherent theme in her books about the role of women in Victorian England being dependent on men and marriage. I wanted to make a module that was part parody, in which the main character would have the ability to maintain her agency (perhaps at a cost, as was generally the case in those times). I wrote the story, and the dialogue, first, and called it *Belle of the Ball*. The narrative stuff is the part that's easy for me. What I had not done before was to create the environment that the story took place in, and I was excited for the opportunity!

CREATING THE STORY

You are dropped into the middle of the first ball of the season being held by a country lord and his wife. They are determined that their daughter, Parissa, should marry, and intend to announce her engagement at the end of the evening. There are several people assembled, with suitors among them including Sir Uppington-Downs (a self-involved, rich twit), Professor Smegley (an old man who will treat her well but will die soon), Colonel Brisket (a powerful but evil military officer who only wants the lord's money), and the butler (who is kind and helpful but crestfallen, and upon further review, in love with Parissa from afar but without the class to compliment hers). Your first order of business is to meet and talk to everyone, all without alerting anyone to the fact that you are a crasher... how scandalous!

When a scandal erupts involving Parissa's lost dance card, you must help her by causing a bigger scandal in the room to keep Parissa from experiencing embarrassment at her own engagement ball. These scandal choices might involve a young lady who is hopelessly in love with shy Rufus, who is at the refreshment table making a pig of himself, a family cousin whose hat fell apart at the last ball and is terrified of it happening again, or tensions building between men in the room. You must also find Parissa's dance card and discover which of the women are true and trustworthy friends of Parissa's and can help with her predicament.

You can:

- Try to matchmake between Rufus and the young lady, but he is so shy and nervous, he throws up on her. She leaves crying, with her brother, Sir Uppington-Downs, and Rufus is asked to leave.

- Use feathers on the floor beside the bird cage to make it look like the cousin's hat is molting. If you get caught, you can blame it on the little old lady standing beside the birdcage to avoid getting thrown out yourself. If the ruse works, the cousin leaves in embarrassment, asking Uppington-Downs and his sister to take her home. Rufus escorts the old lady home.

- You stir up enough trouble to cause a fistfight between Rufus and Sir Uppington-Downs. They are both asked to leave, and the women they gave rides to also leave.

(Note that I found a way to make sure that all the same characters leave the ball, no matter what scandal happens. That way, in the postscandal scene, there's only one version of the room that needs to be accessed.)

After a scandal has taken place (and everyone in the room has things to say about that), the Lord of the Manor announces that it will soon be time to announce Parissa's engagement. You need to talk to the suitors and to Parissa in order to help her understand what's up with each of the suitors. Once you have done so, you are encouraged to talk to the Lord again, who says, "I am very interested in an objective viewpoint. To whom should I marry my daughter?" You can, at that point, decide which of the three remaining suitors (Colonel Brisket, Professor Smegley, or the butler) she should marry—or, you can leave it up to Parissa. When you indicate that you've talked to everyone and are ready to proceed, you tell the Lord your choice, and then receive one of four endings:

- Parissa becomes engaged to Professor Smegley, leaving Parissa financially secure and able to find love once the Professor passes.

- Parissa becomes engaged to Colonel Brisket, who the Lord approves of only because he does not know of his womanizing, gambling ways. Brisket makes a side comment about bumping Parissa off after she bears him a child and secures his fortune, if she cannot behave in a less spirited manner.

- Parissa becomes engaged to the butler, a good man who truly loves her, but who is only a butler. The Lord flies into a rage and refuses to allow it, until the grandmother steps forward and explains that the money and the house are still hers—not his—as long as she is alive, and she will see her granddaughter happy. The Lord allows the engagement and Parissa is very happy, but it is obvious that she will probably be financially cut off upon the death of her grandmother.

- Parissa, allowed to choose for herself, decides that she is not ready to get married yet. Her father is furious, her mother faints, but her grandmother steps forward and says that young women should have at least one adventure before they are forced to marry, and she offers to take Parissa on a trip to America to meet the friends and relatives living there. Parissa might find a husband she loves there.

I was super proud of this story and now had to create the 3D environment for it to play out in.

CREATING THE SPACE

To prepare myself for creating the space, I watched *Emma, Pride and Prejudice,* and *Sense and Sensibility* again.* I paid attention to details in the architecture and in the scene, so I could create a ballroom from our assets that people would think believable.

I started with a large hall, with fancy wallpaper, chandeliers at certain points around the ceiling, molding, and a large chandelier hanging down from the ceiling. Then, I filled out the features of the room with things that were both important to the story and congruent with the décor of ball-rooms in Austen novels and movies, leaving a large space in the middle for where the dancing would take place (Figure 4.1) Then, I placed all the characters (Figure 4.2.) The final placement of characters happened once I put in all the dialogue. I tested it out to see whether the character placements made as much sense and felt right with the amount of dialogue the player needed to have with people.

FAIL?!

I tested *Belle of the Ball* with members of my family and a few folks at Schell Games who understood what I was trying to do. My family absolutely loved the story. I made a few tweaks based on dialogue flow, character, and camera placement. I was so proud of my module! I turned it in for the contest, sure I'd win the right to have my module ship with *The World of Lexica.* I'd created an accurate environment to Victorian England and Jane Austen, I'd put in several levels of intrigue that had to be solved with eavesdropping and conversation, and I put in enough player choice over the ending that it would be fun to replay.

When the contest results were announced, *Belle of the Ball* was not going to be shipped, but I was given a gift card to a coffee shop for having entered. I was sad, and not just because I hate and don't drink coffee. I did not understand why. I had worked on this for three straight weekends and was super proud of it, and thought I had represented Austen effectively and presented an engaging story. I needed to fail in order to learn about level design—you'll see what I mean in a moment. It sucked at the time, but the most important thing was that I was unwilling to give up. I needed

---

* Which, you guys, I'm a total sucker for Mr. Darcy, so this was not exactly an arm-twister for me.

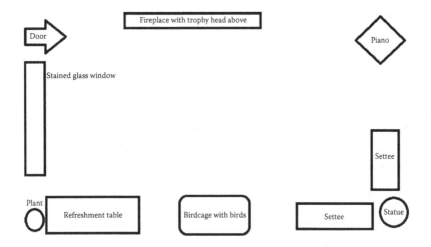

FIGURE 4.1   The ballroom with only furniture placed.

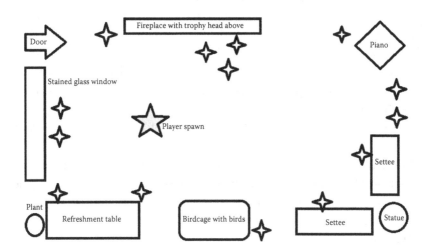

FIGURE 4.2   The ballroom with the characters and player spawn point placed.

to know why I had failed, to see what lessons I could take forward from this experience.

I decided to talk with my manager about this, because I needed to know where I went wrong. "You never had level design, did you?" she asked. I had not. She directed me to a book in the company library, *Level Design for Games: Creating Compelling Game Experiences* by Phil Co, which I took home. I skimmed through the book but ultimately still didn't understand why my module had not been good enough. I had something of a crisis of confidence right then about whether I actually belonged in this job at all.

Fortunately, I was due to go on vacation the following week. What I did not realize was that this particular vacation would not just show me with great clarity why my module hadn't been chosen, but it would also completely rearrange my understanding of level design as I had understood it to that point. And it would renew my love of making games so that any doubt I felt would be replaced with a new drive to build engaging experiences for players.

ENTER THE DRAGON

Now, anyone who has ever read one of my articles or heard one of my conference talks knows that *Dragon Age* is my very favorite game series, mainly for story reasons, and also for romance reasons (because most of my conference talks have been about romance in games, and *Dragon Age* is an example of a AAA title that does romance extremely well). I am absolutely hardcore when it comes to this game. When I got the release date of *Dragon Age: Inquisition* (the third in BioWare's series behind *Dragon Age: Origins* and *Dragon Age II*), I immediately logged a request with HR to take a week's vacation time. On the vacation request, under "Reason," I wrote "DRAGON AGE!"

The HR representative said, "You really want to put that under your reason?"

I explained, "Look, I can either do what everyone else does and call in sick for two days upon its release, or I can call this what it is, take the whole week, and play the crap out of my favorite game in the hardcore manner that I do." The request was approved.

The release date arrived, and I downloaded *Dragon Age: Inquisition* at exactly midnight, its first availability. My kids were already on notice not to open my office door unless the house was on fire. My husband was already prepped with what times he needed to show up with food and drinks, and my minifridge had already been stocked. In the first three days, I played 58 hours. I think that scared the hell out of my family.

There is a sequence that takes three to four hours to play, around level 20, where you as the Inquisitor must attend a ball in Orlais, thrown by the Queen. There is intrigue afoot that you must unravel by talking to people and eavesdropping. You have to avoid scandal, and thereby avoid being kicked out of the ball....

SOUND FAMILIAR!?!!?

Damned right, it did. I could not believe it—here was a situation in my favorite game ever which was pretty close to the one I'd tried to create in my module, *Belle of the Ball*! There was even an achievement you could earn at the Orlesian ball, called "Belle of the Ball"! That three and a half hours I spent playing the Orlesian Ball sequence in *Dragon Age: Inquisition* went on to be my favorite stretch of gameplay ever, not just because of how cool and awesome it was, but because it completely rearranged my thinking as a game designer in ways that had never been obvious to me before.

Here's why.

The Orlesian Ball

You, as the Inquisitor, show up at the Orlesian ball. A few things are made immediately clear:

- A coup is imminent in the Orlesian palace, and you can choose to support the current Queen, her cousin, or another contender you learn about later on.

- Your ability to remain at the ball depends on your approval rating with members of the Orlesian court not dropping below a certain point (Figure 4.3), which mainly has to do with conversations you hold with folks and how visible you are at the party. If it drops that low, you are thrown out of the ball, it is a game fail, and you must reload.*

- There are things here to collect: coins, halla statues, and supplies in areas you really have to explore in order to find, pieces of lore (and I'm a total lore nerd with this series, I READ EVERYTHING). Tossing coins into the fountain will gain you court approval points, and collecting enough halla statues will allow you to unlock certain doors. There are 10 halla statuettes to find, but to unlock all the doors unlockable in this manner, you would need 23 statuettes. Therefore, the player must make a choice about which areas to unlock: treasure/gear; the ability to complete the banner achievement; and the ability to blackmail the Queen and get another ending to the Orlesian Ball sequence.

---

* I have often thought that if there were mod tools for *Dragon Age: Inquisition*, I would want to make a module that added content for people to experience if they got thrown out of the ball; perhaps an added challenge that got them to the natural end of the ball. My Qunari mage Inquisitor, on my second playthrough, is someone I would describe as Chaotic Neutral, and I would disrupt the ball for the hell of it if I thought I could do it without dying, because that's what my character would totally do. She's not the type to think fancy dances are all that. Anyway.

FIGURE 4.3   Interacting well with those you meet at the Orlesian Ball helps your court approval rating.

- As you traverse the area, you see circles projected onto the floor by the game (Figure 4.4). Stand within these circles for enough time, and you will overhear something important. These overheard tidbits are collectable. The circles are placed all over the grounds. Gather as many tidbits as you can, relay them to Leiliana, and you are rewarded with court approval points.

FIGURE 4.4   Eavesdropping to hear important tidbits of information translates into a higher court approval rating.

- The palace is an opulent place with many levels, side courts, and rooms to explore. In fact, in order to accomplish everything, you need to run around the palace awhile. This might include scaling the occasional trellis (Figure 4.5), jumping railings, and going through open windows, for sneaking into a room you're not supposed to enter.

In my module, I got the story right, the characters right, and the dialogue right—but that's not all a good level needs. So, what did I notice about the differences in the ball episode that I'd done, versus this amazing, kick-ass AAA version of basically the same concept? A few things!

- *An explorable environment is paramount. Belle of the Ball* took place in a single room. While this was historically accurate, I might have set up my space a lot differently: included more rooms, spaced characters in different places in the different rooms. Part of why the Orlesian ball was more fun was because I had to search for things in a vast, beautiful space (Figure 4.6). What I would change in my module based on this lesson: the layout of the space.

- *The environment should be part of the puzzle. Belle of the Ball*, again, happened in a single room. Even in a single room, the player's traversal was simply back and forth across that room, and there may have been ways I could have made things more challenging for the player by forcing them to jump on or over things in order to find people or information. At the Orlesian ball, I had to climb staircases and

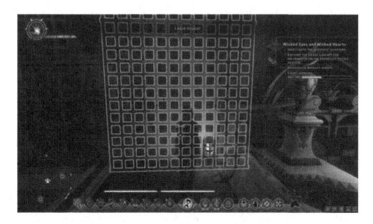

FIGURE 4.5 Scaling the trellis in the courtyard will allow you access to areas of the palace that are supposedly off-limits.

FIGURE 4.6 The main ballroom in the Orlesian Winter Palace has two levels and many side areas to explore.

a trellis and look inside and behind furniture to find certain things. This was more engaging, for sure. *What I would change in my module based on this lesson*: I'd have had physical puzzles the player had to navigate and more places they had to actually physically search.

- *Music matters. Belle of the Ball* had no background music going on, despite the fact that I could have chosen some. The music at the Orlesian Ball was so good that I can still hum it in my head, and it added a lot to the environment. *What I would change in my module based on this lesson*: I'd add background music.

- *Collectables offer more to do. Belle of the Ball* had only conversations in which to move the story ahead and gain information, but the Orlesian ball had things you could collect in order to advance your performance. Now, in our Scriptus tool there wasn't an option to put a script in there to count items collected, so in that case, you would just have to leave things around and hope the player found them. Also, in the Orlesian ball, the collectables had a purpose; you could trade them for something that made a difference. Using the tool I had to use, I would have to design a way to give any collectables real value and not just be busywork for the player, because having them running around aimlessly collecting things for no reason does not move the game forward. *What I would change in my module based on this lesson*: I'd possibly add some notes around to collect, so that some of the clues about the story happened in ways other than conversation.

Armed with these new lessons, I created a new module called *Mutiny on the HMS Rapscallion*, a pirate adventure narrated by the fictional voice of Robert Louis Stevenson. You find yourself stowed in the belly of what turns out to be a pirate ship, and there is trouble afoot. Speaking to the various people on the ship, you find that a mutiny is brewing. You can support the mutineers, support the captain, or work to a truce. In all three cases, you have to recruit three crewmembers to your cause before you can move on. Neither the mutineers nor the captain are as bad as the other believes; it's all a big misunderstanding. However, you're not able to understand that until you fully explore the ship and talk to everyone aboard.

Things I did differently with this second module:

- *There were several physical puzzles.* You had to jump over boxes to get to certain areas, and you had to jump between objects to reach the first mate up on the mast.

- *There were multiple levels of the ship to explore.* You had the belly of the ship, the main deck, and the captain's quarters. All three had to be explored for you to understand the true nature of what was going on aboard the Rapscallion. For players not interested in that much exploring who just wanted to play through the story, it was also possible to finish without knowing everything.

- I had music playing at all times, different types in the different areas of the ship. I feel it added a lot.

- I didn't put in any collectables, but, I did increase the amount of lore and clues you could randomly find around the ship. I fixed it so that one character might complain of dizziness, and later you find an orange, and choose to take the orange with you, and you can opt to give the orange to that character, helping the character support whichever side of the mutiny you intend to.

- Certain characters had allegiances you could discover by interacting with them, but other characters were able to be swayed to your position just through your behavior toward them. This is a different approach than I'd had with *Belle of the Ball*, and was influenced by the Court Approval feature of the Orlesian Ball in *Dragon Age: Inquisition*.

Shortly after creating Rapscallion, I was put on a different project. It made me sad that I did not have the chance to fine-tune that module a bit better and submit it to be shipped. It was a much better module than *Belle of the Ball*, thanks to all the lessons I learned about level design while playing the Orlesian Ball sequence in *Dragon Age: Inquisition*. I will carry these lessons forward in all my future work, plus, am now much more able to identify the presence of actual levels in the RPGs I favor. In the meantime, I love designing levels with my son on *King of Thieves* and *Super Mario Maker*, because it's helping me to piece together the gaps in my gaming knowledge. Level design wasn't something I initially knew much about or thought of a lot, but it turned out to be something I actually enjoy. Who knew?

CONCLUSION

I am not someone who can call myself a dyed-in-the-wool level designer, at least not without a lot more practice. However, it was really super helpful to have this experience. I am better-rounded as a designer, even if those two modules never shipped.

I guess my final advice to folks who want to get better with their level design is: Think about games you have enjoyed, and begin to identify what factors change from one level to the next. How do they build upon each other, or do they? How does each level impact your overall progress in the game? What did you like, or find frustrating, about levels you've played? These are all things that once I started noticing them, they made me a better game developer. Certainly, there are also tons of good books and Internet tutorials available as well, but I came by my knowledge in a bit of a different way. That seems to fit, seeing as I'm a bit of an edge case in the games industry. Regardless of what path you take to get in, I wish you luck, I hope my story has helped and inspired you, and just, I guess…never stop trying to improve your skills, no matter what. You got this, I promise*!

---

* Just…don't play PONG, okay? That game won't teach you anything but how to be sad.

II

Designing Levels

CHAPTER 5

Hell, Hyboria, and Disneyland

The Origins and Inspirations of Themed Video Game Level Design

Scott Rogers

CONTENTS

OUR HERO RACES THROUGH a labyrinth of fiery death; deftly leaping over constantly shifting floors that reveal molten pits, dodging gouts of flames that lick at his heels, and battles against horrifying creatures whose very bodies drip with white-hot magma. The hero finally crosses the threshold of the dungeon's portals and throws open the gates only to realize yet another trap-laden castle stands before him—one with spires of glistening ice where slippery chasms, dagger-sharp icicles, and flesh-hungry yetis await. Without a second thought, the hero charges on.

Our hero, of course, is the avatar of a video game player; a fictitious character risking life and limb within a virtual world of fantasy. While these virtual worlds can be literally any place and any time, they are limited only by the hardware in which they are created. But video game worlds are not just the product of technology, but also of cultural influences on the game creators. What the average video game player doesn't realize is that his or her player avatar is double-jumping in the pioneering footsteps of creators who never even played a video game in their life: Dante Alighieri, Robert E. Howard, and Walt Disney.

By examining the evolution of the technology of games and the cultural influences on the game creators, we can gain greater insight to how themed video game levels began and why certain aesthetic choices have been made. We might even discover why certain themes become prevalent in video games to the point of becoming tropes within the short period of time that the medium has been in existence.

WHAT IS A THEMED VIDEO GAME LEVEL?

While a *video game world* encompasses the player's entire experience during an entire game, a *video game level* can be defined by the environment where the game player performs activities and/or travels through while performing said activities. To further complicate the definition, in video game developer jargon, a level can refer to physical location as in "I must have died a dozen times on the fire level." A level can also be used as a counting system as in "I'm up to level 20 on *Tetris.*" My own book *Level Up! The Guide to Great Video Game Design* tries to make sense of the confusion:

> A possible explanation for level having four definitions in the video game industry is that video game developers have extremely limited vocabularies. Another reason for the multiple definitions is that developers have used the term "level" in different contexts for so long it's too late to get everyone to agree to call it something else like a "floobit" or a "placenheimer." So level it is. But why? Most ancient game designers believe that the term came from *Dungeons and Dragons*, when players would travel down many dungeon levels (like floors of a building) to reach the dragon. (Hence the title of the game.) Why no one thought to call it "floors" is beyond me [1].

Ultimately, a level is a confined area of play activity—they can be as closed in as a single chamber, such as in the mobile game *The Room* or as sprawling as the programmatically created worlds *of No Man's Sky*. Levels were created as workarounds for game designers who needed to cut up their game worlds into smaller segments due to the loading limitations of early games. It was also easier for game designers to break the game's story and the player's progression (known as ramping) into smaller segments rather than tackling it all at once as a complete whole.

A ***themed*** *video game level* is a video game level themed to a particular subject matter or physical location. It helps to think of them as the genres of movies (drama, horror, western, etc.) but skewed toward subject matter appealing to the game developer and the game player. The subject matter could have bearing to the game's story or be completely devoid of logic as to why it exists. Themed video game levels feature elements that have been designed to bring together the following elements: character, location, story, enemies, mechanics, hazards, art, events, and music.

Where did this concept of themed game levels come from? What inspired themed video game levels? What games first had themed levels? Why are some themes more prevalent than others? The answer, of course, is to start with the classics.

IN THE BEGINNING, THERE WAS THE DARKNESS AND THE LIGHT

Like all creative endeavors, the origins of the themed video game levels started with a blank canvas. In this case, the canvas was the black screen of a cathode ray tube (CRT). In particular, the cathode ray tube of an oscilloscope in the Brookhaven National Laboratory that housed the game *Tennis for Two** (1958). Created by William Higinbotham and Robery Devork, *Tennis for Two* was an abstraction for the real-world game of table tennis. A single glowing line represented the floor of a ping-pong table and two cursors were the paddles that moved by control sticks. The ball was a bright spot that bounced back and forth as long as the player's cursors intersected with it before it bounced offscreen.

That white dot on that black screen must have served as inspiration to Steve Russell, Martin Graetz, and Wayne Wiitanen when they created *Spacewar!* (1961). The game allowed players to control one of two spaceships that could thrust, rotate, and shoot missiles at each other. The

---

* For the record, *Tennis for Two* was not the first electronic game. That distinction belongs to *OXO*, a tic-tac-toe simulator created on the University of Cambridge's EDSAC computer by Alexander Douglas in 1952. However, *Tennis for Two* was the first game with elements that could be controlled by both players.

earliest version of the game featured a randomly generated background of stars. The programmers working in MIT's lab created their code in an open-source environment, which meant that they shared and modified each other's code. That was how Peter Samson "wrote a program based on real star charts that scrolled slowly at any one time, 45% of the night sky was visible, every star down to the fifth magnitude" [2]. The addition of Samson's "expensive planetarium" hack was the first time a game creator designed an environment not tied to the play of a game. It was solely created to make the game feel more like a place.

Themed Video Game Level Trope #1—Outer Space: One can easily see how a black television screen could serve as inspiration to early game developers as the perfect stand-in for outer space. Brightly displayed vector-drawn stars looked great on those early CRT screens. Player-controlled spaceships meant no animations. Spaceships could be rendered in simple geometric shapes. Gameplay could be based primarily on physics. All these elements were advantages to those early programmers during predesigner/preartist days of game development. As the earliest game genre—the shooter—evolved,* outer space continued to be a popular locale for video game battles to be waged. Even as graphics evolved, the outer space environment continued to appear in the flying and shooter genres Space Harrier *(Sega, 1985),* Star Fox *(Nintendo, 1993),* Star Wars: Jedi Starfighter *(Lucas arts, 2002), and* Geometry Wars *(Microsoft Game Studios, 2003).*

During the infancy of video games, most arcade games remained abstractions, as seen in *OXO* (Douglas, 1952) and *PONG* (Atari, 1972). The focus of these early games was solely on the gameplay, not where it took place. Even as color started appearing in games, the environments of games like *Breakout*† (Atari, 1976), *Bomb Bee* (Namco, 1979), and *Galaxian* (Namco, 1979) still closely resembled the abstract black space environments of their forerunners.

A sole exception was *Gun Fight* (Midway, 1975), the first nonspace-, nonsports-themed video game. Players moved a gunslinger up and down the screen shooting bullets at their opponent trying to score as many hits as possible with a limited amount of ammo. Despite its best efforts, *Gun Fight's* theming didn't extend too far past the game's marquee as the play environment was a basic black background. In an attempt to create a Wild

---

* Raph Koster in his book, *A Theory of Fun for Game Design*, has a most excellent illustration showing the evolution of the early video game shoot-em-up from *Spacewar!* to *Sinistar* and beyond.

† The color on *Breakout* was actually a colored cellophane overlay.

West environment, an occasional cactus or a wagon served as a barricade for players to hide behind.

What *Gun Fight* did do was help push video games into new genres. *Warrior* (Cinematronics, 1979) was one of the first fantasy-themed arcade games. Players controlled a vector-drawn knight who bashed an opponent with a two-handed sword into a pit in the center of the screen. A colored, printed screen overlay represented a dungeon chamber in which the warriors battled.*

The first step to establishing a physical location with gameplay came with *Lunar Lander* (Atari, 1979). Simple vector lines created the game's rocky moonscape. The environment's presence is almost completely functional as the basis of the gameplay was to keep the Lander from crashing into the rocky moon surface while navigating toward point-earning landing pads. Now that video games had a ground floor on which to build upon, other land-locked games soon appeared, such as *Space Invaders* (Taito, 1978) and *Missile Command* (Atari, 1980).

The elements of these newly minted worlds still didn't quite match up. The elements of games like *Cutie Q* (Namco, 1979) and *King and Balloon* (Namco, 1980) still felt a bit random, possibly the product of a limited graphical palette and a general lack of artists working in games.

Themed Video Game Level Trope #2—The Elements; Fire and Ice: *The Fire level debuted when Dirk the Daring leapt through a wall of lava in* Dragon's Lair *(Cinematronics, 1983) while the ice level appeared a few years later in* Ghost 'N Goblins (G'nG) *(Capcom, 1984). These treacherous elemental locations swiftly became popular for three reasons: First, killing players with fire was just an art overlay on a collision box. Low-friction surfaces were just a simple tweak to the existing game physics. These hazardous terrains created perfect timing puzzles that caused the players to break their rhythm—making the level more challenging. Second, fire and ice environments lend themselves toward a wide array of deadly inhabitants, from lava-men and flame-breathing dragons to snowmen, both of the abominable and frosty varieties. And third, fire and ice levels added color (red and blue) to the palette of gameplay worlds, especially important to distinguish screenshots on the back of home console boxes in those early 8-bit days.*

---

* This overlay system was abandoned as soon as games developed 16-bit color graphics. The last hurrah of the color overlays on vector games was when Smith Engineering's Vectrex home game system was forced from the commercial market after the crash of the video game industry in 1984.

EVEN IN HELL, THERE ARE ICE LEVELS

As video game themes expanded past technological demos and physics simulation proving grounds, game developers started embracing cultural references and reflecting them into their games. However, before we dive headlong into that, let's back up to the narrative origins of the themed level. First stop: the Underworld of Homer's *Odyssey*. When incorporating ancient Greek myths into his work, Homer doesn't give many topographical details about the underworld—he's mostly concerned about who is in the underworld than what it looks like. A few mythological characters like Sisyphus and his rock show up but for the most part Homer's underworld is relatively free of environmental hazards. Odysseus as he questions his dead companions on how to get home is more nervous about the threat of attack from both spirits and Persephone, the Queen of the underworld, than any environmental dangers the land of the dead might hold:

> I would fain have seen—Theseus and Peirithoos glorious children of the gods, but so many thousands of ghosts came round me and uttered such appalling cries, that I was panic stricken lest Persephone should send up from the house of Hades the head of that awful monster Gorgon [3].

It is important to note that Homer plants the seeds that the underworld is a mysterious place populated by mythological and undead beings.

Centuries later, Virgil's *Aeneid book VI* (19 BC) expands on Homer's underworld, adding both locations; the rivers Lethe and Styx, Plato's palace and the Elysian Fields, and reintroduces characters from classic Greek mythology including the ferryman Charon and the three-headed guard dog Cerberus. Does Virgil realize that thousands of years later how these characters will resonate with video game designers who are looking for horrors to populate their own virtual underworlds?

But while Virgil fleshed out the fantasy of Hell, Dante made it a real place. Taking the *Aeneid* as his inspiration, Dante Alighieri defined the Inferno in his 1308 *Divine Comedy* and provided three major contributions to themed video game design.

The first influence comes when Dante's Hell is broken into nine *bolgie* or circles, each representing a sin (or family of sins) of humanity. Dante describes locations later found in abundance in video games: ice bolgia, fire bolgia, and forest bolgia. We can theorize that this compartmentalization inspired Western game designers (and possibly even with Eastern developers in the case of *G'nG*) into organizing their worlds by thematic categories. While not necessarily true to the source material, modern popular culture sources inaccurately refer to Dante's circles as "levels"—a common term found in video game jargon.

Each of the levels of hell is grossly diverse from one another and populated with horrors and punishments that fit the crimes of its sinners. The lustful are burned by fire, the traitors are trapped in a field of ice, the dark forest of the suicides, with its trees made from twisted human figures and inhabited by dangerous harpies. These fantastic locations would inspire levels found in many video games.

Dante's final (and inadvertent) contribution to video games is the concept of the boss. In video games, a boss or boss monster is traditionally a gigantic monster that is encountered at the end of the game and is themed to its location. Due to early code and creative restrictions, boss monsters tended to dominate a central stationary location in the level, attacking the player with projectile attacks or grasping limbs. When Dante reached the bottom of the ninth level of Hell, he finds Satan, the ultimate boss monster of Christian mythology. Satan is a three-faced, bat-winged horror mired up to his waist in the ice of Cocytus. He beats his huge wings, creating winds that refreeze the ice he is trapped in—much like a boss's attack that would push a player back from his or her goal of reaching and slaying the final creature. Dante and Virgil have to cross the ice to reach Satan and climb up his body (shades of *Shadow of the Colossus!*) to escape to the world of the living. While Dante's influences would prove to be great, the next major influence on themed video game level design wouldn't happen for another 700 years.

Themed Video Game Level Trope #3—Dungeon/Cavern/Tomb: Inspired by spelunking and dungeon crawls from fantasy role-playing games (RPGs), video game heroes have been braving subterranean locations since Colossal Cave Adventure *(CRL, 1976) and* Rogue *(Toy and Wichman, 1980). Dungeon locations offer game designers many advantages; cave wall textures could be made from easily repeatable (or tiled) art on early gaming systems. The gameplay environment could be festooned with traps to avoid and enemies to battle without explanation as to why they were there, and of course, there was always lots of collectable treasure to be had. With the success of modern fantasy games like* World of Warcraft *(Blizzard, 2006) and its randomly generated instanced dungeons, the popularity of dungeon levels shows no signs of going away.*

THE BIG HOP FORWARD

As we have already seen, the earliest avatars in video games were angular spaceships and white blocks. With the arrival of 16-bit color and multiframe animations came characters inspired by cartoon characters. Namco's *Pac-Man* (Namco, 1980) was a yellow eating-machine. While Pac-Man was cute, he was devoid of character outside of a few cute bleeps upon death. However, it was with Pac-Man's adversaries, the four ghosts, that true video game characterization started to emerge.

Displayed on the game's attract screen, Shadow, Speedy, Bashful, and Pokey's names fit their personalities. Shadow would follow you like a shadow, Speedy was definitely the fastest ghost, Bashful would shy away when you turned Pac-Man toward him, and Pokey was just slow. As Pac-Man fever swept the globe, developers quickly realized that players responded to cartoon characters. The brightly colored characters of Pac-Man inspired game protagonists like *Dig Dug* (Namco, 1982) and *Mr. Do!* (Universal, 1982).

But despite its charming characters, Pac-Man (and 1981's *Ms. Pac-Man*) gameplay took place in an abstract maze that had nothing to do with eating, let alone ghosts. If we are to define a themed video game level as one that features a protagonist, antagonist, environment, and hazards that all share a common theme, then this design idea truly found its start with *Frogger* (Konami, 1981).

The lead character of *Frogger* is a frog who just wants to cross the road to get back to his home in the swamp. A highway of cars, tractors, and trucks and a river of logs and turtles stand in his way. While the Frogger avatar has about as much personality as Pac-Man—all he does is hop and go "splat" when run over—the arcade cabinet of *Frogger* depicts a briefcase-carrying frog based on the stereotypes of the Japanese salary man and American businessman. At this point video game developers are starting to develop their game heroes into characters rather than just avatars. While Frogger's enemies of cars and trucks don't have the personality of Pac-Man's ghosts, later gameplay boards add otters, snakes, dogs, and a hungry crocodile who randomly appears in one of Frogger's home stalls.

What makes *Frogger* a milestone is the completeness of its theme in relationship to its gameplay. *Frogger* was the first game to tell a true narrative: "There once was a frog who wanted to cross the road to get home..." Thematically, unlike previous video games, there isn't a mechanic or power-up that feels out of place in *Frogger*. Bonus points can be collected by gulping up dragonflies and pink frogs can be escorted back to the swamp for some extra points. With most of the elements in place, the age of the unified theme has almost arrived.

Themed Video Game Level Trope #4—Factory: With mechanics taken right out of Charlie Chaplin's film Modern Times *(1936), factory levels are constantly moving obstacle courses for players. First seen in* Donkey Kong *(Nintendo, 1981), factory levels became a staple of platform games, especially as platform game genre exploded onto home gaming systems. The dynamic mechanics offered game developers easily created, combined, and repurposed hazards that could be tuned to a wide variety of difficulty levels. The adaptable factory mechanics quickly spread to locations: moving platforms, conveyer belts, and turning gears could be found in the tombs, circuses, and space stations of just about every platforming game. True factory themed levels can still be found in best-selling games like* Super Mario Galaxy *(Nintendo, 2007),* Star Wars: The Force Unleashed *(LucasArts, 2008), and* Little Big Planet *(SCEE, 2007).*

Released in 1981, Nintendo's *Donkey Kong*'s platform gameplay takes place on a skeletal building* consisting of pink, blue, and orange girders and ladders that Jumpman would ascend in his attempt to rescue his girlfriend.† Like *Frogger*, themed props populated the level and contributed to the gameplay: rolling barrels, oil cans that burst into flame, creating fiery enemies, and springs that threatened to bounce on the player's head. This pattern of high action gameplay, particularly in the platform game genre, quickly became commonplace.

By the early 1980s the video game phenomenon had exploded worldwide. In the battle for arcade player's quarters, video game developers designed more sophisticated gameplay, and more important, attractive graphics to escalate the competition for those quarters. Four important deviations start to emerge in 1983.

First, themed, narrative driven games are increasingly edging out abstract games at the arcades. Rather than seeking high scores, players now want to reach the endings of games like *Dragon's Lair* and *Space Ace* (Cinematronics, 1984).

---

* The buildings in *Donkey Kong* always looked like a construction site to me. As Jumpman had an immigrant Italian appearance and name and given that the game's inspiration (King Kong) takes place in New York City, shouldn't Jumpman's occupation have been a construction worker, not a carpenter?

† Whatever happened to ol' Lady anyway? Jumpman–who was later christened Mario–obviously dumped her when he met Princess Peach.

Second, licensed games based on movie and comic properties like *Tron* (Atari, 1982) and *Popeye* (Nintendo, 1982) start to reach the arcades. *Star Wars* (Sega, 1983) is notable for attempting to retell the story from the movie rather than being thematically related as in the case of *Tron* or *Star Trek* (Sega, 1983).

Third, the video game arms race extends to technology. Scrolling screens (gaming environments that extended beyond a single screen or fixed camera view) are introduced in Williams' 1982 *Moon Patrol. Scramble* (Konami, 1981) and *Zaxxon* (Sega, 1982) feature scrolling environments that make their way into the increasingly popular platform genre. As a result, more real estate is required and more gameplay mechanics are created to fill the space. In *Paperboy* (Atari, 1984), "The player must stay alive by avoiding obstacles that appear along the street. Some obstacles include everyday nuisances such as bees, fire hydrants, storm drains, break dancers, cars, skateboarders, drunks, and kids playing with radio controlled toys and even rather bizarre foes such as a tornado, oversized house cats, and even the Grim Reaper himself" [4].

Subgenres quickly form as game creators make more colorful, attention-grabbing art that caters to gamers' increasingly diversifying tastes. In 1983, you could play as an explorer in animal-infested jungles (*Congo Bongo*, Sega, 1983), a knight battling medieval fantasy creatures (*Crossbow*, Exidy, 1983), as a stalwart space hero (*Major Havoc*, Atari, 1983), or a crime-stopping mouse (*Mappy*, Namco, 1983). Games even inspired themselves as the virtual heroes of *Tron* (Bally/Midway 1982) and *I, Robot* (Atari, 1983) battled against power-mad central processing units in out-of-control video games.

Themed Video Game Level Trope #5—Jungle: All jungle levels begin with Activision's 1982 home game Pitfall! *Creator David Crane describes the game's origin:*

> I sat down with a blank sheet of paper and drew a stick figure in the center. I said, "Okay, I have a little running man and let's put him on a path [two more lines drawn on the paper]. Where is the path? Let's put it in a jungle [draw some trees]. Why is he running [draw treasures to collect, enemies to avoid, etc.]?" And *Pitfall!* was born. This entire process took about ten minutes. About 1,000 hours of programming later, the game was complete. It's no surprise that the film *Raiders of the Lost Ark*, which was released in 1981, influenced the design of *Pitfall!*, and there was another apparent nod to Tarzan with the presence of the swinging vines [5].

The jungle theme allows video game designers the flexibility of the dungeon but without the dull colors and right angles. With its exotic traps (quicksand and pongee-knife-lined pits) and exotic creatures (crocodiles, snakes, and scorpions) and set in a colorful outdoor environment, jungle levels quickly became a prevalent video game level theme. The mechanics often found in jungle levels—swinging vines, tree branch platforms from which to leap from, and rivers with moving logs a la *Frogger*—created fluid game movement that kept the player's heart beating like a jungle drum. Jungle environments continue to be popular as advanced game engines are able to render ultrarealistic jungle environments as seen in recent titles like *Crysis* (EA, 2007) and *Uncharted: Drake's Fortune* (SCE, 2007).

HYBORIA: THE ORIGINAL *LITTLE BIG PLANET*

Fantasy lands were not unknown in 1932 when pulp writer Robert E. Howard introduced Conan the Barbarian in *Weird Tales* magazine. Almost 30 years earlier, L. Frank Baum had penned over a dozen tales about the *Marvelous Land of Oz* (1900), a magical world that was split in five distinct zones, and later J.M. Barrie created his Never Land in *Peter Pan* (1911) with areas controlled by pirates, Indians, mermaids, and other groups. While both of these lands were populated with wonders, their contents and population didn't always match their surroundings. What they did do was introduce the fantasy map to the public.

Over the course of 17 stories, Conan the Barbarian battles, pillages, and plunders his way through the world of Hyboria, an amalgam of ancient civilizations all tightly packed into a Europe-sized continent. Howard's compact world served two purposes: (1) as an excuse to allow Conan to have adventures within any culture Howard felt like writing, and (2) to realistically allow Conan to travel the world within a few days or months. Hyboria's cultures were represented by themed lands. For example, Kush was an African analog with fierce warriors and even fiercer animals, Stygia was an analog for Egypt, a desert filled with haunted pyramids and evil sorcerers, Conan's homeland of Cimmeria bares resemblance to the Celtic and Irish lands of Northern England, and so on. Soon other worlds of fantasy sprang up, including J.R.R. Tolkien's Middle Earth (1937), C.S. Lewis' Narnia (1949), and Ursula Le Guin's Earthsea (1964).

While its influence on fantasy fiction can be debated, Howard's Hyboria had a profound influence on the role-playing game *Dungeons and Dragons (D&D)* (Gygax and Arneson, 1974). *D&D*'s content was clearly influenced by Howard's fantasy world and Hyborian characters and deities even appeared in its early game manuals.* And in turn, *D&D* was a huge impact on early video game creators. Many young programmers' first code were 20-sided dice rollers and random encounter generators. *D&D*'s influence can be seen throughout the history of video games in titles like *Gauntlet* (Atari, 1985), *Dungeon Siege* (Microsoft, 2002), and *Everquest* (SCEA, 1999). Many adventure games of the 1980s came with premium world maps while *D&D*-inspired *World of Warcraft* is a real world to millions of players who live, die, and even get married in the fictional realm of Azeroth.

Themed Video Game Level Trope #6—Spooky: The first spooky-themed game was Midway's 1972 Haunted House. Haunted House *was an electromechanical arcade game where players would shoot at black cat, witch, and grave robber targets with a light-emitting rifle. While ghosts were the antagonists of Pac-Man, it wasn't until G'nG (Capcom, 1984) that saw the return of the spooky-themed level. In G'nG, King Arthur jumps his way past gravestones and gnarled trees and into a town haunted by zombies, ravens, and demons. Spooky-themed levels are particularly useful when developing mood and story. As the sophistication of game graphics increased, spooky environments became commonplace. The spooky theme is the most adaptable of all the video game tropes—easily combined with other themes to make new locations. Combine outer space and spooky to make a derelict spaceship or mix equal parts fire and spooky to recreate Hell. The spooky theme can be found in all genres of games, including puzzle games, such as* Uninvited *(Mindscape, 1986) and* The 7th Guest *(Virgin Games, 1993), shooters, such as* Fatal Frame *(Tecmo, 2001) and* F.E.A.R. *(Vivendi, 2005), and educational games, such as* Typing of the Dead *(Sega, 1999). The spooky trope eventually developed its own game genre—survival horror—starting with Capcom's 1989* Sweet Home. *The genre is going strong with both the* Biohazard/Resident Evil *series (Capcom, 1996) and the* Silent Hill *series (Konami, 1999).*

DISNEY'S LAND AND THE CREATION OF A NARRATIVE-BASED WORLD

In 1954, motion picture producer Walt Disney announced to the world his plans for Disneyland, an amusement park like no other. Disney, an avid miniature-scale train hobbyist, had originally planned the park as an eight-acre expansion of his own backyard model railroad. Soon, the

---

* All Hyborian references were later removed after *D&D*'s publisher was sued by Howard's estate.

project grew into a 160-acre theme park built in the orange groves of Anaheim, California.

Influenced by the World's Fair, Disney's unique design for his park grew within the confines of the railroad track. The lands that lay within were based on Disney's interests in history, science, adventure, fantasy, and nostalgia. The goal was for Disneyland's guests to be completely immersed in the artificial environments of Frontierland, Adventureland, Tomorrowland, Fantasyland, and Main Street USA. Disney's Imagineers (Disney's name for the artists and engineers who designed and built the park) crafted wholly complete environments, from buildings to trashcans. As Disney himself said "I don't want the public to see the real world they live in while they're in the park, I want them to feel like they are in another world" [6]. While theme parks weren't an original concept to Southern California,* what made Disneyland so unique was the way it blended storytelling seamlessly with its environment.

> When we began designing Disneyland, we looked at it just as we do a motion picture. We had to tell a story, or in this case, a series of stories. In filmmaking, we develop a logical flow of events or scenes that will take our audience from point to point through a story. If I were to "leapfrog" from Scene One to Scene Three, leaving out Scene Two, it would be like sending the entire audience out to the lobby for popcorn in the middle of the film. When they came back, how could we expect them to understand what was happening? There was another thing we had to keep in mind in developing our Disneyland "story." In filmmaking, although we can control the sequence of events, the viewer might walk in late and, through no fault of our own, miss Scene One and never catch up to the story. But in Disneyland, we had more control. We designed the entire Park so that a guest couldn't miss Scene One or Two. From the moment he entered our "theatre," that is, our front gate, Scene One would begin for him [7].

The layout of Disneyland and more important, the themes of its attractions, would greatly influence video game designers in the future. While *Pac-Land* (Namco, 1984) and *G'nG* introduced the themed lands

---

* Walter Knott created the theme park when he built a ghost town on his berry farm in 1940.

concepts to video gaming, their successors *Pac-Man World* (Namco, 1999) and *Maximo: Ghosts to Glory* (Capcom, 2001) would feature game levels directly inspired by Disneyland's attractions.*

The stars of Disneyland were its attractions—dark rides based on popular Disney animated features like *Peter Pan* and *Snow White and the Seven Dwarves*, as well as original adventures like *Jungle Cruise* and *Trip to the Moon*. In 1964, the Imagineers debuted audio-animatronics—lifelike robot figures synched to move to a prerecorded audio track. New attractions like the *Pirates of the Caribbean* and the *Haunted Mansion* took guests[†] on immersive journeys through temperature-controlled environments in vehicles that directed their view of carousing pirates and waltzing ghosts. These burning cities and musty graveyards were some of the first virtual worlds.

Themed Video Game Level Trope #7—Pirate: Due to the relationship of Disneyland's two beloved New Orleans Square attractions, the Haunted Mansion *and the* Pirates of the Caribbean, *the pirate theme will always be the brother of the spooky theme. Featuring scenes of piracy including cannon-firing galleon, drunken buccaneers, and skeletal pirates, the ride was an influence on the designers of* The Secret of Monkey Island *(Lucasfilm Games, 1990) and* Pac-Man World. *The pirate theme is perfect for high-action gameplay, melee combat, and of course, lots and lots of treasure. And then there are the pirate skeletons. Much like the spooky theme, the pirate theme is treated as a catchall theme—one that can be applied to any genre of game to increase its sales. There have been pirate simulation games* (Sid Meier's Pirates, *Microprose, 1987), pirate platform games* (Hook, *Sony Imagesoft, 1992), pirate action games* (Pirates: The Legend of Black Kat, *EA, 2002), pirate puzzle games* (Zack & Wiki: The Quest for Barbados Treasure, *Capcom, 2007), and even games that simulate tabletop games.* (Age of Booty, *Capcom, 2008 and* Dead Man's Draw, *Stardock, 2014).*

THE SCREEN BECOMES A WORLD

Up through 1983, video games were composed of boards—single-screen environments on which gameplay occurred. Players would have to clear boards to progress. In games like *Ms. Pac-Man* (Namco, 1981) or *Donkey Kong Jr.* (Nintendo, 1982), the boards would change content and

---

* I should know this fact as I was the lead designer on both of these games and I was definitely influenced by Disneyland.
† Guest is Disneyland's term for customers.

configuration, adding some variety to the game. Scrolling environments were not unknown—shooters *Defender* (Williams, 1980) and *Moon Patrol* (Williams, 1982) both featured scrolling landscapes—but their worlds were unremarkable; barren moonscapes without even a sea of tranquility or Shackleton crater to distinguish their surfaces. In 1984, two landmark games in the development of themed levels arrived: Namco's *Pac-Land* and Capcom's *G'nG*. What these two games bring is themed lands that are parts of an extended world.

In the advertisement to Namco's *Pac-Land*, we see Pac-Man standing next to a map of Pac-Land, a Disneyland-inspired environment complete with its very own Wild West town, croc-infested jungle, and a mountain a la Disneyland's Matterhorn. Namco founder Mayasa Nakamura is a well-known admirer of Walt Disney who created his own theme park in Tokyo called Namja Town.

Capcom's *G'nG* pushed the themed world concept even further. In what may be the most difficult game of the arcade era, designer Tokuro Fujiwara's game is as deadly as the monsters inhabiting it. King Arthur jumped and battled his way through a graveyard, an icy palace, a rocky cavern, a fiery dungeon, and finally to the gates of a castle tower—only to be told the princess was in the next tower over! *G'nG* changed the landscape of platform games as other game developers started imitating *G'nG's* level design. Platform games became scrolling death traps of spiked pits, lava spouts, shifting platforms, and perilous jumps.

In the mid-1980s, the platform game genre took hold as home video gaming exploded, particularly in Japan with the arrival of the NES/Famicon in 1985. *Super Mario Bros.*, a platform game designed by *Donkey Kong's* designer Shiguru Miyamoto, blended the ideas found in *Pac-Land* and *G'nG* to create a wholly original classic. The pastoral landscapes found in *Pac-Land* were now brimming with hazards a la *G'nG*. Fire dungeons, underground sewers, and floating clouds were added to the game designer's lexicon of play environments.

Themed Video Game Level Trope #8—**Gritty Urban:** *While the fighting genre started with the fantasy game* Warriors, *it lay dormant for five years until Data East brought it back with two titles:* Karate Champ *and* Kung-Fu Master. *With these two games, the fighting genre split into two different directions.* Karate Champ *featured a single-screen play environment while* Kung Fu Master *had players fight through scrolling environments known as a brawler or beat-em-up. No beat-em-up was more popular than the* Double Dragon *series (Technos Japan, 1987), in which two brothers* *stalk the mean streets of a postapocalyptic New York; beating punks and gang members senseless as they attempt to rescue their girlfriend from criminals.* The game's designer was inspired by movies like* Streets of Fire *(1984) and the manga/anime* Fist of the Northstar *(1984).† Soon imitators sprang up like* Final Fight *(Capcom, 1989) and* Streets of Rage *(Sega, 1991).*

When the shooter NARC *(Midway, 1988) came out, the urban trope was already popular in movies like* Escape from New York *(1981) and* Robocop *(1987) and in comic books like the* Dark Knight Returns *and* Watchmen *(1986). However,* NARC's *digitized graphics were created from photographic reference rather than hand-drawn art. The result was a sleazier environment taken directly from real life. It was a perfect match for the game's ultraviolent gameplay that kicked off a new era of violent video gaming.‡*

The gritty urban theme exploded with the advent of the gangster game genre, including the Grand Theft Auto *(Rockstar, 1997) and* Saints Row *series (THQ, 2006), which take place in sandbox worlds modeled on real and fictitious cities. The powerful graphic processor systems of the PlayStation 2 and XBOX allowed for developers to create more visually detailed worlds. Players become immersed in realistic environments and can easily understand the context of the gritty urban theme as many of us live in such environments in the real world. The genre serves as an outlet for players who live in these urban settings since they can choose to improve or destroy it.*

MANGA MAKES ITS MARK

As with Western culture, comic books have had a powerful influence on video game developers. In Japan, it is called manga. One of the earliest popular heroes of manga was Jiro Kuwata's *8th Man* (Weekly Shonen Magazine, 1963). When detective Yokota is murdered by criminals, he is transformed by scientists into the cyborg the 8th Man, who continues Yokota's battle against crime and giant robots. A few years later, Kuwata drew the manga version of *Batman* to capitalize on the 1966 live-action television show. Both of these manga were a huge influence on Keiji Inafune, a young game designer, when he created *Rock Man* (rechristened *Mega Man* in the West) for Capcom in 1987. Like 8th Man, Mega Man is

---

* The two-player mode of *Double Dragon* has one of the most unexpected twist endings in a video game. The brothers—controlled by the players—have to battle each other for the love of Marian in the game's final battle.

† Which, in turn, was inspired by the dystopian future action movie *Mad Max* (1979).

‡ Midway, the publisher of *NARC*, went on to create *Mortal Kombat* in 1992, the poster child for video game violence.

a cyborg who battles villainous robot masters. Like Batman villains Two-Face and the Joker, Mega Man's foes' lairs matched their appearances. For example, Fire Man lived in a volcanic furnace, Ice Man lived in a frigid lair, and Bubble Man lived underwater. *Mega Man* set the trend and soon themed environments with matching bosses were found in every action platform game.

Found at the end of the game, a boss enemy is a (usually) super-powered opponent that is very hard to defeat. Inspired by supervillains from comic books, the title monsters from horror movies, and the archenemies found in the Bond films, the term "boss enemy" or "boss" is taken from the Bruce Lee Kung Fu action film, *The Big Boss* (1971). Ironically, the first arcade game boss arrived not in a fighting game, but with the mother ship in the shooter *Phoenix* (Taito, 1980).

As early as *Donkey Kong* and *Dragon's Lair*, we find the boss enemy becoming a beloved game design trope embraced by the video game development community. Soon bosses are appearing in every genre of video game. The list of bosses is legendary. Their names are both famous and infamous: Bowser, Ganon, Akuma, Dr. Robotnik, Psycho Mantis, Ares, LeChuck.

Bosses not only provide the player with a good* antagonist, but boss enemies can inspire and become intertwined with the very theme of a level. Have a pirate captain threatening the seven seas? Then fight your way through a pirate ship level to stop him. The player finds himself or herself in a space station? Good luck defeating that horrible alien boss that has eaten the crew.† It is safe to say that boss enemies will always be found in video games. After all, every dungeon needs a dragon.

Themed Video Game Level Trope #9—Space Station: *As early video games started trending toward playable (and merchandisable) characters and leaving the personality-less spaceships behind, these new heroes needed places to go and space stations fit the bill nicely. One of the earliest of these space station adventurers was Major Havoc, the hero of the titular game and leader of a clone army against the vile Vaxxian invaders. In the game, Major Havoc has to dock his ship Lunar Lander style into the space station in order to start the shooting gameplay sequences. Other titles quickly followed suit and the space station became a common location in games, as seen in* Space Ace, Xenophobe *(Bally Midway, 1987), and* Mega Man. *The*

---

* I guess that should be a "bad" antagonist.
† Or, more likely, turned them into zombies.

space station has become the stand-in for the dungeon in sci-fi games, especially in the first person shooter (FPS) and survival horror genres that were strongly influenced by the 1986 film Aliens. *In video games, most space station halls are infested with horrible aliens and malfunctioning robots. The space station theme lends itself to a variety of tech-based mechanics including laser-based force fields and factory-style moving platforms. Space stations allow the art team to show off when creating spectacular visual effects, such as holographic computer displays or stunning starscapes, as seen in games like* System Shock *(Origin, 1994), the* Halo *series (Microsoft Game Studios, 2001), and* Super Mario Galaxy.

Themed Video Game Level Trope #10—Sewer: A variation on the dungeon and jungle themes, the sewer was first introduced to players in Mario Bros. *(Nintendo, 1983). According to Miyamoto, the occupation of his lead character and carpenter Mario didn't feel right:*

> A colleague told Miyamoto that his little sprite looked more like a plumber. Accordingly, Miyamoto put Mario in a crab/turtle/firefly-infested sewer for his third outing. Further inspiration came from *Joust*, an early co-op game where players worked together or, alternatively, wiped each other out [8].

Miyamoto drew simple pipes for his enemies to emerge from, a mechanic that he reused in Super Mario Bros. *(Nintendo, 1985) on the Nintendo home game system. The sewers soon became the modern stand-in for the dungeon and as more game creators turned to Miyamoto for their inspiration, game sewers grew more complex, filled with deadly hazards such as giant rats, mutant alligators, and fetid water that falling into caused instant death. Factory-like mechanics such as whirling ventilation fans and sinking platforms could be found to challenge players.*

Sewer levels have become a popular location for game developers to place into their games. The theme has become a staple of action, RPG, FPS, and platform games like the Metal Gear Solid *series (Konami, 1998),* Oblivion *(2K games, 2006),* Left 4 Dead *(Valve, 2008), and* Lego Batman *(WBI, 2008).*

MEXICAN PIZZAS

In 2009, Electronic Arts published an action game based on the poem of *Dante's Inferno.* In the game, Dante wields not poetry, but a scythe made out of demon bones as he slices his way through Hell's nine levels to save

Beatrice from the grip of Lucifer and his demonic minions. On the game's blog, the game's designer talks about their goal—to fully realize Dante's vision into a real place, a living world:

> An important part about building a fantasy world is sustaining disbelief. Some of the best games I've worked on or played have one thing in common; you feel like the world was there despite you. It was running along just fine and then you just happened to come along [9].

Game creators continue to create themed levels but since many of the old tropes can feel stale after decades of games, they use what I call the Mexican pizza* technique. This is when you take two different tropes and put them together to create something new. I made my first Mexican pizza level when working on *Maximo: Ghosts to Glory* (Capcom, 2001), where I mashed up a fire level with a graveyard level. Graves spit out both flames and attacking skeletons and coffins floated on pools of lava. I was quite pleased with the results.

I have seen this duel-theme approach to level design become more common in recent years: *The Last of Us* (Sony, 2013) and *Enslaved: Odyssey to the West* (Namco, 2010) have beautifully rendered jungles growing out of urban streets and skyscrapers. Pirates have invaded the worlds of *Plants vs. Zombies* (*Plants vs. Zombies 2*, Pop Cap, 2013) and *Assassin's Creed* (*Assassin's Creed: Black Flag*, Ubi Soft, 2013). Players still battle through hellscapes both medieval and futuristic in *Shadows of the Damned* (Capcom, 2011) and *Doom* (ID, 2016).

And this is why I know that themed video game levels will continue to be part of the gaming experience. These levels help the developer invent a play environment from nothing but words and ideas like those written by Homer and Dante. Themed levels can take the player on journeys around virtual worlds of those found in Howard's stories of Conan and the Indiana Jones films. Themed levels allow the player to experience locations that are made real through technology and storytelling like those

---

* In 2001, Taco Bell introduced the Mexican pizza to the world. My curiosity was peaked. Growing up in San Diego, I knew what Mexican food was and growing up in an Italian household, I knew what pizza was. But what the heck was a Mexican pizza? It turned out to be a tostada with the meat and beans on the bottom and another tortilla with cheese and tomato on the top.

crafted by Disney's Imagineers. These themed levels are the playgrounds of our dreams.

REFERENCES

1. *Level Up! The Guide to Great Video Game Design*, 2nd Edition, Scott Rogers, Wiley and Sons, Chichester, United Kingdom, 2014.
2. http://en.wikipedia.org/wiki/Spacewar!
3. *The Odyssey*, XI.628, Homer.
4. http://en.wikipedia.org/wiki/Paperboy_(video_game)
5. The Making of: Pitfall! *Edge Magazine* online, 2009.
6. *Walt Disney's Disneyland: A Pictorial Souvenir*, Walt Disney Productions, 1978.
7. *Disneyland: The First Quarter Century*, Walt Disney Productions, 1979.
8. http://en.wikipedia.org/wiki/Street_Fighter_(video_game)
9. IGN presents the history of Super Mario Bros., Rus McLaughlin, 2007, www.IGN.com.

CHAPTER 6

Level Design Practices for Independent Games

Fares Kayali and Josef Ortner

CONTENTS

INTRODUCTION

The last few years have seen a great rise in popularity for independent games (games created by mostly small publisher-independent teams). This phenomenon can be partially attributed to the emergence of novel distribution platforms and lightweight development tools resulting in a significantly lowered entry barrier. At the same time we see an academic focus on independent games manifested through dedicated special issues in journals,[1] the newly coined term indie game studies,[2] and academics advocating for "engagement with the technical, creative and social obstacles independent developers deal with in their productive life."[3]

Many examples of independent games presented in this chapter feature 2D content and provide fun through strong, innovative, and playful game mechanics. The often-resulting combination of retro flair with modern, focused gameplay is what makes the contemporary retro game. This chapter argues that game and especially level design have evolved over time and provides insights on contemporary level design practice.

The level designer operates at a unique position at the intersection between programming, design, and art.[4] These aspects are usually combined to evoke a certain mood in the player.[5] An important skill for level designers is to distill ideas into solid, workable games[6] while leading players through the experience of the game without revealing their designer's presence in a way that distracts the players from their own virtual destiny.[4] Level design can be regarded as the process that implements the game design as well as all kinds of assets in the game. This chapter helps clarify the prevalent view that often equates many tasks of game and level design by isolating and situating aspects of level design practice.

The contemporary retro game helps to illustrate a newly found focus on level design and on building level design elements on strong core game mechanics. A methodology will be used that combines a qualitative analysis of several examples of such games with a reflection on the authors' own practice as game and level designers. As a result of this analysis, this chapter will present a series of distinct level design practices that relate to the design of contemporary retro games.

CORE MECHANICS

This chapter sees level design elements or patterns[7] as a result of building on game and core game mechanics. Especially contemporary retro games seem to build on one or more strong core mechanics that are explored and expanded through gameplay. This emergent approach is primarily made possible through level design that playfully experiments with the possibilities that are opened up through a game's set of mechanics. Therefore, understanding what game and core mechanics are is the basis for analyzing how these mechanics shape level design practice.

Järvinen describes game mechanics through verbs, regarding them as the actions that are available to the player.[8] Similarly, in their definition of the mechanics, dynamics, aesthetics (MDA) framework Hunicke et al. state that "Mechanics are the various actions, behaviors and control mechanisms afforded to the player within a game context."[9]

Building on these definitions, Sicart describes core mechanics as the game mechanics needed to "achieve a systemically rewarded end-game state"[10] while Salen and Zimmerman see them as "the essential play activity players perform again and again in a game."[11]

For the purpose of this examination, core mechanics are regarded as the defining game mechanics of a game. They can be seen as the building blocks around which a level designer can grow a level that plays with these mechanics. For example, the platformer *VVVVVV's*[12] core mechanic is that the player can reverse the direction of gravity but is not able to jump. A simple pattern based on this mechanic would be to place obstacles on the floor that the player has to evade by switching gravity to run on the ceiling. Expanding on this mechanic, the player later even navigates between and below moving platforms by switching gravity. The understanding of the importance of core mechanics in combination with the following account on what good level design practice is builds the foundation for our analysis of level design in contemporary retro games.

QUALITIES OF GOOD LEVEL DESIGN PRACTICE

As a starting point for the research of different approaches to level design, the following section explains which qualities of good design practice have to be satisfied to build engaging and well-balanced game levels. The authors' regard level design as a tool to expose the game design vision, centering on the purpose of engaging the player, similarly to Cliff Bleszinski's[13] carrot on a stick metaphor (which means to always provide a clear incentive for players) and on handling player expectations[14] (which means to consciously fulfill and subvert player expectations when designing a level). The defining qualities of good level design include:

- To maintain the delicate balance between difficulty and challenge. By avoiding anxiety and boredom players should be kept within an ideal flow channel.[15,16]

- To achieve a balance between giving players freedom to explore while imposing constraints to ensure continuity and fluent play, thereby giving players the illusion of control.[17]

- To provide the possibility to recombine game elements and actions and to achieve elusive mastery of the game. This also results in emergent gameplay and provides an incentive to replay levels. In a way this relates to the quality of malleability that Golan Levin describes for electronic instruments.[18]

- To balance risk and reward to give players risk incentive.[19] A level always should include easier and harder options that are rewarded proportionally.

- To drive the game's narrative. Level design has to ensure individual levels are aligned within the overall progress through the game. To ensure continuity, a level can only introduce new elements as described in the asset revelation schedule.

- To guide the player.[20,21] *Mirror's Edge*[22] with its distinct use of the color red to mark things the player can cling to is the prime example here.[23]

These are some methods found in academic and industry literature on games. The next section will present methods to expand this list by analyzing level design practices of independent games.

METHODS

By a qualitative analysis of contemporary retro game examples and the reflection of the authors' own practice, this chapter defines a series of distinct level design practices. The qualitative analysis uses a playing research approach,[24] where games are played reflectively with specific analysis criteria in mind. This approach is combined with a reflection of an explorative design[25] or design as research[26,27] methodology that involves the authors' own games. In explorative design, the design process itself is a means of knowledge generation.

To have an approach that combines play with practice, the authors asked themselves the following questions. The same questions are used as a basis to look at the qualitative examples.

- How did you approach the level design of your game?

- What led you to the specific level design practice used in the game?

- What are the benefits of this practice?

- What are the drawbacks?

- How do core gameplay and level design relate to each other?

- At what point in the game production process did most of the level design take place?

- How did constraints (time, budget, assets) shape the level design (practice)?

- How does your level design practice shape player experience?

- How is your game retro/what retro game genre would you align it with?

- How does your game combine retro flair with contemporary gameplay and concepts?

- How did the game controller and interface influence the level design?

PRACTICE: ANALYSIS OF THE AUTHORS' OWN WORK

The purpose of this section is to give a deeper understanding of details of the actual design practice that cannot be derived from just playing a game. The authors tried to step back from their own work and act as qualified observers[28] in the following two sections.

Radio Flare REDUX

Radio Flare Redux[29] (Figure 6.1) is a side-scrolling shoot 'em up with multitouch controls and a music-based game where each level is a song. All game elements, from background animations to enemy movement and shooting patterns, are tied to the rhythm of a level's soundtrack. All sound effects triggered by the gameplay blend with the music.

Consequently the game's level design process was tightly connected to the music. The first step of designing a level always meant listening to the respective song many times to identify things like sections, recurring elements, and different themes. The level files of the game consequently read like a musical score. All events scripted in the level files are already quantized to the beat,[30] meaning that the time index used in level files uses bars and beats as measures. This also means that levels would play slower or faster if used with a song with different beats per minute (BPM). Overall *Radio Flare Redux* combines the retro style and basic gameplay

FIGURE 6.1 *Radio Flare REDUX.*

of a side-scroller with the concept of synesthesia (a neurological condition where the stimulation of one sense triggers another sense, e.g., hearing colors or painting music) and interactive music (a musical composition that can be affected by the audience). The game's multitouch controls are tailored to the iPhone and iPad platforms.

In the game you use one thumb to control the ship and the other to target enemies with a swiping motion. When you release your thumb all targeted enemies are destroyed in sync with the music. *Radio Flare Redux*'s core gameplay means alternating between queuing up as many enemies as possible and dodging forward to collect the radio flares released by destroyed enemies. In a sense this core gameplay also happens in rhythm, as does everything else in the game. The rhythmic interaction is designed to connect to the overall synchronicity between music and visuals to deeply immerse players. The level design follows the music not only in rhythm but also in structure and themes. Ideally different sections of a level read like variations on a theme. The combination of the repetitiveness of enemy waves with timed variations of these patterns is an analogy to a level's electronic music soundtrack that evolves similarly.

What is beneficial about this approach is that the possibility to plan everything exactly tightens the connection between music, visuals, and gameplay. It enables the level designer to create a dramaturgy of enemy waves and events that support the flow of a level's music. At the same time this approach results in a very linear and static experience that mostly voids emergent gameplay situations.

Most of the level design for *Radio Flare Redux* was done close to release. This was a necessity because it was only then that all music licenses were cleared and the soundtrack definitive. The game would have benefited from starting earlier, which might have produced a deeper and more varied pool of enemy patterns and game elements to draw from. How many elements are needed to build a good, varied level is something that is hard to judge in advance. Also, many good ideas arise during the level design process that are mostly lost if the design is done late in the production cycle. The bottom line is that the approach to level design worked very well in connecting the gameplay to the music and thereby providing an immersive experience but had serious drawbacks in terms of gameplay variety and depth.

Hue Shift

Hue Shift[31] (Figure 6.2) is an endless action platformer. The player uses the arrow keys to control an oversized pixel that can shift its color between red, green, and blue. The goal is to climb as high as possible while matching the pixel's color to the color of the platforms. Only platforms that have the same color as the player remain solid. If the color does not match, the pixel will fall through the platform and the player has to start again.

Both level design and core gameplay are closely related because the level has to react to the player's actions and change itself accordingly. As

FIGURE 6.2 *Hue Shift*.

a consequence, level and gameplay design happened simultaneously and affected each other during the whole design process.

The first approach used in *Hue Shift* was level-based. Challenges were designed manually and the goal for the player was to finish each level as quickly as possible. Due to the fact that the player speed is constant, early user testing did show that there is a maximum high score, which does not motivate players. An article by Adam Saltsman inspired a new approach to the level design, which suggested an endless, self-generated level.[32] With this approach, players were able to play the game until a mistake ended the run—a practice that led to an active battle for high scores.

The level itself was generated out of 50 predefined blocks, each containing between two and six platforms. These blocks were split into three categories: easy, medium, and hard. Figure 6.2 shows a medium-level block. The first few tiers of the level were designed to be easy, followed by medium and later hard blocks. After a while, blocks were chosen randomly from all difficulties. The biggest challenge was keeping the level solvable. The blocks had to be designed in a specific way so every block could be combined with every other block.

Despite the fact that solving the level design problem took longer than expected, the overall time of the level design process was short and cheap compared to those of other projects, mainly because only a small amount of predefined blocks needed to be designed to ensure a challenging and diversified gameplay experience.

User testing showed that randomized level generation increased player motivation. When a mistake was made, players hoped for a better random level on their next run. Conversely, some players were frustrated after experiencing some tricky random levels. However, they still hoped for a better level in subsequent tries.

Hue Shift is often compared to retro games because it has a very low-end graphic style and limits the player to two actions—jump and change color. Contrary to retro games, one of the major goals of the game was to somehow limit the playtime for each run to approximately five to eight minutes, an approach adopted by many mobile games like *Doodle Jump*[33] or *Canabalt*.[34]

The level design itself also follows a retro approach. For each run, the level is self-generated by combining predefined blocks that are picked randomly. Using only a small number of chunks and combining them as often and as varied as possible is a method which was often used by games that only had very limited disc space at their disposal.

PLAY: QUALITATIVE EXAMPLES

Using literature research and the insights gained from the previous reflection of the authors' own practical work, we identified a series of representative game examples that are analyzed in this section (see Table 6.1). All five selected games are from the contemporary retro game genre. The elegant simplicity of their core game mechanics makes them easy to understand and each of the five games has been selected to illustrate a specific level design practice. The subsequent table aligns the authors' two games and the five qualitative examples with classic game genres. A description of each game's level design practice is given. Contemporary concepts are described to give an understanding of why the chosen games, while having a retro game flair, still are modern games that build upon established modern gameplay paradigms and use novel features. The core mechanic is described to understand its importance to the level design.

LEVEL DESIGN PRACTICES

Building on the analysis of qualitative examples, the following level design practices used in contemporary retro games could be identified: expand on strong core mechanics, iterative level design, design game modes not levels, sandboxes and emergent gameplay, and object-oriented level design. In the following we discuss each of these practices with more detail.

Expand on Strong Core Mechanics

> VVVVVV explores one simple game mechanic: you cannot jump—instead, you reverse your own gravity at the press of a button. The game focuses on playing with this mechanic in a variety of interesting ways.[12]

The self-description of *VVVVVV* from its product page on the Steam download platform gives a good summary of the game's core gameplay: It is a classic platformer game that builds its potential out of exploring a single and simple core mechanic. It constrains input to left and right movement and to switching gravity between up and down. By reversing gravity players suddenly find themselves running on the ceiling or having to walk across the bottom side of moving platforms. *VVVVVV* has very difficult yet fair gameplay. Playing is based on retrying small sections very often. To support this the game makes frequent use of well-placed checkpoints so that players never have to replay longer sections to get to the place where

TABLE 6.1   Overview of Presented Game Examples

Game	Retro Genre	Level Design Practice	Contemporary Concept	Core Mechanic
VVVVVV	Jump'n'run	Expand on strong core mechanics	Accelerated retries and negating the importance of lives and game over	Switch gravity
Galcon	Real-time strategy	Design game modes not levels	Ad hoc online multiplayer, competitive high scores	Send units to conquer planets
Canabalt	Automatically scrolling platformer	Iterative level design	One-button game	Control speed and jump across collapsing buildings
Sleep is Death	Text adventure with graphical user interface (GUI)	Sandboxes and emergent gameplay	Network play and ad hoc user-generated content	Play in a world dynamically created by another player
Bit.Trip Beat	Pong for one player	Object-oriented level design	Play along with the music	Reflect patterns of objects in rhythm
Hue Shift	Automatically scrolling platformer	Iterative level design	In-game score comparison with friends and other players	Match player and platform color
Radio Flare REDUX	Side-scrolling shoot 'em up	Object-oriented level design	Interactive music	Swipe to target multiple enemies

they failed. There also are no lives and no game over. Each section presents either a new or slightly refined challenge that builds on using the game's core mechanic the right way and by using exact timing in doing so. The game's reduced graphical style and the use of basic platformer building blocks contribute to *VVVVVV* being a very focused example of how contemporary retro games can combine a distinct retro style with modern gameplay that is grown out of exploring a strong core mechanic through the game's level design. Similarly, physics-based gameplay often relies on one core mechanic; for example, rotating the whole game world with the Wii remote in order to find a path through the indie puzzle platformer game *And Yet It Moves*.[35]

Iterative Level Design

Canabalt is an automatically scrolling platformer in which the player needs to escape an unknown threat. The player is only able to jump across gaps, obstacles, or boxes and cannot stop the movement at any time. Only the speed can be slightly modified by running into boxes to slow down a little bit. Otherwise, the movement speed is increased over time.

The game contains only one endless level, which changes every time a new session is started and contains only a few distinguishing elements:

1. Nonmoving platforms (in various forms like rooftops and annunciator panels)

2. Moving platforms (collapsing buildings)

3. Bottlenecks (large buildings where you can only cross through one floor)

4. Random enemy encounters (objects that suddenly fall from the sky)

These elements are generated procedurally in a similar manner like the levels in *Hue Shift*, which was described above. Adam Saltsman, the creator of *Canabalt*, defines procedurally generated content as "anything that exists in a game that wasn't strictly scripted that way by a designer. It might be a dynamically generated dungeon or a randomly rolled adventurer."[32] He describes various systems that can be used for computer-generated levels and writes that he uses a tile-based system in *Canabalt* himself. He states that "tiles are randomly arranged (though frequently with some constraints) to create the terrain or playspace of the game."

Although these methods are comfortable to use once they are designed, there are several things to keep in mind when using them.

> All these systems, despite their obvious promise, are fraught with potential disasters, many due to the players' aforementioned need for pseudo-predictable surprises. If your algorithm is too predictable and well ordered, players will become bored or hack the system. If it's too obtuse and unpredictable, players can't explain inconsistencies and will be frustrated or overwhelmed.[32]

The control of the play in *Canabalt* happens by using the touchscreen as one single button. This type of control became popular among small flash and mobile games and even inspired a one-button game programming competition during the Game Developers Conference in March 2010. Simple rules like "Use a single button as your player input, in a unique or experimental way. Be creative"[36] inspired developers to make games that can be picked up and played immediately. Simple control concepts like only pressing one button can also be found in early arcade and videogames that used a joystick and a maximum of two or three buttons as input method.

Design Game Modes Not Levels

Daniel Cook argues that designing interesting game modes eliminates the need to design levels and makes play varied each session.[37] This is evidenced by his game *Steambirds: Survival*.[38] The authors used pool-based approaches (drawing from a subset of enemy formations at random) in *Radio Flare*[39] and *Zombies vs. Sheep*[40] to provide variation within a game mode as opposed to the linear wave-based approach in *Radio Flare REDUX*.

The real-time strategy game *Galcon*[41] uses a very simple game mechanic with a variety of game modes. The game consists of a map with randomly placed planets in different sizes. These are generated procedurally with a node-based system and use a grid as described by Saltsman.[32] The player starts on a planet and can drag his or her units (represented by triangles) to other planets. If the amount of sent units is larger than the amount of units on the new planet, the player takes over this planet and produces units on it. The bigger the planet is, the bigger is its production rate. Once all enemy troops are gone, the player wins.

Because of these simple mechanics, various modes of the game can be played.

1. *Classic mode*: The player and one artificial intelligence (AI)-controlled player start on the same map, both with one planet under their control

2. *Three-way*: The player plays against two AI-controlled players

3. *Vacuum mode*: Only the player starts on the map and has to conquer all planets before a timer runs out

4. *Stealth mode*: Stealth mode follows the same rules as classic mode with the difference that enemy ships cannot be seen

All these modes can be played immediately once the player understands the core mechanic of the game. After the success of *Galcon*, another game named *Galcon Labs*[42] was released. It introduces even more game modes without changing the core mechanics themselves. As such, game modes can provide variety by, for example, changing the game rules, starting conditions, scoring mechanics (how points are awarded), or win conditions, while leaving a game's core mechanics, levels, and level design patterns unchanged.

Sandboxes and Emergent Gameplay

Many examples exist where level design is given to the user as a toolbox. Games like the arcade racing game *Trackmania*,[43] the four-player creative jump'n'run *Little Big Planet*,[44] or the overwhelming success of *Minecraft*[45] show that passing a good toolbox of level design elements to players can yield endless amounts of interesting levels with emergent gameplay. Examples even include working computers that can be built using the tools provided by both *Minecraft* as well as *Little Big Planet*. *Trackmania* gave birth to the idea of press forward sections of a racetrack; a predefined spectacle that relies on the player to accelerate without steering or braking.

The most interesting example in the context of contemporary retro games is Jason Rohrer's online adventure game *Sleep Is Death*.[46] It is a very retro style game both in appearance and gameplay. It uses pixel graphics and the world is presented from a pseudo-top-down view. There is no scrolling; the game only switches between individual scenes. *Sleep Is Death* is a text adventure at its core. It has a graphical user interface but player action is determined by typing sentences to trigger actions and dialogue. The novel thing about the game is that two players play it with one of them designing the levels on the fly. The game comes with a large set of scenery, building, and character items. Players take turns that are limited to 30 seconds each. One player types in an action and/or something he or she wants to say while the other (who represents the game) has to react within 30 seconds by moving characters and objects, introducing new things, or by responding through dialogue. The game does not impose any limits on what players can try out. By passing level design on to the players, playing *Sleep Is Death* always results in a novel experience with endless potential for emergent gameplay that is only limited by the players' imagination. The most intriguing potential of *Sleep Is Death* is its capability to provide a means for interactive storytelling to players.

The strength of the game's design does not lie in the level design itself but in providing a set of level design tools and objects that are easy to use but open up a wide space of possibilities through recombination. The provided level design tools for players can be simple and, for example, provide sets of primitives, some larger building blocks, or templates and interactive elements (e.g., switches or triggers). Complexity ideally does not show in the palette of provided tools but is a result of the combination of simple elements.

Object-Oriented Level Design

Object-oriented level design (OOLD) is a term coined by Rudolf Kremers.[47] The concept, as the name already implies, is derived from the practice of object-oriented programming. It is an incremental technique where assets are introduced and then reused with variations. The player first learns basic patterns. These are then expanded and varied during the course of a level (and the game).

Bit.Trip Beat[48] is a simple action game where the gameplay is a one-player variant of Pong[49] meshed with rhythm-based gameplay. The player controls a paddle to reflect incoming patterns of abstract shapes. Different shapes and colors of objects have distinct movement patterns. The reflection of objects is aligned to the rhythm of the music. Sound effects triggered by the paddle blend into it. New patterns are in most cases introduced by a single object first, and then there are waves of the same objects and combinations of these waves. They are either combined with waves of the same kind or with previously introduced patterns. The game uses a simple 8-bit retro style in both its graphics and music. The repetitive but engaging gameplay is tied to the music beautifully and together an immersive experience is created.

Not incidentally both the qualitative example of *Bit.Trip Beat* and the authors' own *Radio Flare Redux* relate object-oriented level design with music. The introduction and subsequent variation of patterns is something naturally found in music and can form a coherent gameplay experience by using an OOLD approach to introduce level design patterns.

Summarized, OOLD is a technique that allows for varied gameplay while at the same time saving resources. The drawback of this technique is that it easily leads to levels feeling repetitive. This can be partially overcome by altering not only gameplay but also graphical and acoustic representation of game elements that are subject to an object-oriented design approach. If used well (by employing a balanced ratio of repetition and variation) this practice poses a cognitive challenge through variation while also giving a sense of reward because players know part of the solution. Consequently this balance can be compared to the delicate balance that keeps players in the aforementioned flow channel,[16] with too much repetition potentially leading to boredom while too many new elements might induce anxiety.

SUMMARY

This chapter presented the level design practices of expanding on strong core mechanics, iterative level design, designing game modes instead of levels, emergent gameplay and sandboxes, as well as OOLD. These approaches are not meant to be mutually exclusive. In fact, most games might have been shaped by aspects of several of these practices. In particular, building on strong core mechanics is also a quality of good game design itself.

Choosing the correct level design practice is an important part of the level design process. As shown in *Hue Shift*, the whole design process can be accelerated after making a good decision on an approach to level design.

For good level design it is essential to start the design process as early as possible in the production timeline. If the level design process starts too late, it cannot be iterated often enough. By observing the level design process of *Radio Flare* one can see that the process started too late and new ideas had to be left out. It is important to detect circumstances that delay the level design process so they can be bypassed as early as possible.

In addition, early user testing has proven to be an important aspect of level design. It can demonstrate problems that can be missed by developers like the maximum high score from the level-based approach in an early *Hue Shift* version.

Actually all of the distinct approaches to level design call for level design being considered in early stages of the game design process.[50] When building on core mechanics there is a very tight connection between shaping that mechanic and the process of designing individual levels. When using a game mode, sandbox, or iterative level design strategy the boundary between game and level design becomes blurred. Game design ideally defines a rich toolbox for level designers that supports the discussed qualities like flow, balance, and malleability, resulting in more refined gameplay-oriented experiences for the player.

OUTLOOK

This chapter presented a strictly analytical approach to level design. Although reflective insights on the authors' own practice as designers were presented, a truly explorative approach would benefit the topic. Focused experiments or prototypes could be used to test individual practices and shed more light on specific benefits and drawbacks.

Overall, this chapter, as can future research into the topic of level design, contributed to form terminologies for game studies to understand the importance of actual design practice to level design.

REFERENCES

1. Simon, B. Indie Eh? Some kind of game studies, *Loading...* The Journal of the Canadian Game Studies Association, Vol. 7, No. 11, 2013.
2. Parker, F. Indie game studies year eleven, Proceedings of DiGRA 2013 Conference: DeFragging Game Studies, 2013.
3. Guevara-Villalobos, O. Independent gamework and identity: Problems and subjective nuances, Proceedings of DiGRA 2011 Conference: Think Design Play, 2011.
4. Byrne, E. *Game Level Design*, Charles River Media, Hingham, MA, 2004.
5. Logas, H., and Muller, D. Mise-en-scène applied to level design: Adapting a holistic approach to level design. In DiGRA 2005, Vancouver, CA, 2005.
6. Feil, J. H., and Scattergood, M. *Beginning Game Level Design*, Boston: Course Technology PTR, 2005.
7. Björk, S., Lundgren, S., and Holopainen, J. Game design patterns. In Level Up – 1st International Digital Games Research Conference, November 4–6, Utrecht, 2003.
8. Järvinen, A. Games without frontiers: Theories and methods for game studies and design. PhD thesis, University of Tampere, 2008.
9. Hunicke, R., LeBlanc, M., and Zubek, R. MDA: A formal approach to game design and game research. In Challenges in Game AI Workshop, San Jose, CA, 2004.

10. Sicart, M. Defining game mechanics. Game Studies Vol. 8, No. 2, 2008.

11. Salen, K., and Zimmerman, E. *Rules of Play.* Cambridge, MA: MIT Press, 2004.

12. Cavanagh, T. VVVVVV [PC game] Terry Cavanagh, 2010.

13. Bleszinski, C. The art and science of level design, 2000. Available at http://www.cliffyb.com/art-sci-ld.html (accessed Jan. 11, 2016).

14. Kayali, F., and Pichlmair, M. Intentions, expectations and the player. In [player] conference, 2008. Copenhagen, 2008.

15. Csikszentmihalyi, M. *Flow: The Psychology of Optimal Experience.* New York: Harper, 1990.

16. Chen, J. Flow in games (and everything else). *Communications of the ACM,* Vol. 50, No. 4, 2007, pp. 31–34.

17. Kayali, F., and Purgathofer, P. Two halves of play—Simulation versus abstraction and transformation in sports videogames design. *Eludamos. Journal for Computer Game Culture,* Vol. 2, No. 1, 2008.

18. Levin, G. Painterly interfaces for audiovisual performance. Master's thesis, Massachusetts Institute of Technology, 2000.

19. Ryan, T. Beginning level design. Gamasutra, 1999. Available at http://www.gamasutra.com/view/feature/3329/beginning_level_design_part_1.php (accessed Jan. 11, 2016).

20. Van Best, M. A trail of breadcrumbs: Level design and player experience. Nisute, 2010. Available at http://www.nisute.com/2010/08/18/needs-images-a-trail-of-breadcrumbs-level-design-and-player-experience/ (accessed Jan. 11, 2016).

21. Schuh, J. Beyond the Map: Navigation Systems for Virtual Worlds. Master thesis. Vienna University of Technology, 2008.

22. D.I.C.E. *Mirror's Edge* (multiplatform), 2008, Electronic Arts.

23. Silli, E. *Mirror's Edge*—Level design challenges & solutions. Game Developers Conference 2010. Available at http://www.slideshare.net/DICEStudio/e-silli-taome (accessed Jan. 11, 2016).

24. Aarseth, E. Playing research: Methodological approaches to game analysis. Game Approaches Conference. Spilforskning, Denmark, 2003.

25. Ehn, P., and Löwgren, J., eds. design [x] research: Essays on interaction design as knowledge construction. Vol. 3, Studies in Arts and Communication, Malmö University, 2004.

26. Burdick, A. Design (as) research. In *Design Research: Methods and Perspectives,* B. Laurel, ed. Cambridge, MA: MIT Press, 2003.

27. Stapleton, A. J. Research as design-design as research. Digital Games Research Association 2005 Conference—Changing Views: Worlds in Play, edited by Akira Baba. Vancouver, 2005.

28. Lammes, S. Approaching game-studies: Towards a reflexive methodology of games as situated cultures. Digital Games Research Association 2007 Conference—Situated Play, edited by Akira Baba. Tokyo, Japan: University of Tokyo, 2007.

29. Kayali, F., and Pichlmair, M. *Radio Flare Redux* (iPhone game), studio radiolaris/Chillingo, 2010.

30. Pichlmair, M., and Kayali, F. Levels of sound: On the principles of interactivity in music video games. Digital Games Research Association 2007 Conference—Situated Play, edited by Akira Baba. Tokyo, Japan: University of Tokyo, 2007.
31. Schuh, J. *Hue Shift* (PC game), All Civilised Planets, 2010.
32. Saltsman, A. Constructed procedural generation. *Game Developer Magazine*, No. 2/2010, 2010.
33. Lima Sky. *Doodle Jump* (iPhone game), Lima Sky, 2009.
34. Saltsman, A. *Canabalt* (PC game), Semi-Secret Software, 2009.
35. Broken Rules. *And yet It Moves* (PC game), Broken Rules, 2009.
36. http://switchgaming.blogspot.com/2009/12/gamma-4-one-button-game-competition.html (accessed Jan. 11, 2016).
37. Cook, D. *Steambirds: Survival*: Goodbye handcrafted levels, 2011. Available at http://www.lostgarden.com/2010/12/steambirds-survival-goodbye-hand crafted.html (accessed Jan. 11, 2016).
38. Radial Games, and Spry Fox. *Steambirds: Survival* (PC game), 2011.
39. Pichlmair, M., and Kayali, F. *Radio Flare* (iPhone game) studio radiolaris, 2008.
40. Pichlmair, M., and Kayali, F. *Zombies Vs. Sheep* (iPhone game), studio radiolaris/Clickgamer, 2009.
41. Hassey, P. *Galcon* (iPhone game), galcon.com, 2008.
42. Hassey, P. *Galcon Labs* (iPhone game), galcon.com, 2009.
43. Nadeo. *Trackmania* (PC game), Valve, 2003.
44. Media Molecule. *Little Big Planet* (PS3 game), Sony Computer Entertainment Europe, 2008.
45. Mojang. *Minecraft* (PC game), Mojang, 2009.
46. Rohrer, J. *Sleep Is Death* (Geisterfahrer) (PC game), 2010
47. Kremers, R. *Level Design: Concept, Theory, and Practice*, Natick, MA: AK Peters, 2009.
48. Gajin Games. *Bit.Trip Beat* (Wii game), Aksys Games, 2009.
49. Alcorn, A. *Pong* (arcade game), Atari, 1972.
50. Crawford, C. *The Art of Computer Game Design*. New York: McGraw-Hill/Osborne Media, 1984.

Making the Most of Audio in Characterization, Narrative Structure, and Level Design

Chanel Summers

CONTENTS

A UDIO IS AN EXTREMELY powerful storytelling, design, and communicative agent, but too often it gets relegated to an afterthought. Even worse, many see audio as a bunch of assets intended only to support visible game elements without considering its potential for storytelling and characterization. When this happens, the emotional and psychological functions of sound that could cause the game's audio design to rise to the level of art are often sacrificed in the name of utility.

Randy Thom, an Oscar-winning sound designer who has worked on such creative *tours de force* as *The Right Stuff, Cast Away, Contact, Backdraft, Forest Gump,* and *Return of the Jedi,* was one of the first to take a stand in protest of this systematic and unparalleled abuse when he wrote,

> Many directors who like to think they appreciate sound still have a pretty narrow idea of the potential for sound in storytelling. The generally accepted view is that it's useful to have "good" (meaning, "technically proficient") sound in order to enhance the visuals and root the images in a kind of temporal reality. But that isn't collaboration, it's slavery. And the product it yields is bound to be less complex and interesting than it would be if sound could somehow be set free to be an active player in the process.[1]

Thoughtful game designers and audio professionals realize the potential of audio to impact an audience when they set it free. Thom continued, "Only when each craft influences every other craft does the movie begin to take on a life of its own. A dramatic film which really works is, in some senses, almost alive, a complex web of elements which are interconnected, almost like living tissues, and which despite their complexity work together to present a more-or-less coherent set of behaviors. It doesn't make any sense," he concluded, "to set up a process in which the role of one craft, sound, is simply to react, to follow, to be pre-empted from giving feedback to the system it is a part of."

When thought of as an extension of the overall game design process, audio can be skillfully manipulated within a game to further the design goals of the entire production. To do so, however, it is vital to comprehend the power of sound, what well-designed audio can do for the choreography of level design, how to combat listener fatigue by creating a wide dynamic range of audio, and perhaps most important, how to make the most of audio's power to impact an audience by mapping audio design to level design.

THE POWER OF SOUND

Audio has the ability to affect individuals on a deeper level than most might expect—often on a subliminal level that they aren't even aware of. Sound is an immensely powerful narrative device that plays a crucial role in our emotional lives. It can imply actions or items that cannot be depicted through graphics. It can also alter our perception of events on a deeper level than graphics, story, or character. Sound affects us on a deep emotional level because we are continually experiencing it. Unlike our eyes, the ears never blink.

In *Game Sound Technology and Player Interaction*, Mark Grimshaw describes an experiment at the University of Waterloo where participants playing a game saw a losing outcome but heard a sound associated with winning played concurrently with the visual. In that experiment, the sound dominated the players' emotional response. "In a sense, the sound overrules our eyes and leads the emotional (and physiological) response to the event."[2]

However, Michel Chion, an innovator in the field of experimental music and author of *L'audio-vision*, considered by many to be the definitive author on the relationship between sound and images, demonstrated this same principle several decades earlier. In Chion's experiment, which he dubbed, "Forced Marriage," he paired a relatively neutral visual film sequence with two completely different soundtracks, altering both the sound effects and music, in order to observe the very different relationships that develop in the mind of the audience. Although the visuals remained the same, the experience of the viewers was radically different depending on the soundtrack. Chion observed that, "There will always be a few that create amazing points of synchronization and moving or comical juxtapositions, which always come as a surprise."[3]

In recent years, a number of clever editors have shown off their skills on YouTube by recutting trailers for classic films in a style that is completely different from the original film itself. For example, in one such recut trailer entitled *Scary Mary*,[4] the children's classic *Mary Poppins* becomes a tense thriller with elements of horror. The fact that the viewer is completely aware of the story of the original *Mary Poppins* makes their emotional reaction to the very different story implied by the trailer that much more delicious. By pairing a family-friendly musical comedy with the conventions of a horror film, and in particular that genre's audio signatures, the editors are walking the same path as Chion.

Chion and others demonstrate that the power of audio is such that in a conflict between sound and images, the audience's perceptions of the images are almost always altered by the sound and almost never the other way around. When artists combine images and sound, they can create associations and convey concepts and emotions that are more powerful than those conveyed simply by one or the other, providing additional narrative details and impacting the audience's experience in an understated fashion that affects them to a much more significant degree.

For this reason, audio is a great way to communicate messages, meaning, metaphors, pacing, and mood. Think of the mother in *Psycho* or the wizard in *The Wizard of Oz*. These powerful characters are introduced initially entirely through sound. The audience hears them long before they ever see them, and through misdirection, the audience is forced to create their own personal, larger-than-life, mental image of the character. When eventually revealed, of course, the characters are significantly reduced in stature in comparison to the audience's expectation. We have been tricked by the audio and the trick is revealed by the image.

In summary, well-designed audio has the potential to craft the story elements of a product, control the pacing of an experience, enforce the narrative, elicit and influence emotion, create mood, shape perception, and reinforce the way people experience characters. As such, audio must be considered a fundamental storytelling, characterization, communicative, and design mechanic.

INTEGRATING SOUND DESIGN INTO LEVEL DESIGN

The mark of a superior sound design, like any superlative work of art—whether painting, sculpture, stage play, film, novel, or any other art form—is one that the audience doesn't consciously notice. It works on the subconscious, playing with silence, subtlety, and tension. It manipulates players' moods and draws them into the game world. It takes advantage of the basic elements of audio aesthetics and utilizes devices such as ambiguity, juxtaposition, counterfunctional sounds, and misdirection. It enhances all other game elements, creating a cohesive and comprehensive player experience.

In order to achieve this, the time for a creative director, game designer, or producer to begin thinking about audio must occur at the moment the initial design process begins. As the creative team begins envisioning the style of gameplay and the environments in which the game will take place, the team must consider the aural aspects of the game and make plans for the audio to help communicate the game's narrative, allowing the team to design opportunities for sound to contribute to a deeper meaning within the production, perhaps even driving the game design itself.

By following a character's emotional journey and a game's story structure, audio can do as much as any other single production element, if not even more, to create mood and intensity, control the pacing of the game, and introduce subtle and powerful dynamics.

However, just as the emotional arc of a game's narrative structure can be visualized and mapped out based on the intensity, emotion, and feel of player interaction, those same elements of the audio design must also be mapped out, creating a meaningful and dynamic emotional state while remaining flexible enough to follow where the user chooses to take the action. Choreographing emotional resonance, characterization, and intensity levels across the narrative structure of the level also can yield many additional benefits, such as helping to combat listener fatigue, allowing players to hear clearly all the various audio textures, and enabling them to understand what is important or is the focus within the level at any given time.

COMBATTING LISTENER FATIGUE

An audio map is also critical to the prevention of sensory overload, particularly in action games where many loud sound sources might be present at the same time. It is crucial, even in such games, to develop an audio design that choreographs emotional resonance and intensity levels across the narrative structure of the game level. If a player is constantly bombarded with noise at full volume, the audio turns into a sort of sonic sludge without any element of dynamics and with no potential for even greater intensity in moments where an extra layer of intensity might be needed. If the sound is always at maximum loudness, two things happen. On a physiological basis, players become fatigued and desensitized. On a narrative basis, the game has already established its maximum intensity level and can go no higher.

One of the most fundamental and yet most underutilized techniques to prevent fatigue and extend a game's dynamic range is the clever and tasteful use of silence. Contrasting moments of intense auditory stimulus with moments of relative silence conveys greater meaning to both extremes. However, since complete silence would be disruptive in most game scenarios, silence does not have to mean absolute silence, or the complete absence of sound. For instance, Chion stated:

> ...the impression of silence in a film scene does not simply come from an absence of noise. It can only be produced as a result of context and preparation. The simplest of cases consists in preceding it with a noise-filled sequence. So silence is never a neutral emptiness. It is the negative of sound we've heard beforehand or imagined; it is the product of a contrast. Another way to express silence, which might or might not be associated with the procedures I have just described, consists in subjecting the listener to... noises. But I mean here the subtle kind of noises like the ticking of an alarm clock, naturally associated with calmness. These do not attract attention; they are not even audible unless other sounds (of traffic, conversation, the workplace) cease.
>
> Film uses other sounds as synonyms of silence: faraway animal calls, clocks in an adjoining room, rustlings, and all the intimate noises of immediate space. Also, and somewhat strangely, a hint of reverberation added to isolated sounds (for example, footsteps in a street) can reinforce the feeling of emptiness and silence. We cannot perceive reverb like this when other sounds (e.g., daytime traffic) are heard at the same time.*

The insightful designer will look for opportunities to create moments of high dynamic contrast, even if it is not a faithful representation of what the actual sound of the game environment would be in reality. For example, by focusing on a specific sound such as breathing or a ticking clock, the game gives specific prominence to the action and meaning associated with that sound. Similarly, by eliminating all sounds entirely except for music, the game can imply the subjective perception of the main character.

Taken to such an extreme, silence (whether complete silence or relative silence) can draw the player's attention to specific auditory elements, elevate moments of drama, and enhance the game's narrative and stylistic direction, but it must be utilized thoughtfully in order to have the desired impact, whether that is to enhance or to contrast with the visuals.

---

* See Ref. 3, p. 57.

This thoughtful approach is particularly critical during climactic moments of gameplay. While the natural instinct at such times might be to go big, layering sound upon sound so that the loudness of the audio matches the intensity of emotion, a judicious introduction of silence at just the right time creates a moment of contrast that emphasizes specific elements of narrative.

Limbo, a beautiful game from Danish game company Playdead, deftly utilizes the device of silence. The title focuses on minimalism, with an emphasis on silence and subtlety. Rather than relying on a traditional music soundtrack that could be seen as overtly manipulative, the game instead uses sound effects for their musical qualities. These sounds, with their unique sonic attributes and rhythms, serve the same purpose that a traditional musical score would in a more straightforward game, but at the same time the subtlety of the sounds and the surrounding moments of silence make the "score" even more intrinsic to the game.

NARRATIVE MAPS AND GRAPHICAL VISUALIZATION TOOLS: A FOUNDATION FOR CRAFTING DEEPER EMOTIONAL RESONANCE

Narrative audio maps are graphical tools and techniques that provide a visual foundation or roadmap for crafting deep emotional resonance, great drama, smooth transitions, continuity, and flow within a game level. These techniques allow the team to see where things might be breaking down in the level and where adjustments need to be made. They also help develop the structure and pacing of the gameplay's narrative and action and aid in the creation of smooth changes in intensity and musical styles, as well as natural transitions to other narrative moments. The process of detailing the narrative arc of a level's audio—dialogue, music, and sound effects—follows the exact same steps as mapping the story and gameplay elements within a level (Figure 7.1).

Music already lends itself to this kind of exercise most naturally, as Michael Sweet has remarked in his book, *Writing Interactive Music for Video Games: A Composer's Guide*:

> Many composers choose to draw out on paper the intensity of the music arc level by level, and throughout the game, to see where tension and release occur. In the composition process, they can then keep these points in mind to create the most effective music for each level. This process, which is known as emotional arc mapping, is common in narrative experiences.[5]

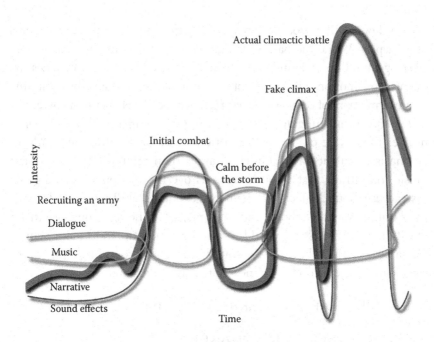

FIGURE 7.1   An example of the narrative arc of audio within a game level.

However, taken a step further, this same technique can also help determine for instance whether sound design, rather than music, should drive the audio in a scene or game level and also ensure that if some combination of sound effects, music, and dialogue all coexist within a scene, the audio elements do not step on each other. The player should always be able to hear dialogue clearly, as it generally must be given the highest priority in a mix, yet still experience the full impact of all other audio elements. These maps also provide an opportunity to plan so that the frequency properties and ranges of the sound effects and the musical instruments in the score do not collide with each other (Figure 7.2).

Even open-world games, which are more about free wandering and player styles and less about scripted interactions, can benefit from generalized, high-level concept maps that represent the various overarching outcomes and achievements within the game. In this case, these broad maps should then be refined to include all smaller goals and actions the player will encounter within the game world, such as character evolution, obstacle avoidance, puzzle solving, exploration of vast lands, collecting items or treasure, or combatting the big boss. Finally, these categorized submaps should be then detailed with finer elements, exploring each map's

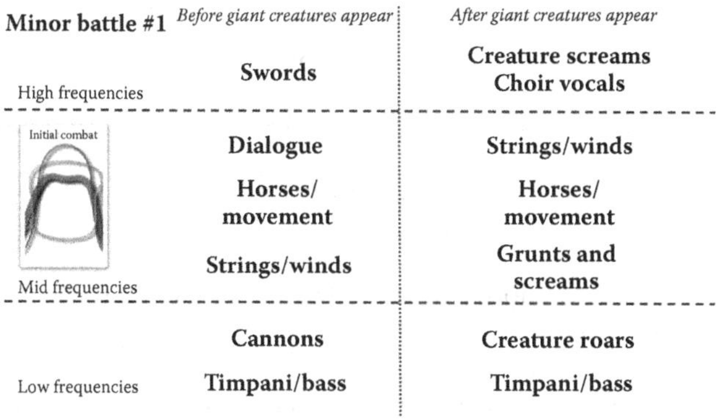

Minor battle #1	*Before giant creatures appear*	*After giant creatures appear*
High frequencies	Swords	Creature screams Choir vocals
	Dialogue	Strings/winds
	Horses/ movement	Horses/ movement
	Strings/winds	Grunts and screams
Mid frequencies		
	Cannons	Creature roars
Low frequencies	Timpani/bass	Timpani/bass

FIGURE 7.2 Narrative audio maps can ensure a thoughtful balance of emphasis between the various elements that comprise a game's soundtrack.

particular set of moods, intensity levels, pacing, dynamics, and transitions (Figure 7.3).

Regardless of the type of game, every narrative map should answer the following questions:

- How do you want to create the tension?

- What will be involved in illustrating the climax?

- How will the resolution be reflected?

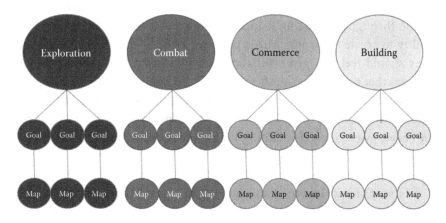

FIGURE 7.3 Audio maps for open-world games establish guidelines for how audio will function within principal game mechanics rather than in response to narrative-driven story elements.

- For each of these elements, will you use the audio to support or be in opposition to the visuals and gameplay?

- How will the transitions be handled between all these phases?

- How can you better utilize and integrate the audio to make an emotional impact?

- Do you want the audio to drive the gameplay or to be reflected or emerge from it?

- Is the audio paced out enough so that it doesn't suffocate the story and that there are quiet moments where it breathes along with the story?

If produced correctly, these narrative maps will form a set of blueprints that dictate how all audio elements will function together and how they will convey story, mood, and emotion. The maps will efficiently create levels of intensity, with multiple tension layers within each intensity level to provide more variation in the soundtrack. The maps will allow for moments of calm, chaos, conflict, and resolution, as well as creating smooth transitions in between.

MUSIC AND THE NARRATIVE ARC

Music plays a special role in surveying the overall sonic landscape of a game. It must be carefully placed within the context of each level in order to achieve maximum emotional impact. When a game liberally applies music throughout, pasting it in every corner like wallpaper, it loses the ability to create emphasis. Music provides a cue to the player about how they should feel in a given situation but by using it thoughtfully it also denotes that something significant is about to happen or is happening, or that something is unique or different about that section of the game. Using music for emotionally significant scenarios increases the impact that it can have. Sweet suggests defining the role of music within a game in two stages:

> First, it's important to establish what the "role" of the music will be by thinking of the music as an invisible actor. Will it be an active participant, or will it be part of the background? Next, the creative vision should include stylistic notes, plans for instrumentation, information about the genre, an outline for the main dramatic

goals, the interactive plan, and the way in which the music will be structured.*

In each narrative map, the role of music must be examined, understood, and optimized:

1. What are the roles that music will play in this level? What is its purpose? Or are we just using it to compensate for a lack of other things?

2. What instruments in the music compete with the sounds and dialogue?

3. Is the rhythm too complex or fast that it distracts from the importance of the dialogue?

4. What happens if we utilize silence instead of music? What is the balance overall between silence, music, sound, and dialogue?

5. Most important, how are we effectively conveying the narrative through the music?

In other words, rather than incorporating music simply for its own sake, be thoughtful of how it can represent or drive the narrative and gameplay within the level, while taking into consideration the following:

- *Pacing of narrative and gameplay.* Peaks and troughs, levels of tension and relaxation, conflict and resolution, and representing elements of great drama through how you choreograph the level with music (for instance, the journey, exploration and discovery, obstacles or challenges, conflict and resolution).

- *Emotions, moods, tones, intensity levels, and musical styles.* What are the various moods, intensities, themes, and musical styles that need to be represented within the level? They will change and be shifted based on various game state changes and variables. For example, encountering enemies, defeating the big boss, finding treasure, depleting health, gaining super powers or enhancements, and so on.

- *Flow.* Effective transitions that smoothly and seamlessly change intensities and musical styles within a level or between levels. Also, consider employing *stingers:* short musical motifs that can be triggered based

---

* See Ref. 5, p. 56.

on certain actions the player takes or in order to call attention to brief but significant game events without requiring a more extreme musical transition.

USING NARRATIVE MAPS TO INFORM THE GAME DESIGN PROCESS

While in most cases the game design will inform the creation of audio narrative maps, in many instances the process of mapping will uncover opportunities for the audio to inform the play mechanics. Because the maps give the entire design team a clear visual guide to the ebb and flow of the game's soundtrack and its relationship to the action within the entire game, they create associations and actually demonstrate how all the various events in a level all work together. For example, it should be clear whether the audio is functioning in support of, or in opposition to, the gameplay and visuals. The team may decide to amplify that support or opposition by emphasizing elements of gameplay or visuals that make the association even more extreme (see Figure 7.4).

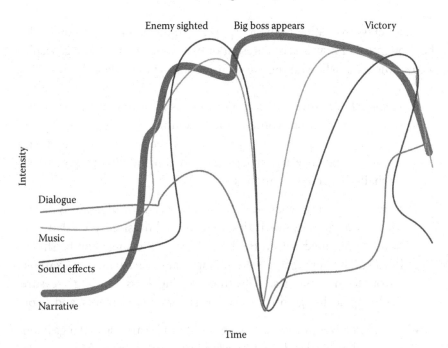

FIGURE 7.4 In this example of audio elements playing against the intensity level of the visuals, when the big boss appears, everything goes silent for a moment and then only the music can be heard.

This process will also ultimately yield dividends when determining how to mix the various audio elements. For instance, where does the sound and music need to be ducked down under the dialogue? Where does the music need to take priority? Using these maps as a focal point gets the whole team on the same page and fosters communication and collaboration throughout the team by forcing other members of the team to talk about and plan for the audio even if it is not their specialization. This, in turn, also makes them feel more invested in the audio and less mystified by it.

EXPANDING YOUR MAPS THROUGH AUDIO CONCEPTING

Once a complete set of narrative maps has been developed, it is time to begin testing, experimenting with, and iterating upon those sketches through a process of audio concepting (or iterative sonic storyboarding) in which pieces of audio are created that enable the entire design team to test how these notions work in an active and more realized, albeit highly selective, implementation. Audio concepts can take a variety of forms, depending on how the creative team works together most effectively. They can range from a set of draft auditory character and environment sketches that are each quite short in length to a complete audio track that accompanies an animatic. A musical framework can serve as an audio concept as can a complete sound narrative or soundscape: a story without pictures.

Audio concepts force the team to concentrate on emotive qualities and feelings rather than focusing entirely on impersonal acoustic properties, and to empathize with characters through deeply personal sensations that bring individual meanings to the piece of work. Doing so allows for more creative and experimental exploration that can further the creative objectives of the story more effectively than would ever be possible with pure focus on very specific and very technical audio strategies.

Once these narrative sketches have been realized into audio forms, the team can listen to various segments of the game and determine if the soundtrack is achieving the goals that were set out, confirm that the more experimental elements do indeed work, that the transitions are smooth, and that the effect of the audio mirrors how it was imagined. Audio concepts also yield further insights into how to implement changes that need to be made, provide ample creative ideas for further exploration, and demonstrate how the various elements within the end product will work together and be mixed together.

Furthermore, just as with visual narrative roadmaps, an entire team is able to gain a clearer and more tangible understanding of how audio is being utilized within each game level, but now that understanding is reinforced by an entire working system. For instance, audio concept work can enable a creative team to explore the personality and emotional makeup of each character through the sounds that accompany them. The iterative approach of audio concepting will enable a thoughtful team to continue to refine and improve on a game's audio plan by exploring, implementing, and perhaps even discarding a wide range of techniques.

CONSIDER DYNAMICS!

The first of these techniques is to consider removing all but the most essential audio elements used to communicate the scene or level. Among other outcomes, this will focus the player's attention on specific or significant occurrences or events.

If removing elements is impractical or too extreme, moments of contrast will also attract a player's attention and assist with creating a wide dynamic audio range within the level. This is most commonly achieved by utilizing a moment of silence to precede a number of major sound events such as an explosion or the appearance of a significant opponent.

PLANNING FOR FORESHADOWING AND PLAYING WITH PLAYER EXPECTATIONS

Narrative audio maps and sonic storyboards also enable the design team to play on the audience's subjective experience of the game's audio by considering their expectations—and then delivering the exact opposite. The audio aesthetics of these narrative dynamics can either play with the action gameplay maps or play against them, potentially even deceiving the player. For example, loud and frenetic audio can force a player to expect conflict, heightening the tension they feel in a moment when in fact there's no threat at all. When used in this way, thoughtful audio design becomes a highly efficient way to influence player psychology.

In evaluating the results of the experiments described earlier, Michel Chion concluded that there are two ways sound can evoke a specific emotion based on what the audience sees on screen: the *empathetic* and the *anempathetic*.* Empathetic sound occurs when the generally accepted mood of the sound matches the overt mood of the scene, reinforcing the visuals with complementary rhythms and tones. Nearly all games (and most films, for that matter) incorporate empathetic sound. However,

---

* See Ref. 3, pp. 8–9.

occasionally artists employ anempathetic sound by combining visuals with audio that is the opposite of what is expected, affecting the audience on a more profound level by hinting at a deeper meaning that lies beneath the action's surface. Anempathetic sound becomes overtly tragic, for example, when it subtlety informs us that what we might expect to transpire in a game's plot will not come to pass. Taken a step further, audio that contradicts on-screen actions or the character's overt emotions can even create a sense of irony.

CREATING AMBIGUITY

Narrative audio maps and sonic storyboards will also indicate where to create moments of intentional ambiguity. Rather than directly influencing the player's emotions, ambiguity leaves things open to interpretation and allows players to project their own feelings and emotions into the experience.

All works of art, including games, must anticipate that they will be experienced, interpreted, and understood by their audience, often in a manner that is very different from that which was intended by their creator. The best works of art—whether they are films, paintings, pieces of music, stage plays, novels, or whatever—create a lens through which the audience can, or even must, imbue the art with meaning based on their own interpretation of the art. These creative endeavors require the audience to make certain very personal assumptions about the work they are encountering based on their own life experiences, viewpoints, and memories, triggering associations that the artist never could have foreseen. This sort of ambiguous creative direction can be inspiring because it forces the designer to make associations that they otherwise would not, if solely focused on the superficial, by thinking about the audio design in terms of feelings and emotions instead of just acoustic properties.

Ambiguous sound can even create frustration or fear in players by presenting sound that is unfamiliar or unintelligible. In French comic filmmaker Jacques Tati's landmark film *Mon Oncle,* the audio track is comprised entirely of sound effects that correspond to the on-screen action, but the sounds are not what the viewer would expect to hear in reality.[6] Tati even uses silence or the suspension of certain sounds at key moments in order to emphasize other sounds, effectively accentuating their impact.

There are many, many ways to interpret the audio choices in this scene: the absurdity of their "ideal" suburban life, the dysfunction of their relationship, the silliness of their traditional gender roles, and perhaps even a statement by Tati about the nature of filmmaking.

Regardless, combining images with sound that initially seems to be out of context or against expectations creates a metaphor that, of necessity, requires the audience to search for their own personal interpretation. In this case, by juxtaposing the "wrong" sounds against the visuals, Tati forces the audience to interpret what they are seeing and hearing in order to try and make sense of something that is ultimately nonsensical.

So, if sounds always correspond exactly to that which is seen on-screen ("see dog, hear dog"), the audience isn't challenged and the meaning is only surface-deep. But conversely, it's ludicrous to suggest that all sound must be ambiguous in order to achieve art or something meaningful. Not all game concepts speak to this aesthetic device.

A good compromise might be to introduce some element of ambiguity, but ultimately resolving and explaining it. Doing so does not rob the work of its artistic ethic. Rather, the level of ambiguity and the circumstances under which it's introduced should be refined and manipulated in order to maximize its impact on the player. A great example of sound design that relies almost entirely on ambiguity is the aforementioned *Limbo*.

> Many can think back to sections of Limbo where they were struck by a certain feeling or sense for what the boy was doing in that place. But one thing Limbo never allowed the player to do was fully understand what was happening. Andersen achieved this by intentionally distorting the sounds of objects in an attempt to make the player think more about what's going on and how they're meant to react. This gave it a level of ambiguity that allows the player to "be there and make their own interpretation."[7]

According to Martin Stig Andersen, who was responsible for the game's audio,

> "The more identity the sounds had, the more I would distort them," Andersen said. "So I wouldn't include sounds that gave too strong associations. If we added something that had a strong identity like a voice or an animal, then it would almost destroy the atmosphere. So with that style, Limbo offered an audio and visual

atmosphere that can really get into the player's mind, and make them feel scared, worried or on edge."*

POINT OF VIEW OR SUBJECTIVE CHARACTER PERCEPTION

The subjective perception of sound is a crucial device when attempting to intensify the narrative qualities of a game. It builds a stronger connection to characters by playing sounds from the perspective of the character. Essentially, the player hears what the protagonist hears—whether real or imagined, or using real-time effects such as filters, delays, and reverbs to model that perspective. Doing so gives players direct access to the character's mental state and enables them to hear things as the character *interprets* them, even to the point of including hallucinations and altered states of consciousness, perceptual distortions, internal voices, or character memories brought on by stress, trauma, or even through the ingestion of mind-altering substances. By hearing the audio as the character does, not as the objective outside world does, players can even be made to explore the psychological processes of the character's mental state and how it affects what they're hearing.

Subjective character perception can also emphasize the scale of an environment. For example, shifting from an extremely immersive ambient sound world to the personal sonic experience of an individual within that environment presents players with a subjective audio experience from the character's perspective. This means the game can effectively compress the scale of the game world down to a single individual—the player's character—in order to present a degree of focus and then later expand that space again when leaving the mind of the character, creating a wide dynamic range within the level and giving the player's ears a rest in order to renew the impact of other sounds within the entire game landscape.

In summary, subjective character perception leads to a deeper sense of who the character is and builds a stronger connection to the character by allowing players to identify much more intimately with the character on a deeper level, making for a much more immersive and visceral experience and may become particularly crucial in a virtual reality experience when *assuming* the role of a character.

---

* See Ref. 7.

THE UNSEEN, OR PLANNING FOR ACOUSMATIC AUDIO

Additionally, the easiest way to build on the subjective perception of audio and to create a seamless game world is through the use of acousmatic audio: sounds whose sources are intentionally not visible.

Obviously, all games include some degree of acousmatic audio, although almost always unintentionally, since it's almost guaranteed to be impossible for a player to see absolutely everything generating the sounds within a game. In this context, acousmatic audio is meant to refer to the intentional manipulation of offscreen sounds in order, for example, to maintain suspense or preserve mystery.

When we hear a sound without seeing its source we are forced to interpret what we're hearing—perhaps even subconsciously. In this way, acousmatic audio can communicate meaning, metaphors, or even game elements that do not exist visually. Since the player cannot see the source or cause of the sound, this can create a sense of mystery and apprehension: a great way to communicate messages, meaning, pacing, and mood in a nonvisual way.

Acousmatic audio is also a fantastic way to create ambiguity. Just as known sounds can force the player to recall memories and experiences, unknown sounds can create confusion and possibly fear.

CONCLUSION

All too often, game designers begin to plan for audio after the fact—so late in the design process that it's impossible to integrate audio into anything more than a purely functional role. Audio can and should be an integral design element from the start, conveying elements of narrative, characterization, or gameplay by itself and in concert with other game elements. Audio must be more than a list of assets to be compiled and assembled like items on a shopping list.

Rather than just coupling each of the visual elements of a game with a corresponding functional sound element, audio should always further the goals of story, characterization, and the creation of a holistic ecosystem. Well-executed sounds and a brilliantly composed soundtrack have minimal value when accompanied by nothing more than surface meaning. The techniques discussed provide ways for an entire production team to work together in order to create a cohesive, holistic unit of all the elements as well as a rhythm within a game level.

Games can and should aspire to deliver more impactful experiences by taking into account that sound enhances the underlying meaning of the experience in a very personal way and contributes to a deeper meaning within a game.

REFERENCES

1. Thom, Randy. Designing a movie for sound. FilmSound.org., http://film sound.org/articles/designing_for_sound.htm. 1999.
2. Grimshaw, Mark. *Game Sound Technology and Player Interaction: Concepts and Developments.* Hershey, PA: Information Science Reference, 2011, p. 14.
3. Chion, Michel. *Audio-vision: Sound on Screen.* New York: Columbia University Press, 1994, p. 188.
4. Rule, Christopher. *THE ORIGINAL Scary* Mary Poppins *Recut Trailer.* YouTube, https://www.youtube.com/watch?v=2T5_0AGdFic. October 8, 2006.
5. Sweet, Michael. *Writing Interactive Music for Video Games: A Composer's Guide.* Upper Saddle River, NJ: Addison-Wesley, 2014, p. 60.
6. Tati, Jacques. *Tati mon oncle extrait 01.* YouTube, https://www.youtube.com/watch?v=gkvtE1AS6Qo. March 14, 2008.
7. Bridge, Caleb. Creating audio that matters. Gamasutra, http://www.gamasutra.com/view/feature/174227/creating_audio_that_matters.php. July 17, 2012.

CHAPTER 8

Procedural Content Generation

An Overview

Gillian Smith

CONTENTS

This chapter first appeared in Game AI Pro 2 *edited by Steve Rabin* (CRC Press, 2015)

INTRODUCTION

Procedural content generation (PCG) is the process of using an artificial intelligence (AI) system to author aspects of a game that a human designer would typically be responsible for creating, from textures and natural effects to levels and quests, and even to the game rules themselves. Therefore, the creator of a PCG system is responsible for capturing some aspect of a designer's expertise—a challenging task for an AI!

PCG has been used in many games for several different purposes. Two popular motivations are replayability and adaptability. PCG can provide large amounts of content so that each time the player starts the game they will have a different experience. In combination with an AI system that can infer player skill, PCG can be used as a form of dynamic difficulty adjustment, shifting the content the player will see in order to adapt to their skill level.

One of the first examples of PCG was in the game *Elite* [Braben and Bell 1984], where entire galaxies were generated by the computer so that there could be an expansive universe for players to explore without running afoul of memory requirements. However, unlike most modern games that incorporate PCG, *Elite*'s content generation was entirely deterministic, allowing the designers to have complete control over the resulting experience. In other words, *Elite* is really a game where PCG is used as a form of data compression. This tradition is continued in demoscenes, such as *.kkrieger* [.theprodukkt 2004], which have the goal of maximizing the complexity of interactive scenes with a minimal code footprint. However, this is no longer the major goal for PCG systems.

Regardless of whether creation is deterministic, one of the main tensions when creating a game with PCG is retaining some amount of control over the final product. It can be tempting to use PCG in a game because of a desire to reduce the authoring burden or make up for missing expertise—for example, a small indie team wanting to make a game with a massive world may choose to use PCG to avoid needing to painstakingly hand-author that world. But while it is relatively simple to create a system that can generate highly varied content, the challenge comes in ensuring the content's quality and ability to meet the needs of the game.

There are several major approaches to PCG that offer different means for this control, as well as supporting different extents to which the control can take place. There are also many reasons for why PCG may be used in a game, which can help inform a game designer's and/or developer's choice about what technique to use when creating the system. *Civilization* [MicroProse 1991], *Rogue* [Toy et al. 1980], *Minecraft* [Persson 2011], and *Borderlands* [Gearbox Software and Feral Interactive 2009] are all examples of popular games that use PCG, but with completely different approaches and purposes.

For the sake of scope, this article focuses on creating content that a player somehow interacts with as part of gameplay—think levels and quests rather than textures and trees.* It will also avoid a discussion of procedural generation of game rules—that is, research that is really still in its infancy as of this book's publication [Smith and Mateas 2010; Togelius and Schmidhuber 2008]. The focus is on the procedural creation of content (e.g., what would be created by a level designer) rather than on storytelling and NPC behavior, although there are many relationships between these systems. However, while we won't delve into systems that create game rules, for many PCG systems it is still necessary to find ways to formally specify aspects of the game's rules in order to guarantee that playable content will be generated.

This chapter will give an overview of PCG, survey different techniques for creating content generators, examine how PCG fits into a game's design, and

---

* There are several resources dedicated to explaining approaches to procedural modeling and texturing. Ebert et al.'s textbook on the subject is a good entry point [Ebert 2003].

give some advice for how to choose an appropriate method for a game. At the end, there are pointers to literature and resources where the reader can find more details on PCG and learn how to stay up to date on PCG research.

TECHNICAL APPROACHES TO CONTENT GENERATION

While there are no off-the-shelf tools or frameworks for creating your own PCG system, there are several common approaches and methods for knowledge representation. This section will give an overview of these approaches and methods and discuss some trade-offs between them.

Algorithms and Approaches

One of the primary considerations when choosing an approach to designing a content generator is the extent and kind of control needed. Approaches to PCG range from purely bottom-up, simulation-based methods that only permit control over the initial state of the world and operators for changing it, to top-down, constraint-driven methods that let the system meet firm authoring constraints but may be more expensive to create and debug.

Simulation-Based

Simulation-based approaches to PCG start with an initial world and a set of operators that can alter that world, and then run a simulation for a pre-determined period of time. For example, a simulation-based approach to creating terrain might start with a single landmass in an ocean, a climate/rainfall model, and an erosion model to create a new terrain with rivers, lakes, cliffs, and beaches. *Dwarf Fortress* [Bay 12 Games 2006] is a game that takes this approach to generation, with a full simulation that creates landmasses, caves, and a history for the world. Simulation-based approaches do not permit any control over the final output of the system without using a generate-and-test paradigm (described further in the section on constructionist systems). While simulation can be a slow process with limited control, it has two potential benefits that may make it a good choice: (1) it provides you with a content history that can be referred to or replayed, and (2) it can be run during gameplay to create a world that reacts to the player's choices and actions.

Constructionist

A constructionist approach is one that pieces together premade building blocks according to an algorithm especially constructed for the game. This algorithm has design knowledge implicitly baked into it—any intelligence in the process exists only in the choices made by this one algorithm rather than more explicitly stated as an optimization function or as a set of design constraints. For example, many *Rogue*-like level generators [Rogue Basin 2012] are constructionist approaches that build different rooms and then construct corridors between them. Constructionist approaches are typically ad hoc, specialized for one particular game with little applicability beyond it, and accessible primarily to developers rather than designers and artists.

Constructionist approaches often rely entirely on their knowledge representation (see "Knowledge Representation" on p. 168). Many, though not all, approaches involve taking large, preauthored pieces of content and placing them next to each other randomly, as in endless runner games like *Robot Unicorn Attack* [[adult swim] games 2010] or *Canabalt* [Saltsman 2009]. This kind of constructionist approach is perhaps more accurately named "content selection," where there is no attempt to make intelligent choices in the *process* that is followed, but there is very tight designer control over the building blocks.

Constructionist systems are difficult to control and difficult to get good variation from; it's easy for all the content to start to feel the same if there's a limited set of building blocks to choose from. Large branching control flow structures can also be difficult to debug, especially if the bug lies in a piece of code that is executed very rarely. And you can spend a huge amount of time tweaking your algorithm to get content that is just right in one situation, without realizing that you're simultaneously breaking the content for some different situation.

Designing your own algorithm from the ground up does have some benefits, however. From a design perspective, content selection is a lightweight approach that is good enough for some games, especially where there aren't a lot of constraints on what constitutes playability (e.g., a simple platforming game such as *Canabalt* just needs the platforms to be reachable, whereas a lock-and-key puzzle game such as Joris Dormans's *Zelda*-like game [Dormans 2010] has deeper constraints).

Grammars

A grammar-based approach starts by specifying the possibility space of content (or generative space) as a formal grammar. Next, an interpreter for that grammar (which will parse and process the rules to create content) is built. This explicit separation of grammar rules from content assembly offers more organization than a constructionist approach, where the rules are often implicitly defined in the code, and can also be useful to technical designers who may be able to edit the grammar rules without needing to touch the content assembly system. Grammars have been used to create levels for platforming games [Smith, G. et al. 2011c] and action-adventure games [Dormans 2010], as well as in tools for rapidly designing buildings [Müller et al. 2006]. Shape grammars are also a useful kind of grammar for creating visual content [Stiny 1980].

When used to create content that is then tested against requirements and discarded if it doesn't pass the tests, this approach strikes a balance between bottom-up emergence from designer-specified rules (in the form of the grammar) and top-down control over content (in the form of the acceptance rules for the generated content). It still allows a computer to explore the design space and come up with surprising and varied results.

Authoring the rules for a grammar-based system is done by breaking down your desired content into increasingly small pieces. The grammar will then specify rules as nonterminal and terminal symbols. Nonterminal symbols can be expanded into more nonterminals and terminals specified by a set of rules. Content creation begins with a single nonterminal symbol, the start symbol, and then repeatedly replaces nonterminals with new symbols (which may be terminals, nonterminals, or a mix of the two) according to a set of expansion rules until only terminal symbols remain. There may also be more than one rule per nonterminal symbol, thus allowing nondeterministic content to be created. Some rules might be weighted toward being selected more frequently than others, which can provide some additional control over the kind of content that will be produced.

The grammar's interpreter is responsible for selecting the next rule to expand. It can be tempting to combine the grammar rules and the interpreter into one big branching control flow, and for simple grammars this can suffice. However, the power of grammars often lies in the ability to quickly add or change rules and see the impact on content, and grammars often change and grow to meet changing design constraints. Thus it is a good idea to keep the interpreter and the grammar separate.

A grammar can produce huge amounts of content, and often very quickly. Unfortunately, grammars are prone to *overgeneration*, where they may create content that was not intended when the grammar rules were designed. If the grammar is too loosely constrained, there is no guarantee that everything it can create will be *good* content. Fixing overgeneration in the grammar rules can sometimes restrict the abilities of the grammar too much, leading to *undergeneration*—all the content may now be considered good, but it will also feel too similar and predictable. Thus, choosing to overgenerate and then running a suite of tests on the results can ensure that surprising content is still generated, but unacceptable content is discarded.

In order to achieve this, some simple-to-measure acceptance criteria (e.g., a level must have at least 15 features) with which the bad content will be culled. These criteria also offer an opportunity to explicitly define criteria that are difficult, or even impossible, to specify in the grammar rules, and provide some ability to have top-down design constraints while still benefiting from the emergent content that comes from using bottom-up rules for generation.

The strength of a grammar-based approach lies in the combination of simple, easy-to-author rules that provide emergent and interesting content with a generate-and-test paradigm that lets the generator meet soft constraints. Grammar rules are also easy to use to express design patterns. Since grammars usually generate content very quickly, generating a great deal of content and throwing much of it away is not expensive. As an example, *Launchpad* [Smith, G. et al. 2011c] is an unoptimized level generator for *Mario*-like platforming levels. Its grammar-based representation is capable of creating 10,000 candidate levels in only a few seconds. The speed of this approach is dependent in large part on the complexity of the grammar rules, but since it is possible to specify recursive rules, speed is also dependent on the allowed recursion depth. The weakness of grammars is their difficulty in meeting hard design constraints and in debugging the rule system, which can become quite complex.

Optimization

An optimization-based generator involves a search process (often unbounded) that seeks out the optimal combination of components according to some evaluation function. This evaluation function is usually specified as a formula that attempts to calculate the desirability, and the search attempts to maximize this value. Alternately, there can be a human in the loop, with a human player or designer selecting their favorite content from among the candidates.

Evolutionary algorithms are a popular approach to optimization-based content generation in academic research. They attempt to mimic natural evolution. An initial population is created and then bred and mutated into a new population that can be evaluated by the fitness function (or by the human in the loop). The best candidates are bred and mutated once again, and their children are evaluated. This cycle continues until there is a piece of content that is a good fit to the evaluation function, or until a maximum number of candidate generations have been created, at which point the candidate with the best evaluation score is chosen.

As a simple example of an evolutionary algorithm, consider the problem of procedurally generating a maze. An evolutionary algorithm might start with a population of 1000 completely random mazes. It would then calculate the fitness score for each maze based on how well that particular candidate meets the evaluation criteria, and would generate a new population of mazes by breeding highly rated mazes together—perhaps by combining the left and right halves of two different mazes into a new one. This process would be repeated until either a predetermined amount of time has passed or until a maze that meets the acceptance criteria has been generated.

There are a lot of nuances to creating genetic algorithms. Optimization-based approaches are also highly sensitive to the knowledge representation used (for example, representing a maze as a set of walls with endpoints and lengths versus as a grid with open and closed cells) [McGuinness 2012], as well as to the particular implementation of the algorithm. What should the mutation and breeding operators be? How should the evaluation function be crafted? How should the percentage of the population that is chosen to breed versus mutate be selected? Should some of the candidates be saved for the next generation without breeding (known as elitism)? There is a survey article on search-based methods for PCG that provides a good entry point to the literature [Togelius et al. 2011].

All optimization-based approaches to PCG must have an evaluation function—some way of quantifying the overall goodness of an arbitrary piece of content. These evaluation functions can be fairly simple approximations, such as the distance from the actual distribution of components in the content to the desired distribution of those components. However, it can be difficult to capture everything important about the content in one evaluation function. *Player experience modeling* [Yannakakis and Togelius 2011] is an attempt to treat the evaluation function more abstractly by learning a model of individual player preferences by having them play some of the content and then applying the model as the fitness function to create personalized content. A simpler use of player modeling is to use the human as the evaluation function. *Galactic Arms Race* is a game that takes a human-in-the-loop approach and uses an inferred simple model of player preference (that weapons the player uses most often are most desirable) to generate new weapons that are personalized to a particular play style [Hastings et al. 2009].

The use of an optimization-based approach relies on a comfort with the notion that there is such a thing as an optimal piece or pieces of content, and that it is possible to express this mathematically. Note that this evaluation function does not necessarily need to be reduced to a mathematical definition of "fun." It can instead be a set of desired properties that the system should aim for. If the generator is being designed with a concrete goal that can be expressed mathematically then this approach may be a good one. It can also work quite well if there is a way to involve a human in guiding the generation process at runtime. Another benefit is that, like the generate-and-test approach used with grammars, optimization-based approaches can be useful for soft constraints—properties of content that are desirable but not crucial to the function of the game. However, evolutionary algorithms that do not have a human in the loop can be slow, and player experience modeling requires the player to be put through training levels, which can be time consuming for the player and must be designed into the game.

Constraint-Driven

Constraint-driven methods are declarative approaches in which hard design constraints are specified, and then a constraint solver is used to find all potential solutions that meet those constraints. All of the content is expressed as variables with ranges of potential values, with constraints dictating the relationships between these variables. This entirely top-down approach allows the specification of knowledge about what the content *should* look like separately from the underlying search algorithm.

Constraint satisfaction has been used for generating room interiors [Tutenel et al. 2009] using semantic constraints, which introduce knowledge about what objects are and how they relate to others (e.g., a table should be surrounded by chairs). Numerical constraint solving has been used for placement of platforms and other level geometry in platformer levels [Smith, G. et al. 2011b]. Answer set programming, a method for specifying constraint problems in first-order logic, has been used for levels in an educational puzzle game [Smith, A. et al. 2012] as well as the real-time strategy game *Warzone 2100* [Smith and Mateas 2011].

The challenge in constraint satisfaction for content generation comes from fully specifying all of the constraints. Common-sense constraints, such as the idea that two objects cannot occupy the same position at the same time, must be specified along with more game-specific constraints. However, constraints are a powerful method for expressing a design space, and this approach works well when there are many constraints that *must* be met in order for the content to be acceptable. Runtime performance for constraint satisfaction approaches to PCG vary drastically based on the size of the problem, how the problem is described, and the number of constraints. Many solvers, such as answer set programming, work by reducing the problem to a Boolean satisfiability problem, which is an NP-complete problem. However, for small-to-medium size domains, such as mazes, grid-based puzzle games [Smith and Mateas 2011], and even simple platformers [Smith, G. et al. 2011b], constraint-based content generation can produce results in a matter of seconds, or a few minutes at worst. What's more, adding constraints can actually improve the runtime performance of some constraint-based systems, as it allows the system to rapidly eliminate portions of the search space that don't contain satisfactory solutions.

Knowledge Representation

Many of the approaches described in the previous section can be further varied by changing the knowledge representation; that is, the building blocks that the content generator will piece together. Here there are four major kinds of building blocks that trade off authoring control against risk of the player recognizing common patterns. They are presented in order from most to least human-authoring.

Experiential Chunks

An experiential chunk captures a sufficiently large amount of content that, on its own and outside the context of the entire piece of content, it could still be experienced by the player as its own entity. An example would be the level chunks used in *Robot Unicorn Attack*. One advantage of this representation is that there is a great deal of artistic and design control over the appearance of the generated content, but there is a significant chance that the player will begin to notice the same chunks repeated again and again. Raph Koster notes that game players are pattern recognition machines [Koster 2004], and this is certainly true for procedural content generation. Unless pattern recognition is desired, experiential chunks should either be avoided or tempered by using a mixture of approaches to designing the generator (see "Mixing and Matching" on p. 170). Experiential chunks are usually used with constructionist algorithms, but can also be used with grammars.

Templates

Templates are a more generalized form of experiential chunk, where the design team can still control the content but leaves blanks for the AI to fill in automatically. Templates are like the *Mad Libs* of PCG, and unless care is taken to construct the template and the rules for what content can fill in the gaps, can have the same quirky consequences as the word game. However, templates can strike a nice balance between authorial control and variety for high-fidelity games.

Templates are a kind of high-level design pattern, and the design patterns literature can be a good place to draw inspiration for templates for a generator. Bjork and Holopainen's book [Bjork and Holopainen 2004] is a good collection of general patterns, but there are also patterns specific to genres such as first-person shooters [Hullett and Whitehead 2010], role-playing game levels and quests [Smith, G. et al. 2011a; Onuczko et al. 2005], and 2D platformers [Smith, G. et al. 2011c], to name a few examples.

Components

Like templates, components are patterns that have been designed by a human. However, unlike templates and experiential chunks, components cannot stand on their own to be experienced as content in their own right. For example, enemies in a first-person shooter have general behavior dictated by a human designer but cannot exist without the broader context of the level that they inhabit. Using components reduces the risk that content patterns will be seen by the player. However, it also means that the generation algorithm needs to play a much stronger role, as it will be almost entirely responsible for the quality of the content that is produced. Component patterns can work well with all of the generation approaches mentioned in this chapter.

Subcomponents

A subcomponent representation uses the smallest possible assets. Subcomponents do not have embedded semantic information about what the content is or how it should be used. They can be imagined as the same kind of building block that humans use to construct their levels, such as art assets from a tileset. Very few generators use this approach to content generation because it is difficult for the generator to understand how to piece things together without some amount of semantic information about the content, and thus it's more common for generators to use a component representation. For example, it is helpful for a generator to understand the concept of a "room" or a "chest" and how they are allowed to fit together. However, *Galactic Arms Race* [Hastings et al. 2009], an experimental game that creates particle system weapons, is one example of a game that uses this representation.

Mixing and Matching

These approaches and knowledge representation techniques can be combined to produce more sophisticated systems and to meet the demands of the game's design. For example, using content selection to create levels at runtime that use pregenerated pieces of content (i.e., experiential chunks) provides the reduced authoring burden and high variety of PCG while still allowing for a lightweight generation algorithm; furthermore, the use of pregenerated content pieces can provide more variety among the chunks than would be easy for human designers to create. *Polymorph* [Jennings-Teats et al. 2010] is an experimental adaptive level generator that uses this approach to create levels that are customized to a player's abilities. Each pregenerated chunk is tagged with a difficulty score, and as the player progresses through the level, chunks with an appropriate difficulty score (based on an estimate of player skill level via observing their failures) are placed in front of the player.

Using different content generation techniques at different layers of abstraction can help balance out human authoring with algorithm complexity. For example, a constructionist, template-based approach to create a dungeon crawler level could be combined with a constraint solver to place items into the rooms in the slots that are left unfilled. This would allow for tight control over the room's overall appearance and ensure that gameplay requirements are met, but still provide a high level of variety in the room's contents. This hypothetical generator is similar to the generation approach taken in the *Tanagra* level design assistant [Smith, G. et al. 2011b], where reactive planning is used in conjunction with a numerical constraint solver to create platformer levels in collaboration with a human designer.

Mixing-and-matching paradigms can be very powerful, but it does have one major drawback: in general, different layers of the generator will not be able to easily communicate with each other. In our dungeon crawler example given above, if the constraint solver is unable to place items into the room to meet all design constraints, the generator must go back and choose another set of room templates, then ask the constraint solver to try again. This is because the constraint solver does not have the power to alter room layout, and the room layout algorithm does not have any knowledge of the kind of constraints that the solver cares about. In a purely constraint-based system, the room layout would potentially be able to shift to meet constraints on the level components.

UNDERSTANDING PCG's RELATIONSHIP TO A GAME

Now that we have an understanding of the different ways to build a PCG system, let's look at how to understand the role that PCG will be taking in the game. This is largely a set of design decisions, but it has a lot of impact on the way that the AI system should be constructed.

PCG's Mechanical Role

There are several important aspects of PCG's mechanical role within the game, including how it is integrated into the overall game, if and how the player will interact with it, and how well it can be controlled by designers and players.

Game Stage

Does content generation need to happen *online*, while the player is playing? Or can it occur *off-line*, while the level is loading or even while the game is being developed? If the generator must run online and frequently, then performance is one of the largest concerns and it may be necessary to compromise quality to some extent. On the other hand, a generator that runs off-line can be slower, but it needs to be able to create content that is flexible enough to support the variety that is inherent in player behavior (that is, content can't be crafted as a response to the player's actions), and it also has to store and load generated content efficiently.

Interaction with the Generator

In games where the player does interact with the generator (as opposed to just with the generated content), there are three main types of interaction the player may have: *parameterized*, *preference*, and *direct manipulation*.

Parameterized control lets the player set some parameters that influence the generator before they interact with content. For example, the *Civilization V* level generator allows the player to set parameters such as world age, temperature, and landmass type.

Preference control means that the player can (directly or indirectly) specify preferences for what content they will see next while they are in the game. For example, *Galactic Arms Race* infers player preferences based on their behavior, allowing them to provide indirect control over the kind of weapons that they will see next.

Direct manipulation lets the player directly interact with the content while the generator runs in the background to assist the player. This kind of control appears in *Spore's* creature creator, where the player builds a model of a creature while the content generator supports the player's choices and augments them by supplying textures and animations.

Control over Player Experience

While it is possible to build a content generator that simply stitches together preauthored chunks of content (i.e., a constructionist approach), it is often desirable to have tight design control over particular aspects of the player's experience. This control can come in two forms: *compositional* and *experiential*.

Compositional control means that the generator can make design guarantees about the presence of particular components in the final product, for example, a platformer level generator that can guarantee that 50% of the challenges in a level will be due to gaps, or a quest generator that can guarantee the quest will involve the player finding two angry shopkeepers.

Experiential control means that the generator has an understanding of some aspect of the player's in-game experience beyond just component placement. For example, a platformer generator that can guarantee level pacing independently from what components are present, or a quest generator that can guarantee that a quest will have a particular difficulty associated with it.

Player Interaction with PCG

The *dynamics* of PCG* are the styles of play that arise from the player's interactions with the generated content. Understanding these patterns can help in selecting which techniques to use and the range of content to create.

PCG Relationship to Other Mechanics

We can first consider the role of PCG in the game relative to the other game mechanics. Will the player's experience revolve around the generated content, or are we creating decorative, incidental content that only

---

* Word usage borrowed from Hunicke et al.'s mechanics, dynamics, and aesthetics framework for analyzing games [Hunicke et al. 2004].

augments the player's experience? Some games use PCG to frame player experience: *Civilization V* is a game where procedurally generated maps give the player something surprising to explore in the early phase of the game, but most of the player's strategies revolve around other aspects of the game (e.g., build order and military strategy)—and indeed, many scenarios with fixed, designer-generated maps exist. Endless runner games such as *Canabalt*, on the other hand, have generators that the player's experience is entirely dependent on. These games have no mechanic other than to interact with the generated content. Understanding the extent to which your generator will influence the player's experience can help you decide how to focus your efforts, how important design guarantees are, and how to ensure that there is sufficient variety for players.

Reacting
PCG is often used to create surprising or unexpected content, forcing the player to react to unforeseen circumstances rather than allowing them to regurgitate memorized actions. This reaction may be related to exploration, as in *Spelunky* [Yu 2009], or it may be a test of reaction time, as in *Robot Unicorn Attack*. Reaction comes from the random elements of PCG, but you may wish to be able to control this somewhat. If the game would benefit from the player being able to practice some aspects but still be a test of reaction in others, then using experiential chunks may be a good choice for your knowledge representation.

Strategizing
The use of a content generator that runs online and can be controlled (either directly or indirectly) by the player leads to situations where the player forms strategies about how to interact with the generator. If this style of play is desirable then consider what these strategies should be when designing the generator. For example, if the player should be able to strategize around the composition of challenges in levels, as in *Endless Web* [Smith, G. et al. 2012], then the generator must be designed such that this can be explicitly controlled.

Searching
Players can do two kinds of searching as a result of PCG. The first is when the content being generated is a world: players will search through it and explore it, looking for surprises and interesting moments, as in *Minecraft*. The second is when the content is smaller and can be found

in the environment, when players may search for interesting or unique content, as in *Borderlands*. The lesson to be learned from this dynamic is the same no matter the kind of searching: the generator should produce content that can be surprising and exciting for the player to find. A generator may be able to produce millions of unique pieces of content, but the quantity is meaningless if those million pieces all *feel* the same to the player. Introducing surprise and variety can be difficult. It may come from incorporating small, hand-authored pieces of content into the generator for the player to find, or from careful construction of grammar rules and weights.

Practicing

Many games use PCG to allow the player to practice game strategies. *Civilization V* (and other strategy games with generated maps) are particularly good examples of this dynamic—the other mechanics of the game provide multiple strategies for success, and the procedural placement of land and resources means that the player can practice selecting from among those strategies and adapting them to many different, but controlled, environments. In such games, especially multiplayer games, the ability for the generator to make design guarantees about resource availability, playability, and balance may be of high importance. Constraint-based generators, or generators that use generate-and-test to approach design requirements, are good techniques for games that need such guarantees.

Community

Finally, PCG can be used to vary the player's experience so as to make it impossible to write a walkthrough for your game. This leads to players having different experiences from each other. When crafting a PCG system it is common to think of a single player's experience with the generated content, but for some games it is also important to think about the *community*'s experience with that content. Fans of games such as *Dwarf Fortress* engage in long, drawn-out discussions and debates based on the results the generator provides, telling stories of their own experiences in their own unique world.

CHOOSING AN APPROACH

This section discusses how to get started with PCG and how to choose an approach, as well as the kinds of design considerations that need to be taken into account.

Getting Started

There are two ways to get started building a PCG system: from the bottom up, or from the top down. Doing both of these at the same time may be helpful, as one method may inspire decisions you make in the other.

A top-down approach starts by mapping out the kinds of content you want to be able to create and developing specific examples of what the generator should be capable of. It can be particularly helpful to start by designing examples of content that represents the extremes of what the generator could produce: what are the easiest and hardest levels, or the quirkiest weapons, or the ugliest and prettiest flowers? If there are parameters that the player should have control over (e.g., the size of the map or the shape of the robot), these are useful starting points for building examples of what the generated content should look like. From these examples, start distilling patterns: these will be the building blocks in the generator.

A bottom-up approach works up from the tools. For example, if you think a grammar approach is an interesting choice, start writing some production rules and see what kind of content you can get out of it. Keep adding rules, and tweaking the ones that you already have, until it starts to feel like you are getting what you want. If a constraint system interests you, start writing simple playability constraints, look at how they can go wrong, and then iterate on them, adding more or changing the ones you have until you get the sort of content that you want to see.

For both approaches, remember that the algorithms you use and building blocks you are piecing together define a large probability space, where each point in that space is an individual piece of content. The space may have some strange twists and turns—there may be kinds of content that you can never produce without changing your knowledge representation or your algorithm, and there may be kinds that you overproduce until you rein in the generator. Rather than thinking about how to create a single perfect piece of content, think about the space of potential content that can come out of your generator.

Game Design Constraints

One of the difficulties that comes with procedural content generation is the need to relinquish some amount of authorial control. The ability for the human designer to control the content that the player will see is limited by the need to allow it to be generated dynamically. With this in mind, when selecting PCG techniques you should consider (1) what kind of design control is needed, and (2) is there a need for tight design guarantees, or is it sufficient to come close? For example, a level generator probably has a need to absolutely guarantee that levels are playable, but it may be sufficient for the levels to just come close to meeting difficulty or pacing requirements. For that matter, even the playability guarantee might not be required if the player is given tools to morph the environment or if the playability issues occur infrequently. These constraints may be dealt with in a different way depending on how important they are. For example, the *Launchpad* level generator [Smith, G. et al. 2011c] guarantees level playability by baking it in to the generation algorithm, allowing only legal placement of level geometry, but it does not guarantee that the desired frequency of different level components will be perfectly met due to its use of generate-and-test for that design constraint.

Other potential game design constraints arise when there is a need to obey rules imposed by some other aspect of the design. For instance, if there is an overarching game narrative that all generated levels must fit into then there must be a way to express the important aspects of narrative as a constraint or rule for the generator.

Relationship with Art

Assuming that some or all of the content that a PCG system produces is visual in nature, the PCG system must be designed in concert with artists. Unless all of the content, including textures, will be generated by the computer (a difficult challenge), artists must create modular assets for the generator to use.

Art is one of the main motivations behind the different kinds of building blocks being chosen: experiential chunks are good when the art direction mandates a rich and detailed world and the artists want tight control over its appearance. Each chunk needs to be designed so that it can fit with others, but otherwise they can stand alone. At the other extreme, a subcomponent representation is useful for a game that uses a tile-based representation, such as a 2D side-scroller, so each subcomponent has a single tile art asset that can be associated with it.

It may still be important for the generator to incorporate some sense of art direction so that the structure of generated content is suitable to be skinned by human-created art assets. For instance, in a *Mario*-like game, a long, flat platform punctuated by only coins and gaps may be playable and even provide an enjoyable challenge, but will likely not be visually interesting.

Engineering Constraints

Finally, there are important engineering constraints to consider when building a generator. Algorithm speed and efficiency is a big concern. While none of the approaches presented here are *unusable* for content generation, some are certainly better than others for specific domains. Simulation-based and evolutionary approaches tend to be fairly slow unless they are running alongside the player in real time. Constraint-based approaches are more difficult to predict. Depending on the number of variables and the kind of constraints that are expressed, constraint systems can actually solve some content generation problems quite quickly. Grammars usually generate content very quickly, but may need slightly more expensive generate-and-test loops to cull undesirable content.

There is also the concern of how long it will take to create the system, and importantly, test and debug it. Content generators are massively emergent, so bugs can be hard to find, even when following debugging practices such as generating from known random seeds. Constraint-based systems reduce concerns about whether the system will accidentally create unplayable content, but can be more difficult to author and debug. Most current constraint solving methods cannot tell you which combination of constraints are causing an unsatisfactory answer, although it is possible to build in debugging methods. On the other end of the spectrum, approaches that build content from relatively simple rules, such as simulations and grammars, do not make it so easy to make design guarantees but can be easier to author.

TUNING AND DEBUGGING A CONTENT GENERATOR

Because of their emergent nature, debugging PCG systems usually requires more than simply spot-checking different pieces of content that are produced. Standard practices for debugging systems that use a lot of randomness apply; for example, keeping track of random seeds so that bugs can be reproduced more easily and logging decisions made during generation (if possible, given the method used) to get an explanation from the system of what it's doing. For complex PCG systems, however, this alone is not enough to get a sense of what the system is doing and how changes made to the generator influence the content being produced.

Expressive range refers to the shape of the space of content that a PCG system can produce, as well as how easily that space can be controlled [Smith and Whitehead 2010]. A good method for understanding expressive range is to define important, measurable qualities (metrics) of the content being generated, and produce a graph or other visualization of those metrics to see what kind of content is being created. By generating a large amount of content and evaluating each piece using those metrics, it is possible to get a view of the generator's performance. A first step is to look just at the minima, maxima, and medians for each metric—this will show examples of content that are at the extremes of the generator's abilities. For example, this is a quick way to see what the easiest and hardest levels are (for some approximation of difficulty), as well as a level at average difficulty. The metrics can be simple approximations, such as assigning scores to different level components based on their difficulty and averaging them together. More sophisticated metrics, including automated playtesting techniques [Salge et al. 2008], are also possible.

We can also use expressive range analysis to see if the generator seems biased to making any particular kinds of content by looking at the data in a histogram. Are there some bins that have more content in them than others? The generator may be biased toward creating that content over other kinds. A heatmap visualization can be applied to a two-dimensional histogram to visualize hot spots in the generator and quickly see changes in the expressive range from different versions of the generator.

By investing in creating a system like this up front, it is possible to see how small changes to the generator lead to changes in the qualities of the content by rerunning the metrics and seeing new expressive range charts. Expressive range can also be used to compare different generators [Horn et al. 2014].

SUMMARY AND RESOURCES

This chapter has given an overview of techniques for content generation and discussed their trade-offs, described the many roles that PCG can have in a game and how to use those roles to guide decisions about which technique is best, and given some advice for getting started and for debugging your PCG system. This is only an overview of the field of PCG, and there are many more resources available for learning specific techniques or finding how other games have implemented their own content generators. Consequently, this chapter will close with a list of resources to point you toward more information.

Tools and Frameworks

While most off-the-shelf tools are not appropriate for use in large game projects, these tools and frameworks can be used as a prototype for your generator to experiment and see what is possible.

- *Context Free Art* [Context Free Art 2014] and its cousin *StructureSynth* [Christensen 2010] are accessible and well-documented tools for using shape grammars. They are intended for use by digital artists, but can be used to mock up game content generators.

- *Choco* is a free and open-source Java-based numerical constraint solver [Choco Team 2008].

- The *Potassco* suite of tools, particularly *clingo*, are good tools for getting started with answer set programming [Gebser et al. 2011].

Reading and Community

- *Procedural Content Generation in Games: A Textbook and Overview of Current Research* is a book with chapters written by prominent researchers in the PCG community [Shaker et al. 2014].

- The PCG wiki is a community effort to create a central repository for articles and algorithms [PCG Wiki 2014].

- The PCG Google group is an active community of developers and academics who share an interest in procedural content generation [PCG Group 2014].

- There is a great deal of academic research into PCG. Common venues for PCG research are the Foundations of Digital Games (FDG) conference, the Procedural Content Generation (PCG) workshop, and the Artificial Intelligence in Interactive Digital Entertainment (AIIDE) conference. Papers from AIIDE are available for free online through AAAI's digital library. Many FDG and PCG papers are archived in the ACM digital library.

REFERENCES

.theprodukkt. 2004. *.kkrieger* (PC game).

[adult swim] games. 2010. *Robot Unicorn Attack* (PC game).

Bay 12 Games. 2006. *Slaves to Armok: God of Blood Chapter II: Dwarf Fortress* (PC game).

Bjork, Staffan, and Jussi Holopainen. 2004. *Patterns in Game Design* (Game Development Series), Charles River Media, Boston.

Braben, David, and Ian Bell. 1984. *Elite* (BBC Micro). Acornsoft.

Choco Team. 2008. Choco: An open source Java constraint programming library. In *White Paper, 14th International Conference on Principles and Practice of Constraint Programming, CPAI08 Competition*. Sydney, Australia.

Christensen, Mikael Hvidtfeldt. 2010. StructureSynth. Available: http://structure-synth.sourceforge.net (accessed: June 22, 2014).

Context Free Art, software. Available: http://www.contextfreeart.org (accessed: June 22, 2014).

Dormans, Joris. 2010. Adventures in level design: Generating missions and spaces for action adventure games. In *Proceedings of the 2010 Workshop on Procedural Content Generation in Games (colocated with FDG 2010)*. Monterey, CA.

Ebert, David S. 2003. *Texturing & Modeling: A Procedural Approach*. San Francisco: Morgan Kaufmann.

Gearbox Software, and Feral Interactive. 2009. *Borderlands* (XBox 360). 2K Games.

Gebser, Martin, Roland, Kaminski, Benjamin Kaufmann, Max Ostrowski, Torsten Schaub, and Marius Schneider. 2011. Potassco: The Potsdam Answer Set Solving Collection. *AI Communications* 24(2): 105–24.

Hastings, Erin J., Ratan K. Guha, and Kenneth O. Stanley. 2009. Automatic content generation in the *Galactic Arms Race* video game. *IEEE Transactions on Computational Intelligence and AI in Games* 1(4): 245–63. doi:10.1109/TCIAIG.2009.2038365.

Horn, Britton, Steve Dahlskog, Noor Shaker, Gillian Smith, and Julian Togelius. 2014. A comparative evaluation of procedural level generators in the Mario AI framework. In *Proceedings of the Foundations of Digital Games 2014*. Fort Lauderdale, FL.

Hullett, Kenneth, and Jim Whitehead. 2010. Design patterns in FPS levels. In *Proceedings of the 2010 International Conference on the Foundations of Digital Games* (FDG 2010). Monterey, CA.

Hunicke, Robin, Marc LeBlanc, and Robert Zubek. 2004. MDA: A formal approach to game design and game research. In *Proceedings of the 2004 AAAI Workshop on Challenges in Game Artificial Intelligence*. San Jose, CA: AAAI Press.

Jennings-Teats, Martin, Gillian Smith, and Noah Wardrip-Fruin. 2010. Polymorph: A Model for Dynamic Level Generation. In *Proceedings of the Sixth Artificial Intelligence and Interactive Digital Entertainment Conference*. Palo Alto, CA: AAAI Press.

Koster, Raph. 2004. *A Theory of Fun for Game Design*. Paraglyph Press, Scottsdale, AZ.

Persson, Marcus. 2011. *Minecraft* (PC game).

McGuinness, Cameron. 2012. Statistical analyses of representation choice in level generation. In *2012 IEEE Conference on Computational Intelligence and Games* (CIG), 312–19. doi:10.1109/CIG.2012.6374171.

MicroProse. 1991. *Sid Meier's Civilization* (PC game).

Müller, Pascal, Peter Wonka, Simon Haegler, Andreas Ulmer, and Luc Van Gool. 2006. Procedural modeling of buildings. *ACM Transactions on Graphics* 25(3): 614–23.

Onuczko, C., M. Cutumisu, D. Szafron, J. Schaeffer, M. McNaughton, T. Roy, K. Waugh, M. Carbonaro, and J. Siegel. 2005. A pattern catalog for computer role playing games. *GameOn North America*, 33–8.

Procedural Content Generation Google Group. https://groups.google.com/forum /#!forum/proceduralcontent (accessed: June 22, 2014).

The Procedural Content Generation Wiki. http://pcg.wikidot.com/ (accessed: June 22, 2014).

Rogue Basin. 2012. Articles on implementation techniques. (accessed: April 28, 2014). http://roguebasin.roguelikedevelopment.org/index.php?title=Articles #Implementation.

Salge, Christoph, Christian Lipski, Tobias Mahlmann, and Brigitte Mathiak. 2008. Using genetically optimized artificial intelligence to improve gameplaying fun for strategical games. In *Proceedings of the 2008 ACM SIGGRAPH Sandbox Symposium on Video Games*, 7–14. Sandbox '08. Los Angeles: ACM.

Saltsman, Adam. 2009. *Canabalt* (PC game). Adam Atomic. (accessed: August 14, 2014.) http://www.adamatomic.com/canabalt/.

Shaker, Noor, Julian Togelius, and Mark J. Nelson. 2014. *Procedural Content Generation in Games: A Textbook and an Overview of Current Research.* Springer. http://pcgbook.com.

Smith, Adam M., and Michael Mateas. 2010. Variations forever: Flexibly generating rulesets from a sculptable design space of mini-games. In *Proceedings of the IEEE Conference on Computational Intelligence and Games* (CIG). Copenhagen, Denmark.

Smith, Adam M., and Michael Mateas. 2011. Answer set programming for procedural content generation: A design space approach. *Computational Intelligence and AI in Games, IEEE Transactions on* 3(3): 187–200.

Smith, Adam M., Erik Andersen, Michael Mateas, and Zoran Popovic. 2012. A case study of expressively constrainable level design automation tools for a puzzle game. In *Proceedings of the 2012 Conference on the Foundations of Digital Games*. Raleigh, NC.

Smith, Gillian, Ryan Anderson, Brian Kopleck, Zach Lindblad, Lauren Scott, Adam Wardell, Jim Whitehead, and Michael Mateas. 2011a. Situating quests: Design patterns for quest and level design in role-playing games. In *Proceedings of the 4th International Conference on Interactive Digital Storytelling (ICIDS 2011)*. Vancouver, Canada, November 28–December 1, 2011.

Smith, Gillian, and Jim Whitehead. 2010. Analyzing the expressive range of a level generator. In *Proceedings of the Workshop on Procedural Content Generation in Games, Co-Located with FDG 2010*. Monterey, CA.

Smith, Gillian, Jim Whitehead, and Michael Mateas. 2011b. Tanagra: Reactive planning and constraint solving for mixed-initiative level design. *IEEE Transactions on Computational Intelligence and AI in Games* (TCIAIG), Special Issue on Procedural Content Generation 3(3).

Smith, Gillian, Jim Whitehead, Michael Mateas, Mike Treanor, Jameka March, and Mee Cha. 2011c. Launchpad: A rhythm-based level generator for 2D platformers. *IEEE Transactions on Computational Intelligence and AI in Games (TCIAIG)* 3(1).

Smith, Gillian, Alexei Othenin-Girard, Jim Whitehead, and Noah Wardrip-Fruin. 2012. PCG-based game design: Creating endless web. In *Proceedings of the International Conference on the Foundations of Digital Games*, 188–95. FDG '12. Raleigh, NC: ACM.

Stiny, George. 1980. Introduction to shape and shape grammars. *Environment and Planning B* 7(3): 343–51.

Togelius, J., and J. Schmidhuber. 2008. An experiment in automatic game design. In *Computational Intelligence and Games, 2008. CIG'08. IEEE Symposium On*, 111–18.

Togelius, Julian, Georgios N. Yannakakis, Kenneth O. Stanley, and Cameron Browne. 2011. Search-based procedural content generation: A taxonomy and survey. *Computational Intelligence and AI in Games, IEEE Transactions on* 3(3): 172–86.

Toy, Michael, Glenn Wichman, Ken Arnold, and Jon Lane. 1980. *Rogue* (PC game).

Tutenel, Tim, Ruben M. Smelik, Rafael Bidarra, and Klaas Jan de Kraker. 2009. Using semantics to improve the design of game worlds. In *Proceedings of the Fifth Artificial Intelligence in Interactive Digital Entertainment Conference* (AIIDE09). Palo Alto, CA.

Yannakakis, Georgios N., and Julian Togelius. 2011. Experience-driven procedural content generation. *IEEE Transactions on Affective Computing* 2(3): 147–61. doi:10.1109/T-AFFC.2011.6.

Yu, Derek. 2009. *Spelunky* (PC game).

III

Constructing Levels

CHAPTER 9

P.T. and the Play of Stillness

Brian Upton

CONTENTS

I<small>N GAME SCHOLARSHIP, IT'S</small> taken as a given that interactivity is an essential element of play. Interactivity is used to distinguish games from traditional passive art forms such as painting, literature, or film. When we play a game, there is a give-and-take that doesn't exist in other mediums, and this give-and-take is often presented as the primary thing that separates games from these other sorts of aesthetic experiences.

This critical stance has been very useful for carving out a separate discourse for analyzing games. While games themselves are very old, the scholarship of games is very young. Literary theory can draw on a 2000-year tradition dating back to Aristotle, but the notion that games can be studied and interpreted as cultural artifacts is considerably newer, tracing its origin only to the publication of *Homo Ludens* in 1938. And the field of game design theory is newer still. Until recently (in a historical sense) there were no treatises on how to design games. New games were created by gut instinct and trial and error, and were often the product of decades or centuries of innovations and tweaks by anonymous designers. This lack of a historical tradition left game studies ripe for colonization by older critical approaches. (This tension lay at the heart of the narratology/ludology arguments of a decade ago.) By emphasizing the unique interactive nature of games, game scholars created a powerful weapon to defend themselves from being absorbed into mainstream literary theory. Games are fundamentally interactive, and that means older critical traditions don't apply to them. Or so the argument goes.

However, there's a problem with this stance. When we define interactivity as being fundamental to play, it makes it difficult to talk or theorize about the intervals during a play experience when no interaction is occurring. Design theory becomes centered on transactions: What does the player do to the system, and what does the system do to the player in return? As a result of this definitional move, the idea that meaningful play might unfold in nontransactional moments becomes quite literally unthinkable. Experimental games with minimal interactivity such as *Dear Esther* are pushed outside the circle of play—instead of being treated as games, they're dismissed as walking simulators or audio books.

This emphasis on interactive essentialism also skews the design of more mainstream games. How do you make a turn-based game fun for its off-turn players? How do you build suspense during a horror game? How do you design an e-sport that will be as fun to watch as it is to play? How do you design a good stealth mission? How do you insure a player's actions carry narrative weight? Answering these sorts of design questions requires an understanding (either formal or intuitive) of the way that play flows during moments when the player is not interacting with the game. They're difficult to grapple with if you take interactivity as your starting point.

Level design also depends on a good understanding of noninteractive play. The amount of interactivity required to simply navigate a virtual space is minimal. We push the joystick and we move forward. We press the "use" button and a door opens. Unless we're playing a platformer, navigating a game level is about as ergodic as turning the pages of a book. And yet, some game levels are interesting to explore, while others are boring. The difference between a good and a bad level is often not a matter of how its interactions are doled out, but how its level geometry supports noninteractive play.

In the rest of this chapter, I'll explore the ramifications of this proposition. I'll start by laying out a general theory for understanding noninteractive play. And then I'll show how this theory can be applied to specific challenges in level design by examining how the physical layout of the horror game *P.T.* drives player experience.

PLAYING IN OUR HEADS

If you watch two people playing chess, you'll notice that most of their time is not spent moving pieces. It's spent staring at the board. The actual moments of interaction in chess, when they occur, are intermittent interruptions to the general stillness of the experience.

But if you actually play a game of chess, your feeling of play isn't intermittent. It's continuous. You spend the time between moves considering the future unfolding of the game. In fact, the play of chess lives in this elaborated process of anticipation, not in the brief moments when you actually move your pieces. When your turn comes around, you don't rush to move as quickly as possible. You don't rush to interact. Instead you hold off interacting until you've finished your anticipatory play. And your move, when you finally do make it, is largely a matter of bookkeeping. It's a way to tick forward the state of the game and trigger a new cascade of anticipation in the minds of both players.

This sort of anticipatory play exists even in games that are more action-packed than chess. If you're playing a first-person shooter, part of the fun is placing your crosshairs on a target and pulling the trigger. But there's also fun to be had in reading the situation around you and anticipating threats before they appear. A good first-person shooter is more than just a shooting gallery. If threats pop up at random—if there isn't any way to anticipate a firefight before it occurs—then the game will quickly degenerate into a repetitive aiming challenge. The deepest play in a first-person shooter doesn't occurs when you're not shooting. It occurs when you're trying to anticipate the threats that lie ahead of you. It occurs when you're trying to position yourself and your weapon to give yourself an edge when the bullets do start flying.

So, how do we design good anticipatory play spaces?

Stillness

One of the problems with tightly linking play and interactivity is that it encourages designers to design games that keep the player busy all the time. Levels are packed with encounters and collectables and quests, so from moment to moment there's always something that needs to be done. But if players are always kept busy doing things, they don't have the mental bandwidth to stop and consider what they're doing or why they're doing it. You can't strategize in the middle of a frantic firefight, even if strategizing would be a fun thing to do.

I first discovered this when I was working on the sequel to the original *Rainbow Six*. We took a look at the levels that were the most fun in the original game, and we discovered that all of them had one thing in common: They didn't throw the player straight into the action. Instead, they had a long approach to the main encounter area. Furthermore, these approaches offered hints of what lay ahead: a view of a sentry's patrol path, a glimpse of how the combat zone was laid out. Often this approach was as large (in terms of level geometry) as the combat zone itself.

What made these approaches work as locations for anticipatory play was that they were largely empty of combat. Players felt relatively safe, and that feeling of relative safety meant they were free to explore, observe, and analyze. They were free to anticipate. If you want players to engage in anticipatory play, you have to be willing to create areas in your level where nothing much is happening. And the more anticipatory play there is, the larger and longer these areas need to be.

You can see this same principle at work in 2D platformers. Often right before a hard jumping challenge, there will be a safe platform for the player to stand on while considering what lies ahead. Players may actually spend longer standing on the safe platform thinking about what they're going to do than actually doing it. The more engrossing the anticipatory play, the longer the player holds still.

Choice

A situation is interesting to consider only if it can play out in a variety of different ways—if it contains some degree of ambiguity. Anticipatory play involves sifting through potentialities, weighing their likelihood, and imagining their possible consequences. There's no play value in a situation where we can tell immediately how things are going to unfold. A corridor with one door at the far end is boring. A corridor with two doors isn't. A corridor with two doors can be longer than a corridor with only one door—it can offer the player a longer stretch of stillness—because the player has something to consider while traversing it.

But a choice only counts as a choice if the player recognizes it as such. If the player believes one of the doors is locked, or thinks both doors lead to the same place, or has learned that all paths through the level play pretty much the same, then the feeling of choice evaporates. So, doors that look different offer more of a choice than doors that look the same. And doors that clearly lead to distinctive rooms offer more of a choice than doors that lead to similar corridors. When designing a space to offer anticipatory play, you have to give the player meaningful alternatives—alternatives that offer (or at least appear to offer) to differing outcomes.

Variety

A choice ceases to be a choice if we make it over and over again. If we repeatedly encounter the same situation, we remember how our anticipatory play previously played out and instead of experiencing the fun of sifting through potentialities, we converge instantly on a familiar resolution. The first time we encounter a strange idol in the jungle, we approach it warily; is it a trap, a clue, a reward, a puzzle? The unexpected is always an invitation to play. But if every jungle clearing contains the same idol, we quickly lose interest. The statue may still have some gameplay function—indicating a save point for example, or marking the entrance to an underground tunnel—but the space around it stops being a locus of anticipatory play.

The economics of game production often preclude the creation of large numbers of single-use game assets. So variety is usually more a product of how objects are arranged than what those objects are. One powerful way to introduce variety is to establish a familiar pattern and then break it. If every door in a game is open, then encountering one more open door doesn't mean much. But if every door is closed, then coming across the one door that's slightly open is a significant moment. It sets the mind racing: Why is it open? Who's in there? Am I in danger? The idea is not to eliminate repetition entirely. The idea is to use targeted instants of interrupted repetition to call the player's attention to the uncertainty of their current situation and set off a cascade of anticipatory play.

Consequence

An ambiguous situation is more interesting to consider if its possible outcomes generate new ambiguities of their own. A strategic game like *Go* supports long runs of anticipatory play not just because each turn offers a large number of possible moves, but because each move leads to a fresh board position that invites further anticipatory play. If you place your next stone here, your opponent might respond in this way, and if you place your next stone there, your opponent might respond in that way. A meaningful choice is a choice that offers different outcomes, and the difference that matters between different outcomes is the difference in future choices they allow you to make.

So a junction is more interesting than a straight corridor because it offers the player a choice. A junction that leads to two different rooms is more interesting than a junction that leads to two identical ones. But even better is a junction that leads to two different rooms that themselves invite additional anticipatory analysis: If I run straight through the door I might be able to dash across the open courtyard before the guards see me, but if I climb up to the balcony I might be able to sneak past them. This sort of choice is not a simple either/or proposition, but the first link in a long chain of choices that lead to a wide variety of different outcomes.

Predictability

In order for players to form a reliable chain of cause and effect linking one choice to another, they need to be able to correctly anticipate the likely consequences of their actions. If I try to jump this chasm, I'll probably make it. If I climb up to that door, it will probably lead me to the throne room. If I crouch down behind this wall, the guard probably won't see me. Anticipatory play requires your game to have a consistent grammar that the player can learn and depend on. If it looks like you should be able to make a jump, you should be able to make it. Locked and unlocked doors should be distinguishable from a distance. And so on.

But it also means foreshadowing. At its simplest it might merely be a matter of putting up signs at intersections: "This way to the dungeon!"

But it also means creating vistas and overlooks that show what lies ahead if you take a particular path. If a particularly tough monster is lurking behind a door, let the players catch a glimpse of it through a crack or window. The approach to a boss battle should be designed to put players on their guard—a grand staircase, an impressive door. You feel dread when you know something difficult is coming up but it hasn't happened yet. Part of what makes a boss feel like a boss is the sense of apprehension that you develop during the approach and take with you into the encounter.

Uncertainty

While some predictability is good, too much ruins play. If the outcome of a situation is too predictable then actually playing through it will feel anticlimactic. So while the design of a level should give the player a sense of the potentialities represented by different choices, those potentialities should never harden into certainties. Elaborated anticipatory play depends on the player sifting through a range of consequential choices that chain together with future opportunities to choose. But if the outcome of choices is too certain, then the play potential of those future opportunities will be exhausted before the player actually reaches them. If your initial anticipatory play allows you to work out the perfect plan in advance, then there's no further anticipatory play left to be had while you execute it.

A good anticipatory play space should balance on the knife edge between knowledge and ignorance. You believe you've figured out the right choice, but the shifting circumstances around you continually call that belief into question. Sustaining anticipatory play requires that there be some uncertainty in the system that thwarts unbounded causal analysis. So if you're designing a courtyard full of sentries, you don't give the players a birds-eye view that shows them all the sentries at once. Instead you give them a glimpse that reveals part of the patrol path of one or two sentries—just enough information for them to form a provisional plan. Then as they move forward, their changing sightlines reveal more information, causing that provisional plan to be continually questioned and revised. Anticipatory play is sustained.

There are a number of different ways to introduce uncertainty into a game system: incomplete information, randomness, other players. Poker uses all of these—cards are assigned randomly, other player's hands are hidden from view, and you can't be certain if they're bluffing or not. The result is a very fertile anticipatory play space. You have a sense of the possible ways that a hand might play out, but the uncertainty keeps your mind spinning as the hand progresses.

Satisfaction

All of the other principles don't matter if players think the task in front of them is impossible or pointless. You may design an inviting level with interesting choices, nicely chained cues, and just the right balance of predictability and uncertainty, but players will still reject it if the challenge seems too daunting. Anticipatory play always needs to resolve successfully, even if that success is conditional and temporary. Players don't need to solve every puzzle the first time they see it, but they do need to be able to converge on something that feels like a solution. "Maybe this is it!" is a much better place for a player to occupy than "I have no idea."

Considered collectively, these principles allow us to sketch out a design pattern for creating levels that encourage anticipatory play: You want to create a period of stillness where players aren't distracted by immediate interactive demands. The players don't have to remain stationary, but movement challenges should be kept to a minimum. While inside this stillness, they should be presented with a choice that is unfamiliar enough to require extended consideration. The consequences of this choice should be both clear and elaborated. The outcome of choosing a particular path should be obvious, and it should lead to new choices to consider. But the players' knowledge shouldn't be absolute—as the game continues to unfold, they should feel compelled to continually reassess the decisions they've previously made. Is this really the right path to take? Do I really understand what's going on? And, at all times, they should feel like it's possible for them to arrive at a provisional solution to the challenge at hand, even if they later abandon that solution as new information comes along.

In describing these design principles, I've couched them in terms that make it seem as though anticipatory play is always about pausing to plan our future actions. And it often is. But just as often, it's directed toward analyzing the significance of our past actions or interpreting our current circumstances. Whether the choice is "What should I do?" or "What does this mean?" such moments play out in the same way. This is how experiential games like *Dear Esther* work. There's almost no interactivity as we move through *Dear Esther*. There aren't any future actions for us to plan. But the shifting landscape around us and the unfolding monologue of the narrator trigger a series of interpretive moves in our heads as we play. These interpretive moves executed in the stillness of the overall experience are where the play of *Dear Esther* resides, much as the play of a game of chess resides in the moments of analysis between the moves of the pieces. Playing with meaning is also a thing for players to do, and this sort of play can only exist if the player isn't distracted by interactive busywork.

Now that we have a general theory of anticipatory play, let's see how the theory can be used to understand the level design of an actual game.

ANTICIPATING DOOM

P.T. is a short horror game that was released as a free download on the PlayStation Network in August 2014. It was originally intended as a playable teaser for the game *Silent Hills*, but it worked as a self-contained horror experience in its own right. With the cancellation of *Silent Hills*, it was pulled from distribution. Fortunately it still survives on the PlayStations of the people who originally downloaded it and in video walkthroughs on the Internet. And while watching a walkthrough won't give you the same experience as actually playing the game yourself, it can at least give you a sense of how *P.T.* manages to create its scares.

Horror games have always been an interesting counterexample to the notion that interactivity is essential to good play. Most nonhorror games try to make the player's core actions feel as frictionless and satisfying as possible. So a good first-person shooter will have a crisp, consistent aiming mechanic. A good platformer will have a tight, predictable jump. A good cart racing game will have a vehicle physics system that makes the carts feel responsive and lively. The feedback loops in all these games are quick and predictable, giving the player a powerful feeling of agency in the immediate moment.

However, horror game mechanics are different. They're often designed to deliberately thwart the player's sense of agency. Movement is slow and mushy, aiming (if it exists at all) is inaccurate and often ineffective, hand-to-hand attacks are awkward and dangerous. Anticipatory play in a non-horror game is usually directed toward figuring out a route to success. But anticipatory play in a horror game is directed toward dread of failure. It's claustrophobic, and not merely in the sense of feeling trapped in a too-small physical space. It's metaphysically claustrophobic—you feel trapped in a too-small possibility space. Your options for action all feel dangerous and bad (even if some of them are slightly less dangerous and bad than others).

The thwarting of satisfaction usually destroys play. But horror game players deliberately seek it out, much in the same way that people who ride roller-coasters deliberately seek out dizziness and vertigo. There's nothing intrinsically enjoyable about being frightened or disoriented. But if you enter into the experience knowing that the apparent danger is safely contained—you're not really falling to your death, you're not really being threatened by a murderer—then the negative emotional response the experience triggers becomes a source of satisfaction in and of itself. You don't win a scary game by overcoming its challenges. You win a scary game by allowing it to thwart you.

So, in analyzing the level design of a game like *P.T.* what we're really looking at is how the level geometry can be used to trigger dread: How does the physical layout of the play space lead to feelings of hopelessness, doom, and frustration? How do we create stretches of claustrophobic anticipatory play where all the choices available to the player seem to lead to bad outcomes? And how do we do this without actually making the game feel frustrating or pointless?

The Level Layout

The physical layout of the play space of *P.T.* is very simple. Most of the game takes place in a simple L-shaped corridor. (Figure 9.1) There are one-way doors at both ends; leaving through the one-way exit door at the end of the corridor transports you back to the one-way entrance door at the beginning. The result is an endless loop that you can only move through in one direction. Every time you step through the exit door you're moving deeper and deeper into *P.T.*'s labyrinth with no possibility of retracing your steps—it acts as a one-way *ratchet* on your progress.

Halfway down the corridor, just after the bend in the L, there's a door leading to a small bathroom. Sometimes this door is shut and locked and sometimes it's open, but you can't tell which until you turn the corner of the L. Further along the corridor, just before you reach the exit, the corridor widens to form an entry hall. There's a permanently locked door to your left that apparently leads outside. Straight ahead, another door leads to the stairs down to the exit. This door can lock as well, allowing it to function as a *valve*, allowing or blocking forward movement as necessary. The ceiling is twice as high in this part of the corridor, and if you look up you can see an inaccessible dark balcony, part of a second floor you can never reach.

The level is sparsely furnished. A few unremarkable pictures hang on the walls. The only furniture is three low cabinets and a coat tree. The tops of the cabinets are covered in debris—candy wrappers, used ashtrays,

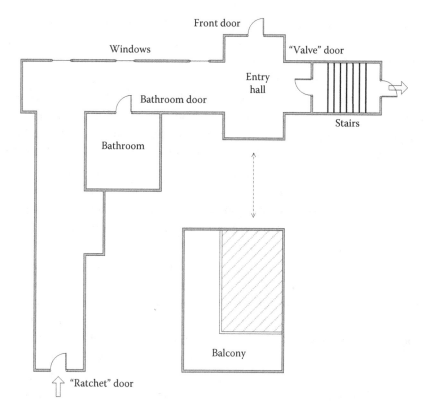

FIGURE 9.1 *P.T.* floor plan.

empty bottles—as well as a few other significant props—family portraits, a dusty radio, a digital clock that seems to be perpetually stuck at one minute before midnight. But that's it. It's not a large palette to work with. Nevertheless, *P.T.* manages to be very scary indeed.

The Corner

The shape of the corridor is central to how *P.T.* functions as a horror game. Each time you reenter the level, you're faced with a short walk from the entrance door to the corner of the L. You can clearly see everything ahead of you in the first half of the corridor. While it may be gloomy or dingy, you feel relatively safe. But you can't see the second half of the L. It's the rising dread you experience as you approach this single turn that forms the foundation of *P.T.*'s horror gameplay.

It's the turn in the corridor that creates the ambiguity required to transform the level into an anticipatory play space. If we could see all the way from the beginning of the corridor to the end then we would know exactly what lay ahead of us and there would be no space for our imaginations to explore. By hiding what waits in the second half of the corridor, the turn invites us to speculate. And the simplicity of the approach to the turn gives us the stillness we need for this speculation to grow into dread.

Corners are always significant gameplay beats. Like doors, corners are liminal—they mark the transition from one set of circumstances to another. As a result, they're always proceeded by a rising sense of anticipation as we approach them, followed by a rush of interpretation as the new vista reveals itself. But while doors tend to be binary—they're either open or closed, you're either inside or outside—corners are analog. Turning a corner is a continuous process, a nuanced and interruptible unfolding. It can be done quickly or slowly. We can venture a quick peak and pull back, or plunge blindly forward into the unknown.

It's important that the transition between the first and second halves of the corridor in *P.T.* is a corner and not a door. A door in the middle of a straight corridor would still hide what's ahead, allowing us to speculate about what lay beyond it, but the abruptness of the reveal that comes from opening a door would rob the moment of much of its dread. A door has an inevitability to it that a corner lacks. Opening a door is a commitment to moving forward. A corner, by contrast, is much more tentative. We hesitate, we slow down, we draw out the transition, allowing our anticipatory play to build toward a climax as the reveal plays out.

Now, there are lots of corners in lots of games. What is it about the corner in *P.T.* that makes approaching it and turning it so particularly scary? The first ingredient is repetition. Most of the time when we come to a corner in a game, we either know too much or too little about what's around it. If it's a familiar part of the level, we know exactly what to expect as we approach the reveal; there's not enough ambiguity to trigger significant anticipatory play. Or, if it's a part of the level we've never visited before, the ambiguity is so large that it's hard to converge on a specific expectation.

P.T. loops us through the same corridor over and over again. At first, when this happens, turning the corner doesn't seem that interesting. We know exactly what's beyond the turn and there's not much anticipatory play as we approach it. But after completing the loop a few times, things change. There's a startling thumping noise from the closed door to the bathroom. The next time through the loop there's a more powerful jump scare at the bathroom door. The time after that, there's a glimpse of a spooky apparition waiting at the end of the corridor. The lighting changes, getting dimmer and dimmer, and eventually turning blood red.

The game trains us that bad things happen in the second half of the corridor. Once this has been accomplished, anticipatory play kicks into high gear, and *P.T.* has us at its mercy. It no longer needs to do anything overt to scare us. Just walking toward the corner and making the turn is enough to fill us with dread. It doesn't matter that most of the time nothing at all is waiting for us after we make the turn. The idea that something might be there is enough to put us on edge. The early jump scares combined with the corner's inherent uncertainty open up a large and disturbing possibility space for us to explore. And it is primarily toward the exploration of this possibility space that our attention is directed as we move through the stillness of the first half of the L.

Essentially, *P.T.* asks us to repeatedly walk to our doom, and it is the sustained feeling of dread that accompanies this walk that becomes the carrier wave that boosts and sustains the game's other scares. *P.T.* is scary not just because of its unsettling encounters, but because of how the level geometry keeps us perpetually on edge.

The Ratchet Door

The placement of the turn in the corridor is not the only important level design choice in *P.T.* The use of doors also play a major role in building the sense of anxiety that we feel moving through the level. There are four doors: the one-way ratchet entrance/exit door, a lockable valve door near the end of the corridor that sometimes blocks progress, the door to the bathroom, and the front door in the entry hall. Each of these doors has a very specific function that we're going to explore in detail through the filter of anticipatory play.

The most important of the four is the one-way entrance/exit door at the beginning and ending of the corridor. The one-way door is the ratchet that ticks the state of the game forward. When we pass through it, we literally are unable to turn back. Because of this, the one-way door focuses and amplifies our dread as we walk toward the corner. It's not just that we're moving forward into danger—we're moving forward into danger with the knowledge that there's nowhere else to for us to go. The implacable barrier of the one-way door behind us removes the temptation for us to treat our situation as a puzzle to be solved. If the level geometry allowed us more freedom, we might start looking for ways to avoid the ominous corner—maybe there's a safer way around, maybe we can backtrack, maybe there's a hidden trigger we missed. But the stark simplicity of our situation—the empty corridor, the locked door at our backs—precludes that sort of play. Without our attention being diverted into problem-solving, we can concentrate entirely on imagining what awful things lie ahead of us.

The one-way door in *P.T.* is important because it's a powerful example of how reducing interaction can increase the playfulness of a game. If there were more things for the player to interact with in the first half of the corridor, if backtracking offered the hope of finding a safer route, if there were more meaningful gameplay choices to make, then thinking our options would crowd out the interpretive choices that make *P.T.* scary. The use of a one-way door to eliminate the possibility of backtracking directs our attention away from planning our escape and toward interpreting our ominous situation.

The Valve Door

While the one-way door ratchets you forward through the experience, the door just past the entry hall is the valve that works to block your progress. Most of the time this door is open, but sometimes it swings shut, trapping you in the current iteration of the L. When you're trapped, you have to activate some unknown trigger in order to open this door and progress again.

One of *P.T.*'s most interesting design choices is that it uses one door as the ratchet and another door as the valve when a single door could have served both functions. There are several subtle reasons why two doors work better than one in this situation. The first is that since the valve is a separate door, the block state can be communicated visually. If the game blocked progress by locking the ratchet door, then players could only learn they'd been blocked by going to the door and trying to open it. With a separate door as the valve, players can tell from anywhere in the second half of the corridor if they're blocked or not.

Using a clear visual cue to indicate whether our progress is blocked has an important effect on how our attention is directed during sequences where we're trapped. If we had to walk to the exit door to determine its state, we'd spend as much time wondering if the door was locked as we spend wondering about how to unlock it. But directing the player's attention toward the question of whether the door is locked or not undermines play. Anticipatory play requires choice, and there's no choice involved in verifying a game state. By making the state of the valve clearly visible, *P.T.* keeps our attention squarely focused on what's important—the fear of the fresh horrors we imagine are awaiting us.

The second reason that the valve works better as a separate door is that it makes the operation of the ratchet absolutely unambiguous. We quickly learn in *P.T.* that the entrance/exit door always functions exactly the same way: It's a one-way gate that always allows passage forward and never allows passage back. If it changed its state by locking and unlocking, that would imply that it might change its state in other ways. Backtracking returns as a possibility to consider. If we can't backtrack now, it might not be because backtracking is impossible, but merely because we haven't discovered the correct trigger yet.

Making the valve and the ratchet separate doors doesn't just keep the player from wasting time wondering about the lock state of the valve. It also keeps the player from wasting time trying to figure out how to defeat the ratchet. It reinforces that idea that the entrance/exit door is an inviolable rule and not a negotiable puzzle. And, as we've seen previously, the nonnegotiable nature of the ratchet (you can't turn back, no matter what) is essential for creating the strong sense of dread that accompanies each iteration of the loop.

The Bathroom Door

Almost equal in importance to the door at the end of the corridor is the door to the bathroom just after the turn in the L. Early on the game establishes that while bad things can happen in the second half of the corridor, the source of these bad things is the bathroom. The bathroom's danger is built up through a well-designed sequence of scripted events. The first jump scare in the game comes when something pounds on the bathroom door as you walk past. Shortly after that, the door opens just a crack, inviting the player to peek inside. Doing so triggers a stronger jump scare, the second in the game. By the time the bathroom door opens fully, allowing us to go in, we've been trained to feel apprehensive about crossing its threshold into the darkness beyond.

When the door to the bathroom is open, it functions like a more intense version of the turn in the corridor. We know we have to go inside (the valve door is shut, leaving us no choice) but we also know we don't want to. Again, the primary scare of this sequence isn't what we find inside the bathroom. It's the anticipatory dread of knowing we have to go look.

Once we're inside the bathroom, the door closes, trapping us inside. The bathroom door is locked in terms of game mechanics—the player can't open it and leave. But when something outside in the corridor turns the handle and tries to push its way in, it becomes apparent that while the door is locked mechanically, it's not locked metaphorically. Metaphorically, it doesn't feel like we're trapped in the bathroom. Rather it feels as though we're hiding in the bathroom, holding the door shut against some horror that's trying to force its way in.

Forced Choices

This is an interesting example of how the right combination of situation, structure, and mechanics can trigger meaningful interpretive play that departs from the demands of goal-oriented problem solving. If there's a problem to be solved at this stage in *P.T.*, it's "How do I open the door and escape the bathroom?" But at the moment we see the handle start to turn, we don't want the door to open. We want to hold the door closed, even though that's not something the game allows us to do.

The game creates a situation where there's a particular action we want to take. It then responds as though we had done what we wanted to do, even though there's no way for us to do it. The correlation between desire and outcome creates a feeling of cause and effect where none actually exists. Instead of feeling like we're trapped in the bathroom, we feel like we're hiding in the bathroom. The inevitability of the forced choice makes the fear of what lies outside the door even stronger. We're hiding from something so awful that we can't imagine opening the door. We're in a situation where being brave enough to open the door isn't possible. The fact that the real reason we can't open the door is because the game scripting doesn't allow it is immaterial. What matters in the moment is the interpretation that we assign to the situation as it unfolds around us.

The use of forced choice to drive interpretive play is more common than we realize. It pops up in a wide variety of different games and gameplay situations. The most obvious example is the use of mainline quests in role-playing games. Most role-playing games have some set of primary quests that the player must complete in order for the game to progress. While the game seems to offers players complete control over their actions, when it comes to these primary quests, this agency is an illusion. You storm the castle and rescue the princess because that's the only option the game gives you (other than putting down the controller and walking away). But you interpret this forced choice as agency. You aren't rescuing the princess because the game doesn't leave you any other options (even though that's true). You're rescuing the princess because you're the sort of person who rescues people in danger—you're a hero.

This observation has profound implications for level designers. Level designers don't merely create things for players to do. They create situations that invite players to interpret who they are. Striding boldly through the main gate doesn't mean the same thing as sneaking in through the sewers, even though in mechanical terms both get you inside the castle. A door that resists your attempts to force it open doesn't mean the same thing as a door that looks like it's being forced from the other side, even though, in mechanical terms, both keep you trapped.

Played-Out Situations

There's a second scare in the bathroom, and it's one of *P.T.*'s few missteps. It doesn't pay off, and it doesn't pay off because of a failure of interpretive play. Soon after you're trapped, you discover there's something awful in the sink—a deformed fetus-like creature that squirms and mewls as you look at it. The first time you see this thing you're shocked and disturbed, and these feelings are magnified by the fact that the bathroom door is closed. You're confined in a small space with something horrible, and the urge to run away is strong. But the door is locked, and you can't run away. It's a powerful moment.

But, the longer you're trapped with the fetus, the less scary it becomes. Interpretive play demands variety—the situation that we're working to understand needs to evolve so that that we continually reassess and reevaluate our conclusions. When we first glimpse the fetus, we experience a powerful cascade of interpretative play as we struggle to fit its presence into our previous understanding of the game world. Its deep strangeness and the monstrousness of what that strangeness implies drives our initial burst of fear. But after a few seconds of horror, we assimilate the presence of the fetus into our understanding of the world and our fear begins to ebb. The longer we're trapped in the bathroom, the less scary the fetus becomes—it's played out as a locus of interpretive play.

In order for the fetus to remain scary while we're trapped in the bathroom with it, it would have to change—grow, retreat, move, talk to us… whatever. Exactly what it does isn't important so long as the ambiguity of the encounter is sustained. It needs to teeter on the edge of comprehensibility, even though we can't currently comprehend it. We should feel drawn to invent a provisional understanding of what we're experiencing and then reassess that understanding as the changing circumstances undermine it. But because the fetus holds still epistemologically—because its situation stops evolving—our thoughts quickly converge on a settled interpretation and our fear begins to retreat. And so, the locked door of the bathroom actually winds up working against the scariness of the fetus encounter. By prolonging our exposure to the thing in the sink, it allows the initial rush of terror we feel to trickle away and dissipate.

The Balcony

It's interesting to contrast the fetus with the other sinister entity in *P.T.*— the ghost of Lisa. Lisa is a bloodied, emaciated woman in a long gray gown who moves with a jittery jerkiness. The ghost can appear in a variety of places in the level. Sometimes she's deployed as an abrupt jump scare, while at other times she's an ominous watcher. Our encounters with her are always brief, however. Unlike the fetus, she's never in view long enough for her to become played out, and she stays scary to the end.

One of the more interesting Lisa encounters takes place in the entry hall near the front door. The ceiling is higher in this part of the corridor, and there's a dark, inaccessible balcony overlooking the play area. During one iteration of the loop about halfway through the game, there's a jump scare in the entry hall—one of the windows shatters unexpectedly. If you look up immediately after the scare, you'll see Lisa's ghost leering down at you from the balcony. After a second or two, she slowly retreats into the darkness behind her. The encounter ends before our understanding of the ghost can converge onto a fixed (and therefore safe) accommodation.

The layout of the balcony contributes to the power of this scare. We can't reach the balcony and we can only see part of it—the back is obscured by darkness. Besides giving Lisa someplace to retreat to, the hidden back of the balcony functions in much the same way as the second half of the L-shaped corridor—as an ambiguous canvas on which we can paint our fears. The game prevents the corridor from becoming played out by changing it in ominous ways as we pass through successive iterations of the loop. The game prevents the balcony from becoming played out by keeping it out of our normal line of sight as we move through the corridor. Most of the time we don't look up as we pass through the entry hall, so even though the balcony is fully visible on every iteration, we don't become overly familiar with it. There's still the potential for a twinge of apprehensive anticipatory play whenever we glance up and glimpse the darkness behind the railing.

This visible/invisible nature of the balcony pays off dramatically when we look up to see the ghost. It means that instead of the encounter beginning with the ghost moving into view, the reveal comes from us turning to find the source of the breaking glass. We see her there, already staring down at us, and immediately jump to the terrifying realization that she was there all along, we just didn't know it. Being secretly watched is a different flavor of fear than being directly attacked, and the careful positioning of the balcony and the game's control of sight lines is what makes this particular scare possible.

The Front Door

The entry hall is also the location of the front door, the last of *P.T.*'s four doors. Unlike the other three, the front door is completely noninteractive. It remains solidly locked from the start of the game to the end. Even when the player finally escapes the corridor, the exit is through the one-way door at the bottom of the stairs and not the front door, even though the latter seems to be the most obvious way out. So why have this door at all? What is the point of including a noninteractive door in the game?

The front door in *P.T.* functions as a spur to yet another sort of anticipatory play. It's there to direct our thoughts toward the possibility of escape. Without this door, the continual repetitions of the same corridor would feel oppressively claustrophobic. One of the elements of successful anticipatory play is satisfaction, the sense that our situation isn't hopeless and that a positive resolution is possible. The locked front door is a note of hope. It's a subtle reminder that escape is not off the table. But at the same time that hope is offered, it's also deliberately withheld. The horror of being confined in the corridor is amplified by the sense that our deliverance is so tantalizingly close—always in view, but never achievable.

Like the self-blocking bathroom door that encourages us to roleplay hiding, the noninteractive front door encourages us to roleplay being trapped. By continually directing our attention toward the possibility of escape, it directs our attention away from other possible roles—explorer, for example, or hero. We're not pushing bravely forward into the unknown to uncover its mysteries and master them. We're locked inside in a nightmare and our ultimate goal is not to defeat it, but to flee.

In level design terms, this means that if you want players to feel trapped, you need to tantalize them with escape routes. You need to engage anticipatory play around the process of escape, encourage them to consider the contingencies of freedom, even if such contingencies always ground out in failure. When players stop thinking about how to escape, they no longer feel trapped. It's this tension that the front door in *P.T.* exploits, and the reason that it's such an important noninteractive gameplay element.

The L-shaped corridor, the bathroom, the four doors, the balcony—these are the major architectural features that *P.T.* uses to create its scares.

Each functions in a specific way to trigger the interpretive play that produces the powerful sense of dread that is the game's hallmark. There are other minor level design touches that contribute as well. For example, the black windows along the second half of the corridor are similar to the blackness at the back of the balcony; they function as a blank canvas on which to paint our fears of the unknown. The coat rack is positioned in the front hall so that it's easy to mistake for a human figure out of the corner of your eye. The cluttered cabinet tops invite close inspection, but when you narrow your focus to examine them, you're also reducing your awareness of your surroundings, increasing your anxiety over what's behind you. Each of these small level design touches adds to the game's powerful impact.

CLOSING THOUGHTS

This chapter isn't intended to be an exhaustive survey of all the tools that *P.T.* deploys scare players. Rather, it's intended to show how moving away from thinking exclusively in terms of interactivity makes it easier to grasp the underlying processes that produce many of these scares. Once we recognize the power of this sort of play, we can start to design levels that explicitly exploit it. We can deliberately design moments of stillness that are just as engaging as moments of interaction.

Level design is not merely a matter of arranging things for players to do. It's also a matter of constructing situations that encourage players to hold still while they plan or interpret. Furthermore, if we want to create games that are meaningful—games that affect players in deep and profound ways, games that linger in player's minds long after they've finished playing them—then we need to create games that are rich in interpretive play. If we want games to grow into their full potential as an art form, it's not enough to just give players interesting gameplay mechanics. We need to give them interesting ideas to play with, both in the immediacy of the experience and in the stillness that follows after the game ends.

CHAPTER 10

The Illusion of Choice

How to Hide the Linearity of Levels from Players

João Raza and Benjamin Carter

CONTENTS

THE PREDIGITAL ERA OF FILM depended on the facade of the moving image; that a series of still photographs, when sped at a sufficiently high frame rate, provide the illusion of motion. Similarly, a narrative-driven game must sustain the illusion not of motion, but of free will. Effectively, a successful game must hide the contrivances of its level design: go down this corridor and not that one, open this door but not that one, and so on, without making the player feel his or her hand is forced. However, whereas the illusion of motion in film is a trick of the brain that works every time, hiding the artifice in a game depends on distraction and psychological suggestion utilizing both specific techniques of level design and narrative direction. Arguably, it is as important that a player is directed through the level as it is that the player feels he or she is choosing the direction. A hallway that would otherwise be freely available to explore in reality may, in a game, result in a dead end with an impenetrable locked door, be conveniently blocked by misplaced furniture, or perhaps most unimpressive, by apparently impenetrable yellow police tape as seen in

Warner Bros' *Batman: Arkham Origins* (2013). Having the path blocked by such a flimsy excuse takes the player out of the experience with the reminder that this is a game and that rules may be arbitrarily imposed. But there are better ways to accomplish this task and sustain the illusion that the gamer is in control.

This chapter will explore how level designers may disguise linearity through a variety of methods. We will start by examining the most straightforward method; namely, the use of coerced player movement in two-dimensional scrollers, as well as 3D games in the shooter genre. Following suit, we'll get into freer player movement being guided by explicit indicators in the game such as signage, optional pathways, and the usefulness of non-player characters (NPCs) as a guide, whether a mutual companion or a vulnerable target to be escorted by the player. Further widening the scope, architectural elements and audio or graphical cues that can be incorporated will be explored, as well as the narrative conditions that are implied by landmarks in the game. Lastly, the ways that games can go awry will be discussed, as well as a few exceptional cases where design decisions that are conspicuous to the gamer can even be appropriate in certain narrative contexts.

COERCED PLAYER PROGRESSION

To begin, it is appropriate to dig into the earlier history of games to understand the foundations of pushing the player forward, especially without giving them time to doubt their path. As some of the most linear games historically, two-dimensional side-scrollers also have a variety of methods for hiding linearity. Typically, these games are able to avoid the problem of driving the player forward, as the format only allows for two distinct directions, with one plainly more obvious than the other. Traditionally, players are to head right toward a goal, although various titles will play with the rules of this expectation. Nonetheless, we can find in certain side-scrollers one of the simplest ways to motivate the player toward the intended destination: the threat of impending failure. The airship levels of Nintendo's *Super Mario Bros. 3* (1988), for example, utilize continually scrolling screens to create this threat. Normally, the screen moves in accordance with the player, but in these scenarios, the screen moves independently, forcing the player to engage the obstacles preventing him or her from moving forward. If the player fails to do so, the left side of the screen will eventually catch up, forcing death on the player and causing a redo of the level. In this case, the player hardly has time to consider whether he or she is in control, as they are too busy struggling to stay alive to debate whether it would be prudent to backtrack or explore. There simply is no time.

This tool has also been used effectively in three-dimensional spaces, such as early in Valve's *Half-Life 2* (2004). In the beginning of the game, the player is unarmed and forced to flee guards intent on killing the player. The game leaves no option but to run in the most convenient path, which is of course the one the designer deliberately intends. For example, the player may be initially presented with a fork in the road and two seemingly viable paths. As the player approaches, he or she may arbitrarily decide on going left when the designer intends for the player to go right. In order to facilitate this, then, the designer can set up an event such that an overwhelming force of soldiers appear, so the player is routed to the right. Rather than the scenario being made of one long corridor, the player is at least given the illusion of another road to take, if only it wasn't blockaded by the well-established urgency of pursuing soldiers. A similar example is Infinity Ward's *Call of Duty* (2003), in which the player assumes the role of a Russian soldier during the events of World War II. It begins with the siege of Stalingrad, in which Russian forces cross a river by boat and run up the hill to the city proper, which is well fortified by German forces. The player queues up with NPC soldiers with the intent of receiving ammunition, but in the rush is quickly passed over and pushed onto the battlefield. As Soviet forces were infamous for at the time, any retreating of soldiers was treated as a traitorous act and were shot by commanding officers. Thus, in the game, the player is forced to move forward without a means to fight off enemy forces, lest he return to the level's beginning, only to be shot anyway, and is pushed forward into a fight under threat of being fired on by commanding officers should he or she retreat. Sure enough, if the player does retreat, he or she is killed and forced to replay the opening of the level. This effectively instills urgency in the player's actions, leaving little time to idly wander and explore the boundaries of the gamespace.

DIRECTING THE PLAYER WITH LIMITED FREEDOM

While a convenient method for propelling the player forward, coerced movement is not a method that can be routinely relied on, especially when the overall pacing of the game is taken into consideration. There are a variety of ways to tackle these calmer scenarios. Some games will quite literally point the way, and this may prove satisfactory to most (though not all) players. Even something as conspicuous as a sign can lend the player an appropriate sense of place and direction. The opening of Valve's *Half-Life* (1998) asks the player to navigate through a benign set of corridors without fear of hostilities. The player is technically free to explore, and should he or she do so, will find a few Easter eggs to discover, such as a microwave in the breakroom that will turn on if interacted with, but otherwise serves no meaningful purpose for gameplay. There are corridors that terminate into a dead end, but often a narrative excuse is employed: in this case, a security guard insisting that Gordon Freeman (the player's avatar) does not have the clearance to move further. Nonetheless, the player is led by the nose thanks to handy signage painted on the wall. The player can follow each corresponding line to its endpoint, and so rather than being forced on a rail, or otherwise forced through a cut-scene, the player is permitted some range of movement but is still given subtle prodding in the "right" direction in an organic way that makes sense in the context of the world. A more explicit method is found in *Half-Life 2*, which contains a level that is quite literally a road. The player is told that the destination being sought (which is reinforced prior to this point by the story) is at the end of Highway 17. The player is never left in the position of wondering where to go, as the road is always leading onward.

We can also find various examples of developers employing guidance that are not necessarily built into the art and architecture of the level itself, but which guide players through a level in imaginative ways while hiding linearity. A level type known as escort missions contain examples of nongeometric guidance. Escort missions task the player with keeping a typically vulnerable NPC alive. In the process, the NPC will guide the player and help him or her around certain obstacles that are otherwise insurmountable alone. As it pertains to guiding the player, NPCs at their most base level serve as gatekeepers. For example, the security guards and scientists in *Half-Life* are uniquely capable of unlocking doors that the player otherwise cannot, using the narrative device of a retinal scan as a logical obstacle of the player's progress. This is an effectively organic way of gating the player without feeling like the gates are arbitrary. However, the effect is not as subtle as literally being guided by an NPC sometimes can be. *Half-Life 2* and its follow-up, *Episode 1*, utilizes the NPC Alyx, both as a companion in combat and a tour guide of sorts, who helps navigate the level for the player at certain key moments and provides narrative motivation for moving in a certain direction. We see similar mechanics in games like Rare's *Goldeneye* (1997), in which the character of Natalya shows the way and acts as gatekeeper at certain moments; or, most recently, in Naughty Dog's *The Last of Us* (2013), in which the character of Ellie will verbally lambaste the player for either idling too long or spending onerous amounts of time exploring otherwise meaningless areas of the level. Both examples provide due incentive for the player to continue moving forward in the intended direction. However, while these are examples of encouraging lures, there's also ways of using a perceived opponent to guide the player forward. A key example can be found in DICE's *Mirror's Edge* (2008). While the game frequently compels urgency much in the same way as *Super Mario Bros. 3*'s airship levels, namely by having the relatively helpless-in-combat player be chased down by well-armed guards, the more pressing example is a specific level in which Faith, the player's avatar, is tasked with chasing down an enemy of similar abilities to the player. The result is a similar urgency to that of being chased, except if you tarry for too long, the pursued enemy will eventually be out of reach. In this way, NPCs can not only cooperate with the player to help guide him or her forward, but literally lead the way while being oppositional. However, an NPC can be difficult to implement and is not always the most convenient solution.

NARRATIVE LURES BUILT INTO THE LEVEL

Being escorted by an NPC is one way of using a narrative lure, but such lures can also be built into the levels themselves. This can range from small graphical cues to large physical objects that dominate the level's presentation. In the case of *Mirror's Edge*, the main character Faith is said to have a natural ability to sense objects of opportunity, which is employed in the game by highlighting climbable pipes, ramps useful for jumping off of, zip cords that can be slid down, and so on, in a bright red color. Especially on the deliberately plain white aesthetic of the game's world, the red highlight serves as a de facto guiding light. If the designer does not want the player leaving the intended path, the red objects simply won't be available to take him or her in the wrong direction. Of course, *Mirror's Edge* often benefits from another narrative circumstance: much of the game takes place on the roof tops of tall buildings, and so the wrong path is often a very large drop to one's death. But rather than just having a long row of roof after roof, the designers incorporated multiple traversal paths that are then indicated to the player through the red highlights. This opens up a way to both gate the level and also open it up sufficiently such that the player still feels he or she maintains control.

Architectural centerpieces can be used as a sort of guiding light. Returning to *Half-Life 2*, nearly the entire gameworld is built around the monolithic Citadel, an impossibly tall blue structure that serves in the literal background as the foreboding symbol of the game's antagonist, but more importantly toward the latter half of the game as the ultimate objective of the player. Visible virtually from anywhere in the game's main setting, it rarely leaves the player questioning in which direction he or she should proceed. It provides a focus, whereas if the game lacked such a prominent structure, the player may find him or herself sufficiently aimless as to wander into the artificial barriers of the levels. Therefore, rather than being guided by the level's geometry, such as unclimbable walls, the player is lured to the relevant direction, with the Citadel acting like a compass. We can find that same narrative lure used in thatgamecompany's *Journey* (2012), the very premise of which is to surmount a mighty mountain that works as a beacon throughout the entire game, and like *Half-Life 2*'s Citadel, is visible from most anywhere. The player could very well choose to head in various other directions, but only the mountain serves to give a proper point to navigate toward.

Of course, it's not necessary for lures to be so epic in scale. An exceptional refinement of narrative lures is on display in Kojima Productions' *P.T.* (2014), ostensibly a playable teaser for the now-canceled *Silent Hills*. Architecturally, *P.T.* is nothing more than a single L-shaped corridor, and passing through the door at one end will simply take you to the beginning of that exact corridor. However, with each pass, a new hint or clue is subtly dropped. Initially, it begins with a radio newscast about a murder that is eventually revealed to have taken place in the house that contains the corridor in question. Over time, through creative use of graphical effects (e.g., animated cockroaches, flickering lights) and audio cues (quiet rumblings, faint voices), *P.T.* gradually ramps up the tension, both engaging the player and removing any reason to doubt why one door may be locked or any desire for there to be a more nonlinear path through the house. It provides a terrifying experience without need of leaving the single L-shaped corridor. Generally, this terror serves as the motivation for the player: it becomes increasingly irrelevant as to the seeming inanity of walking the same hall over and over again, as the player is nonetheless tense and stressed out by the escalating horror of the scenario. It arguably gets to the point that the player is too frightened to stay in one iteration of the corridor but too intrigued to decline progressing through the next iteration. Ultimately, it succeeds in distracting from the fact that the player has no real choice.

Unfortunately, *P.T.* serves as a rare exception of narrative lures being used exclusively to direct the player through a three-dimensional space. Ultimately, it's prudent to work in certain architectural characteristics in the level in order to facilitate directed passage without feeling forced. In contrast to *P.T.*'s strict linearity, a game can foster the player's desire for more flexibility by offering branching paths, some of which may possess certain incentives, and others that function as a fork in a road, but both paths ultimately lead to the same place. Providing the player with some choice can alleviate the reality of having no choices whatsoever, or in the case of games, disguise the reality that, regardless of the path you take, all roads in any given level typically lead to the same end. Examples can be frequently found in RPGs like Bioware's *Dragon Age* (2009) franchise or in Irrational Game's *Bioshock Infinite* (2013), both of which offer hidden rewards off the beaten path, such as a chest with loot that is useful to the player, or a simple detour that loop players back onto the main path.

Location-based features provide opportunities for designers to create architectural obstacles that can both direct player movement while providing daring players opportunities for exploration. With the earlier example of *Half-Life 2*'s Highway 17, the road is explicitly a coastal one, and so it would make sense in that context that one side of the path is always guarded by an ocean, and that the other may be shadowed by cliffs, as is common in the real world. In the case of the ocean, it is filled with hostile creatures as per *Half-Life*'s setting. The player *can* choose to wade out into the water, but will be faced with imminent death thanks to attacks by said hostile creatures. The player can never get very far, but at least the illusion is maintained that there is something more out there if only the player wasn't so vulnerable to the circumstances. A similar example of such a risk-based boundary can be found in *Call of Duty*. Progressing through many levels, it seems as though the player could conceivably walk toward the horizon. However, in making the attempt, the player will run afoul of landmines, as would be expected on the battlefield, should he or she stray too far from the path intended by the level designer. The result, naturally, is death. This serves as a justified fiction, whereas a simple wall would be all too obvious a barricade and risks alienating the player in the midst of the experience. The physical blocking of the player should always come off as functionally relevant to whatever setting is established in the narrative.

Barriers can also be built behind the player in order to push him or her forward. Square Enix's *Tomb Raider* (2013) or Naughty Dog's *Uncharted* (2007) franchise frequently put the player character in a precarious situation, such as balancing high up on a wooden beam or scaling a wall or cliff side, in which an emergency scenario occurs: the beam is teetering, implying that it will (and does) eventually collapse, there's a rock slide on the cliff or an avalanche on a mountain side. The end result is twofold. First, the player is given urgency in the crisis of the moment, driving them forward through what could otherwise be a boring series of linear jumping puzzles; as Lara in *Tomb Raider*, the player is running along a rooftop of an ancient dilapidated building that is in the process of collapsing, so if the player is not quick about traversing the obstacle, he or she will be caught in its destruction. Second, once the player escapes, the path behind them is closed off. The building that Lara has now vacated has become rubble and the path back is physically blocked. We see examples of the latter in many games, such as a doorway that conveniently collapses behind a player, or simply jumping off a ledge that is otherwise too high to jump back up to. Without being unnecessarily explicit, the reality is clear to the player: he or she must move forward.

MISTAKES THAT BREAK THE ILLUSION

It's easy to demonstrate how any of these methods can be misused, such that the illusion is broken and the player becomes too conscious of the designers' intentions, ruining any sense that the player has choice. Where poor level design runs astray, as far as it concerns the illusory experience intended for the player, is when the necessary contrivances are so conspicuous that the player recognizes them upon playing. It can often be as simple as the unbreakable yellow police tape in the earlier example from *Batman: Arkham Origins*, which will leave almost every player wondering why a character as powerful as Batman, who at one point in the game secretly infiltrates an actual police station, is nonetheless beholden to the power of their yellow tape. But while the yellow tape serves as an inconvenience to the player, such obvious tactics by the level designer can be observed in layouts intended for the very opposite purpose. In the case of Bethesda's *Skyrim* (2011), the player must frequently venture into dungeons, usually at the behest of a narrative lure such as a quest granted by an NPC or promises of treasure to be found. In a clear design choice, the end of every dungeon typically winds back to the entrance, so once the player is finished, he or she can easily exit and promptly continue onward. Insofar as this convenience is found in virtually every dungeon in the game, it becomes obvious that the circuitous layout of the dungeon was intended deliberately by the level designer. The illusion is ruined, if only because it has made itself too well known to the player; the player is thus removed from the experience. But it's important to understand within the narrative context why this is an issue that warrants attention.

The problem in *Skyrim* is perhaps a betrayal of what is otherwise supposed to be a natural world. In the context of the story, it isn't prudent, for whoever in the *Skyrim* universe designed the dungeon, to make it so his or her final chamber naturally pours right into the entrance, especially if the intention is to barricade the length between the entrance and final chamber with a series of traps and guards—objects that function as obstacles to the player to be tackled by gameplay, but are also serving the narrative purpose—that is, the player is not supposed to be here and is trespassing. But such a routine and obvious exit to every dungeon only make sense in the context of game design rather than in the context of the narrative. It serves as an example of how the level's layout can incidentally incur ludonarrative dissonance. In other words, the player should never be patently aware of design choices made outside of the game, and any layout of levels in the game should suit the narrative. If *Skyrim* held to this rule, then the player wouldn't expect dungeons to consistently loop in on themselves, or at the least, the player would have the reasonable expectation that instead of traversing all the traps and obstacles, the player could just as well take the backdoor that is otherwise intended to bring the dungeon to a quick end once completed. Being faced with the same contrivance over and over again dispels any illusion the player would otherwise have of being free to act in this game world—they are reminded that all they are doing is following the path created by the designers. It might have been better to let the player backtrack through dungeons, to use the backdoor sparingly, or to come up with more elegant solutions, as long as it avoids repetition that is the result of obvious (to the player) design choices.

Similar to *Skyrim*, a contradiction in style can lead to such dissonance. In id Software's *Doom 3* (2003), we see somewhat of an adoption of *Half-Life*'s style of level design. Similar to Valve's magnum opus, *Doom 3* opens with the player character entering his or her new job in a science facility and finding their way through a nonhostile environment. For all intents and purposes, the game is establishing a certain logic and order to things: there's a check-in desk with a security guard, bathrooms where you would expect them, benches for idling scientists, and so on. This world is, ostensibly, real. However, as you progress through the game and tackle its many enemies, you begin to see callbacks to design choices that were only really relevant in the 1990s, especially in the case of monster closets—that is to say, trap doors in the wall whose only purpose is to ambush the player with a previously unseen monster. In the logic of the first two games in the *Doom* series, this was appropriate, but in the realistic setting of *Doom 3*, it's a contradiction—why would whoever designed the science lab seemingly place a hidden wall slot, behind which was an empty space devoid of purpose except to house a monster? And why does that monster only become revealed when a new weapon, conspicuously placed in front of the closet, is picked up by the player? This is a clear choice of the level designer, and a poorly hidden one of that. Again, we find a case where the designer runs afoul of ludonarrative dissonance, and the player is yet again reminded that he or she is following the path intended by the designer and tackling obstacles placed by the designer rather than obstacles that make sense in the narrative context. It could be said that *Doom 3* would be better off without the monster closets, or at least throw in a bucket and mop so that the closet now belongs to a janitor and just so happens to have a monster in it.

An infamous example of conspicuous design choices is the much-maligned early levels of Square Enix's *Final Fantasy XIII* (2009). Arguably, the game leverages most of its worth on the gameplay, and so level design takes a secondary role: it's merely an aesthetically pleasing place in which to facilitate the combat. As a result, levels are quite literally comprised of long hallway after long hallway, with little option for branching off or even offering to the player consideration that one could, at least in theory, explore a larger world. As a quick contrast, consider again *Half-Life 2*, and how, while not necessarily in practice, the player could, at least in theory, walk the streets of City 17 and explore. Whereas Valve would implement a variety of methods to divert the player, *Final Fantasy XIII* does not even presume this to be a problem: just a straight-shot corridor. Even worse, the game fails to utilize any appropriate narrative lures early on. It proffers next to no information on the motivations of the characters, lacks any hint at the larger lore of the world, and fails to provide direction for the player other than the literal line in front of them that is the only available avenue. As such, the player does not know what they are doing, why they are doing it, or where they're heading. Even previous installments of the *Final Fantasy* franchise, despite being technologically more primitive, are given sufficient motivation to navigate such linear levels: consider *Final Fantasy VII* (1997), in which from the get-go the player is actively encouraged by NPCs to tackle the task at hand, which is infiltration and sabotage of a facility thought to be causing environmental harm.

That all said, sometimes conspicuous level design can be used as an advantage if framed appropriately within the narrative context. Titles such as Valve's *Portal* (2007) or Croteam's *The Talos Principle* (2014) work on the premise that the player character is being tested in a series of puzzles contrived by the antagonist in each respective title. The result is that each level in either game has design choices that deliberately show contrivance: boxy rooms, restrictively linear paths, and conspicuous blockage of other routes with simple walls. Some even feature the same circuitous routes that would otherwise be criticized in a game like *Skyrim*. Puzzles in the narrative exist for their own sake, just as they do to the actual designer, and are not hidden behind a facade or ostensibly for some practical real-world purpose. Instead, they exist as they actually do: solely to be solved for the player. This is no pretension, so there is no reason for the level designer to hide this fact, save to let any narrative elements to provide compensation accordingly: in the case of *Portal*, the villainous GLaDOS insists the tests are necessary for whatever function she as a computer was created for, and in the case of *The Talos Principle*, the self-declared God, Elohim, insists that it is the player character's purpose to be tested. Arguably, both these titles are using narrative elements as a dodge for disguising their experience, but really, they both serve as clever satires of gaming in general, and turning the conventions outlined in this article on their ear. So just as understanding these methods can be used to create an experience for the player that hides the designer's intent, they can also be used to make the designer's intent obvious for the purpose of the story. In the case of *Portal*, the designers and GLaDOS are one and the same, and ditto Elohim in *The Talos Principle*.

CONCLUSION

One of the greatest achievements that a narratively driven linear game can hope to accomplish is to completely divest the player of the reality that he or she is in a videogame and that the experience itself takes priority rather than his or her awareness of the virtual reality that is being enacted. In practice, the designer cannot reasonably be expected to fully simulate the world, whether fantasy or a depiction of our own reality, in a manner that completely fulfills the expectations of the player. So it remains prudent that the designer takes into consideration both the general methods outlined in this article, as well as any we failed to account for, in order to essentially deceive the player into believing he or she is acting out in an ostensibly naturally occurring world, and not one that has a creator (the designer) who has made conscious decisions that are easily detected by the player. A designer failing to appreciate these concerns ultimately results in a player who, rather than responding organically to the problems within the gamespace, is instead trying to predict why the designer has made one decision over another. This is the breakdown of the illusion.

If the player is forced to move, as per the airship levels in *Super Mario Bros. 3* or the pursuit of the player by soldiers in *Half-Life 2*, then the player does not have time to consider any path but the most convenient one. If the player is busy escorting an NPC who insists on pressing forward, the player is too committed to the urgency of the objective to wander off elsewhere. If the player has an overwhelming beacon presented to them, such as the Citadel in *Half-Life 2*, it dominates not just their literal view, but their figurative one as they decide how to progress further. If the player is too terrified to stay in place, as in *P.T.*, they are propelled forward, and more important, feel they *choose* to, even though the reality is that there is no choice. And therein lies the point: games are ultimately a set of rules as determined by the designers in order to guide the players to some conclusion. There may be leeway into what precisely that conclusion is, as in the case of games with multiple different endings, but not necessarily an unlimited freedom. At some point, the designers must make a decision and gate the world accordingly. The trick, then, is how to hide the fact from the player that the world is gated, such that the player feels his or her progress is a natural extension of how they would really act in that situation in real life.

Ultimately, the designer cannot account for everything. There is no amount of tricks or tools of the trade that can stop the most inquisitive player from deciding to ignore all impetus and instead push the boundaries that should otherwise be beneath consideration. A player could very well decline to save the princess, and instead toy with the geometry of the level and glitch through walls that are supposed to be impenetrable. The player may even find a way to solve a level such that they skip portions that were conceived by the designer as vital. It is the nature of video games that not all scenarios can be anticipated, and for such players as outlined above, the game will always be that—just a game—rather than the involved experience originally intended. For all the methods outlined in this chapter, the designer must nonetheless have a player who is willing to suspend disbelief and to accept the illusion.

CHAPTER 11

Integrating Procedural and Handmade Level Design

Mark R. Johnson

CONTENTS

INTRODUCTION

At first glance, procedural content generation (PCG) and handmade design seem markedly dichotomous. One produces a near-infinite volume of permutations while the other only offers a single instance. One appears focused on replayability while the other seems to offer little that is new to the player who returns for a second playthrough. One is designed by an algorithm designed by humans; the other is designed directly by humans. One can only be learned in terms of the algorithm's outputs while the other can be precisely rote-learned. One is used in only a small fraction of all computer games, while the other is so near-universal that many players may not even recognize that the first kind even exists. Despite these gulfs of difference, a significant number of games (including the author's) choose to integrate these two design rationales in an attempt to have the best of both worlds and/or utilize procedural content to produce game experiences that are difficult to hand-make (and vice versa), resulting in patchwork level designs that are not entirely one thing or the other. This style of probabilistically varied level design—the absolute singularity of the handmade combined with the vastly unpredictable of the procedural— merits a close examination in order to understand the respective benefits of both procedural and handmade content, the different methods of over-laying these rationales, the gameplay experiences created by these meth-ods, and the (un)intended consequences of creating such multilayered game design architectures.

This chapter consists of four substantive parts. The first proposes three major rationales for procedural content generation in terms of player experience—enabling replay value and novelty, offering significant game-play challenge, and the development of gameplay focused around explo-ration and discovery of the unknown. The second section then argues for two particular benefits of handmade design that are specifically rel-evant to our discussion of procedural-handmade integration: the creation of precise and exact gameplay instances and the creation of puzzles and narratives (which procedural generation systems, at the time of writing, struggle with). The chapter will not seek to assess the validity or merit of any of these rationales toward procedural and handmade design, but rather to serve as a review of five common design philosophies (three pro-cedural, two handmade) that have strongly influenced the design of the four games examined in the subsequent part of the chapter. With these reasons for both design rationales established, the third section then examines four games that have attempted different methods of integrating the two: *Faster Than Light* (2012), *Dungeon Crawl Stone Soup* (2006), *Spelunky* (2008/2012), and the author's *Ultima Ratio Regum* (2012). The fourth and final section places these four games into a binary typology (*vertical integration* and *horizontal integration*), examines whether integration should be hidden or explicit, and summarizes the state of the field and the potential of future games that stray from the seemingly polar extremes of the procedural-handmade spectrum. In doing so the chapter serves as both a theoretical analysis of games of this type, and a practical guide to the design (and pitfalls) of integrated games and integrated levels.

PCG BENEFITS

This section explores three primary rationales for procedurally generated level design: ensuring replay value and prolonging novelty, creating challenging gameplay experiences, and creating gameplay experiences focused around the theme or mechanic of exploration.

Replay and Novelty

Replay value has been an integral part of the discourses of procedural benefits: procedural generation is routinely cited in a large volume of work as a method for giving games "higher replay value,"[1] "close to infinite replay value,"[2] "massive replay value,"[3] boundless replay value,[4] and so on. By utilizing procedural generation the specific instances of gameplay differ each time the game is played—enemies are in new locations, quests might differ, crucial items are in distinct places, level layouts are different, and things the player encountered in one playthrough may not even appear in the next—and this should give such games significantly more replay value for the player than their handmade equivalents where nothing changes on each new playthrough. This benefit of procedural generation also ties in to a related claim: that one game which can be enjoyed for longer than another game is inherently better.[5-8] Unpacking this venerable yet problematic gaming discourse is beyond the scope of this chapter, but replay value can be readily understood as a subset of this argument—a longer game is generally perceived as being superior to a shorter game, so a game one can replay hundreds of times and still get something new from the experience must be preferable (all other things being equal) to a game that only offers variety over a dozen iterations (which, in turn, is more desirable than a game that can only be enjoyed once). Replays will seem more distinct if they contain something novel and noteworthy in each iteration, and therefore procedurally generated games (with their algorithmically selected orientation of component) seem to offer significant novelty. This in turn encourages replay and prevents each playthrough from blending into the others (for one procedurally generated dungeon floor can look rather like another). However accurate, and whether representative of genuine experiential difference or nothing more than advertising claims, this combination of interrelated claims and factors—higher replay value, higher novelty, a longer period of overall playtime—is a clear and oft-stated encouragement toward the development of PCG games.

Challenge

Procedural generation—in large part perhaps due to its very close association with roguelikes (procedurally generated dungeon crawls with a high level of complexity and difficulty)—is also seen as a method for creating challenging games and creating forms of challenge that are not necessarily easily replicated in handmade games. Challenge is recognized as an integral part of the gameplay experience as defined by a range of conceptual models[9-12] and procedural generation offers a particular and distinctive method for offering long-term consistent challenges to players. Although handmade games can have areas of particular challenge, the challenge of any gameplay scenario is most significant the first time the player encounters it even if the player is aware of all the mechanics or game systems relevant to that encounter; upon death or defeat the player knows the particular challenge (or knows at least some of it), can adjust their strategy for a second attempt, and continue doing this until victory is achieved (this is not to discount the role of physical reflex skill in game challenge as well as strategic decision making, but this assumes a player who has a level of reflex skill appropriate to the game they are playing). In a procedurally generated game, however, the player does not know what will happen next, and thus is forced to respond correctly the *first time*[13] they ever encounter a particular gameplay scenario (since that first time will also be the *only* time), thereby demanding significantly greater decision-making ability and decision making with less information—the player cannot play out the entire scenario before deciding their strategy for their second attempt, but must determine their strategy from the immediate information presented when the gameplay scenario is entered. Most procedurally generated games are turn-based, which gives the player ample time to compose a strategy in response to a challenging gameplay scenario, although a small number (e.g., *The Binding of Isaac* [2011], *Terraria* [2011], *Risk of Rain* [2013]) are in real time, requiring not just strong strategic decisions in unknown scenarios, but *immediate* strong strategic decisions. In order to create this form of procedurally generated challenge, both the unexpected nature of the situation and the challenge of the situation must be combined. A situation that is unexpected but nonchallenging is trivial (although naturally not all PCG games strive for challenge, e.g., *Proteus* [2013]), just as a situation that is expected but challenging also becomes trivial with enough trial and error and time granted to reach the correct solution. This is not, of course, to suggest that handmade level design cannot be challenging even upon multiple replays (as players of the *Souls* series and many others will attest), but rather that procedurally generated games in most cases excel at producing strategic and tactical challenges rather than reflex or execution challenges (although some games, as above, offer both). When the exact layout of a game cannot be rote-learned, challenge is preserved to a greater extent across multiple playthroughs—although the player of course comes to learn the *potential* challenges that may arise—in a way that handmade games are unable to match, leading to a game whose challenges remain challenging and fresh for a longer period of time and which will always maintain some interest for even the most skilled and experienced players.

Exploration and Discovery

Procedural generation can also yield significant player benefits in games focused on exploration and discovery.[14,15] Examples of such PCG-focused games include *Minecraft* (2011), *Terraria* (2011), *Ultima Ratio Regum* (2012), *No Man's Sky* (2016), and arguably even *Civilization* (1991–Present) or *Alpha Centauri* (1999), when we recognize that exploration is essential to placing one's cities, locating and fighting one's enemies, making informed choices in the technology tree (vis-à-vis the layout of land, ocean, and the units capable of traversing each), and so on. These games are specifically about the discovery of objects beyond the player's immediate starting area, exploration as a means of information gathering, or where exploration and the uncertainty of what will be uncovered (through a complex and detailed PCG system) is an integral selling point of the game. The game world that differs each time is a game world that is explored anew each time, even if the player has an inkling of what it *might* contain. There is therefore an interesting observation here about discovery in a handmade game and a procedural game: when one completes the former (assuming these are linear, not sandbox, games), one is most likely aware that the overwhelming majority of that game has now been seen. There may be secrets or alternative levels, but in most linear game narratives, completing the game once means that very little has not been discovered or experienced. By contrast, in a procedurally generated game, the player ordinarily doesn't know how much has been seen, although a small number of games (e.g., *The Binding of Isaac* [2011], *Risk of Rain* [2013]) do give explicit metrics of increasing player completion. Perhaps the PCG systems are sufficiently constrained and unvarying that a single playthrough will already display a quarter of all the possible variation in the game or perhaps the PCG systems are so many and so diverse that no playthrough will even show a hundredth of what the game has to offer—but the player *doesn't know which it is* until the game has been played repeatedly (an obvious overlap here with the *replay value* benefit explored above; many of these benefits are interwoven). A single playthrough is an inadequate sample size to assess the possibility space of the game's permutations, even if it may offer hints to the analytically minded player toward the nature of other, as-of-yet unseen permutations. For the player, therefore, procedural generation can be a major benefit in exploration-focused games, ensuring uncertainty about what lies over the horizon and allowing for level design that stresses the constant and endless encounter with the new. This section has outlined the primary benefits of PCG content, and we will next examine the benefits of handmade content in order to then assess how much they may be utilized together.

HANDMADE BENEFITS

We have now identified what are arguably the three most-cited benefits of procedural generation: replay value and the creation of repeated novelty, procedural generation as a method for the creation of challenge and difficulty, and PCG as fundamental to games focused around exploration and discovery. The chapter will now examine two benefits of handmade level design that procedural generation struggles to reproduce to a quality equivalent to a handmade level design, which are very distinct from the procedural benefits outlined above. These are the crafting of specific gameplay instances and the accompanying pedagogic and narratological control such crafting offers, and the *inability* for PCG systems (generally speaking) to produce compelling narratives or detailed puzzles. There are naturally many other benefits of handmade level design that could serve as a book in their own right, let alone a chapter, and therefore this discussion will be limited to a brief summary of these two particular benefits of handmade level design that are strongly reflected in PCG-handmade integrations, instead of listing all the benefits of handmade design per se.

Crafting Specific Gameplay Instances

Handmade design is well-suited to the careful and deliberate crafting of specific moments of gameplay. This might be an integral piece of story, a major challenge to the player, a moment in the narrative into which all players are funneled regardless of their previous actions, a specific item or enemy that is particularly noteworthy, or small section of a level (the rest of which would otherwise be algorithmically created). By definition, in fact, procedural content generation cannot achieve such exactitude, for if the requirements and parameters of the generating algorithm were set to such restrictive limits that the outcome was the same every time, that is effectively indistinguishable from simply creating and then saving the particular gameplay moment the designer wants to include. For PCG to be genuinely procedural there must be leeway and variation; in some cases this could still enable variation while ensuring the necessary (and identical between playthroughs) components are always present (a nonprocedural enemy who is always spawned, but spawned within a procedurally designed level, for example), and thus there is a spectrum between procedurality and handcraftedness along which all such design choices lie. Nevertheless, such a placement of a specific enemy in a non-specific spatial environment, as in the above example, still contains a handmade element, and an element which (as the section below demonstrates) is fairly easy for procedural generation to integrate. A story element, for example, or a particular cinematic sequence, remains extremely challenging to generate, and thus handmade design is required to craft such moments of gameplay that the game's otherwise-adequate PCG system presumably cannot (or where the game seeks to tell a specific story in a specific way, and thus exact narrative elements must be included). As such, some predominantly PCG games—such as *NetHack* (1987), *DCSS* (2006), *Faster Than Light* (2012), *XCOM: Enemy Unknown* (2012), *Darkest Dungeon* (2015), and others, depending on how wide or narrow a definition of a handmade segment we adopt—deploy a range of handmade segments designed to offer precisely tuned and balanced instances of gameplay amidst the far more variable but inevitably less perfected procedural content surrounding them. Several of these will be examined later in "Four Case Studies of Integration" section of this chapter.

Narratives and Puzzles

Despite its well explored and seemingly near-limitless potential for what we might term the generation of space and place—the creation of solar systems, placements of buildings, layouts of dungeons, and so on—there are other aspects of contemporary games that procedural generation tends to struggle with. Perhaps the most well known of these is *narrative*—the few games that have attempted detailed procedural narratives often are composed of bizarre behavior on the part of their characters, idiosyncrasies, and contradictions, and moments of rare lucidity tend to be more down to unfounded apophenia on the part of the player than intention and design on the part of the developer. This is in contrast to generating landscapes, for example, as humans are more readily equipped to notice holes in stories than unusual geological formations. A growing body of scholarly work on generating narratives does exist,[16-19] but the techniques for generating narratives and puzzles remain in their early stages compared to those for the generation of gameplay spaces and have yet to find their way into games to the same extent.[20] Procedural narratives require a great deal of engagement with other game factors that may themselves *also* be generated—geographies, factions, other characters, and so on—and must respond fluidly and adaptively to in-game events[21] rather than (as with a procedural dungeon) being an unchanging backdrop that is generated once and then played *upon* rather than played *with*. A procedural narrative must adapt to a (likely) generated world and to the (likely) significant actions of the player, which are often unpredictable, if there is to be any hope of creating narratives and characters as convincing and well-rounded (and able to impact the game world) as handmade equivalents. In other instances a *procedurally* generated game might seek to tell a *handmade* story, and therefore actually doesn't want the narrative to be generated; but if it were to be generated, it would encounter the set of problems described above. Many games, therefore, opt to hand-make their narrative segments, either because there is a specific narrative they want to tell or because the task of procedural narrative generation appears too daunting (or too prone to yielding bizarre stories) and it is simpler to write it beforehand.

Just like narratives, procedural puzzle generation is less commonly seen in procedural systems, and when we examine what we might call the formal properties of a good puzzle we can readily perceive why. There are a number of interrelated issues that make puzzles particularly problematic for procedural generation, which we will now explore, and it is these issues that have encouraged a number of games into placing handmade (or semi-handmade) puzzles into otherwise procedural worlds. Just as with narrative, work is nevertheless underway into procedural puzzle generation,[22-26] but it similarly remains comparatively incipient, challenging, often comparatively simplistic to more complex handmade puzzles, and underused in the wider game industry.

Good puzzles (or sequences of puzzles) have a range of requirements that procedural generation, at the time of writing, struggles to work around. First, in almost all cases a more challenging puzzle is one with more steps (computer games tend to prioritize puzzles based on multiple actions over riddle-based puzzles) from initiation to completion. This therefore necessitates a PCG system that does not just create puzzles of multiple steps, but ensures that the puzzle must be solved with those multiple steps, which is to say that no easier solution presents itself. In a given possibility space of mechanics and systems, the more steps a puzzle requires the more intricately it must be constructed, and the fewer hypothetical puzzles are possible (consider the creation of a chess problem or a Go *tsumego* that has a one-step solution and must have only one answer, and the creation of a puzzle that must also have only *one* solution but must require a hundred steps—the latter is immeasurably more challenging to construct without accidentally allowing easier solutions to appear). A puzzle-creating PCG system must therefore be able to generate puzzles with a range of steps (assuming that the designers want difficulty to increase with time, which is a reasonably implicit hypothesis) and ensure that the many-step puzzles can only be solved with the many-step solutions. This means that the algorithm must have the ability to exhaustively assess *all possible sequences* that might lead to the winning outcome, and either generate puzzles with only one solution or puzzles with a precise number of allowed solutions (or a number within a range of acceptable numbers). However, this second possibility—puzzles with many valid solutions—raises another interrelated issue: most puzzles require *parity between solutions*. It is hard to conceive of a design situation where a designer would actively seek a puzzle with some easy solutions and some hard solutions: the pace of the game will be upset for some players, the experiences between players will rarely be comparable, and difficulty will not climb steadily if the local difficulty of any given puzzle is dependent on which particular solution hypothesis players happen to start off pursuing (and whether that hypothesis yields an easy or a hard solution). A PCG system must therefore ensure that if it is designed to offer multiple solutions, it can recognize when these generated solutions are of *roughly equal difficulty*. This is complex enough when trying to generate multiple solutions of the same number of steps, but a more detailed system would be able to recognize steps that are easier or harder, and thereby make allowances for solutions with few very difficult steps or a greater number of less difficult steps. Either way: it is a significant programming challenge. There is a final additional subset of outcomes here—where a puzzle has multiple solutions, and some solutions offer better rewards than others—but such systems are extremely rare, although in such a case the PCG system would also have to assign higher challenges to higher outcomes.

There is one other issue with PCG puzzle generation, unrelated to multiple steps, multiple solutions, and intergeneration parity. Playing through the most carefully-designed of puzzle games, it is not hard to see that many puzzles are designed to be *viewed* by the player in a particular sequence: to have the player notice certain features before others, to show the player the components in a certain order based on the ability of the player to traverse the environment in which those components exist, or to offer the player aspects of a puzzle that might only fully make sense once the player has spent a few moments contemplating or engaging with another component. Some puzzles offer seemingly innocuous aspects of the puzzle that only attain meaning once the player has learned they might be noteworthy, such as small portions of portal-able walls in the *Portal* games that at first appear to be only an environmental detail, or systems that are active before the player is able to view the environment surrounding them and interact with them, such as many of the monster generators in *Braid* (2008). A PCG system that reflects this would therefore require the ability to deduce the player's lines of sight (fairly trivial) and potentially extrapolate as to the order the player will observe and consider items within the space of the puzzle (far from trivial), and these are significant challenges for contemporary PCG at the time of writing. As such, some predominantly PCG games—such as *NetHack* (1987), *Brogue* (2009), *Spelunky* (2008/2012), and others, depending again on how wide or narrow a definition of "puzzle" we adopt—choose to integrate handmade (or predominantly handmade) puzzle segments into predominantly generated game worlds rather than generate a puzzle from scratch.

COMBINING PROCEDURAL AND HANDMADE

We have now outlined three major benefits of procedural generation and two aspects of handmade level design that are particularly relevant to our discussion, for they focus on the inability or difficulty of generating certain aspects of level design. We established that procedural generation is a design technique that emphasizes replay value, the length of interesting play, and the importance of novelty; that PCG can create both strategic and reflex challenges of a sort not readily found in handmade games, and certainly not across multiple playthroughs; and that games that emphasize exploration and discovery are well suited to a model of the world where the player understands the unpredictability of the unseen and/or the uncertain scope of the game's permutations. However, procedural content generation cannot produce specific instances of guaranteed gameplay and struggles with generating the narratological or the puzzling—things handmade design tends to excel at.

FOUR CASE STUDIES OF INTEGRATION

This chapter will now examine four particular case studies of integration between procedural and handmade content: the modern roguelike game *Faster Than Light* (2012), the classic[27] roguelike game *Dungeon Crawl Stone Soup* (2006), the platformer-roguelike *Spelunky* (2008/2012), and classic roguelike game *Ultima Ratio Regum*. In doing so the chapter will both look closely at the different methods these games use to combine the two forms of contents, the benefits and drawbacks of these varied approaches, and subsequently utilize these examples to build a two-part typology of procedural-handmade integration: *vertical* integration, where a single thread of handmade content runs through the game, and *horizontal* integration, where handmade content can be readily exchanged for procedural content at any point in the game and vice versa.

Faster Than Light

In *Faster Than Light* (FTL), the player controls a spacecraft and its crew who move through eight sectors of space, each of which consists of a nodal map of checkpoints, with each node representing a particular place, event, or encounter and containing a planet, a sun, an asteroid field, or another stellar landmark in the background. The player is free to move between nodes within a given sector until advancing to the next sector, after which the previous sector cannot be revisited. As the player moves within a sector, the Rebel Fleet advances, shown by a curved line drawn across the map of nodes, and the player moving into any node behind the line results in a far more challenging battle than any in a nonoccupied node. In this manner the player moves from node to node, and in turn from sector to sector, while being pursued by the Rebel Fleet, which slowly but surely renders previous nodes and sectors unsafe for player travel. The majority of these nodes are one-off events: a single battle, a single event, a single planet, a shop, or something else noteworthy but unconnected to anything else on the nodal map(s). However, a small number feature handmade quests. These quests consist of multiple stages that are distributed, in a particular order, to multiple nodes, resulting in a small number of nodes being nonindependent and having the content accessed at that node connected to that at other nodes. In some of these quests rewards are distributed only when the final node is completed, and in others there are intermittent rewards at multiple nodes. In this regard brief moments of handmade narrative—as we have seen, traditionally a weakness of PCG—are interspersed with the otherwise procedurally generated occurrences at each node; certain nodes gain structure and importance over others, encouraging the player toward pursuing these minor stories (with the lure of greater rewards) over merely selecting nodes in order to reach the exit of each sector and maximize the number of nodes visited before moving on.

However, a problem arises in *FTL*—sometimes not all checkpoints required for a particular multinodal narrative are actually generated by the system-generating algorithm, *and* sometimes the player doesn't know which node subsequent to the first is important and which is not, and is therefore forced to gamble on picking the narratologically significant node over its one-off equivalents. This highlights a crucial necessity for games that seeks to place handmade content into otherwise procedural worlds when that handmade content might stretch over several areas of the game—a system needs to ensure that the full piece of handmade content can be placed and completed. Procedural level generation has a similar technique to this, known as floodfill, which is used to ensure that all parts of a generated level meet up and that no part of the level is cut off from the rest; similarly, a kind of narrative floodfill (whereby the game ensures the entire narrative can be placed before placing any of it) is necessary in an *FTL*-style scenario to ensure that the full handmade sequence can be successfully placed (or has been successfully placed). For those aiming to integrate this kind of handmade sequence in future games, two solutions seem to present themselves: either don't spawn any of the quest unless it can be completed (i.e., all the required categories of nodes/sectors are present), or have the game retroactively change later parts of the game world so that the quest can be finished, while also marking future parts of the quest so that the player never feels cheated out of the narrative segment by the bad luck of selecting the wrong nodes. This might not have functioned for *FTL*, since the player can see all the sectors in advance and would notice if they suddenly changed, but for games where the entire map is *not* visible beforehand, a method of this sort would work. Nevertheless, in the majority of situations where the multinodal quest system works, this integration of a multiple-step narrative segment distinguishes playthroughs from one another, changes up the pace and tone of the game from the otherwise universal sequence of procedural nodes, and encourages the player toward other considerations when choosing the next node or sector to travel to, even if this same system highlights a difficulty in a game like *FTL*.

Dungeon Crawl Stone Soup

Dungeon Crawl Stone Soup (*DCSS*) is a classic roguelike game where the player descends through dozens of PCG levels in search of the fabled Orb of Zot. On each floor the game's algorithms procedurally place rooms and corridors in a pattern unique to each playthrough, and subsequently distribute items, monsters, and dungeon features across these levels. The area of the dungeon the player is in and the depth to which they have descended combine to determine the possible choices of the algorithm in the placing of enemies, items, and so on. Although the majority of the individual rooms in *DCSS* are procedurally generated, a small number are handmade. These handmade rooms are called vaults. Each vault generally contains a particularly challenging gameplay scenario, a carefully crafted piece of thematic content, or a combination of the two. They offer a break from both the standard randomized distribution of monsters and items in the main dungeon and the lack of deeper meaning or coordination in the distribution of these elements. In vaults the player knows that each enemy and feature has been specifically placed with an intended meaning and purpose to collectively construct a planned whole.

The presence of a vault is almost always apparent in *DCSS* before the player enters. Most are of a distinctive shape that could rarely be mistaken for a procedural dungeon area; others have special doors, or initial hallways, or symmetrical layouts of features and patterns that likewise wouldn't be generated by algorithm. Once inside, vaults in *DCSS* of the gameplay-challenge variety tend to offer the player a choice: greater risk for greater reward, knowing that a human designer will have placed a more challenging selection of foes within the fault than the random placement of an algorithm, but also that a superior reward is likely present at the end of the trial (loot, as well as enemies, tends to be procedurally distributed in roguelikes). Vaults can generally be explored at any point the player desires; the staircase to the next floor will never be found within a vault, and thus the player knows these areas are optional. Just as the narrative nodes in *FTL* break up the sequence of procedural nodes, the vaults in *DCSS* serve a comparable purpose: they break up both the level aesthetics (it is immediately apparent which segments are handmade and which are procedural) and the flow of gameplay by encouraging the player to sometimes pause and consider whether to investigate the vault rather than continuing through the procedural melee. Additionally, and unlike *FTL*, *DCSS* is a game where the player can move freely between dungeon levels as often as desired. Vaults therefore also serve as a method for the player to track progress and register floors in the dungeon as distinct—one procedural level looks broadly like another, unless the player remembers a certain level as the level with a particularly deadly vault, or recognizes the unusual shape of another vault when looking back over the levels previously explored.

Spelunky

In *Spelunky* the player explores a sequence of procedurally generated platform levels. Each level has an entrance near the top from which the player's character emerges and an exit placed somewhere in the lower segments of the level. The player can run, jump, and deploy ropes in order to ascend to higher places or bombs in order to destroy segments of the level and descend to lower places (or damage enemies, break various objects, etc.). Each level consists of 16 rooms in a four-by-four grid—although the exact boundaries of these rooms is deliberately blurred in the hope of obfuscating the generative process—which are first placed in a sequence from entrance to exit to ensure that the level can actually be completed, and then additional rooms with additional paths are placed around the periphery. Each room, as defined by which sides of the room are open (so a room with an open ceiling and floor is distinct from a room with an open left side and an open floor) has around a dozen variations that can be selected. The precise tiles in each room (10 tiles horizontally, eight tiles vertically) are then also procedurally varied so that the same room across two levels should never appear to the player to be the same room, even if the macro-scale structure of that room is the same. There are also many overlying thematic differences between levels generated at certain stages of the game—The Mines, The Jungle, The Ice Caves, etc.—that affect the types of terrain, object, and enemy appearing in each level. There are also level feelings (a concept taken from classic roguelikes) that shift the generator in a certain single level in a certain way; the generator might decide to generate a level full of gravestones and undead enemies, for example, and give the player the message "The dead are restless!" as a clue upon entering that area. In summary, therefore, the player will almost certainly never visit the same generated level twice (either at the macro layer or the micro layer, though the former is a little more likely than the latter) and there are many layers of procedural generation that combine to make each playthrough highly distinctive.

Woven into these procedural levels is a handmade thread of secrets, consisting of a range of special items, special enemies, and special actions that must be performed by the player, all in a particular order, in order to access a secret level at the end of the game. The player must first find a key and a locked chest in the first world of the game (The Mines) and combine them to acquire the Udjat Eye item from the chest. This then enables the player to find the Black Market, a secret level where the player can purchase the Ankh item, which must then be taken to the third world, The Ice Caves, and upon reaching the level containing a large Moai statue, players must kill themselves in order to be resurrected and collect the Hedjet item. This must then be taken to The Temple and upon slaying a monster called Anubis, the player collects his or her scepter, which is then sacrificed to pass through a door into The City of Gold, wherein the player can locate the Book of the Dead. Lastly, the player progresses to what appears to be the final boss, who must then be manipulated (using the Book of the Dead as a kind of compass) into a particular sequence of actions that will unveil the entrance to Hell, the secret final area. This sequence must be followed precisely because each step is dependent on all prior steps, and once the player leaves a level, that level cannot be returned to; if a step is missed, Hell cannot be accessed on that playthrough. This sequence is always identical, and the possibility space of where each component might be found is the same—the key and chest are always somewhere in the earliest stages, the Moai always somewhere within the third world, and so on—but the specific challenges that must be overcome to acquire or complete each level varies depending on the PCG layouts of each level. This handmade quest plays out across otherwise algorithmic levels, offering a unique and handmade challenge for the most skilled and experienced players, and also a puzzle of sorts which contains a range of distinctive elements that would be difficult to generate via a procedural system.

Ultima Ratio Regum

Ultima Ratio Regum (URR) (2012), my own work, is a roguelike game in ongoing development based on the work of Umberto Eco, Jorge Borges, and the Italian literary collective Luther Blissett/Wu Ming. The player explores a vast procedurally generated world in search of scattered clues hinting toward an intellectual conspiracy hidden beneath the surface of the generated planet's societies. Whereas the above three games focus on what we might term quantitative procedural generation—creating levels, spaces, and areas of play, whether nodal, top-down, or platformer—*URR* instead emphasizes what I have come to define as qualitative procedural generation: the creation of cultural semantics, modes of speech, social norms, and so on. A detailed description and analysis of these processes is due to be published in future work, but it suffices to say that developing for the first time a class of algorithms capable of creating these more abstract concepts has been a challenging (if extremely fulfilling) design process, which has lead to a particular form of integration between the handmade and the procedural in *URR*. Almost all the generation systems in the game can output *either* a procedural output or a handmade one, which is to say that when the game considers what the altar for a particular religion should look like, for example, the game will normally generate the altar from a vast database (in the hundreds of millions) of potential altars, but will also sometimes select an altar from a far smaller (but *more rarely accessed*) database of handmade altars (Figure 11.1). When generating a coat of arms the game might piece together a range of components or select a handmade predesigned instance; when generating nicknames for important characters there is a spectrum of possibilities from a range of handmade nicknames to those constituted from thousands of randomly selected elements; when generating clothing the game selects from a range of archetypes with varying levels of procedurality (Figure 11.2); and this method is repeated across the majority of the game's generation systems.

The use of this system can be seen most strongly in the generation of *URR*'s buildings. Although primarily a traditional spatial form of procedural

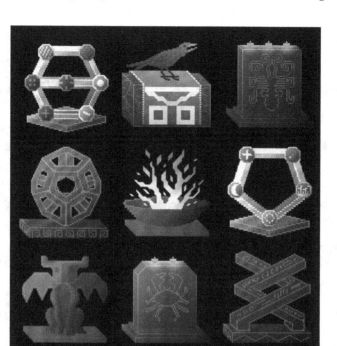

FIGURE 11.1　Range of religious altars from *URR*. Some are heavily procedurally generated with dozens of parts and variations, while others are closer to being entirely handmade. All three *URR* screenshots have been brightened slightly to improve their printed quality.

generation, the algorithms access the qualitative architectural preferences of each nation, and the buildings that are subsequently generated aim to reflect these; the religious buildings of a given religion should always be similar to each other and distinct from other places of worship; the fortresses of one nomadic people should not look anything like those of another but all should still be identifiable as belonging to the superset of fortresses; and so on. However, in the game's development it became clear that some buildings were easier to write in algorithmic form than others, an issue epitomized in the difference between cathedrals (the largest

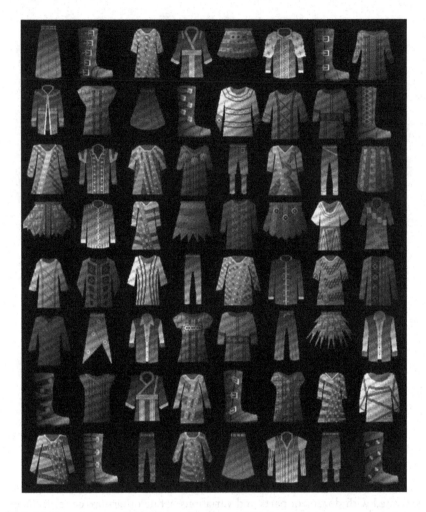

FIGURE 11.2 Range of clothing styles from *URR*. As with altars, some are heavily procedural, others less so, but the combination gives rise to upward of tens of millions of variations that are distributed to the game's nations and cultures.

religious buildings for any in-game religion, Figure 11.3) and mansions (the houses of the wealthiest individuals in any of the game's nations, Figure 11.4). Cathedrals were designed to be sprawling and expansive, and only *had* to contain a small number of things (crypts, altars, and so forth), allowing for great algorithmic freedom in their design and layout. In contrast, mansions were designed to be large but had a range of requirements for a range of important rooms and necessities, bedrooms, servant quarters, libraries, studies, dining halls, and the like. Cathedrals also proved simpler to generate because they tend to be large open structures with a

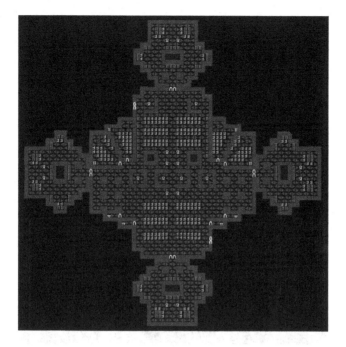

FIGURE 11.3 Screenshot of *URR* showing a cathedral. These structures are highly modular and vary widely in their layouts, interior decoration and design, the placement of furniture and relevant items, and so on.

small number of grand chambers; in contrast, a mansion would be full of corridors and smaller rooms that had to fit into the space available, generate every room required, and place themselves in a layout that actually looked as if an architect had designed it, instead of the far looser constraints on the placement of rooms and corridors in *DCSS* or other traditional dungeon crawl roguelikes. As discussed earlier in the chapter—the stronger the constraints, the more similar the generations, and every mansion generation was beginning to look far too similar. It therefore became apparent that cathedrals should be procedurally generated at both the macro and the micro level—in the placement of rooms and chambers and the contents of those chambers—whereas mansions should perhaps be handmade at the macro level while still ensuring a level of microprocedural generation to maximize their variation (similar to the rooms and in-room layouts of *Spelunky*). All buildings are a mixture of the handmade and the procedural, depending on both the requirements of that building and the complexity of those requirements, and this system also applies to the generation of almost everything else in the game world.

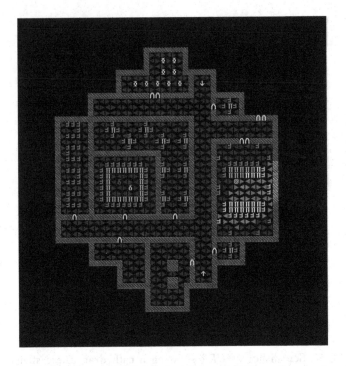

FIGURE 11.4 Screenshot of *URR* showing the ground floor of a mansion. In contrast to cathedrals, these vary less from playthrough to playthrough, and instead draw recourse to a large database of handmade variants.

An interesting observation was made in the process of pursuing this form of level design: players *cannot generally spot the difference.* As the game's designer I have received a range of comments from players asking me how the game procedurally generates something that is actually handmade, and how many handmade variations I sat down and wrote out for something that is actually procedural. The game has been designed such that *each can pass for the other.* It is important to note that this is not inherently true of this kind of integration—in *DCSS* the procedural and handmade rooms are obvious, and masking this difference is considered unimportant or perhaps even considered actively undesirable—but in *URR* the game's algorithms have been specifically built so that one looks indistinguishable from the other. The design rationale here was twofold: first, to ensure that the handmade variants could potentially be perceived as procedural, and in turn that the procedural variants are of a sufficient quality and level of detail that a player could mistake them for handmade, and second, that interspersing procedural variations with handmade ones allows the designer to ensure that at least some variations of a particular factor (cultures, religions, etc.) are guaranteed to yield interesting gameplay (although obviously the intention is that the procedural variations are, ideally, no less compelling). Further details of this blurring in player experience and perception between the procedural and the handmade remains a question for future research, but it is nevertheless apparent that this system has achieved the two goals above and is another model of procedural-handmade integration distinct from the three other case studies explored here. Having now explored all four case studies, the chapter will now examine what conclusions can be drawn from these varied yet comparable experiences of procedural-handmade integration.

DISCUSSION

We have now examined the rationales for procedural and handmade content, and introduced four games that have combined the two in a variety of ways. *Faster Than Light* distributes a quest across a range of nodes that the player will (under ideal conditions) encounter in a linear order as they move through the game; *Dungeon Crawl Stone Soup* contains algorithms that select sometimes from handmade vaults instead of simpler procedural rooms and makes the differences between these two explicit to any observant player; *Spelunky* distributes a guaranteed secret quest throughout the entire game even if the particular components of that quest are procedurally *placed* anew in each playthrough; *Ultima Ratio Regum* contains procedural systems designed to look handmade, and vice versa, simultaneously blurring the boundaries between these and allowing the designer to implement greater gameplay control than is traditionally associated with procedural content. Having previously identified three core rationales behind procedural content generation and two rationales for handmade design that deal with the shortcomings of PCG, we can now consider what rationales do these four games embody when they consider their procedural-handmade designs? *FTL* utilizes procedural generation to create replay and challenge, and handmade content for the imposition of narrative elements; *DCSS* also uses PCG for replay and challenge, but uses handmade content both to create narrative/thematic elements and to guarantee the placement of specific handmade instances of gameplay; *Spelunky* once again uses PCG for replay and challenge, but uses handmade content to place a complex and distinctive puzzle throughout its PCG levels; *Ultima Ratio Regum* uses PCG to assist in both replay and *exploration*, and deploys handmade content to guarantee specific instances of gameplay but not narrative or puzzle design.

Although the four games examined here offer four distinct methods of handmade/procedural integration, there are subsequently two clear higher-level models visible, which I term *vertical* and *horizontal* integration. The *vertical* model sees a single thread of the handmade running throughout the game (or part of the game), as in the chain of secrets in *Spelunky* or the multiple-node or multiple-system quests in *FTL*. The *horizontal* model, meanwhile, sees procedural and handmade content as readily interchangeable modules[28] in a given scenario of gameplay, as in the mix of procedural and handmade rooms and areas in *DCSS* or the author's own attempts to shuffle and interweave the two in almost all the content of *URR*. Vertical integration has handmade content following the linear progression of the game, while horizontal integration allows for procedural and handmade content to be switched out and exchanged in a given design slot—an item, an enemy, a room, and so on. A player engaging with vertical content is likely to find meaning and consistency that stretches across more of the game than a single instance (though what an instance consists of, and how we might define this, will naturally vary from game to game), while horizontal content tends to vary the nature of a specific instance of gameplay in situations where both procedural content, and previously handmade content, are equally valid (in terms of both programming and design).

Is one form of integration more suited to some tasks than the other? This question remains largely speculative with so few games of this sort to draw upon, and this chapter is naturally not an exhaustive survey of all such games, but there is nevertheless a pattern that can be identified from the four case studies here: the two games with vertical integration utilize handmade content to create narratives and puzzles, whereas the two games with horizontal integration seem more concerned by guaranteeing certain precise moments of gameplay and not leaving everything to the whim of the algorithm. These differences of course blur at the edges, but it is tougher to conceive of a system capable of switching out between handmade and procedural narrative or puzzle *elements* (especially the latter), or somehow deploying a single handmade gameplay scenario that stretches vertically throughout the entire game (while still making the rest of the game procedural), than it is to imagine long-running puzzles or narratives that the procedural elements are constructed around (*FTL* and *Spelunky*) or the ready exchangeability of distinct components contained within a certain moment or location of gameplay (*DCSS* and *URR*). In this regard it points toward two potential future paths for the development of procedural generation: improving and developing the generation of horizontally exchangeable narrative and puzzle elements, and the generation of larger vertical structures and patterns that are consistent throughout a game (e.g., Ref. 29). As this chapter has illustrated these are both currently almost exclusively the realm of handmade content and its integration into otherwise procedural gameplay experiences, but there remains significant ongoing work in these areas.

The design philosophies of *DCSS* and *URR* also raise another pertinent question: should designers make *overt* the differences between procedural and handmade elements (as in *DCSS*) or mask these as much as possible (as in *URR*)? A player who knows *FTL* and *Spelunky* in detail will readily identify the handmade and procedural segments, but playing these games it is clear that no particular intention exists to make the divide explicit. In *FTL* handmade nodes look just like procedural nodes until the player explores them; in *Spelunky* the handmade secrets are hidden (as befitting their *secret* status) but until the player knows the nature of the secret segments, it is not apparent that these are anything other than items, enemies, or levels procedurally distributed across the game world (which—albeit within strict and sequential constraints—they are). By contrast, both *DCSS* and *URR* take an explicit stance on this front: *DCSS* makes it extremely clear where the dividing line lies and uses this to aid in visual variation of the game world, the pacing of gameplay, and offering the player risk/reward choices; *URR* tries to blur the line between the procedural and handmade so that players cannot identify which is which, and does so in order to both ensure moments of particular gameplay and push upward the average quality of output from the game's predominantly procedural systems. In both of these cases the explicit decision to blur or not blur these lines has a particular gameplay purpose, and therefore this decision appears to be one of significant importance for game designers seeking to integrate both procedural and handmade design; "Should players be able to see which is which?" is an important question to consider before creating any PCG systems, as it will inevitably influence the design of those systems. Such a decision is ultimately dependent on how procedural and handmade content are combined, and what the gameplay effects of making this divide obvious will be. In some games this may be very desirable, while in others it may give the player information about important and unimportant aspects of the game world that the designers would rather leave players to *discover* rather than simply *notice*. Future work in the field might seek to categorize the nature of handmade content in all procedural games and attempt to codify and define additional design rationales for making this divide clear or covert.

This chapter has examined the rationales behind the use of procedurally generated content in level design, outlined the gaps filled by handmade content in otherwise procedurally generated games and why handmade content is used in this way, examined four case studies of such procedural-handmade integration, analyzed these four different models, their similarities and differences, and the rationales they speak to, and codified these models into a two-part typology and highlighted the differences between these two approaches. In doing so it has sought to serve as both a theoretical analysis of the ways to integrate procedural and handmade content and the advantages and disadvantages of these techniques, and the unexpected complexities and considerations in taking such an approach (primarily the question of whether each type of content should be explicit as belonging to one form or the other), and has touched on the player-side experiences of experiencing these games and engaging with both kinds of content during gameplay. Equally, this chapter also has a practical design-oriented agenda, seeking to concisely explore a wide range of issues around procedural-handmade integration and serve as a guide to best practice (and potential pitfalls) for developers pursuing a mixed design, while simultaneously identifying future agendas for research into both procedural-handmade integration and procedural generation in its own right (primarily for narrative and puzzle generation), and how such techniques might be combined with existing research and practice into both PCG and vertical and horizontal PCG-handmade integrations.

REFERENCES

1. Prachyabrued, Mores, Timothy E. Roden, and Ryan G. Benton. Procedural generation of stylized 2d maps. *Proceedings of the International Conference on Advances in Computer Entertainment Technology*. ACM, 2007:147–150.
2. Togelius, Julian, Georgios N. Yannakakis, Kenneth O. Staney, and Cameron Browne. Search-based procedural content generation: A taxonomy and survey. *IEEE Transactions on Computational Intelligence and AI in Games*, 2010, 3.3:172–186.
3. Zafar, Adeel. An experiment in automatic content generation for platform games. *IEEE 9th International Conference on Emerging Technologies*, 2013:1–5.

4. Dawson, Adam. How procedural generation is making games more interesting. *METALEATER*, 2010. Accessed online, available at http://metaleater .com/video-games/feature/how-procedural-generation-is-making-games -more-interesting.

5. Blake, Boston. Game Rant asks: What's the ideal length of a video game? *GameRant*, 2015. Accessed online, available at http://gamerant.com/video -game-completion-time-length-discussion-the-order/.

6. Khan, Zarmena. Quality vs quantity: The growing dilemma of video game length, *Playstation Lifestyle*, 2015. Accessed online, available at http://www .playstationlifestyle.net/2015/01/12/dilemma-of-video-game-length/.

7. Makuch, Eddie. Does game length matter? *Gamespot*, 2015. Accessed online, available at http://www.gamespot.com/articles/does-game-length -matter/1100-6425375/.

8. Tassi, Paul. The Witcher 3' and game length as a mountain to climb. *Forbes*, 2015. Accessed online, available at http://www.playstationlifestyle .net/2015/01/12/dilemma-of-video-game-length/.

9. Ermi, Laura, and Frans Mäyrä. Fundamental components of the gameplay experience: Analysing immersion. *Worlds in Play: International Perspectives on Digital Games Research*, 2005, 37:37–55.

10. Gilleade, Kiel, Alan Dix, and Jen Allanson. Affective videogames and modes of affective gaming: Assist me, challenge me, emote me. *DiGRA 2005: Changing Views—Worlds in Play*, 2005.

11. Sweetser, Penelope, and Peta Wyeth. GameFlow: A model for evaluating player enjoyment in games. *Computers in Entertainment (CIE)*, 2005, 3:3:1–24.

12. Juul, Jesper, and Marleigh Norton. Easy to use and incredibly difficult: On the mythical border between interface and gameplay. In *Proceedings of the 4th International Conference on Foundations of Digital Games*, 2009:107–112.

13. Yu, Derek. The full spelunky on Spelunky. *Make Games*. Accessed on 31/10/2015, available at http://makegames.tumblr.com/post/4061040007/the -full-spelunky-on-spelunky.

14. Kelly, George, and Hugh McCabe. A survey of procedural techniques for city generation. *Institute of Technology Blanchardstown Journal*, 2006, 14:87–130.

15. Lauro, Christina. MMO mechanics: Procedural generation is the future. *Engadget*, 2014. Accessed online, available at http://www.engadget.com /2014/02/26/mmo-mechanics-procedural-generation-is-the-future/.

16. Lendvai, Piroska, Thierry Declerck, Sándor Darányi, Pablo Gervás, Raquel Hervás, Scott Malec, and Federico Peinado. Integration of linguistic markup into semantic models of folk narratives: The fairy tale use case. In *Proceedings of the Seventh conference on International Language Resources and Evaluation (LREC'10)*, 2010.

17. Fernández-Vara, Clara, and Alec Thomson. Procedural generation of narrative puzzles in adventure games: The puzzle-dice system. In *Proceedings of the Third Workshop on Procedural Content Generation in Games*, 2012.

18. Kybartas, Ben, and Clark Verbrugge. Analysis of ReGEN as a graph-rewriting system for Quest Generation. *IEEE Transactions on Computational Intelligence and AI in Games*, 2014, 6(2):228–242.
19. Li, Boyang, and Mark Riedl. Scheherazade: Crowd-powered interactive narrative generation. In *Twenty-Ninth AAAI Conference on Artificial Intelligence*, 2015.
20. Tearse, Brandon Robert, Noah Wardrip-Fruin, and Michael Mateas. Minstrel remixed: Procedurally generating stories. In *AIIDE*, 2010.
21. Chang, Hsueh-Min, and Von-Wun Soo. Planning-based narrative generation in simulated game universes. *IEEE Transactions on Computational Intelligence and AI in Games*, 2009, 3:200–213.
22. Colton, Simon. Automated puzzle generation. In *Proceedings of the AISB'02 Symposium on AI and Creativity in the Arts and Science*, 2002.
23. Nitsche, Michael, Calvin Ashmore, Will Hankinson, Rob Fitzpatrick, John Kelly, and Kurt Margenau. Designing procedural game spaces: A case study. *Proceedings of FuturePlay 2006*, 2006.
24. Hendrikx, Mark, Sebastiaan Meijer, Joeri Van Der Velden, and Alexandru Iosup. Procedural content generation for games: A survey. *ACM Transactions on Multimedia Computing, Communications, and Applications (TOMM)*, 2013, 9(1):1.
25. Smith, Adam M., Eric Butler, and Zoran Popovic. Quantifying over play: Constraining undesirable solutions in puzzle design. In *FDG*, 2013, pp. 221–228.
26. Thomson, Alec. A system for procedurally generating puzzles for games. PhD dissertation, Massachusetts Institute of Technology, 2013.
27. Johnson, M. R. The use of ASCII graphics in roguelikes. In *Games and Culture*, published online, available at http://gac.sagepub.com/content/early/2015/05/15/1555412015585884.
28. Cook, Michael, and Simon Colton. A rogue dream: Automatically generating meaningful content for games. *Papers from the 2014 AIIDE Workshop*, 2014:2–8. Accessed online, available at http://popelka.ms.mff.cuni.cz/~cerny/WS-14-16.pdf.
29. Kerssemakers, Manuel et al. "A procedural level generator." *2012 IEEE Conference on Computational Intelligence and Games* (CIG). IEEE, 2012.

CHAPTER 12

Level Design Planning for Open-World Games

Joel Burgess

CONTENTS

THIS CHAPTER IS ABOUT A TECHNIQUE for planning and organizing the development of any video game with a large number of individual locations spread around a big environment. These are often called *open-world* games, including examples from the *Grand Theft Auto* and *Assassin's Creed* series, and some that I have worked on, such as *Fallout 4* and *The Elder Scrolls V: Skyrim*.

There is no definitive way to build any particular creative work, including—and perhaps especially—those of significant enough scale to require a large team of collaborators. The techniques I have used in my own career have constantly changed, evolved, been scuttled, reconsidered, and revisited. When I began working on open-world games, there was no manual for creating them, none exists today, nor do I presume to create one now. I have only tried to learn from what has come before and apply new ideas and techniques, keeping what works, and discarding or modifying what doesn't. I also try to remain open to the fact that the creative goals of a game should shape the process of creating it, not the other way around. By this standard, assuming that every game is unique and distinct, there cannot be any process that will serve one game's development process as well as it will the next.

That said, this chapter will attempt to represent accumulated knowledge from my career thus far. This includes wisdom as it applied to specific games, but presented in a way I hope will be generalized enough to make the distillation of principles as easy as possible, allowing the reader to adapt the information to his or her own projects.

THE THREE ELEMENTS OF WORLD PLANNING

The technique I'm describing will take advantage of three elements, each of which is essentially a piece of living documentation that can be used to plan and track the level design for a large-scale, open-world game. Further, I will briefly outline an implementation process that relies on these elements as the foundation for a workflow with iteration as a core value.

The Map

The main spatial feature of an open-world game is, as you might guess, the world. The map is the most literal representation of the game in its physical sense, and will be a central tool for understanding and creating the game world.

The Master List

A master list of locations, often put together in a program like Microsoft Excel, will also be used to track a wide range of filterable and sortable data per location, and provides the best data-driven view of the game world from a high level. It's an excellent tool for visualizing and comparing data in many forms, making it handy throughout development as an aid for analyzing the game in many ways. While the list can be tracked in whatever software you prefer, this chapter assumes Microsoft Excel.

The Location Directory

While the master list will provide a view from orbit, the directory is a place where each location can have its own dedicated space for expanded information. While you can build the directory in a collaborative software package of your choosing, this chapter assumes a Mediawiki implementation.

THE WORLD MAP

In my experience, a world map (or maps, if your game has multiple open-world areas) is the first and most vital asset for planning a large, free-roaming space. Maps of any kind, never mind those specific to video games, convey a tremendous amount of information. A huge amount of information can be conveyed instantly upon viewing. Your game map can quickly communicate the setting, its general scale, the regions within it, and key anchor locations that will begin to define the exploration points within the space. Studying and internalizing the map throughout development will give you a deep and nuanced familiarity with the world. This section will help guide you through the process of planning the world map and predicting how it will look and feel in-game, and how it will differ from a real-world counterpart.

Because it can summarize a wealth of information in such an intuitive way, the map is perhaps the most vital piece of game design documentation that can exist for an open-world game. In the early stages of development it will help unify the team perceptions of what the identity and scope of the world will be. Throughout development it will help guide decisions such as difficulty curve, quest routes, and density of locations or activities. When the game is done, this same map will likely be presented to players through its in-game counterpart and sometimes a physical map.

The actual creation of the map requires several decisions and considerations that will be described in detail throughout this section:

- Where does the game take place?

- Is this a real-world location or something entirely fictional?

- What subregions exist within the map?

- What is the scale of the map, and how dense will it be?

- Can it be plotted with in-game units to determine the actual playable size?

- What major geographical features exist?

- Does the world contain natural boundary features you can take advantage of?

Where Does the Game Take Place?

It is very likely that you will already know the setting of your game before beginning work on the world map. Try to understand what is important to represent visually. Are you working on a real-world location? If so, what parts of that area are critical to include? If the setting is fictional, are there elements of real locations you hope to include? Do you have key features you know of now, like major geographical features or thoroughfares? Get as much of this information internalized as possible as you prepare.

Working with a real-world location is a double-edged sword. Even the most mundane real-world location will have a great deal of preexisting history and culture to draw from. And unlike a fictional location, you will not need to think too deeply about how and why the geography was formed. But real-world locations can also be a bit of a burden, because you're beholden to accurately represent the location and frequently need to choose between accuracy and gameplay.

In my experience, working with a real-world location requires a significant amount of research and preparation. Achieving an authentic feel requires a slightly deeper understanding of what makes a region feel unique than can be accomplished with an afternoon of Internet research, especially if your project will take significant license with the specifics. This is often necessary because a 100% accurate, street-for-street recreation will almost never translate to a great gameplay experience. Creating compelling versions of

Boston and Washington, DC for the *Fallout* series, for example, was more an exercise in getting the relative positions and surroundings correct for certain landmarks while highlighting the most evocative elements possible and omitting less useful details. *Fallout 3* often feels most familiar when exploring the visually distinct metro system, for example, and *Fallout 4* placed a lot of emphasis on the series of corridor avenues throughout Back Bay.

Subregions

A fantasy location such as Skyrim, however, has almost no requirement to stick to a predefined set of characteristics (caveat: there is *some* of this in the form of fictional canon) but also demands more from the creators in terms of determining how the landmass should be composed and made to feel like a believable place with a distinct sense of identity. When development on *Skyrim* was at its earliest stages, some members of the development team had a hard time picturing how the frozen north of Tamriel—a location mostly described in text only thus far—would be an interesting enough world to explore for dozens of hours. It fell to the environment art team to research and present the surprising variety of subarctic climates that would be represented as the many regions of Skyrim, only a minority of which would be the snow-choked landscape originally pictured by many.

Many of the subregions in Skyrim are actually based on seasonal changes, even though there are no seasons simulated in the game. The Rift region is always autumnal, Haafingar invokes a bleak winterscape, and Falkreath's pine forests are perennially in springtime. These kinds of subregions offer variety within the larger scope of your open world.

Creating a believable transition from one subregion to another can be challenging, so be sure to leave ample room to blend between them, otherwise the regions may not feel credible. It's sometimes possible to use geographical features to transition more quickly, however. The top of a sheer cliff ridge could be region A, while region B below may feel very different, even though they are topographically adjacent. Bodies of water also neatly bisect region boundaries and can make it easier for players to tolerate rapid shifts. In Skyrim, Riverwood's titular river eases the transition from the relatively verdant town area into the snow-choked mountain trail to Bleak Falls Barrow. Similarly, the Charles River in *Fallout 4* helps to contain the urban sprawl of Boston. Elsewhere in *Fallout 4*, areas of heavy destruction (e.g., craters) were used to quickly cut off an area that otherwise would have required lengthy tapering of architectural features from heavily urban to open wilderness.

As important as it is to establish the world map to a high level of detail early on, there is no real need to do this for the interior locations that will exist within that world. It's good to know a bit of information about each, which we'll explore next with the directory. The physical specifics of interiors have much less impact at this point, so there's no real benefit in spending time on their maps and layouts until the creation of a specific location is ready to begin.

Scale and Density

The scale of your world can be measured in a few different ways. The most obvious is the physical extent of the map and its boundaries. How big is your world compared to the size of the player and his or her ability to traverse it? If your game engine has a known, core unit of measurement, use this as early as possible to make sure you're generally aware of how your map scale will translate to in-game dimensions.

If representing a real-world location, consider the boundaries as they would exist on an actual world map. How large or small a segment of the world are you hoping to represent? Will the location need to be dramatically compressed to fit your game scale? What natural boundaries exist that might be useful as world boundaries in your game?

Another sort of scale to consider is point of interest (POI) density, or the general frequency with which players will be encountering hot spots of interest, geographical or otherwise. When analyzing an open-world game, I personally consider this to be the most useful metric to keep in mind. There is no best POI density to aim for, but be mindful that it will have a strong impact on the pacing of exploration in your game. A high POI density (especially when combined with high visibility) will result in a world with a theme park feel, while a low POI density can result in a world that feels very sparse and vast. It's up to you where along the spectrum your game should end up.

A few examples of POI density in action: the *Just Cause* games have a relatively sparse density; getting from one place to the next often involves navigating roadways through relative emptiness, just as one would expect in the type of environment they represent. *Grand Theft Auto* (*GTA*) games are denser, with the locations of (their primarily urban) worlds pushed generally closer together than in the real world. *GTA* games assume players use vehicles to move around them quickly, however, so the POI density of a *GTA* world would feel much sparser if the game was on-foot only. The *Legend of Zelda* games, as another example, tend to have very high POI density, with almost no buffer area between points of interest. *Ocarina of Time*, however, introduces horseback riding, and those portions of the world have much lower POI density. Many games have this kind of non-uniform POI density. The downtown regions of both *GTAV* and *Fallout 4* are highly dense, while the outlying areas are much sparser, with small pockets of density representing rural towns. This results in areas of the map that not only look different for world-building reasons, but can also play very differently.

Major Geographical Features

When choosing your location, it's likely you are already aware of certain geographical features that are going to influence the map. These kinds of features will have trickle-down impact on the world, often beyond what you may initially anticipate.

Whether your location is based on the real world or entirely fictional, it's good to understand how the geography was formed so physical characteristics of the landscape feel like they belong. You should also think about the various eras of the land. How has it been used by people? Where is the terrain unforgiving, and where is travel easy? What natural disasters and other landscape-altering phenomena have occurred? How high is the water table, and where will water need to deal with elevation changes?

Try to include orienting features in the landscape, if possible. The tallest mountain in Skyrim, High Hrothgar, lies at the center of the playable area, allowing players to orient themselves in relation to this from almost anywhere in the exterior world. Likewise, the Boston skyline in *Fallout 4* is designed to be recognizable from a distance. The height of Boston's financial district acts as a natural anchor for the harbor area, and the fictional Mass Fusion building, the tallest skyscraper, features a distinctive crown shape to stand out in silhouette. This pairs with Trinity Tower (loosely based on the real-world Hancock Building) in Back Bay, which sits apart from the financial district and offers a two-point system of orientation.

Water features are powerful for navigation, as well. Rivers create natural highways for players to discover and follow. Water flow can indicate direction and lead toward or away from a point of interest. Water also tends to serve as a natural barrier, and a span of water will tend to feel like a further distance than that same span of dry land. Note that player aversion to water can vary, depending on your game mechanics. Water in *Fallout 3* and *Fallout 4* typically carries the threat of radiation exposure, for example. Another game may treat water as a powerful place to evade detection or hide secrets, however, drawing players not only toward water, but into it.

Boundaries

Because water tends to be a natural repellant in open-world games, it's often the ideal world boundary. Many open-world games feature coastal or island environments, in part because of how useful water is as an alternative to a more artificial boundary type.

Artificial boundaries are generally considered undesirable in open-world games, but sometimes they are unavoidable. It's possible in most Bethesda Game Studios' games, for example, to reach the edge of the playable area, collide with an invisible wall, and be presented with a simple "You cannot go that way" notification.

Water, as mentioned, works well. Games such as *Jak & Daxter* or *GTAV* will allow players to swim into deep, world-bounding bodies of water, only to be pursued (and eventually eaten) by some invincible sea monster. *Ark: Survival Evolved* will eventually present players with an invisible go-no-further wall in the ocean, but features difficult marine enemies and exhaustion mechanics that make reaching the artificial boundary unlikely for a player to do under normal circumstances.

Other geographic features, such as cliffs or thick marshes, can provide additional natural world boundaries. Certain manmade elements can work as well. Exercise caution with these, however. Relying on structural boundaries, such as fences or retaining walls, can have an adverse impact if the structure ends up drawing the curious player toward it. Respecting a buffer of boring space prior to the world boundary may be the better option. Also be sure that the area *beyond* the boundary, if players are able to look into it, has no landmark or other attraction object (including wandering enemies) that may make the boundary more frustrating.

Keep all of this in mind when determining the world map. The more natural boundaries your location permits, the better equipped you will be to provide an overall positive player experience in the final game.

THE LOCATION MASTER LIST

While the map is being defined, you can also begin working on a master list of locations that will appear on the map.

This master list can be tracked however you wish. I have found that Excel works best for keeping information central, sortable, and easy to update. This chapter will refer to some specific tips for Excel, but most of the techniques should be adaptable to other tools.

The first thing necessary is defining a plotting system, which for most maps can be a simple *X/Y* coordinate (or longitude/latitude) grid. I recommend using a unit of measurement that corresponds to the native units of your game. In Bethesda's Creation Engine, for example, a cell is a conceptual unit (similar to an acre) that has remained relatively consistent since *Morrowind*. (The master list is actually called the cell list at Bethesda Game Studios.) This consistency will make the locations easy to track in the game and also provide a sense of knowable scale for dev team members.

There are many things to consider when structuring and using the master list. This section will explore the types of information you need to gather before working in Excel, and the steps to take when making your own master list:

- Anchor locations

- Other key locations

- Draw the map

- Wish list of locations

- Plot for desired density

- Add footprint radii

- Distribute encounters and art styles

- Chart activity routes

Anchor Locations

Chances are that you will be aware of certain key locations very early on, which must exist for reasons like story, navigation, or real-world accuracy. For example, you may know that the game will include a mountain stronghold for the villain, a gigantic tree that is visible from all points on the map, or a major tourist attraction.

These locations can be thought of as anchors. Their relative position to each other and other features (such as coastline) will be a point of early consideration. Even at the earliest stage of planning, a loosely sketched map indicating the relative position of each anchor location is probably possible. You may be confident that a certain key point will be situated in the southeastern extent of the map, for example, or that a particular house must be along the north shore of a particular lake.

Anchor locations aren't the only ones that can be documented and planned for at this stage. The master list can be expanded to include virtually every location that will appear in the final game.

Other Key Locations

In addition to your anchor locations, there may be other sites within the game map that are vital but don't require a lot of early specifics in terms of physical location. This may be some location where a key story event must take place, for example. It's important to be sure these key locations are accounted for on your master list, even if their exact position will not be nailed down until later. This is because the list will be used for scheduling, planning, and organization. This can also be important if you are interested in tracking the progression of a particular series of events through the game world.

For example, the *Fallout 4* master list included a column in which a location could be associated with a quest line (if applicable) and the numerical identifier for that quest. With that information, it was trivial to visualize the physical journey that quest line would take the player on. This made it easy to catch potential problems, such as an early-game quest attempting to send the player into a location balanced for end-game difficulty, and vice versa, or realizing that certain regions of the world were over- or underutilized by quests.

Draw the Map

Actually creating the visual for a map can be a difficult and time-consuming artistic process. It's nice to have a beautiful piece of cartography at this point, if that's available. But if not, that's okay. The main requirements for a drawn map right now are relatively simple. Any line drawing with roughly accurate proportions will do. As long as the height:width ratio is reliable, you can update the visual map as it evolves. That is, if your final world map is likely to be an equilateral square, mimic that shape now. If it's a widescreen rectangle, mimic that. It's not the end of the world if this must change later, but it's best to avoid this, as it can introduce some hassles down the line. Also note that this map should *not* include any visual information plotting specific locations on it. This is because we'll be feeding location data to Excel, which will overlay visual plots at the appropriate coordinates. It's okay to have these markers for other reasons, but be sure those redundant details are removed from the version you use in Excel. The reasons for this will become clearer later in this section.

Wish List of Locations

With all anchor and other key locations accounted for, you may have a wish list of additional locations. These are locations that command lower priority but would be nice to have. Examples could include a minor landmark from the real world, a novel idea for a specific point of interest, infrastructure sites that build world credibility, or any other tempting idea you want to account for ahead of time.

If you have a target number of overall locations, build your wish list large enough to, when taken with the anchor/key locations, roughly equal that target. This will help you overscoping the project early on and maintain your ability to meet scheduling goals.

Create Spreadsheet and Chart

At this point, you're ready to create your Excel document.

First, create a worksheet/tab in which each location is documented on its own row, with columns for (at least) the name, horizontal coordinate, and vertical coordinate (I use x/y for horiz/vert). You will probably want to use additional columns for additional data, as seen in this example (Table 12.1). We'll add and use some more columns like this as we refine the spreadsheet.

The second worksheet will house a scatter graph. Scatter graphs are used to plot data on both the horizontal *and* vertical axes, making them useful for simulation of a two-dimensional map. Ours will use coordinates identified in the first worksheet and produce a chart that will be placed over our sketched map, which will be used as a background in the plot area. Therefore, you should populate this chart with X/Y data from the corresponding columns in your locations worksheet. For this example, we will continue to use the UK (and Ireland) sample from above. With default settings, the initial scatter graph will look something like Figure 12.1.

There are several steps you can take to improve the visual quality of this chart. Most of these functions are accessed in Excel by right-clicking the area of the chart you wish to modify, and choosing Format.

TABLE 12.1   Basic Location List with Coordinates and Data

Name	X	Y	Designer	Quest
London	5	−6	Brutus of Troy	AN101
Dublin	−2	−3	Brian Boru	AN208
Manchester	3	−2	Roger Poitou	N/A
Edinburgh	1	2	David Choluim	N/A
Isle of Man	0	−1	Magnus Haakonsson	VK302

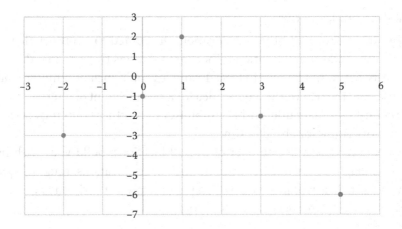

FIGURE 12.1   Scatter graph of locations before modification.

Set manual min/max bounds on both axes. These should be set to perfectly match the aspect ratio of the playable-area map you have. My example map of the United Kingdom has eight horizontal cells and 10 vertical,
so I can make sure those line up well.

Also on each axis: set the Label Position to Low, High, or None, depending on your preferences.

Format Plot Area and set to "Picture or texture fill," then use the "Insert
picture from file" option to choose your map image.

Scale your chart area (you can eyeball this or manually enter values in
Excel to ensure precision) so that individual grids are equilateral squares.
If this is giving you trouble, consider adding gridlines to the background
image you are using and employ those as guides.

Format Data Series plot points, if you would like something more leg-
ible than the default. It's possible to use icon images, if you have specific
plot images you would like to see. I prefer a simple white circle (from the
built-in marker shapes) with a dark gray outline, which provides good
contrast against most backgrounds.

At this point your chart may look something like the example in
Figure 12.2.

Plot for Desired Density

Once the spreadsheet is set up and working, you're ready to fill out your
locations worksheet with all of the anchor, key, and wish list locations.
You'll begin to get a feel for the POI density of the world simply by studying

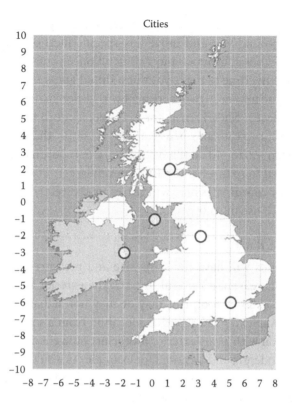

FIGURE 12.2 An example UK/Ireland map with simple location plots rendered as scatter graph data.

the location plots appearing on the scatter map as you type. You can watch this happen in real time by creating an additional view.

In Excel, choose View > New Window, then Arrange All > Vertical > Windows of active workbook > OK, and use the new window to display the map's worksheet.

Note that if your map isn't updating, check the data range in your scatter chart and ensure it encompasses a large number of fields in your respective columns for horizontal/vertical coordinates. I usually ask Excel to plot from about twice as many row entries as I expect I'll need, to minimize the odds I'll ever enter values outside the data range and be confused as to why they are not appearing.

Keep an eye on how compressed or sparse your map feels, and compare this to your expectations for the desired POI density of the game. It's very quick and easy to move things around in this spreadsheet, so play with coordinates and find a distribution that feels right to you. Use your anchor locations to ground you and move less-specific locations around freely. Relocating a POI will be much more difficult once you begin building the world, so take the time to make your best initial guess at this stage.

Note that you may need to experiment with different unit scales depending on your needs. My UK map, for example, is much too compressed if our goal were to create an open-world game set in that area. Instead of spanning from −10 to +10 on the vertical axis, my coordinates for the same space may need to span −100 to +100, or even larger. Try, if at all possible, to ensure your coordinates here will correspond directly to the coordinate system you will use in your game!

Add Footprint Radii

Not all locations will have the same size and presence in your physical world. For this reason, it's useful to track the exterior footprint of each. Note that the exterior footprint may or may not actually correspond to the overall complexity and scope of a location from a scheduling point of view. A location with a tiny exterior footprint could entail a lot of work if it hides a vast underground location, for example, as would a location where a complicated scripted event takes place. That kind of scope is useful to track as well, but in a separate column.

I've added a few new locations to my worksheet for the UK/Ireland example, and given them all footprint values according to a loose standard I've chosen of small, medium, or large (Sm, Md, Lg), as seen in Table 12.2.

While I can already use column filtering to hide or show all locations of a certain footprint, it's also useful to have this information available at

TABLE 12.2   Location List with Footprint Data Column

Name	X	Y	Footprint
London	5	−6	Lg
Dublin	−2	−3	Md
Manchester	3	−2	Md
Edinburgh	1	2	Lg
Isle of Man	0	−1	Sm
Aberdeen	3	4	Sm
Cork	−5	−5	Sm
Belfast	−2	−1	Md
Plymouth	1	−8	Sm
Inverness	0	4	Sm
Newcastle	3	0	Md

a glance. For this, we can set up footprint rings. The process is relatively simple, but requires a little bit of setup in Excel. Those interested in following along can refer to a brief tutorial at the end of this chapter.[i]

When done correctly, designers should have a sheet containing only the X/Y values of locations with an Md footprint, as seen in Table 12.3.

Note that you can use conditional formatting to hide the N/A values, making them a little less intrusive. While handy for work-checking I do *not* recommend leaving conditional formatting rules in place. They can significantly affect performance when used with big, processing-intensive documents like this one will become for a very large game. I've had complex Excel files crash my computer just as often as complex, in-development games have.

Next, repeat the whole process to create two more columns, this time looking for Lg footprint values. We needn't worry about Sm values for now. You'll see why soon. The example in Table 12.4 shows this completed (more advanced Excel users will realize there are much faster ways to propagate this work across the new columns; for the sake of brevity I am leaving that out).

With such a separate, filtered list of coordinates, we can plot these as new data series in the map chart. Tutorial steps for this are also available at the end of the chapter.[ii]

Figure 12.3 shows what my example map looks like with these radii displayed.

Here is a version of the map with simple circles to indicate large and medium footprints. This is really just a clever trick. Excel doesn't know anything about our location sizes, but by creating our data the way we have, it will now keep everything in sync automatically. If we wanted to

TABLE 12.3   A Formula-Filtered List, in Which Only the Coordinates for "Md" Spaces Are Referenced

Md X	Md Y
N/A	N/A
−2	−3
3	−2
N/A	N/A
N/A	N/A
N/A	N/A
N/A	N/A
−2	−1
N/A	N/A
N/A	N/A
3	0

TABLE 12.4 Formula-Filtered Lists for both "Md" and "Lg" Coordinate Sets

Md X	Md Y	Lg X	Lg Y
N/A	N/A	5	−6
−2	−3	N/A	N/A
3	−2	N/A	N/A
N/A	N/A	1	2
N/A	N/A	N/A	N/A
N/A	N/A	N/A	N/A
N/A	N/A	N/A	N/A
−2	−1	N/A	N/A
N/A	N/A	N/A	N/A
N/A	N/A	N/A	N/A
3	0	N/A	N/A

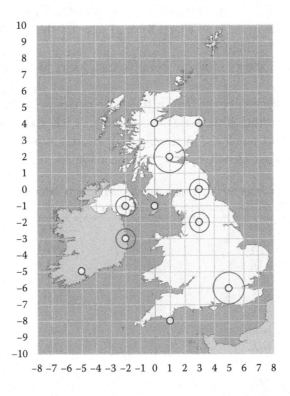

FIGURE 12.3 Secondary chart plots can be used to render a radius marker around medium and large locations.

add a new radius type it would be necessary to go through the same steps. Note that you can also hide these radii if they are ever in the way. Excel experts familiar with the VBScript language can create a custom button to do this. The simplest way, however, is simply to right-click the map, edit data, and uncheck the radii data series you wish to hide temporarily.

Distribute Encounters and Art Styles

This is a good time to introduce new columns to the locations worksheet for tracking additional data such as architectural style, overall scope, difficulty, activity, enemy type, or whatever other distinguishing information is important for your game's locations. You can then filter via these columns in the locations worksheet, which will automatically filter and hide the corresponding plots in your map. This is extremely useful for checking on many aspects of your map, such as making sure your zombie dungeons are well-distributed, or visualizing clusters of factory locations specific to a certain industrial subregion of the map. In my experience, this spreadsheet is one of the most useful pieces of documentation throughout the duration of an open-world project, in large part because of the power it grants to visualize and analyze information in response to a variety of questions and problems that may arise during implementation and playtesting.

It's entirely possible to add a new data series to your map to display this kind of information with unique plot icons. However, I generally rely on filtering for this. I have also set up alternate maps with entirely unique sets of data and custom icons for things like enemy or difficulty tracking. This can be done using the same exact method shown for the footprint radii above. It's all a matter of what information matters to you.

Chart Activity Routes

One example of an alternate map would be one which charts the route through the world that a player will follow during a certain activity or questline. See Figure 12.4 for an idea of what the end result of such a map might look like.

To set this up, I created a new worksheet with a simple set of data for a series of quests defined as AN, in the order they appear to the player. That list looks something like Table 12.5.

I then created a new data series that plots this information and customized the series to show no marker, but display a dotted line. These controls are also in the format data series menu. I also changed the sort order in the Select Data window to visually layer this series below all others.

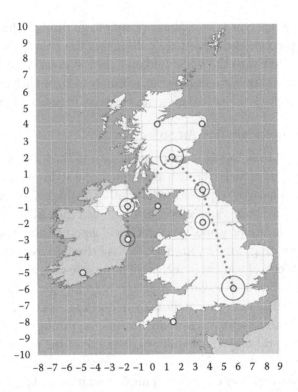

FIGURE 12.4   A simple line element can be generated to chart a basic routing map between key points in the world, such as locations visited during a quest line.

TABLE 12.5   A Custom List of Quest Destinations, in Chronological Order

Quest ID	Location	X	Y
AN101	London	5	−6
AN102	Newcastle	3	0
AN201	Edinburgh	1	2
AN202	Belfast	−2	−1
AN301	Dublin	−2	−3

Note that I've chosen *not* to reference my main list of locations. Instead, I created the new list above, using copy and paste. There are two main reasons for this.

First: order matters. When using marker lines, Excel looks at the order in which data appears to know where each line in the series must originate and terminate. My primary location list is ordered by location ID, not quest ID. Quests change a lot during development, and I don't want to keep reordering my list. Doing so can wreck your data, sometimes in ways that are not obvious until it's too late to reverse the damage, especially if multiple users need to access and alter this file. Rather than take the risk of accidentally creating and saving a bad filter, I create a "dumb" data set. (I've simply had too many instances of bad luck to be less paranoid! Consider this a reminder to always use version control software for critical documents like this one.)

The second reason I do this is simple: I don't need constant access to this visualization. Charting a quest route can be a very useful aid to certain conversations and analyses, like cross referencing a quest route against the difficulty of regions in the map. Since I only need this kind of information once in a while, it's a lot easier and less risky to just set it up dumb. If and when I need to revisit, I just need to update the data set manually. If I did require frequent access to this kind of visualization, I would be more likely to spend the additional time and attention setting it up as a dynamic version of the main master list.

This is just one example of how the master list can come in handy for analyzing data. There are many times I've needed to analyze and discuss world location data and been glad to have a robust master list to use as the foundation for understanding and presenting information that would otherwise be difficult to discern.

The master list is an excellent tool for high-level understanding and sweeping manipulation of locations in the game. For deeper analysis of individual locations, however, it's better to use a secondary resource in which each location can be detailed out and tracked, preferably by the individual(s) implementing the location. This is the general premise behind the directory.

THE DIRECTORY

The directory is essentially a longer-form version of the master list. While the master list is useful for reviewing and planning from orbit, the directory of locations is where individual content creators can dive deeper and track more specific information about each individual space. The directory can be set up in whatever software you prefer: it could be a series of individual documents in a network folder, a collaborative spreadsheet, or anything else. For team collaboration, an online wiki or wikilike implementation works well. My experience is based on using Mediawiki, the same platform most web users will be familiar with as the platform used to build Wikipedia.

Whatever software you choose to host your directory, be prepared to create an individual entry for every location on your master list. These entries can be used to track whatever information you deem necessary. They should follow as standard a format as possible. Mediawiki-specific tools such as templates and categories can be very useful to sort and filter entries together when searching and organizing. (If you're using another system, look into any features that would allow you to sort and organize entries.) Here are some of the items that can be tracked, many of which may also be tracked on the master list.

- Current status of work

- Contributing developers

- World coordinates

- Debug commands for testing

- Enemy/encounter type

- Associated quest(s) or activities

- Walkthrough steps for testing

- Known bugs, issues, and workarounds

- Backstory and fiction

- Notes from playtesting, peer review, etc.

- Personal to-do list of implementing developer

When setting up a directory, establish a naming convention for tracking each individual location. These identifying codes should also be used in the master list for sorting and can become a general shorthand for tracking specific locations. The convention I've used tends to be very, very simple: something like DN004 would simply stand for Dungeon #4. When using Mediawiki, for example, I can then create a page simply called DN004, which corresponds to this location in both the master list and directory.

Here's a simple, hypothetical example of what such a document may look like (Figure 12.5).

This page includes several useful elements.

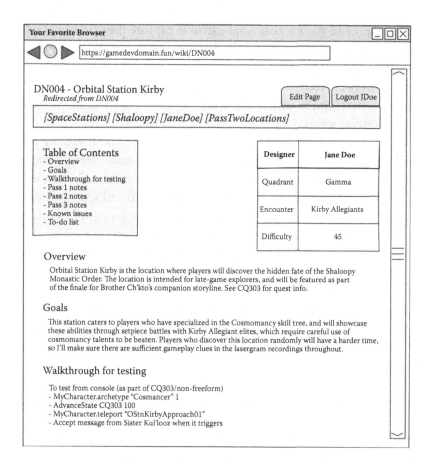

FIGURE 12.5   Wiki pages are a useful way to create and organize directory pages for locations, especially in a collaborative environment.

Category tags have been used to associate this entry with keywords that can be used to search and organize pages. The tag PassTwoLocations in this example (assuming Mediawiki) can be clicked to show all pages that are currently in pass two, for example, while the tag JaneDoe makes it easy to organize all location pages owned by that developer.

The table of contents, which Mediawiki can auto-generate, is a straight-forward way to organize pages with many headings.

The table of data on the right of the example page can be set up using a Mediawiki template. Templates are good for tracking a standard (and potentially changing) data set, and can also be used to automatically cat-egorize pages while maintaining an orderly appearance.

Overview and goals sections are useful to capture the primacy of intent for a specific location; the original vision and goals for a location will usually not change dramatically over the course of a project, and it's good to have a way to reference these throughout development, especially with long-term iteration, in which case it can be easy to lose sight of the original, underlying goals.

Walkthrough steps are vital for content that will be tested by other developers or members of a quality assurance (QA) staff (professional testers). Initial walkthrough steps will tend to be very technical, often working around incomplete or broken parts of the game and specific content. A well-maintained walkthrough will become more straightforward over time, however, as there are fewer workarounds and issues to compensate for. This information will also be useful if your game is eventually the subject of a strategy guidebook, as these walkthroughs will become less technical in nature as the content becomes more complete, and can be given to strategy guide writers as a starting point and reference guide for their work.

Pass notes, if your game is developed over a number of iterative passes, are useful for tracking notes gathered from playtesting and peer review at each pass.

Known issues can be useful for content with a lot of QA attention. Existing bugs and problems can be posted here, with specific links to database entries, depending on your bug tracking software. This is helpful for avoiding duplicate issues; a developer or QA staffer using the walkthrough can glance at this section when running into trouble. The designer can also provide temporary workarounds to known issues in this section, preventing testers from becoming blocked by the issue.

A to-do list is a nice place for the responsible designer to keep track of his or her intentions on a space. Iterative passes can be scheduled quite far apart. This list provides a central, easily remembered location to jot down anything the designer would like to do on future passes, especially if a thought occurs to him or her when they aren't able to work on it immediately.

As mentioned before, there are a lot of things you can choose to include on each directory document, and these are just a handful. Try to anticipate your needs and establish a format early so you can ensure uniformity in how pages are structured and organized.

Note that it can be easy for the master list and directory to get out of sync with each other over time. This is okay to a certain extent, depending on your development priorities and where you are in the development of the game. You can create tools to help keep the two in sync, however.

Fallout 4, for example, briefly used a custom tool to push data from the master list spreadsheet into the directory wiki. While extraordinarily useful in early development, this tool became cumbersome and unreliable as time went on, and was abandoned. This was okay, because by this point the tool had served its main purpose of generating directory wiki pages and making large-scale updates to their formatting before individual creators were taking over the pages. The time and effort that could have been spent maintaining and updating the python tool was better spent elsewhere. It is important to understand the role of your documentation and tools so you know when it's okay to let them go fallow.

As an aside, consider this saying, oft repeated by game developers: "We ship games, not documents." Clean and robust documentation, such as we're describing here, can go a long way toward planning work, communicating vision, and improving the overall quality of a game. Or, more specifically, it can go a long way toward improving the organization and quality of life for the developers creating the game, which will, in turn, result in a better game. Conversely, however, keeping complex optimization up to date can become a tedious distraction, taking up time and attention better spent on efforts that more directly impact the game's final quality.

Keep this in mind throughout development, and be sensitive to the costs and benefits of documentation, and don't be afraid to let documents go fallow once they've fulfilled their purpose.

With this in mind, consider to whom the directory is most beneficial. The nature of the directory (a collection of many documents, unlike the single master list document) lends itself as a personal record for the designer(s) directly responsible for the content.

APPLIED: WORKFLOW AND PROCESS

The techniques I'm describing here are not strictly for high-level, preproduction planning, but also work well with an approach to scheduling for iteration. This system is designed to let world design occur in as organic a way as possible. I want to take a little bit of time to describe this workflow and demonstrate how it incorporates with the planning method described so far.

It is fundamental to understand that game development is messy and complicated, and some old adages apply, such as "expect (and plan for) the unexpected," or "hope for the best, but plan for the worst." Responsible scheduling often involves accounting for major overages in terms of time spent on tasks. There are bound to be unforeseen problems and opportunities that arise throughout development. If your metrics suggest that a task will take 5 days, and there are 10 instances of that task, don't assume the work will be done in 50 days. It's much wiser, in this example, to allow 100–150 days for that work. To borrow another old adage: "No plan survives first contact with the enemy." Or, if you prefer Mike Tyson to Kaiser Wilhelm II: "Everyone has a plan until they get punched in the mouth."

Well-informed guidelines (or metrics) will help you understand how to allocate time for the iterative passes that are at the core of this workflow. Be sure that the time set aside for each task is based on a sampling of designers working at average or below-average standards. Creating metrics based on your best designer in optimum conditions will only set the team up for failure. Even with generous metrics, remember to plan for the worst, as mentioned above, and leave ample free time tucked away for emergencies and unforeseen opportunities.

With reliable guidelines established, you can begin to estimate how much time is required overall to implement the workflow described here. This overall level/world design process assumes a series of focused passes, each of which are designed to coordinate with the overall development schedule, as well as permitting a healthy creative process for level designers and the content creators they collaborate with. The general breakdown of these passes, very briefly outlined, is thus:

Pass zero or pitch pass: Occurs during or immediately after conception/ preproduction. Pass zero is essentially a pitch pass. It has no technical requirements. All that's needed is a relatively well-defined master list of locations (and/or events) that require level designers and a template the team is happy using for tracking individual locations (i.e., the directory described in this chapter). Try to ensure, as much as possible, that the designer who handles this pass will handle the same space throughout development. Pride of ownership goes a long way toward helping a creative person feeling motivated, and the designer who spearheaded the original pass zero of a location will understand his or her own intentions and motivations better than anyone who may inherit the space later because of assignment shuffling.

Pass one or layout pass: Occurs during/after creation of core environmental art assets. This pass is similar to the widely accepted graybox stage espoused by many level designers. Because Bethesda Game Studios works with modular, artist-created environment kits (as opposed to brushes or other editor-created primitive geometry common in many editors), level designers must work closely with artists to ensure their schedule is able to prioritize the fundamental pieces of art required to construct a basic layout. This requires a shared understanding that a comprehensive set of core pieces is an important priority, and that it's vital to get this art in place before spending time on aesthetic embellishment or one-off art pieces. (Modular kits aren't inherently tied to the overall concepts here, though. For the interested, I've written extensively about the creation and use of modular art for level design elsewhere.*)

Pass two or gameplay pass: Occurs while core gameplay is defined. The gameplay pass comes after first-pass layouts have been defined and agreed on, and key systems (combat, for example) are available in an early form to be used to define the sequence of events players will encounter while exploring a layout. It's important to remember that gameplay at this stage needn't be a comprehensive reflection of the final game. Systems (enemy behaviors, weapon types, player abilities, etc.) are probably only available in their earliest form, and the identity of the game itself may still be unclear. Level designers can think of this phase as an exercise in spatially communicating intention, particularly with regard to pacing. The specifics of moment-to-moment gameplay will change, but this pass should represent a reasonable first draft. Three melee enemies in a narrow corridor—even if those enemies are inanimate or behaviorally very simple—still loosely demonstrates the kind of encounter the level designer has in mind.

Pass three or content complete: This pass is ideally concurrent with first playable. While different teams may use different terms to describe it, there is generally a point in development when all content is accounted for but is still unpolished. Some call this "first playable," some call it "content complete," and some call it "alpha." The flippant term I've used for it is "ship with shame," meaning the game is technically complete, but in such a rough form that you would be embarrassed to actually release it as is. What's important for this methodology is that nearly every aspect of the level is present in a playable form, and those (hopefully few, if any) elements that are not

---

* I have coauthored two talks about modular level design, both with Nathan Purkeypile and originally presented at the Game Developer's conference in San Francisco 2013 and 2016, respectively. The modular level design of Skryim can be found in written form here: http://blog.joelburgess .com/2013/04/skyrims-modular-level-design-gdc-2013.html and the Modular Level Design of Fallout 4 can be found here in video form: https://www.youtube.com/watch?v=QBAM27YbKZg.

present are accounted with a very specific plan for when and how they will be available later.

Art pass or atmospherics, lighting, clutter: This pass occurs between the third/fourth passes, if at all possible. This requires coordination with the art team schedule if level designers rely on artists to do the majority of this work. This may not be necessary in a studio environment where level designers are expected to be expert in these talents. This pass is when the level is visually nailed down. It's important that the artists understand the gameplay intention of the level designer, however, so that their decisions can be in support of (and not conflict with) those intentions. Collaboration is important to this pass, and as insurance against poor communication, it should occur early enough that the level designer has ample time to playtest with the more-polished visuals and identify errors.

Pass four or polish pass(es): This pass is the level designer's final preparation before shipping the game. Every aspect of the gameplay experience must be accounted for and polished. Bugs may be present and are acceptable as long as there's ample time for bug-fixing in the schedule and those bugs are not the result of missing or incomplete work on behalf of the level designer himself or herself. Note that the fourth pass may or may not *actually* be the final pass, however. Certain levels will receive additional passes. This may happen because the level isn't up to expected standards or has other problems that require rework. More often, hopefully, levels are given additional passes because they show unexpected potential that merits further work. Whatever the reason, these additional passes are not planned for ahead of time, instead being a reaction to the state of the game as it is developed. Again, including ample extra time in your schedule is what empowers you to have this freedom. This is especially important toward the end of development, when there's often a frenzied atmosphere in the surge to finishing a game.

Those interested in learning more about this process may wish to refer to a longer discussion on the topic.*

---

* I have also presented on the Iterative Level Design process at GDC. That talk can be found in written form here: http://blog.joelburgess.com/2014/07/gdc-2014-transcript-iterative-level.html and video form here: https://www.youtube.com/watch?v=PhW8CY8XkFg.

CONCLUSION

These passes are just one system for implementation, however, and not inextricably linked with the map, master list, and directory system that serve as their foundation. It's possible and likely that any reader hoping to apply techniques described in this chapter will do so by ignoring certain elements, cherry-picking others, and customizing those to the specific needs of a given project and team.

To best understand which elements you may want to use, it's useful to remember their most basic purpose: the world map makes it possible to visually organize an open world and understand the density of points of interest. The master list provides a tool for quickly organizing and shuffling high-level data about the world. The directory then offers a platform where fine details of each location can be documented and tracked, especially for individual creators.

While this chapter hasn't been too directly concerned with the nitty-gritty of actual level design, it provides a framework for thinking about the needs of level design in the context of a large project. Project planning and scheduling is an important part of game development and must take its cues from the needs of the developers of the game, seeking to empower them rather than asking them to contort their creative process to fit within a project planning methodology that is unaware of how the particular development team works best or the goals of the game they are trying to make.

By organizing data and schedules in a way that is easily understood, permits flexibility, and integrates iteration as a core value, you can lay the groundwork for a game development process that will enable level designers to do their best work, resulting in an all-around better game.

ENDNOTES

i Tutorial instructions for Excel example to set up filtered lists of locations by footprint size:

1. First, create a new worksheet called "Footprint Filtering." We are going to use this spreadsheet to separate our medium- and large-footprint locations into their own minilists. Once the worksheet is created, navigate to it and in cell A2, follow the instructions in endnote 1.

2. Type "=" to begin entering a formula.

3. Excel formulas are a simple way to add basic logic to your spreadsheet. They're less powerful than vbscript, but easier to learn and (crucially, for me) run in real time!

4. Type "IF(" to begin an if-statement.

5. We want to see if the footprint value in a cell on the locations worksheet is "Md," and copy that value if so.

6. Next, type "EXACT(" inside the first parenthesis.

7. This begins an exact() statement, which compares two strings and returns the Boolean value our if() statement will be looking for.

8. In your "Locations" worksheet, click on the footprint column in row 2 (D2 in the example above).

9. You can also enter target cells manually, but the syntax can be confusing. It's usually easier to use the cursor.

10. Enter a comma: ",".

11. The target cell we just chose (D2, if you're following my example) contains a string, and is the first argument of our EXACT() statement. The comma tells Excel we're about to enter the second argument.

12. Enter the text "Md" (with quotations).

13. We're manually entering a string to compare against. You can also use a target cell for this, which is useful if you want to maintain a key in your worksheet and reference that value instead.

14. Enter a closing parenthesis, followed by a comma: "),".

15. The parenthesis ends the EXACT() statement, which serves as the logical_test argument expected by the IF() function. The comma tells Excel we're about to enter the value it should print if that test returns a "true" result.

16. In your "Locations" worksheet, click on the X-coordinate column in row 2 (B2 in the example above).

17. If exact() determined the location in row 2 of "Locations" is a medium footprint, it will copy the x value. That's what we want! More on this shortly.

18. Enter another comma: ",".

19. The IF() statement is ready for it's last argument now.

20. Enter "#N/A" (without quotations).

21. #N/A is an error value in Excel, which we want in this case. Our chart will ignore errors when plotting coordinates.

22. Enter a final closing parenthesis ")" and hit enter to complete the formula.

23. In our example, row 2 is a "Lg" location, so we *expect* to see an #N/A in this column.

24. Select the cell containing the formula we just entered. While holding Control, click the small square in the lower-right corner of the cell and drag downward. Go far enough to encompass as many locations as are in your "Locations" worksheet.

25. This will make Excel copy your formula into each highlighted cell. Excel will automatically increment the row number for every copy, meaning your formula will automatically work for you!

26. Select cell B2 and repeat all of the above, except be sure to copy the "Y" coordinate value instead of the "X" for your second IF() argument.

27. Excel experts may wish to manually update the formula instead. Beginners may find the syntax overly confusing at first, though.

ii Tutorial instructions for Excel to plot new lists of data below existing scatter graph data set:

1. Right-click on the map and choose "Select Data."

2. Choose to "Add" a new series.

3. Name the first series "Medium Radii."

4. For the X Values range, choose the appropriate column in your Footprint Filtering worksheet.

5. Repeat for the Y Values range. You may need to manually remove "={1}" from the field.

6. Repeat all of the above to create a data series for Large Radii.

7. OK to exit. You may see a lot of duplicate plots on the map.

8. Right-click on one of these new plots to "Edit Data Series" for the medium radii.

9. Edit the marker to use a built-in circle icon.

10. Set the marker to use no fill.

11. Set the marker size to a value you see fit (I used 16 in the example pictured in Figure 12.2).

12. Repeat for the large radii data series, choosing a larger marker size (I used 25).

IV

Testing Levels

CHAPTER 13

Play-Personas

Mental Tools for Player-Centered Level Design

Alessandro Canossa

CONTENTS

The limits of my language mean the limits of my world

LUDWIG WITTGENSTEIN,
"TRACTATUS LOGICO-PHILOSOPHICUS"

Uncounted gigabytes of information are now available at a finger's touch on a keyboard, cached in digital memories, out of context. Our problem is not the scarcity of information, but the overwhelming challenge of sorting it, understanding it, and finding relevance, meaning and truth within data.

NEIL GAIMAN, *THE ABSOLUTE SANDMAN*, VOL. 1

INTRODUCTION

Level designers are designing spaces for players to act. Even the most solipsistic auteur working on the most linear and story-driven experience must acknowledge a hypothetical future player lurking behind the corner. Games must be played in order to fully exist. Game and digital culture researcher Espen Aarseth, says

> Playing is integral [to games], not coincidental like the appreciative reader or listener. The creative involvement is a necessary ingredient in the uses of games. The complex nature of simulations is such that a result can't be predicted beforehand; it can vary greatly depending on the player's luck, skill and creativity.[*]

This chapter presents a possible strategy for integrating profiles of players' behavior in the design of game levels by employing play-personas. A similar approach is already in use in interaction design; the method can be improved by complementing the traditional narrative description provided by traditional personas with quantitative, parametric models of hypothetical player behavior.

Tracy Fullerton, in one of the most influential books on game design,[†] maintains that game designers are first and foremost "advocates for the player" and must look at the world of games through the player's eyes focusing solely on player experience.

---

[*] Aarseth, Espen. Computer Games Studies, Year One. *Game Studies Journal*, 2001.
[†] Fullerton, Tracy. Game Design Workshop. San Francisco: CMP Books, 2004.

If a prototype exists, it is easy to look through player's eyes by playtesting as often as possible; but how is it possible to initiate the design process and think and act on behalf of players with wildly differing preferences? Developing conceptual models of player behavior might help greatly in prefiguring possible actions and emotional responses of a wide variety of people. These conceptual models are used to know, understand, or simulate a wide array of possible players.

Computational models of player behavior would also be a good solution if the game already existed and the design wasn't going to change. For example, in a simplified version of the game *Pac-Man*, players can choose between four low-level behaviors: go up, left, right, and down. The map presents 24 decision points or locations where a player has to decide between two possible paths, a comprehensive list of all possible behaviors in that game would amount to 2^{24} or 16.777.216 choices (Figure 13.1).

An alternative solution to envision possible players interacting with the game is to classify the 16 million possible low-level actions as high-level behaviors. High-level behaviors are in this case general representations of preferences that players can display; for example, players that prefer to linger at the center of the play board as opposed to players that spend most of the time in the periphery, players who turn the little ghosts edible by eating the pills at the beginning of the game as opposed to players that save the pills for later in the game, players that maintain a linear trajectory as opposed to players that continuously change direction, and so on. These three sets of polar parameters—center/periphery dweller, early/late

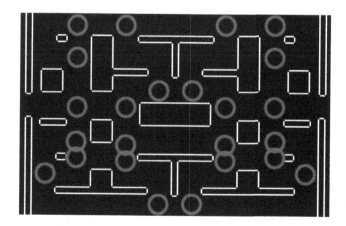

FIGURE 13.1　Decision points in the *Pac-Man* maze.

pill eater, and linear/broken path—give rise to eight behavioral profiles based on concrete ludic affordances provided by the game (Table 13.1).

Thinking in these terms allows designers to make rather educated assumptions before any level is implemented and create informative profiles. For example, a periphery dweller that tends to eat the pills fairly early on and has a linear path (profile 4) could easily be labeled as a fraidy cat; since it is easier to navigate the outskirts of the board, the relative vicinity of the pills casts a sense of security and it's easier to avoid bad surprises in terms of ghosts spawning right in front. Conversely, a player that dwells close to the ghosts' spawn cell, delays the use of the pills, and displays a very broken path (profile 4) can easily be labeled as a risk taker. A designer empowered with the knowledge of these two profiles can create Pac-Man boards that fit both, and include areas that cater specifically to one or the other.

This example shows two of the benefits of play-personas. Initially, before a game is even finished, designers can prefigure possible player behaviors by grouping sets of low-level game mechanics as parameters to inform the definition of the play-personas describing those behaviors. These are the play-personas as metaphors. Afterward, when the game is being played and data can be collected, assumptions about player behavior can be tested and the levels created can be evaluated in terms of the goals set initially by the play-personas. These are the play-personas as lenses.

Play-personas are ways of modeling player behavior and understanding players' relationship to the ludic and aesthetic affordances of specific computer games. Play-personas are defined as patterns of preferential interaction and navigation attitudes; they can be employed as a means of assisting the computer game design process or as an a posteriori method for evaluating designs. Persona-oriented game design can connect quantitative analyses of player behavior (game metrics) as well as psychological studies of player types, studies into game design processes, and analyses of level design in computer games.

This chapter proposes play-personas as a framework to sharpen the focus on player experience when designing and evaluating game levels.

TABLE 13.1 Combinatory Matrix for High-Level Behaviors and Persona Profiles

Profile Number	1	2	3	4	5	6	7	8
Center (1)/periphery (2) dweller	1	1	1	2	2	2	1	2
Early (1)/late (2) pill eater	1	1	2	1	2	1	2	2
Linear (1)/broken (2) path	1	2	1	1	1	2	2	2

Play-personas represent means to imply metaphorically players during the design phase and also serve as lenses to evaluate finished levels. The concept, initially inspired by Cooper's[*,†] work in human computer interaction, attempts to provide tools to model player behavior in a parametric manner, distancing itself from traditional human computer interaction (HCI) personas and their ethnographic legacy. This is particularly useful to help designers get into the mindset of other players with different sets of desires and motivations that may give rise to very different play styles, and be able to design for a wider audience without compromising on the vision of the core experience that the game sets out to deliver.

TAKEAWAYS

- Analyze existing sets of low-level gameplay mechanics and aesthetics to derive high-level behaviors

- Leverage high-level behaviors to obtain a permutation matrix listing all possible play-personas intended as profiles of player behaviors

- Select, among the numerous play-personas, a cast of profiles that fit the vision for the level to be created

- Associate aesthetic and ludic affordances to the selected play-personas, training players to expect a certain set of possibilities of behavior at any given time

- Orchestrate throughout the level the opportunities for players to embody any of the behaviors encapsulated by play-personas

- Utilize play-personas to evaluate whether players' behavior conforms to the intention of the level designers

BACKGROUND: ORIGIN AND HISTORY OF PLAY-PERSONAS

Persona is a Latin word that describes the mask that actors put on before becoming their characters: it is a socially agreed convention used to represent certain types. Currently it refers mostly to social masks or roles

---

[*] Cooper, Alan. *The Inmates Are Ruling the Asylum*. Indianapolis, IN: Sams Publishing, 2004.
[†] Cooper, Alan. *About Face 3: The Essentials of Interaction Design*. Indianapolis, IN: John Wiley & Sons, 2007.

that all humans have to play on the stage of life. Goffman[*] uses the term "fronts" to address the different masks that we have to wear according to the different contexts we are presented with. We must act differently in different settings, as the world is a stage. It is in this sense that Jung listed it as one of the archetypes populating the human unconscious. Personas or fictional identity constructs have been recognized as fundamental in many creative practices. In literary theory, Iser[†] introduced the term "implied reader" to address the certain "reader that a given literary work requires." Within the frame and the context imposed by the text, this implied reader makes assumptions, has expectations, defines meanings that are left unstated, and adds details to characters and settings through a wandering viewpoint. For example, by Joyce's own admission, *Finnegan's Wake* should be read by "that ideal reader suffering from an ideal insomnia." Eco expanded on the concept, introducing the model reader[‡] as "the author's foreshadowing of a reader competent enough to provide the best interpretation of a text." The author tries to prefigure a model reader by imagining what could be the actualization of the text. The author, consciously or not, is concerned with how the text/type becomes interpretation/token. In social sciences, Max Weber introduced the concept of Idealtyp as "formed by one-sided accentuation of one or more points of view and by the synthesis of a great many diffuse, discrete, more or less present and occasionally absent concrete individual phenomena, which are arranged according to those one-sidedly emphasized viewpoints into a unified analytical construct."[§] The ideal type is a pure mental construct used to assess the behavior of social groups. It is totally theoretic, almost fictitious, and generally not empirically found anywhere in reality, it is not backed by statistical data or a model personality profile, it is more used as some sort of unit of measure, standards much like meter, second, or kilogram not really found in nature, but useful to measure it. In similar ways game designers could benefit greatly by making assumptions about the nature of players using personas to map the extreme boundaries of the field of possibilities afforded by their game.

---

[*] Goffman, Erving. *The Presentation of Self in Everyday Life*. London: Penguin, 1990.
[†] Iser, Wolfgang. *The Implied Reader*. London: Johns Hopkins Paperback Editions, 1978.
[‡] Eco, Umberto. *The Role of the Reader*. Bloomington, IN: Indiana University Press, 1984.
[§] Weber, Max. *The Methodology of the Social Sciences*. Edward Shils and Henry Finch (eds.). New York: Free Press, 1949.

Personas in Interaction Design

The practice of creating and using play-personas as proxy models of player behavior has its roots in HCI and it is inspired by Alan Cooper's work. Alan Cooper is an interaction and user experience designer credited with humanizing technology through his groundbreaking approach to software design. Cooper developed a method called goal-directed design. This method makes use of personas—"archetypes that represent distinct groupings of behaviors, attitudes, aptitudes, goals, and motivations"—to help developers understand the end user and to foresee its way of interacting with the product.

Alan Cooper's goal-directed design process starts with the research phase, in which behavior patterns and modes of use of products are identified. These patterns suggest goals and motivations and in turn these inform the creation of personas. Personas are detailed, composite user archetypes and they serve as main characters in narrative, scenario-based descriptions that iteratively inform the design of a product, so that features emerge directly from the goals. Typically a persona is a description of behavior patterns, goals, skills, attitudes, and environment, with a few fictional personal details to make it a realistic character. For each product there should be a set of three to 12 personas, it is not necessary to design for all of them, but an extensive cast helps articulate the user population, the primary focus for the design will be a limited subset of maximum three personas. Persona description should be precise, including as many details as possible, but not necessarily accurate; it does not need to represent a real person. Name, physical appearance, education, and idiosyncrasies should be included. The main benefits of personas for product development purposes are (1) it is easier to relate to a personal human face and name instead of abstract customer data, (2) it is possible to infer user needs not openly stated by drawing on personal people-experience, (3) personas provide a shared, fast, and effective language for communication between engineers and designers, (4) personas state what a user needs and wants so that no stakeholder can reshape the user to their convenience, (5) personas avoid self-referential designs, where designers might unconsciously project their own mental models, (6) personas also work as reality checks, helping designers keep the focus on the limited subset of users that have been deemed primary, and (7) proposed designs, features, and solutions can be evaluated against the needs of individual persona models. Personas have also been criticized mostly because if they are fictional, they have no clear relationship to real customer data and therefore any data gathered cannot be considered scientific. In any case, in order to apply this design method to computer games some changes are necessary.

From Personas to Play-Personas

Play-personas are an evolution of Cooper's personas thanks to three factors. First, the play-persona construct helps modeling both ideal players prior to the encounter with the game as such (a priori metaphor), and also helps modeling empirical players after the play experience (a posteriori lens). This double-headed nature mirrors the creative and performative nature of games as acts of communication that are established around levels or game worlds. Second, the play-persona attempts to describe behaviors procedurally, beside the traditional narrative model proposed by HCI practitioners. Player's preferences, choices, and desires are described in terms of likelihood of choices among all the possibilities that the game as a system of rules affords. Due to the intrinsic numeric nature of procedural descriptions, it is immediately possible to compare different play-personas provided that they are scored according to compatible parameters. Third, data gathered by game telemetry informs the creation of these performative models, the a posteriori lens used to describe behavior of real players. If a model is supposed to indicate a common form shared by separate phenomena, individuating common features and clusters of similarities, then the logical application is to use this model to evaluate the behavior of players looking for groups of similar performances. Play-persona limits itself to assumptions/predictions operating on the temporal and spatial fabric of the game—what, where, and when—and it does not require assumptions that go beyond what can be known.

PLAY-PERSONAS

Play-personas are further defined as clusters of preferential interaction (what) and navigation (where) attitudes, temporally expressed (when), that coalesce around different kinds of inscribed affordances in the artifacts provided by game designers. This means that personas can no longer just be limited to narrative descriptions of motivations, needs, and desires distilled in ethnographic interviews. The persona hypotheses emerge as a relation of parameters from the set of interaction and navigation possibilities that the game rules and gamespaces can afford. Personas can be augmented and strengthened by a quantifiable, parametric, data-driven perspective. Furthermore, if directly coupled with instrumentation data in the form of gameplay metrics gathered from game engine software during play sessions, play-personas can provide a powerful evaluation tool to confirm whether a certain hypothesis also turns out to represent a sizeable slice of players. That is why play-personas are both theoretical models of ideal users (metaphor) and data-driven representations of player behaviors (lens).

Play-Persona as Metaphor

A metaphor is a rhetorical device that allows describing something unknown by transferring attributes from a known entity. Metaphors are utilized before the accumulation of experience, in a similar way personas allow designers to imply unknown player behavior in the process of creating digital games (i.e., by predefining the ideal play patterns possible in the game in question and design to accommodate these). It is the case in *Tomb Raider Underworld*, where players can choose between different identically optimal strategies to progress and express preferences for some modes of interaction and navigation instead of others. Play-personas as design tools represent an expectance of how players would like to craft their experience. As metaphors, play-personas are hypotheses that emerge as relations of parameters from the set of possibilities that the game can afford. Designers can use personas as categories of behaviors prior to a playable version of the game in order to plan coherent navigation and interaction modes. They are also precious as guides to select which variables are interesting enough to monitor as game metrics, which will lead to the creation of play-personas as lens.

Play-Persona as Lens

Lens is here intended as the choice of a context (Ümwelt) from which to sense, categorize, measure, or codify experience. Lenses are utilized to examine the accumulated experience. The concept of lens is somewhat related to how Jesse Schell defined it in his book *The Art of Game Design: A Book of Lenses*, a viewpoint from which a designer can view a game to answer questions about the design. Gameplay metrics data can form the basis of defining data-driven personas during game testing. As lenses, play-personas are derived from game metrics gathered from players after they have been interpreted as clusters of similar behaviors. Personas can be used as tools when evaluating games by comparing the goals set by the designers with those of the players. By comparing designers' and players' goals it is possible to check whether the game design actually supports and facilitates the planned experience in practice and if any new personas emerge from the user interaction with the game software. Analyzing game metrical data with multivariate statistical tools can provide a way of discovering patterns in the usage of game elements and features, thus enabling the building of personas of how players interact with the game, and whether the game design facilitates the specific play patterns of the personas assumed as hypotheses. It is a sense-making perspective, a code that allows extracting meaning from an otherwise unclear list of numbers. Playstyles (or patterns of play) are possible ways in which certain subsets of the rules and mechanics provided by the game can be combined. A player that maintains consistent choices of styles eventually identifies with a play-persona. Personas are aggregate descriptions of possible player behavior both in theory, as an expectation of the designer—an a priori metaphor—and in practice, as a description of what actual, real players do during a play session—an a posteriori lens. What follows is a description of the process in which play-personas are identified and utilized to map out the possibility field of a level even before a single polygon is laid out.

THE PLAY-PERSONA PROCESS

Working with play-personas enables level designers to infer hypothetical players' behavior even when a game prototype does not exist. Play-personas allow the aggregation of large numbers of game variables along dimensions defined by core game mechanics to establish behavioral profiles. It is therefore necessary to have a set of mechanics to work from.

Step One: Gameplay Analysis and High-Level Behaviors

The first step consists of analyzing the list of existing low-level gameplay mechanics and aesthetics and derive high-level behaviors. In *Pac-Man*, for example, the low-level mechanics are walking up, down, left, and right, eating a pill, eating a bonus item, eating a ghost, being eaten by a ghost, and utilizing the shortcut passages. As seen in the example earlier (Table 13.1), these mechanics can be abstracted into high-level behaviors, such as eating pills early or late in the game, occupy the center versus the periphery of the screen, maintaining a linear movement profile versus a convoluted pattern, and always maintaining a certain distance from the ghosts versus allowing them to get close. This process is very subjective; different designers will derive different sets of high-level behaviors from the low-level mechanics. At the same time it is not necessary to define objective high-level behaviors in order to generate a thorough mapping of hypothetical player profiles, as long as all of the low-level mechanics can be subsumed under the high-level behaviors.

Step Two: Play-Persona Matrix

The second step consists of plotting all the high-level behaviors identified into a matrix and plotting all the possible permutations that are possible, as seen in Table 13.1. As seen earlier, high-level behaviors are subjective groupings of low-level mechanics, for example the high-level behavior "linear versus convoluted movement" subsumes the low-level mechanics of move left, move right, move up, and move down; a very quick succession of changes between these four mechanics marks a convoluted movement pattern, while sustained use of each of the four mechanics marks a linear movement pattern. It is possible to assign any number of states to each high-level behavior; for example, "linear versus convoluted movement" could have five states: very linear, rather linear, neither linear nor convoluted, rather convoluted, and very convoluted. In order to keep the possibility space from exploding, usually all the high-level behaviors only have two states; for example, very linear and very convoluted, meaning that the number of possible persona profiles is 2^n where 2 equals the number of states and n equals the number of high-level behaviors.

Step Three: Selecting the Cast of Play-Personas

The third step consists of selecting the cast of personas that are most compatible with the vision for the level to be created. It is not possible nor recommended to design levels for all the play-personas identified, it would create a rather unfocused design trying to cater too broadly of a cast. It is recommended to keep the selected personas to a minimum by filtering out uninteresting profiles or profiles not aligned with the vision for the level to be created. For example, for the *Pac-Man* game, it does not make sense to include the fraidy cat persona as a design target for a level in the advanced stages of the game since a periphery dweller that tends to eat the pills fairly early on and has a linear path would require the level to be too easy, definitely not aligned with the goal to keep players on their toes. It would be more appropriate to design around the risk taker, a player that dwells close to the ghosts' spawn cell, delays the use of the pills, and displays a very broken path. Designing walls that zig-zag would force players to have a broken movement path, constantly changing direction; creating these walls as rays emanating from the center toward the periphery would force players to converge closer to the ghosts' spawn point, and placing pills in walled nooks would make it difficult to access them, meaning that players would not accidentally run into them but deliberately make an effort to seek the pills.

Step Four: Associate Affordances with Behaviors

The fourth step consists of building a thesaurus of associations between ludic and aesthetic affordances and the sets of high-level behaviors identified. This is in order to train players to expect a certain set of possibilities of behavior at any given time. Ludic affordances consist of all the actions that players can undertake, such as being caught by a ghost, acquiring a pill, eating a ghost or bonus fruits, or moving around the level. Aesthetic affordances consist of those possibilities for action that emerge from the sensory-perceptual qualities of the world, such as navigation patterns and viewing ranges; they describe where the avatar can go and what they can see. The aesthetical elements comprise, for example, colors, textures, shapes, lights, ambient sounds, and music; pretty much anything that invests the senses immediately.

For example, placing bonus items (ludic affordances) always close to the center, the most dangerous part of the map, where the ghosts have their spawn point, creates a mental association between high-risk behavior and high rewards; players that choose to pursue bonus items can expect a more difficult experience. Similarly, it is possible to create associations with aesthetic affordances, such as the shape of walls or their colors; for example, the walls of the maze could be blue toward the periphery of the screen and red toward the center to signify increased potential danger.

Step Five: Weave and Orchestrate Play-Personas

It is necessary to modulate the opportunities for players to embody different personas throughout the level. If initially players have the chance to change at a whim from the fraidy cat to the risk taker, removing all bonus items and increasing the aggressiveness and speed of the ghosts is enough to push most players to adopt a more conservative behavior. The designer is in fact in charge of creating interesting modulations in terms of which behavioral profiles are available to players at any given time.

Step Six: Play-Personas as a Tool for User Research

As seen earlier, it is also possible to utilize play-personas to evaluate whether the players' behavior conforms to the intention of the level designers.

In fact, when a prototype exists, it is possible to collect game telemetry and to analyze whether players conform to the intention of the designer; for example, in the later stage of the game when the ghosts have turned more aggressive, are players still enacting risk taker behaviors or have all reverted to the fraidy cat persona as intended? By collecting game telemetry it is possible to analyze player logs and infer if players still tend to spend considerable time close to the ghosts' spawn point, or when, during their play time, they tend to consume pills, or again whether they still move in convoluted patterns. By analyzing players' behaviors through logged telemetry, designers can confirm or disprove their initial hypotheses which were formalized as the initial play-personas.

The process that has been described until now will be applied to a concrete case study of an existing game, *Left 4 Dead*, to show how high-level behaviors can be derived from low-level mechanics and how play-personas can be derived and used to guide the design of a level for an existing game.

CASE STUDY: *LEFT 4 DEAD*

The game *Left 4 Dead* is a first-person, cooperative shooter with a survival horror theme. Players are asked to survive hordes of infected enemies and escape the location to a safer area. The core mechanics are shown in Table 13.2.

TABLE 13.2   Low-level Mechanics for the Game *Left 4 Dead*

Inputs	Outputs
Primary attack (ranged)	Damage to self/enemy/teammate (direct or
Secondary attack (melee)	indirect)
Crouch-shooting (more precise)	Death to self/enemy/teammate (direct or
Crouch	indirect)
Jump	Headshot to self/enemy/teammate
Reload	Heal self/teammate
180-degree spin	Revive teammate
Use (context sensitive)	Being revived by teammate
Walk	Hand out first aid/pills
Run	Receive first aid/pills
Inventory (flashlight, first aid kit, pain pills,	Partial/full reload
Molotov, pipe bomb)	
Change weapons (pistol, dual pistol,	
submachine gun, pump shotgun, auto	
shotgun, assault rifle, hunting rifle)	

Step One

This list of core mechanics can be arbitrarily grouped into four main high-level behaviors:

- Surviving: instantiated by a high or low number of times that players heal themselves, the damage taken, the total number of times players were incapacitated, and the number of deaths. Surviving points toward a selfish skill set aimed only at self-preservation.

- Killing: instantiated by a high count of headshots inflicted, the accuracy, the total number of kills, and the ratio of pipe bombs and Molotovs used versus the amount of infected killed with their use. The killing skill polarizes players according to their ability to dispatch enemies.

- Helping: instantiated by players killing infected people that are dealing damage to teammates and reviving teammates that are under attack. The helping dimension shows players' attentiveness to each other.

- Healing: instantiated by a high count of the times players heal and give health packs/pills to teammates. The healing dimension reveals players that are willing to sacrifice their own survival for the good of others since the items given cannot be used on oneself.

Step Two

As mentioned earlier, this is not the only way to group the core mechanics. These four parameters form the axes of a 4-dimensional space that contains all the possible players' behaviors in the game. At the same time they allow developers to select which game variables should be monitored in order to gather usable game metrics data for evaluating players' behavior, if we assume that players can be scored in each dimension only in two ways: positive and negative, according to whether they instantiate a behavior or not. Exploring the possibility field is a matter of elevating 2 (the possible values: instantiated behavior or not) at the power of 4 (the high-level behaviors), obtaining a total of 16 possible profiles (Table 13.3).

Step Three

Among those profiles there are only few that become interesting because they are so extreme they delimit the possibility field of player behavior.

TABLE 13.3 Example: A Player that Dies More Times than the Average but Kills More Zombies than the Average While Not Helping or Healing Teammates Will Be Classified as a Grunt

	Fugitive	Grunt	Samaritan	Doctor	Rambo	Red Cross	Expert	Rookie
Survive	+	−	−	−	+	−	+	−
Kill	−	+	−	−	+	−	+	−
Help	−	−	+	−	−	+	+	−
Heal	−	−	−	+	−	+	+	−
	H1	H2	H3	H4	H5	H6	H7	H8
Survive	+	−	+	−	+	+	+	−
Kill	−	+	−	+	+	+	−	+
Help	−	+	+	−	+	−	+	+
Heal	+	−	−	+	−	+	+	+

For example, persona profiles H1 to H8 are hybrids that contain already the behaviors listed in the first half of the table; likewise, it is not so interesting to include the Expert and Rookie profiles. This leaves the first six play-personas as interesting profiles to drive the design of a level: Fugitive, Grunt, Samaritan, Doctor, Rambo, and Red Cross. Labeling these profiles is an important part of the process as these labels will become simulacra, metaphors, used by the design team to refer to a collection of behavioral attitudes and preferences.

Step Four

It is now necessary to create a list of associations between each play-persona identified and ludic and aesthetic affordances. For example, we know that the Red Cross persona is both helping downed players and healing them, depriving themselves of rare resources such as pills and health packs. In order to perform these behaviors it is necessary to possess pills or health packs and then find a position covered from enemy attacks that allows for transferring items and restoring teammates back to life. Both procedures require a certain amount of time where players are vulnerable to attacks. Placing healing items and covers is necessary for these behaviors to be performed successfully. Designers could choose to consistently utilize sandbags to create such shelters and indicate the presence of these shelters with a blue light, while a green light could be used to illuminate cabinets containing healing devices. This association between aesthetic affordances, such as the color blue, the material sandbag, and a shelter space, is arbitrary; nothing about the color blue or the

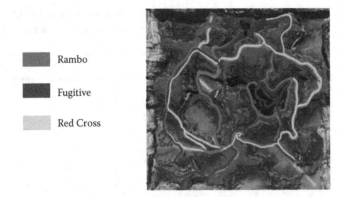

FIGURE 13.2   Projected paths for Rambo, Fugitive, and Red Cross personas.

sandbags necessarily implies a safe place, but designers can train players to expect safety from this association. In a similar manner, the association between cabinets bathed in green and healing devices can be communicated clearly to players with consistent repetition. Eventually, players spotting green cabinets and blue sandbags can safely expect the possibility to enact Red Cross behaviors without being forced to do so. Such associations should be created for each persona profile identified. This thesaurus of associations between play-persona profiles, behavioral attitudes, and ludic/aesthetic affordances becomes essential when designing a level that can enable multiple behaviors. It is in fact possible to quickly draw a layout and color code parallel and alternative traversing routes, as shown in Figure 13.2, automatically distributing aesthetic and ludic affordances.

Step Five

Identifying the six play-personas does not mean necessarily assuming that players will perform consistently as one profile throughout the level, nor does it mean that designers are obliged to cater to all profiles throughout the level. It is in fact recommended for designers to modulate the six profiles identified, deciding in which areas all of them have a chance to play out and in which area only a subset of the six personas is available. In order to control and modulate the possibility to embody different personas throughout the level, it is recommended to divide the whole level in sublocations, and for each one plan which personas will be catered for (Figure 13.3). Sublocations are defined as contiguous, uninterrupted, isotopic spaces that share aesthetic, ludic, and phenomenological features.

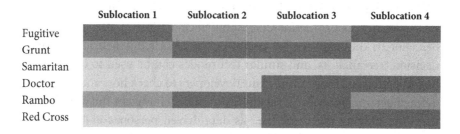

FIGURE 13.3 Example of how the six personas are weaved along the four sub-locations of a level. Gray: preferred persona, playing in this way is encouraged; light gray: it is possible to play in this way but not easy; dark gray: persona non grata, it is very difficult or impossible to play in this way.

Sublocation 1 is designed to encourage Grunt and Rambo play. It is forgiving so that even the most foolhardy approach rarely ends in defeat. There are a few supplies so that Doctor and Red Cross can be instantiated, but there are no shelters so it will not be very easy, while the sheer number of enemies prevents the Fugitive to be performed at all.

Sublocations 2 and 3 swap the numerous but weak enemies of section 1 with fewer almost invincible enemies, meaning that the preferred persona is the Fugitive, leaving no space for the Grunt or Rambo. While section 2 has a few limited supplies, allowing Doctor and Red Cross to exist, section 3 presents no supplies so only the Samaritan can be instantiated but with a certain amount of difficulty because of the lack of shelter.

Sublocation 4 presents players with a new weapon that allows tackling the previously invincible enemies, who must be killed in order to finish the level. The preferred style is Rambo; it would be difficult but possible to play as Grunt or Samaritan, while completely impossible to play as the Fugitive, the Doctor, or Red Cross.

Step Six

The initial hypothesis, the persona-as-metaphor, has a prescriptive nature: after individuating the high-level behaviors emerging from the core mechanics it is possible to define personas as guiding beacons during the design phase. The final analysis, the persona-as-lens, is of a descriptive nature: it allows observing the clusters of players' behaviors and comparing them with the initial hypothesis. For this to happen it is necessary for a game prototype to exist and for it to be able to generate data on player progression and performance along all the game mechanics used to create the high-level behaviors. Via the application of multivariate statistical methods such as cluster analysis, factor analysis, and population statistical methods such as ordination/correspondence analysis, patterns of player behavior in the data can be sought out. Additionally, neural networks, decision tree analysis, and similar techniques can be used to locate data-driven patterns. This permits game developers to check how and if the pre-defined persona models (as metaphor) actually emerge in the way the end users are playing the game (i.e., as data-driven personas-as-lens). Since explaining these methods and techniques would require more space than the present chapter allows, the interested reader can check out a primer on the topic, such as the book *Game Analytics*.*

It is in this phase that persona hypotheses are checked against the numbers. This kind of information generates knowledge that has both short- and long-term effects: on a concrete level, the information provides valuable feedback to level designers, who can use the input to modify a level to achieve better balance and facilitate the different persona models, on a longer term it allows designers to obtain greater insight on the landscape of possible player types and eventually make games that can cater to a broader audience.

The main uses for these aggregate constructs are

- Phenomenological debugging (balancing of experiences); some levels are open in terms of defining what kinds of experience can emerge from the player-game interaction, while some others are closed

- Envisioning possible ways the game can be played; some levels will show the not-so-invisible hand of the designer forcing the player's behavior in a bottleneck, limiting possibility for expression and therefore the depth of the experience

- Verification of hypotheses set forth during design phase (designers imagined a certain way their game could be used, and play patterns can verify or disprove that)

- Ensuring variation and change in gameplay by providing quantifiable proof for a variety of play

- Optimization of features and resources (making sure that no feature in the game is underused or wasted)

---

* Seif El-Nasr, Magy; Drachen, Anders; Canossa, Alessandro. Game Analytics. London: Springer, 2013.

CONCLUSIONS

Much like personas in software development help improve the user experience by shifting the focus from designer to users or a wide variety of users, play-personas can help level designers think about their craft in novel ways. Play-personas are data-driven collections of high-level behaviors that are rooted in a given game's set of low-level mechanics; a cast of play-personas allows a design team to articulate an appropriate language to discuss player behavior without narrowing it down to a monodimensional experiences. This strategy provides immediate inspirations for brainstorming level layouts, iterating design ideas, and evaluating finished levels, provided that the game is instrumented and able to collect logs recording the interaction of players with the game.

CHAPTER 14

Evaluating Level Design Using Public Events

Jonathan Moriarty

CONTENTS

A S A DESIGNER, YOU cannot judge how effective your game is without putting it in the hands of players, and game development as a process always requires iteration. This will lead you to test iterations of your game on a constant crop of new players, always preferring fresh eyes to those who may have become accustomed to odd quirks that might stump a new player. This chapter discusses opportunities and methods for getting playtest feedback at public events. Many developers find that their pool of new testers dries up fast: they quickly exhaust the pool of friends and family readily available to test their game before it is ready to ship. Likewise, your friends and family are personally vested in your success; they are not going to get up and stop playing your game when it becomes too frustrating, making them data points of questionable use. So the problem essentially is, where can you find a steady supply of largely objective people willing to test your game? Gaming continues to take a larger place in public culture, and with this shift, many public events have arisen that provide excellent test grounds for games. These events range from gatherings of fellow developers to public showcases conducted as part of art festivals, concerts, or educational events. This chapter will focus on when and how to use public events to iterate on the levels in your game. This includes the following:

- Determining when your game is ready for events

- Finding events that are a good fit for your game

- Presenting your game at an event

- Interpreting feedback from an event to improve your game

- Putting this into practice through the testing process of *Lost Cave*

DETERMINING WHEN A GAME IS READY FOR EVENTS

Public events can be an important source of feedback on how to improve your game, but before you get to that point, you must first ask yourself if your game is ready for public events. Speaking from personal experience, taking a game to a public event when it is not ready to show can be a painful and stressful experience. However, you have to push past that critical inner voice whispering "The game is not ready, it will never be ready" and actually get your game into the hands of players, which means making a realistic assessment of where your game is in its development. Rather than attempt to define a hard criterion for event readiness, the following can be considered a general set of guidelines to keep in mind. You should never assume that your game is bug-free at any point in its development, but it should be free of any game-breaking bugs that you have noticed and that players are likely to encounter in a short play session. The quality of the visual art in your game can be somewhat flexible depending on the event you are targeting. Developers can be forgiving of temporary art assets, whereas the public at large won't be. Try to make sure that the game has some level of visual interest, even if none of the assets or effects are final. Another thing to keep in mind for a good demo experience is that the art should be communicative of the state of the game, which is to say that everything that the player needs to know while playing is visually accessible to them in some way. As an example, if the player can dodge, there should be a dodge animation, even if it is only a single frame, so that the player can distinguish this functionality visually without being verbally informed. Another element that can go a long way toward making your game presentable is audio; again, nothing needs to be finalized, but there should be music or ambient sound that loosely conveys the tone of your game, and there should be at least place-holder sound effects for important gameplay moments. There should also be a tutorial within the game itself that explains, at minimum, the controls and goal of the game. On a first pass this tutorial will not be perfect, but it will give you something to iterate on. This will also allow you to avoid having to explain the game to each new player and permit you to be more of an observer rather than a guide when conducting play-tests at events.

If your game is ready to be shown publicly, the question becomes "what can you improve about your game through this process?" The design of the levels in your game can be the best tool you have to communicate the mechanics and goals of the game in a way that is natural to the player. Teaching the game in this way can be a balancing act that requires extensive iteration. The arrangement of different elements in your introductory levels should be simple enough that players are able to grasp individual mechanics and concepts as they are introduced; however, these elements also need to be paced fast enough that players do not become bored by the lack of variety and challenge. Through testing your levels at different public events, you can see how players react, and then adapt your level design to better discover that balance of communication within your game. When you have finished iterating on these level designs, players will be able to sit down in front of your game and have direction about what to do without you having to brief them in person. This is a crucial polishing step in taking your work from a prototype to a full game. The start of that process must begin with finding an appropriate public event to use for testing.

FINDING THE RIGHT EVENTS FOR YOUR GAME

There are a wide variety of public events that offer a venue for game show-casing, so it is important to consider what event will be the most useful to you. This requires examining potential events in terms of their scale, audience makeup, and effort required for participation. Larger industry events like PAX, IndieCade, and MAGFest have the advantage of providing a large and diverse audience of potential players for game testing, but these events often have stricter entry requirements and/or fees and tend to require games to be in a more polished state by virtue of the sheer volume of entries they receive. These facts make such events poor candidates for early showings of your game and much better choices for a time when your game and levels are more polished. Although these larger events can be useful for fine-tuning your game to suit a specific audience, they are most useful as opportunities to promote the existence of your game to that specific audience. Conversely, a type of event that can be extremely useful when a game is in early development are gatherings of your fellow game developers. In terms of an audience, game developers are the most forgiving of a lack of polish in level design and gameplay present in early builds, being familiar themselves with the process of polishing and iteration that comes with game development. These events also tend to have a shorter running time than most other types of events, so if a player encounters a game-breaking bug, you will not have to scramble to address it like you would at an event running over several hours and potentially over the course of multiple days. The middle ground between these two types of events is often comprised of game showcases put on as a part of larger events. These showcases are often organized by academic institutions, festivals, or organizations partially related to gaming. They offer a decent-sized audience of average players for game testing, extremely useful for testing and balancing various iterations of your levels once the game has moved beyond the prototype stage, but you must also consider the average age of the people in attendance at these showcases and see how that compares to the age of your intended audience. If there is a drastic difference, then demoing at that event may not be worth your time. There are also other audience factors to consider, such as how familiar the audience at a given event is with the type of game you are making; a general audience might not be familiar with the design tropes associated with a PC real-time strategy game, so unless you are aiming to design the game to appeal to a general audience, you may want to select an event with an audience that is more in line with your target demographic. Presenting at any type of public event can often carry a significant cost in time, money, and personal effort, so any amount of study and analysis you can do beforehand will help ensure that the events you go to are as useful to you as they can be, while reducing the stress that can be caused by presenting at an event that is not a good fit for your current game.

PRESENTING AT AN EVENT

Once you have decided on your target event, you need to determine how to best present your game in a way that allows you to gather meaningful feedback from each player. There are many great resources that cover how to set up an exhibition space for your game in a way that attracts people or how to best demonstrate a game to members of the press or prospective buyers. In this section, however, we will limit our discussion of the presentation space to specifically describing how to construct a good environment for playtesting, and how to best position yourself to gather meaningful feedback. A basic version of a recommended setup can be seen in Figure 14.1. If at all possible, you will want to have the game set up with mirrored displays: one that faces out at the player, and one that is behind the table, *where you should be sitting*. There is a tremendous urge as a designer to sit beside the player when they are playing, to coach them through a tough part or to explain something. You have to fight that urge because people play differently when they are being watched; just ask any popular streamer or Let's Player. Your space should also contain a way for you to quickly take notes. Either have a small notebook on hand for jotting things down, take notes on your phone with an app; use whatever method works best for you. All this being said, if you have enough people available to help, having another person out in front of the table to draw people to your game isn't a bad idea, but that person should be ready to step out of the way when the player begins the game.

FIGURE 14.1 An admittedly simple setup, but it allows you to watch what players are doing without standing over their shoulder.

Encountering Bugs during Playtests

You should also consider how to handle bug discovery in playtests: there is no worse feeling than getting your game set up at a public event and within the first few minutes discovering a player has found a bug you did not even know existed. The severity of a bug and how likely a player will run into it can determine how you should handle this, but typically if you are a singular developer or part of a very small team, you should try to avoid iterating on or fixing a game build during a public event. There are a couple reasons that this is suggested. At an event, you are going to be distracted, and that usually does not lead to fixing problems in a way that permanently addresses them, and a hasty bug fix can often introduce potentially more severe issues. Also, for iteration in general, it pays to have many people test a build and you want a lot of data points to compare; just because you observe something in one playtest that might be a problem or something you might want to tweak, you should avoid the knee-jerk reaction of ceasing to watch the player while you go to make the change. You should instead continue to be available to observe your players. If you have another developer that can devote themselves specifically to dealing with bugs at the event, that would certainly be useful, but unless the bug is a show-stopper, do not drop everything the first time players run into an unexpected issue.

Gathering Feedback during an Event

The feedback you will get from a player when you are sitting or standing next to them will be different than what you would see if you were to observe them playing the game at their home. You want the feedback from that more personal environment because you will not ship with your game, and that environment will be the one where they will truly experience your game. You, as a designer, may squirm watching what a player does in your game when they are struggling or frustrated, especially when it is clear that you have failed to communicate something significant about that game, but you must observe and analyze how a player acts when these difficulties arise. It is more critical than anything a player will do when everything is working as designed. Answer questions about the game when asked, but try to let a player run through the game with as little prompting from you as possible. You are not interested in the interaction between you and the player; your focus should be the interaction between the player and your game. Also try to take notes as discreetly as possible. You do not want the player to act differently because they feel like they are being graded when what you are actually grading is your own game's levels. What you decide to take note of can depend on the specific game, but when trying to make sure that your game and its levels are as communicative as possible, there are some common things to investigate. Take note of when a player asks you a question about the game. What were they doing in the game and what did they ask you? Note when a player takes longer than you would expect in a given level and when they appear to be struggling with something in particular. As hard as it can be, pay close attention to when a player gets up and leaves: where were they in the game, was there something that they failed to do repeatedly, or was there something they did not seem to understand? Also mark down what players have to say about their experience afterward and try to get them to describe any problems they experienced in detail. Record, but do not place emphasis on any advice they might offer, as these are typically offhand suggestions that do not take the entirety of the game into account. When the event has concluded, you should have a decent amount of data describing how players interacted with your game, and by analyzing it, you should be able to greatly improve that interaction.

INTERPRETING FEEDBACK FROM AN EVENT

In addition to good practices to use when gathering feedback at an event, there are good strategies for analyzing that feedback to improve game levels.

Answering the Important Questions

The questions that players asked during a playtest are directly applicable to improving the level design of your game; if a player had to ask you a question about the goals of the game or how one of the systems in the game works, that means that whatever they wanted to know was not made clear through the design of the levels. If the goal of the game was unclear to a player, then adding some kind of visual signpost or landmark that is visible to them early on might help convey your goals (however, a clichéd reliance on actual signposts and arrows is discouraged). Some good examples could be a light off in the distance or a distant mountain peak, as in the case of the game *Journey*. If a player asked a question about some system in the game, one way to address that is to add a new level or level element that conveys that lesson. Adding a skill gate that requires that the player understand this aspect of the system in order to progress may also help.

Balancing for Challenge versus Struggle

Analyzing where players struggled in the game is important, especially if it was clear they were getting frustrated. Challenging players is important. Without any sort of challenge, players will lose interest in your game. However, certain kinds of frustration are just as likely to drive players away. When examining any one instance of struggle, ask yourself if the player was improving with each attempt at progressing or at least learning something in defeat. If the answer is no, then the difficulty of those challenges needs to be lowered to better fit player skill at that point. Another cause of frustrating struggle is competing challenges within the same level. You should ensure that players are taking the right lesson away from each failure. If a player completes a part of the level's challenges correctly, fails a challenge, then begins trying an entirely different strategy, you may need to break up those challenges into separate levels.

Combating Boredom with Better Pacing

If players left without finishing a full playtesting session, yet they appeared to understand or even initially to enjoy the game, they might have left due to lack of interest caused by your game's failure to communicate anything new to them about the mechanics in play. If this is occurring very early in the game, consider reordering your levels to put more interesting challenges earlier. Another method of correcting this situation is to combine earlier levels together, in order to push the introduction of more level elements forward, effectively speeding up the pace of the communication occurring between the player and your game.

Dealing with Drop-Off Points

It is important to assess every recorded instance of a player leaving in the middle of a play session during the event. These drop-off points typically result from a failure to communicate something significant to the player. If the player fails to use or understand a level element correctly when it is first introduced, you may need to simplify the layout of the level that introduces it or be more direct in your in-game explanation of that element. You may also want to examine what you are trying to teach the player with that level and determine if it is one discrete concept or multiple related concepts. If you find that it can be broken down into multiple concepts, then you should add levels preceding the drop-off point for each distinct concept. If a player fails to remember something about a level element in a later level, you might need to add another use of it between when it was introduced and the drop-off point. Another common cause of a drop-off point is introducing a new element in combination with too many other existing elements. After analyzing and incorporating the feedback that you have received, your game will be ready for the next event, and hopefully you will see more players connecting with the game without any coaching on your part.

PUTTING THIS INTO PRACTICE

I will now discuss how I employ these ideas in my personal work. I will begin by describing the game I am currently developing as I write this chapter and explain how its specifics altered aspects of my playtesting approach. *Lost Cave* is a 2D side-scrolling puzzle platformer, so when I talk about level design, I am also talking about puzzle design. While they are related, in most games they can be two different things, such as action adventures where a level may have a single puzzle. *Lost Cave* focuses heavily around a single mechanic; the ability to manipulate the camera perspective on the environment and have that perspective change the level (see Figures 14.2 and 14.3). In order to have the player understand the game, I have to teach them two different things. First, I have to teach them basic platforming, following the tropes of the genre (a button/space key to jump, left control stick on a game pad to move). This can be as simple as presenting a raised obstacle to the player. Playtesting has shown players will figure how to move and jump organically when confronted with a raised platform they have to get past in order to progress with no

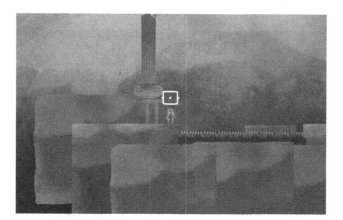

FIGURE 14.2 "Before" screen shot demonstrating the perspective mechanics in *Lost Cave*.

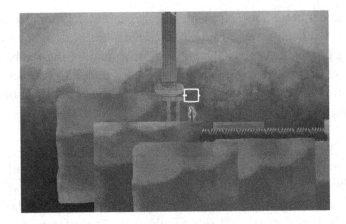

FIGURE 14.3 "After" screen shot demonstrating the perspective mechanics in *Lost Cave.*

prompting text needed. You can see a very basic example of this level layout in Figure 14.4. Having mentioned all this, at events where the typical attendee is experienced with platformers, I disable this level. It adds time between starting the game and introducing the core unique mechanic, and the fact that more experienced players have been trained to know how to jump the same way in countless other games is sufficient.

The real difficulty came in teaching the perspective mechanic to players. *Lost Cave* (originally *Cave*) was prototyped at the 2014 Global Game Jam, and I have to credit my codesigner, Rick Van Tassel, with many of the original concepts for levels. These levels were created to show off a variety

FIGURE 14.4 Basic level layout for teaching the player to jump.

of complex and intricate ways that the perspective shifting mechanic could be used. This worked fine at the game jam, but in taking it to small showcases after the event, it was evident that less than half of people were able to understand the perspective shifting mechanic without an explanation of some kind. Those that did pick up the basics were also likely to stop playing at one of a couple major drop-off points that occurred when level complexity spiked.

This led me to rethink our level designs. I started by breaking down every level we had in the game currently in terms of the different kinds of knowledge of the mechanic that a player would need to complete that level. These categories included requiring a certain degree of platforming skill, needing to know how to rotate the world, and needing to know how to zoom the world in and out. What I realized in doing this analysis was that we were inconsistent in what skills were required across levels—some later levels could be solved with only rotating, while some earlier levels required very precise uses of both rotation and zooming. Reordering the levels according to the number of skills required was helpful, but there were so few levels that each individual level and puzzle required a new skill, leaving the player with no time to get comfortable with an individual skill. So we added levels that required the same skills with different solutions, to make sure our players understood the aspect of the mechanic we were trying to teach them before moving on to the next lesson. I was also careful to avoid adding hazards to a level that was introducing new elements of the shifting mechanic. In Figure 14.5, you can see the level that introduces the concept of moving the environment does not have anything that can

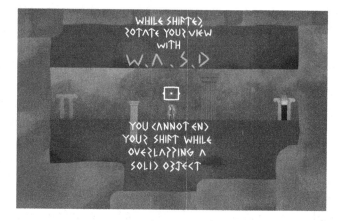

FIGURE 14.5   The level that introduces shifting to the player.

harm the player, it just requires that they use the mechanic to progress while allowing them to experiment with it in safety. In tutorializing these early levels, we added cave writing that explained how to perform each of these functions. I am an ardent opponent of this tactic in most games, but I have yet to find a better way of relating to the player what they can do when it comes to explaining our strange game mechanic. However, we were careful when using this tactic to make sure that we used the writing only to tell the player what they can do, but not what they have to do. That distinction preserves these early levels as puzzle levels in their own right, instead of turning them into an annoying tutorial segment. Testing at later events of this change in level flow and order was really encouraging; more people seemed to be understanding the game and playing to the end of the current set of levels.

Several early playtests also showed that many players did not know which objects in the level were in the foreground or background. This was a source of great confusion for them, causing them to use the perspective mechanic in seemingly random ways, as they could not anticipate what would change about the level as a result of their actions. I addressed this by adding color tints to objects in the environment based on how far into the foreground or background they were, which comes back to the notion of making your art as communicative as possible. This change meant players could see more of the makeup of the puzzle without having to shift everything around randomly to see how every piece of the level moved. The other change I made was to the second puzzle (shown in Figure 14.3). I originally had the platform that the player had to move as a background platform, meaning that moving it to the player required moving the environment in the opposite direction of what would be straightforward. I picked up on this because some players describing what they were doing mentioned that they thought that level pieces moved in the opposite direction of the player when shifting. The ambiguity in this early level had caused them to gain a false understanding of the shifting mechanic.

I tracked another source of player confusion to two critical mistakes I made when building the first level. In this level, I had an imposing cave entrance that players had to walk into to progress to the next level. This was unlike the level goals present in every other area of the game, and they were composed of foreground and background objects that players could move through without shifting, unlike every other level piece in the game. I had violated two rules of the game before I could even teach them to players. I reworked the first level to have a goal like all other levels, and removed the cave entrance level pieces that players could walk through. This way the first level teaches the player what they are looking for in each level, and does not risk imparting them with incorrect information about the rules of the game.

Another problem I observed was in the mixing of the platforming with the shifting mechanic. Often, players would use the shifting mechanics to alter the terrain in the correct way, but would fail the platforming challenge that this shifting would set up. This would send players back to the beginning of the level, and they would then assume that their entire approach had been wrong, leading to players experiencing frustration and asking for hints. As a result of this feedback, I had to decrease the difficulty of the platforming and height and length of jumps required, because the platforming is a part of the game, but it is secondary to the shifting mechanic.

Players also continually found new ways to progress through levels that had never occurred to me. Whenever I observed this, I watched how they beat the level to determine if the way they did it still taught the lesson of that level, and particularly if a player that solved it that way ran into difficulty understanding later levels. If they still learned the lesson, I would leave that solution in, and if not, then I would remove it as a possibility.

CONCLUSION

I have shown games I have worked on, including *Lost Cave*, at a variety of public events over the past several years. These events have ranged in attendance from 20 people to 20,000 people. Showing your game to the public can be exhausting and exhilarating at the same time, but I think it is an invaluable experience for any designer to see how an average player will interact with their game and play through their levels. Gathering feedback at these events allows a designer to identify critical problems and test the effectiveness of their solutions. My understanding of game design and my abilities as a designer have improved greatly as a result of these experiences and this process. I hope that taking your games to public events and using them to iterate on your game design and level design will help you as much as it has helped me.

CHAPTER 15

The Rule of 27s

A Comparative Analysis of 2D Screenspace and Virtual Reality Environment Design

Hadar Silverman

CONTENTS

Y OU'RE LOOKING AT A blank canvas, or napkin, or sheet of paper, and thinking, "Where do I draw that first line?" Maybe after a few seconds you make a decision. Then the second, the third, and so on and so on, and when point becomes line becomes plane becomes something we free-associate with, an image is formed in our minds, open to interpretation on the canvas or drawing medium, and quickly becomes subjected to criticism. As designers, for some inexplicable reason, our minds immediately look for structure within balance, color, contrast, foreground, background, and abstraction. In 1797, John Thomas Smith writes:

> Two distinct, equal lights, should never appear in the same picture: One should be principal, and the rest sub-ordinate, both in dimension and degree: Unequal parts and gradations lead the attention easily from part to part, while parts of equal appearance hold it awkwardly suspended, as if unable to determine which of those parts is to be considered as the subordinate. "And to give the utmost force and solidity to your work, some part of the picture should be as light, and some as dark as possible: These two extremes are then to be harmonized and reconciled to each other. (Reynolds' Annot. on Du Fresnoy.)
>
> Analogous to this "Rule of thirds", (if I may be allowed so to call it) I have presumed to think that, in connecting or in breaking the various lines of a picture, it would likewise be a good rule to do it, in general, by a similar scheme of proportion; for example, in a design of landscape, to determine the sky at about two-thirds; or else at about one-third, so that the material objects might occupy the other two: Again, two thirds of one element, (as of water) to one third of another element (as of land); and then both together to make but one third of the picture, of which the two other thirds should go for the sky and aerial perspectives.

JOHN THOMAS SMITH
Remarks on Rural Scenery, 1797

That doodle or image that we just placed on the canvas exists within a frame of reference. So what happens when that frame of reference no longer exists? Take the image we just created, peel it away from that canvas, and place it somewhere in your field of vision (metaphorically of course, unless you have access to some augmented reality equipment!) Something seems off. There is depth. Colors change because our light and environment is changing. The image we created may become lost in the environment, or our attention is quickly drawn to our peripheral vision where something else caught our attention. We shift our focus elsewhere, and suddenly that doodle once in our field of view is now just a blur against the horizon with our focus captured by another object or thought.

Virtual reality (VR), as a medium to create user experiences in the form of games, movies, or even a utility, is that ever-changing canvas with no specific focus predetermined and no frame or boundary that contains the image. This leads us to believe that designing for VR might be very much like designing for reality. But in reality, the architect depends heavily on time, space, and agency to guide design. Buildings and places are designed to withstand the impact of time. Space, in this case referring to any point in space, be it empty or filled, is subjected to the laws of physics with no two points in space occupying the same point in time. And agency determines what governs that space-time interaction.

In VR, the designer is not constrained by these perceived limitations. We do not have a frame of reference, and when we enter a VR experience, we quickly forget our canvas is actually a technological advancement sitting half an inch in front of our eyes. This is a double-edged sword. On one hand, not having these constraints or reference frames gives our imagination incredible power over our VR design. However, on the other hand, departing from these constraints quickly drives us toward a design that our mind—and body—may not be able to identify with. This chapter discusses differences and similarities between 2D screenspace design and VR environment design that have a direct impact on the way we play or experience digital media in the form of games or interactive art. In the context of this chapter, 2D screenspace design will refer to content that is displayed on monitors, televisions, or mobile devices where the user can still see their external reality around them (i.e., their living room or media room). VR environment design will refer to the opposite case, where our vision is comprised completely of the virtual reality experience through the use of a device that limits our cognizance of our external reality (such as with an Oculus Rift, GearVR, etc.). Furthermore, this chapter proposes a method of designing in VR that applies structure to VR space. By adding a third dimension into John Thomas Smith's rule of thirds, we can create VR experiences that guide users in VR and allow them to make educated decisions in VR through the use of focal points. Through extensive play testing and experimentation on a variety of platforms, it was found that a natural way to develop where these focal points should be is by adding another dimension to the rule of thirds'. We can take full advantage of a boundless canvas surrounding our eyes and ears in all directions and create multidimensional experiences that build drama through the inventive and careful use of scale, navigation, and detail applied to these 27 focal points.

SCALE: DETERMINING OUR BOUNDS (OR LACK THEREOF)

Scale is a great place to start in VR because it establishes or communicates the role that is intended for us in an experience by immediately conveying distance and how much space we occupy. Using architecture as a historical precedent, scale was used to magnify or humble the human experience in various artistic movements. For example, architecture that is designed to fit within the basic range or limitations of human movement gives us a more natural feeling associated with our cultural upbringings. However, when we deliberately deviate from our natural movement limitations and begin to occupy space that is beyond our natural movement capabilities, new feelings are perceived. When the space we occupy is much larger than us, more often than not we feel humbled by what is around us. Using the gothic cathedral as an example, these were designed specifically to evoke a sense of spiritual greatness that superseded the needs of our physical selves. When looking at the reverse case, standing in a space that is claustrophobic is uncomfortable, but also empowers us with the sense of being a giant. This is true of our natural environment as well. Consider standing in a canyon versus standing in a small cave and notice how these two experiences alter the feelings we have about ourselves and our environment.

This remains true in VR design as well, but differs from traditional 2D screenspace on several levels. First, and along the lines of John Thomas Smith's theory, scale on a computer monitor, television, or even canvas, is immediately subjected to the frame of reference in which it is presented. We look at the size of a character in a third-person gaming experience and make sure it is proportionally balanced against the background, giving the player enough time to react to their environment. This depends heavily on how much of the scene is displayed on our computer monitor. Scale is also used to determine the importance or power of the player. Traveling through a traditional framed screen experience, we perceive ourselves to be more powerful during midlevel gameplay progression because we are typically the same scale as our foes, but end bosses are made much larger to increase the drama. We feel less powerful, or feel that we'll have to use some other strategy to overcome the difference in size. All of this is encapsulated within a computer screen's physical dimensions.

In VR design, our frame of reference no longer exists in the same manner. We don't have a screen that creates a reference plane against which we can identify scalar differences. Therefore eye-level and environmental depth references become that much more important. Taking that same third-person example into play, the position of our camera/player perspective in the scene plays a critical role in establishing a frame of reference to help guide player experience. Since our external frame of reference (the computer screen frame) is gone, our background environment needs to serve as that frame of reference or boundary against which we can set our foreground. And this needs to occur not just in front of us, but all around us, which is where *focal-based design* becomes an asset.

Focal-based design alludes to the idea that because we don't have an external frame of reference to establish balance in our designs, we can use focus points at varying depths in an environment to deliberately place objects of interest to help us establish scale and points of reference in an environment or space we are occupying. The scalar differences in these focal points help ground us for one, and begin to serve as pointers in space that become beacons or objects in our periphery, encouraging/guiding us to explore an environment. So now that we've established scale using intermediary points of reference without a framed screen, creating contrast between points in space rather than in relation to a framed canvas or computer screen, the natural question arises, how do we get to that point of interest in VR?

NAVIGATION: HOW DO WE LOOK OR MOVE THROUGH THE EXPERIENCE (IF AT ALL)?

Changing perceived location in VR is undoubtedly one of the most difficult challenges in VR experience design. It is written about quite often in this field and while this chapter doesn't intend to address the scientific causes of VR sickness associated with dissonance in perceived movement, there are some general notions to consider that are generally agreed upon between developers and manufacturers of VR equipment and experiences.

When standing still in a VR environment, we have established that scale helps us understand the bounds of our occupiable space, the role we play within it, and how that makes us feel—like ants, like giants, or maybe just like humans. Or even in the case of the abstract, maybe we just feel... having no real association with what we are experiencing or where we are. As focal pointers are established in our field of view or potential field view (this includes everything behind us), we develop the desire to move and experience more. So how do we get there? Not going too far into Zeno's paradox, our first attempt to get somewhere might involve interpolating between two points, otherwise known as walking. Our second approach takes advantage of VR rulesets, or lack thereof, meaning we can teleport. We don't need to slowly (or quickly) travel from point A to point B. It is important to note that in this case, a VR teleport will refer to the instantaneous shift or replacement of the user's field of vision. To further clarify, in a third-person perspective game, an avatar may teleport to another location in an environment, but the user/player may maintain their same field of view during this action. Thus, a VR teleport is referring to only those cases where the player's view into the virtual world changes location instantaneously. Let's tackle the interpolation method first.

Recommendations for Character Movement in 3D

Walking or moving in general as a means of translocation requires careful consideration in the interest of the user's comfort level during a VR experience. It is generally accepted that movement should be constant when it occurs, meaning little to no acceleration. It should be slow, and it should provide a predictable outcome. Any movement that our body thinks will generate G-forces will create user discomfort. Speeding up, slowing down, and turning should all occur with zero acceleration, meaning the velocity must be constant. Testing this type of movement during all phases of development is an integral part of VR design. Furthermore, testing this content with a new user base should be implemented where possible. As we test our developments and slowly get our VR legs we become slightly more tolerant of the discomforts that improper VR design impose on us. Finding new groups of testers will help facilitate the development of smooth, comfortable VR experiences. While this type of movement is very unnatural in reality, it maintains user comfort in virtual reality translocation. There are pros and cons to this type of translocation. The pro side is that it allows us to create environments open to exploration. We give the user complete control over where and when they want to experience a certain perspective in VR. Similar to say, an open-world experience on a computer monitor, enabling player-controlled movement, gives users a sense of freedom to discover. This approach also maintains immersion at all times. It feels natural, regardless of how slow, to experience the space between two points to arrive at the second point. The downside to this style of movement is that first, those user discomfort warnings come into play, meaning this type of movement will usually be relatively slow. Translocating via interpolation differs greatly from 2D screenspace movement in that our body reacts much differently to movement in VR and so we are limited with how we can move through space. Second, this makes it difficult to predict where a player might travel regardless of how we want to guide them with our environmental focal cues. We would wind up designing and detailing a tremendous amount of space in VR per chance a player may or may not find their way to that point in space. With all of the time in the world, this might not be such a bad idea, and could result in some incredibly well detailed worlds. But in reality, we do have time limitations and giving the player control over movement may not be the best approach.

Teleporting in VR

The second approach, teleporting, is an incredibly useful way of traveling. There are several points to consider when teleporting in VR. The first relates back to 2D screenspace design: avoid leaps of faith (An Architectural Approach to Level Design, Totten, 150). A leap of faith is not seeing enough on your computer monitor and being forced to make a decision out of faith rather than what is present on screen. In VR, if a player is going to teleport, they need to be confident that they will arrive at the location they think they are teleporting to. Second, the environment's key focal points become critical to help maintain a person's familiarity with the place they are teleporting to. This means understanding position, orientation, and distance from their last position/orientation/location immediately on appearing in their new location. Third, the transition of the teleport plays a role as well. Immediately replacing ocular input with a new environment is a bit of a shock to the system, even if we know where we are going. However, integrating a fade or dissolving into that new location in some fashion or another helps give our minds time to mentally acknowledge the passage of time when traveling between two points, even if that time value is relatively low.

There are pros and cons to implementing this method as well. The downside to this approach is that teleporting is not natural to how we experience occupiable space, and therefore breaks immersion to an extent. The upside of this translocation method is that it maintains user comfort. It also allows an experience to be incredibly well controlled with each teleport location predetermined as a means of helping guide production efforts. The set-design approach can be used, meaning we know which points of the environment the camera will always be located at. This makes precalculated visibility culling easier to handle, can establish where to put desired detail into a project early on, and simplifies issues related to environment collision (brought up later in this chapter). So where is that detail, and how far away do we put it to guide us through an experience?

DETAIL, DEPTH, AND DISTANCE: HOW WE PLAN AND INTERPRET SPACE IN VR COMPARED AGAINST 2D SCREENSPACES

As mentioned earlier, when we take the borders away from our drawings or concept art, designing space becomes very similar to the way architects plan space. Regardless of how realistic or unrealistic our design intent is for an environment in VR, being able to communicate this design is essential to creating it. And a time-proven way to do this is with traditional architectural drawing styles: plan, section, elevation, and detail.

Floor Plans

Floor plans help us map out horizontal boundaries VR users should be able to experience. Reflected ceiling plans are just as important because in VR, some of the first actions people take when putting on VR equipment is to look all around them, especially up. This is important in VR design for a variety of reasons and is one of the reasons VR environment design differs heavily from 2D screenspace environment design. Looking back again at the third-person perspective example, when you're following your avatar through an environment, the entire environment is designed to allow space for the camera to travel behind and above the avatar, often looking down. Ceilings don't really play a large role here, because gameplay would be too awkward to have to negotiate what is above the player during critical choice-making processes. The space above us is better used as space for our player cameras. In VR, however, we have a new input mechanism—rotational tracking. Rotational tracking makes it seamless to engage the space above us. Six degrees of freedom (6DoF) refers to movements where vertical and lateral character movements are implemented. Helicopters, for example, are 6DoF vehicles, while labyrinths are much more viable in the third person. Even in first-person cases or cockpit-based games, having rotational head tracking allows a user to make much more educated decisions based on what is above them without compromising their location or situational position. Take the example of *Descent*. While this is a 6DoF flying game, the player is required to move or rotate the ship in the actual direction they wish to travel, which could be a huge risk. In VR games, a player can simply look up while continuing their course.

Architectural Sections

The use of an architectural section relates to scale. A section helps communicate the relationship between our floor plan and ceiling plan, effectively establishing the design intent of the scale in an environment through differences in height. In games that occupy 2D screenspace, a section can be compared to early platformers (Totten, 56). The game is essentially played in sections. In VR, planning with a section drawing is very similar to planning space in 2D screenspace, as it establishes our vertical design intent. Elevations can be used to define vertical differences in background and foreground. They are great for communicating textures, surfaces, and patterns that the player will be exposed to, as well as for planning details.

Architectural Details

Details in the architectural world can mean a few things. But in this case we will focus on the meaning associated with how things come together in the environment. How does the floor meet the wall that meets the ceiling? How does a light fixture fasten to a surface? How does a window or door fit into an opening? These are all points of convergence relating to the physical constraints that follow the rule that no two objects can occupy the same point in space and time. However, in VR environment design, these convergence points relate much more so to John Thomas Smith's rule of thirds applied in all dimensions. We rely heavily on these convergence points to understand and guide our *view direction* through the space we are designing.

It is important to consider certain advantages and limitations of designing details in VR when compared against 2D screenspace environments when using the environment to encourage the player to look around. First, rotational head tracking is no longer implicit of a player turning around. While this is possible and occasionally implemented in games presented in 2D screenspace, this has a pretty big impact on player controls in VR. Taking a first-person experience as an example, *looking* left and right is often implicit of *turning* left and right. In third person, these two actions can be disassociated; however, the result is confusing to gameplay, and many games autocorrect this disassociation by reorienting either the camera or player. In VR, however, the player needs to maintain control over body and head orientation at all times. If there is a dissociation between head movement and body movement that does not correspond to a person's physical movement (in reality), this may result in user discomfort. Given this response, it is important to design details that guide a player's view, but also allow a user time to adjust to their new focus point. And if they desire to move to that point (if the game environment controls permit this), the user needs time to turn and move without being penalized. Without this adjustment time, user discomfort may be incurred.

Viewpoint Considerations in VR

Understanding where the focus details are in a space compared against a user's location is a great planning tool during design development of VR space. Let's look at the viewpoint cases: forward/backward, left/right, above/below. Through extensive testing, it was found that people new to VR would more often than not keep their head looking forward during an entire experience. In many cases, this is the fault of the environment designer. One of the powerful advantages in VR as an environment design medium is that we are not restricted to looking straight ahead at a 2D screen to interact with an experience. Things should be happening to the left, the right, above, and below. So if a player is only looking straight ahead, something needs to occur in the environment that encourages and rewards them for looking in other directions. However, this comes with a caveat rooted back to hardware consideration.

Mobile VR and *tethered VR* have two very distinct differences that may seem obvious, but for argument purposes should be stated to understand their influence in VR experience design. When a designer builds an environment that encourages a player to look around in all directions, a mobile headset would be ideal in that it allows total freedom of movement without any impact on the user's external/physical existence. If a player is encouraged to look around an environment in a tethered experience, immersion does have an impact because of the tether. Turning around causes the headset cable to physically move or wrap around us. We can feel this, and this feeling is not natural, nor does it correspond with what is most likely happening in the VR environment. So while encouraging the player to look around is important and vastly improves user experience in VR, caution needs to be taken on how much they can move around and the impact that movement will have on their physical surroundings.

The last two directions to consider have a huge impact on scale. Looking above and looking below create two very different feelings. Consider walking into a large open atrium. One of the first impulses a person has when entering this space is to look up. The same is true in VR. Putting on a VR headset and entering a world where the space above us is grandiose in nature, we tend to look up. If the space we enter is claustrophobic, then typically the opposite occurs, which leads to another VR challenge: looking down.

In a 2D screenspace game, we are detached from our avatar no matter what. Even in a first-person game, we are cognizant of the room we are sitting in (in reality), and so it's no big deal to look down in our game world in 2D screenspace to see the ground or a ledge from a better perspective. In VR space, this leads to several problems. Looking down in VR space, one of the first things people notice is that their body is missing. This immediately creates a sense of dissonance with the VR experience. In many cases where designers have created a body for players to acknowledge, it is still often an uncomfortable situation to be in because we know it is not our body. We can't feel it, we can't move it, and depending on how body model animation is handled, it can be awkward to move around with. Motion control hardware (and/or positional hand tracking) is helpful in this field, but it's important to know that this is something to be considered when designing an experience in first-person view. An alternative would be third-person view that avoids the situation and makes looking down a positive action to better view the avatar we are controlling. In the case of abstract experiences, looking down has virtually little impact because abstract experiences detach our minds from our body or physical environment anyhow.

Detail distance also plays a key role in VR design when compared against 2D screenspace design. In 2D screenspace, designers often distort scale to fake distance. Known as the parallax effect, a designer can simulate distant mountains in the background by moving them subtly as a player walks quickly through a moving foreground. In VR, the same effect does not work and creates user discomfort. Mesh scale can, however, be altered to simulate distance, as long as the object is static. Using this same scenic outdoor environment as an example, we could design an environment where a mountain is placed somewhere in the background, but rather than place it several kilometers away from the viewer, we can place it within the bounds of our level and simply reduce its scale to fake the distance— as long as the player will never conceivably get close to this object. When viewing distant objects it can be a challenge to give the player feedback that acknowledges or confirms where they are looking. To accommodate for this, reticles can be used with careful consideration. Looking through a scope or using some sort of targeting reticle in VR can induce double vision, causing us to close one eye to aim correctly. To fix this, reticles need to be stereoscopic and exist near the same distance as the object being targeted. In 2D screenspace this effect does not occur, because our eyes are focusing on the physical television or computer monitor rather than simulated depth in a near-eye device (https://www.google.com/design /spec-vr/interactive-patterns/display-reticle.html). In the opposite case, objects being close to the user, another impulse needs to be considered and designed around: the desire to touch objects in VR. This can be problematic if we are not using motion control devices in conjunction with VR headsets. If we get close to an object, we impulsively want to reach out and feel it depending on the aesthetic, and thereby are quickly reminded that we are in a simulation when we don't see our hands or can't feel the object. This leads us to collision in VR.

Collision Considerations in VR

Collision considerations in a VR environment differ from 2D screenspace in several ways. Collision in a 2D screenspace environment is designed with optimization and visual readability in mind. Optimization matters because collision—or hit detection—is a somewhat expensive operation and a lot of information is needed for game-world objects to react in an expected manner from the viewpoint of a player. So quite often, per-poly collision is avoided where it's not needed to help simplify what actually needs to collide in game and to help simplify how things react when colliding. But for the most part, collision is generally simulated in a way where the collision volume closely resembles the render mesh that is visually representing the object to collide with in screenspace. In many cases, this render mesh versus collision mesh is somewhat ignored or flexible to help a game flow. It's OK if players can overlap in many cases, and this is often encouraged to prevent problems in gameplay flow, taking full advantage of the fact the objects in a computer world can occupy the same point in space and time. In VR, however, collision plays a much more critical role in building a sense of immersion and can complicate gameplay design for several reasons. Given that positional tracking is quickly becoming a fundamental aspect of VR space design, the space a player occupies in VR will be subjected to two major collision considerations. First, the protagonist will have a collision volume of sorts designed to stay within the bounds of the world. Second, the camera, or player's head, or any point at which the player sees the game, is subjected to positional tracking freedom, meaning that if a player moves their head in reality, the camera in VR space needs to move as well—no matter what. So if the player hits a wall in VR space but there's still room to lean one's head in reality, stopping that collision from going through a wall will create a disconnect between VR and reality, resulting in user discomfort. However, if the alternative is chosen, which is to allow the player's head in VR to go through the wall based on positional tracking, the world immersion is broken, revealing parts of the world that weren't meant to be seen. The desired solution is therefore to design the world in a way where the player cannot be within positionally tracked physical range of a virtual obstacle. In cases where this virtual/real collision does occur, this can be used to increase immersion by having the VR world react in some way or another to the positionally tracked collision. Maybe the wall in the previous example would crumble or somehow give way, revealing another room to explore. But in cases where this is not intended, it is important to consider a design that naturally encourages players to stay slightly distant from objects they could collide with that might break immersion.

CONCLUSION

Throughout this chapter we have taken a look at scale, movement, and detail in VR space compared against 2D screenspace design. Notable differences have been identified to the point where simply placing a game that was designed for 2D screenspace will not automatically work in VR space. When considering a platform port, it would be advantageous to understand what the fundamental goals and objectives are in the 2D screenspace game, and reevaluate how those objectives might be reinterpreted in a VR environment. Even though there are many limitations in VR design, there are many more advantages that give designers a powerful new medium with which to explore VR interactive environment design.

Furthermore, when designing VR space, we acknowledge we no longer have a frame of reference or border around our environment. The environment we create will completely surround the user, which takes us out of the rule of thirds image composition world and puts us into the architectural world of plan, section, and elevation to plan perceived occupiable space. The constraints that VR no longer has with our physical world opens a lot of doors. But with this comes the need to respect limitations in physical tracking space, body/mind movement disassociations, and virtual collisions that could break immersion or cause user discomfort.

To help manage these trade-offs, especially when transitioning from designing an experience in 2D screenspace to designing an experience in VR space, adding another dimension to the rule of thirds gives the designer structure and guidance to help focus their efforts. It establishes convergence or focal points that are used to build contrast in an environment and consequently drama. Focal-point-based design can be used to channel our efforts into key moments of an environment that help guide designers to build immersive and intuitive VR worlds.

ADDITIONAL REFERENCES

Carrapa, Daniel. 2014. The architect's guide to life in video games. http://architizer
.com/blog/the-architects-guide-to-life-in-video-games/.

Francis, Bryant. 2015. How devs deal with 4 problem areas in VR game design.
http://www.gamasutra.com/view/news/254720/How_devs_deal_with_4
_problem_areas_in_VR_game_design.php.

Gschwari, Andreas. 2015. Designing for virtual reality. http://www.gamesindustry
.biz/articles/2015-02-11-designing-for-virtual-reality.

Hopkins, Casey. 2015. Designing for virtual reality. https://ustwo.com/blog/designing
-for-virtual-reality-google-cardboard/.

Kerr, Chris. 2015. Designing zero-gravity virtual reality in *Adrift*. http://www
.gamasutra.com/view/news/261915/Designing_zerogravity_virtual_reality
_in_Adrift.php.

Oculus documentation. 2016. https://developer.oculus.com/documentation/intro-vr
/latest/concepts/bp_intro/.

Wawro, Alex. 2015. Valve survey suggests most VR experiences will be in the bedroom. http://gamasutra.com/view/news/256128/Valve_survey_suggests_most
_VR_experiences_will_be_in_the_bedroom.php.

CHAPTER 16

Expression Versus Experience

Balancing Art and Usability Needs in Level Design

Christopher W. Totten

CONTENTS

L EVEL DESIGN HAS ELEMENTS of both artistic expression and usability design. As a form of expression in game design, level design involves arranging art assets to create visually compelling and emotionally evocative spaces. As usability design, it involves arranging game objects to communicate the functions of the game and reinforce player behaviors (Totten 2014). Often, reconciling the two is not a concern, as developers set their own expressive and usability goals at the outset of projects. However, when the expressive goals of a game are set by external factors, such as during the creation of artful game projects, the designer must find ways to carefully balance these goals with the usability factors that will allow the game to be playable.

This chapter uses the term "artful games" to generally describe types of games that are created for artistic or expressive purposes. These games include those from the art games movement, which utilized interactive and semiotic elements of games to "challenge cultural stereotypes, offer meaningful social or historical critique, or tell a story in a novel manner" (Holmes 2003). Early examples of these games use devices such as barring players from achieving goals to show the hopelessness of social conflicts (Bogost 2007) or manipulating a player's item reserves to demonstrate the passage of time* (Nintendo 2000). Art historian and game designer John Sharp further delineates these works into art games (previously discussed), game art (nonplayable works that utilize games or elements of games as the medium), and artists' games (playable experiences that address metaphysical themes) (Sharp 2015). In terms of usability and level design, artful games' experiential goals may involve the use of disorienting or nonuser-friendly

---

* These games are often the work of academics or independent (indie) game developers, but can, based on the opinions of critics, include commercial games. It is this author's opinion that certain commercial games can retroactively be called art games based on their inventive storytelling structures or the issues addressed by them and how those issues are supported by gameplay mechanics, and citations in this chapter will reflect that.

design elements that confound players, but ultimately aid the expressive power of the game. Games that take inspiration from the aesthetics of fine arts and other media suffer similar pressures, often having to follow strict formal rules that deny the use of user-friendly design solutions.

This chapter describes the playtesting process I employed for the artful game *Lissitzky's Revenge* (Totten 2015), which translates the visual style and themes of posters by the early twentieth century constructivist designer El Lissitzky and his contemporaries into interactive game levels (Figure 16.1). As pieces of art modeled after Lissitzky's work, these levels had to adhere to the artist's visual and formal language in its representation of game objects, level arrangements, and object interactions. As scenes of gameplay, these levels had to teach players how to operate the game and provide a satisfying experience for these players as they progressed. This chapter will explore the creative goals of both art and games to provide a basis for reconciling areas where they are disparate from one another. It will then examine the playtesting processes utilized during the development of *Lissitzky's Revenge* to gain feedback on the effectiveness of the game's abstract visual elements as gameplay signifiers. Lastly, it will show how I utilized this feedback to maintain the integrity of the artwork's aesthetic and formal elements while eliminating "unfun" (Rogers 2010) portions of the game.

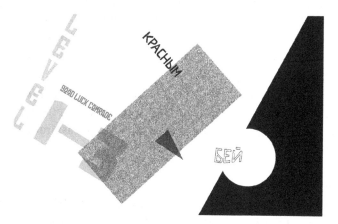

FIGURE 16.1 Screenshot of *Lissitzky's Revenge*, a game based on various works by early twentieth-century graphic designer, El Lissitzky.

THE GOALS OF ART AND GAMES

To find how a game might achieve artistic goals while providing an entertaining game experience, it is important to explore the goals of both expressive art and digital games. While many goals of game development lean heavily toward technical advancement, the considerations we are most concerned with come from software user experience (UX) design: ability for users to determine how to use the game, clear visual signifiers, distinct mapping of actions to feedback, and so on (Norman 2013). These contribute greatly to making entertaining experiences for players. These considerations, from a technical field related to digital games' history as software products, greatly influence the goals of game making.

Compared to the long history of developers approaching games as software applications, the development of games for expressive or artistic purposes is a relatively new phenomenon. As computer hardware power increased in the 1980s, developers such as Cinemaware and Sierra experimented with the abilities of games to tell stories (Donovan 2010). Throughout the 1990s, games of genres such as Japanese role-playing games (RPGs) used strong, authored narratives as a selling point. In the 2000s the notion of strongly authored content in games evolved to include the goals of art house media, such as "the foregrounding of abstract themes through dialogue and direction of the viewer to the image" and concepts of "subjectivity, point of view, reflexivity, and open texture" (Manchel 1990). These goals reflect the aims of much older media such as film, graphic design, and the fine arts but clash with goals of software development that emphasize clarity and easily understood communication to users. This dissonance is one of the reasons that Roger Ebert famously declared that games could not be art (Ebert 2010), as he believed that the notion of players' agency over their experience is at direct odds with authors' intent. In light of these discussions, this section will compare some potential goals of fine art and authored media with those of games to provide a basis for discussing how game developers may balance artistic aspirations with UX considerations.

Goals of Art

It is difficult to discuss goals of art, as there is little agreement on what art is: definitions of art are highly subjective. To Ebert, it would seem that part of what defines art is the uncontested perspective of an individual author. Many consider Ebert's own medium, film, to have been entered in the artistic canon when film studios and cultural institutions included films in collections because it made good business sense for both sides (Decherney 2012). To these critics, curators' and academics' tastes weigh heavily in when and how media is included in the canon, further demonstrating how subjective factors weigh into the goals of art. While highly subjective perspectives seem to make setting goals for art difficult; and indeed, this chapter does not attempt to provide an exhaustive account of goals for artworks, the ones offered here provide examples that level designers may find useful for creating artful and usable game worlds.

Technique

In the shifting goals of art in the past several centuries, we can see different sets of criteria that inform the contemporary artist's goals. The academic era of the seventeenth through nineteenth centuries emphasized technique and a heavily controlled hierarchy of painting types based on the subject and size of the work (Duro 2007). Academies were known for rigorous and prescriptive training: students would begin their education in several stages of drawing from examples—prints of other artists' work, sculptures, and finally nude models. After gaining proficiency in drawing, they could then begin instruction in painting. Students in each stage had to be approved by faculty before entering the next one. Likewise, the previously mentioned hierarchy of painting types—or *genre* system—further reinforced the academies' emphasis on technique: paintings with copied subjects were seen as lower than biblical or mythological scenes composed by students. This rigor extended to the material aspects of how works were created: canvas sizes were chosen based on where in the genre hierarchy a painting was and media was applied to these canvases in very particular ways to fit the standards of the academy.

While some of these practices are applicable today in art schools, especially when students are beginning their instruction, or in industries where realistic styles are valued, the specificity of the older academic style demonstrates the ways that goals may be set based on technique. Artists wanting success in this system had to hone their skills in each level to earn instruction in new techniques. Likewise, being chosen for exhibition had much to do with demonstrating your skill with a medium. In this way, it may be said that mastery of specific techniques or mediums has been a widely influential factor in determining goals for art.

Curation

While many artists worked through the academy system, there were many critics that argued its results were too homogeneous, too derivative, or too restrictive (Murray 2013). This changed when artists began to experiment wildly with style, medium, and composition in the nineteenth century and into the twentieth. Art in this period has been organized through curation based on geographic or cultural conditions, or on how the works were produced. Exhibitions became central not only for showing work, but also for directing how artworks were to be contextualized among other works like it (Ormiston 2014). Even commercial art and illustration—such as the posters of Toulouse-Lautrec (Meggs and Purvis 2011) or the cartoons of Winsor McCay (Braun and McCay 2014)—has been recontextualized as more traditional artworks through curation.

Curation as a goal is distinctly different from judging. Curation in art is the gathering and sorting of works, often for public exhibition or collection. Where the technical or stylistic sophistication of a work may be judged as adhering to a particular set of standards, with winners in competitions being the work that most adequately meets these standards, curation can include works of varying levels of sophistication depending on what a curator is hoping to achieve through their sorting. As a curator for events and exhibitions, I have both begun with a distinct theme in mind for an exhibition and also solicited general calls for submission then chosen to highlight trends I see in the contributed works. In several cases, works that may have not been as polished as others were included because they demonstrated a quality or theme present in other works in the exhibit. For artists, seeking curation as a goal may mean creating work inspired by or referencing the work of past artists so their work may be considered for display with them.

Expression

The last goal we will cover is expression—the intent of an author that their work presents a particular idea or point of view. In this chapter, we have already seen several allusions to the notion of art as an expressive medium by way of film. Siska's notions of "subjectivity, point of view, reflexivity, and open texture" (Manchel 1990) are key to seeing art as able to express ideas beyond the visual elements on the canvas itself. By the 1920s it was common to see visual art express political ideas, such as the work on which *Lissitzky's Revenge* is based, *Beat the Whites with the Red Wedge*,* a Bolshevik propaganda poster. As a film critic, Roger Ebert was likely familiar with *auteur theory*, the notion that the director is the primary apparatus of authorship in filmmaking and that films are based on their individual vision (Ryan 2015). This closely mirrors his view that statements could not be art because player interactions could undermine the author's perspective.

Some of these definitions of expression in art assume that the art medium is passive, meaning that the audience is receiving the argument of an author as in film, literature, or some visual arts. However, more active arts such as architecture can still be expressive, despite the audience having significantly more affordances for directing their experience with the art itself (Totten 2011). Urban designs such as Ebenezer Howard's Garden City (Figure 16.2) and Le Corbusier's Ville Contemporaine express the designers' ideas of separating city functions to allow for wide green spaces. Sacred space design is especially expressive, integrating aspects of religious ceremonies or belief systems into the architecture itself: building orientations, plan designs, artwork, and so on. Architects utilize expressive elements by exploring the physical forms of their buildings or influencing the ways in which occupants interact with them. In these ways, architecture demonstrates how art can be expressive as passive media as a sculptural art and as active media by integrating user interactions into the design.

Holmes's definition of art games prioritizes expression over other art goals that we have discussed here. Likewise, Sharp's criteria for other artful game works include some expression of thematic ideas beyond the work itself, as is common in contemporary art. Therefore, many developers aspiring to create artful games assume their game's goals must be expressive. However, as we have seen, artworks have throughout even the last several centuries had many goals, including technique and curation.

As stated previously, this is but a small sampling of the types of goals artworks might accomplish. With these, however, we can look at the goals of games and find several places where level designers can find crossover and create works that balance artistic and gameplay considerations.

---

* *Beat the Whites with the Red Wedge*. El Lissitzky. 1919. Lithographic poster.

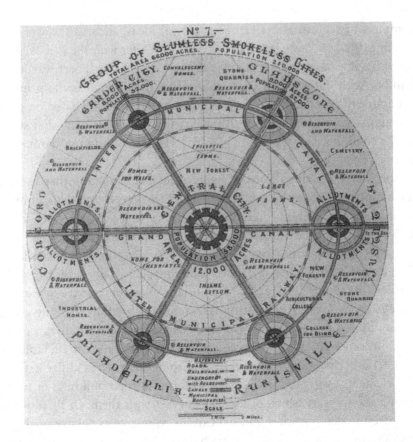

FIGURE 16.2 The plan of Ebenezer Howard's theoretical Garden City design shows how the functions of a city—living, working, commuting, administration, and so on—are isolated from one another. Designers like Howard believed in decentralizing city life and incorporating the automobile and other at-the-time new transportation methods.

Goals of Games

Unlike the fine arts, digital games have a far shorter history and have gone through far fewer evolutions in how they are judged. That games are taking on some of the goals of art might itself be considered a significant evolution, and the transition has not been easy. For much of their early history, digital games were tools for developing or demonstrating other technologies such as artificial intelligence, simulations, or graphics processing (Donovan 2010). Their goals were therefore based on the goals of the technology being developed through the game. The ways in which games are judged today is also a by-product of popular gaming journalism from the 1980s onward and their review methods. These outlets, such as *Nintendo Power, GamePro,* or *IGN,* evaluate games as both pieces of technology and entertainment by how well they worked and how engaging they are for audiences. These reviewers have, like academics or curators of art have for artists, dictated the popular tastes of gamers and set many of these goals for game developers.

Technical Elements

The first major goal of popular game development has been a game's technical quality. The most noticeable in large-industry commercial games is graphic quality: as computers and game consoles advance in graphics processing power, they are capable of generating more realistic images. Less noticeable by consumers* but of great importance to developers is the technical polish of a game: the lack of significant bugs or glitches in the software.

This goal is one of the most divisive in gaming, as critics claim that increased visual fidelity in games is both decreasing the industry's emphasis on building interesting game experiences (Papathanasis 2015) and increasing the obstacles preventing small or diverse developers from gaining industry relevance (Campbell 2013). However, technical achievement in other areas—creating functionally polished games, inventing new interface devices, or building games around new types of simulations—has become a significant force in events such as the Independent Games Festival, Experimental Gameplay Workshop, and Smithsonian American Art Museum Indie Arcade. When considered in this broader way beyond simply the quality of game graphics, technical goals become more about the *craft* of game-making rather than simply demonstrating computing power.

Gameplay

Where the technical goals of games represent how a game is made, the gameplay goals of games represent the experiential elements of games. In the *GamePro* review system, this was best represented by the "Fun Factor" category. It is outside the scope of this chapter to give full commentary on the elements that create an engaging game, but there are some general guidelines

---

* This statement assumes that in-game glitches are relatively minor. AAA games have, in the past several years, become increasingly known for being released with significant visual errors and game-breaking bugs that must be patched with downloadable updates.

that can contribute to the investigation of *Lissitzky's Revenge's* gameplay design and playtesting goals and therefore the goals of artful games.

A core element of creating engaging gameplay is to increase the quality of a game's feel (Swink 2008), which can be roughly defined as the amount of feedback that players are given for their in-game actions. A simple example would be to add a combination of animated particles and sound effects when a player attack collides with an enemy character. Done properly, these additions can make the game not only more understandable, but also more exciting. Other elements include providing players rewards for their actions in the form of power-ups or honing the difficulty level of a game so that players feel that they are being constantly challenged but not overwhelmed.

Player Usability

Related to the goal of keeping players engaged through gameplay is the goal of making a game user-friendly. The game-feel elements that make an engaging experience also assist in giving players signifiers that their actions are meaningful in the game environment. Beyond feedback, however, designers need to teach players how to play their games in the first several minutes. Depending on the goals of the developer, they may choose to include an intensive tutorial or design their levels to direct players to make proper gameplay actions.

Methods for teaching these behaviors include a combination of allowing players to have adequate opportunities to experiment and then rewarding players for actions that lead them toward gameplay goals (Totten 2014). This can be a significant challenge for level designers, who are responsible for directing these gameplay scenarios, but one that can be addressed through extensive playtesting. In this way, they can see which game-feel elements they are using to communicate to players are clear and which ones are not.

Having established the goals for both art and games, we can take a look at *Lissitzky's Revenge* to see how its development was influenced by both. Then, we can see how playtesting helped ensure that these goals were met while balancing the artistic goals of the game and the elements that allow it to be an engaging play experience.

DEVELOPMENT OF *LISSITZKY'S REVENGE*

Now that we've investigated goals of both art and games, we can explore *Lissitzky's Revenge* and the goals game designers might set for themselves when creating a game based on famous artworks. *Lissitzky's Revenge's* development began as part of a larger project, Atelier Games (Pie for Breakfast Studios 2015), where games would be created inspired by pieces of famous artwork. Each game would adopt not only the visual style and themes of the work, but also the generation methods for the art: if a work was created with oil paints, the game's art would be made with oil paint, and so on. The purpose of the project was to evaluate fine art methods for use in game development with the hope of increasing accessibility of game development to those already skilled in the arts.

Core Mechanic Analysis of El Lissitzky's
Beat the Whites with the Red Wedge

For the first game of the Atelier Games series, Lissitzky's *Beat the Whites with the Red Wedge* (Figure 16.3) was chosen as the inspiring artwork. To begin the series, I wanted to create a gateway game that had many of the hallmarks of traditional action games. For this, *Beat the Whites with the Red Wedge*'s violent theme—the Bolsheviks' overthrowing anti-Communist forces (The White Movement) during the Russian Civil War—was ideal. The poster utilizes the concept of figure-ground, where contrasting positive and negative space is used to create the impression

FIGURE 16.3 El Lissitzky's *Beat the Whites with the Red Wedge*, 1919. This Bolshevik propaganda poster utilized ideas of suprematism, which believed in the creation of art from simple shapes for art's sake rather than creating art for external ideologies, and constructivism, which did utilize art to influence social causes.

of shapes (Figure 16.4). Through this, the image creates the impression of the white circle as both a void that can be broken into and an object that the red wedge is stabbing at, which is supported by the flourish of red and white objects around the impact point. The composition of these objects and the way they are juxtaposed gives the impression that if the poster were animated, we would see them in constant motion, overlapping and rearranging themselves continuously.

From the simple formal analysis of *Beat the Whites with the Red Wedge*, I derived the potential core mechanics of attacking, breaking, stabbing, and overlapping. The story of the original work seemed to be that the red wedge

FIGURE 16.4 In figure ground, the contrast between dark and light portions of an image can be used to create multiple images depending on whether the viewer is focusing on the dark portions of the image or the light portions of the image. In this example, the dark shapes form the impression of two faces while the light portions create the impression of a vase.

had broken some sort of barrier (marked either by the gray squares or the black mass itself) that protected the white circle and was victorious. The poster would have us believe that the wedge is a hero, but a colleague of mine suggested that the work is propaganda, so the wedge's heroism is up for debate. The game, therefore, would be one where the player controlled the red wedge, which could move and perform a rushing attack of some sort that would use its sharp point as a weapon. In each level, players would push back a black form to expose the white circle, which would then be attacked.

Artistic Goals of *Lissitzky's Revenge*

For *Lissitzky's Revenge's* artistic goals, I wanted to explore how abstract shapes could become symbols and how gameplay could be used to assign meaning to those symbols. Likewise, I wanted to explore notions of how gameplay itself is propagandistic, molding player actions through symbols and rewards. Lastly, I wanted to pay homage to the aesthetic of El Lissitzky and other constructivists through interactive shapes that players would juxtapose as they played the game.

These goals explore technique, both through the previously discussed desire of the Atelier Games project to evaluate fine art media for game art and because they are about adherence to a particular art style. They also approach expression by embodying my own interpretations of Lissitzky's work in gameplay mechanics. Later in the development of the game, I would also add elements that made arguments about the propaganda-like effects gameplay mechanics can have in some art and persuasive games: early levels establish the morality of the game, while later levels allow the player to question it. Lastly, the game was developed to appear in curated shows rather than as a commercial product. By aligning itself with art popular in museum collections such as the media arts collection at the Smithsonian American Art Museum and others displaying video games, the game walks a line that makes it relevant both as media art and game.

First Prototypes and Finding Other Inspiration

I was easily able to create the first prototypes in Construct 2, an HTML 5 game engine that utilized a visual scripting language to make gameplay behaviors. This was beneficial both because my art skills are much more advanced than my scripting skills and because of the "show that anyone can do it" nature of the Atelier Games project. For this game, I decided to utilize paper cutouts as the art medium. The original poster was a lithographic print, but many of Lissitzky's works utilized either paint on architecturally drafted compositions or collage (Beat the Whites with the Red Wedge 2016). Likewise, paper cutouts were a common medium for graphic artists with similar visual styles (Meggs and Purvis 2011). Lissitzky was trained as an architect, so I used my own architectural training and drafted my cutouts to maintain the proper look (Figure 16.5).

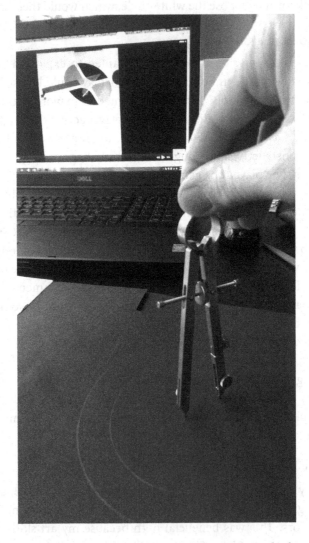

FIGURE 16.5 Drafting a circular-shaped object with a drafting compass. Lissitzky was trained as an architect, so I drafted all the cutout shapes that I made for the game.

The result was a very attractive minimalist game that, beyond using an attack to push back a black barrier and expose your enemy via a cool figure ground trick, had very little to do (Figure 16.6).

Lissitzky's original poster has other elements: the words "beat," "white," "red," and "wedge" in Cyrillic lettering, gray boxes, and particles that emanate from the contact between the wedge and the circle. I thought that these elements might make good game objects but had little idea of what they could do. When I was creating the idea for *Lissitzky's Revenge*, I had thought that the mechanics of breaking through a barrier to get to an enemy agent were a lot like the premise of the Atari 2600 game *Yars' Revenge* (Atari 1981). This similarity even inspired the game's title, so I looked to it again to find a gameplay purpose for the other parts of Lissitzky's poster.

In *Yars' Revenge*, players are a member of the insectoid Yar race trying to defeat the evil Qotile, who is hiding behind a force field. Players can either shoot or ram the barrier to expose the Qotile, then must fire a cannon from across the screen to defeat their enemy. As the player tries to accomplish this goal, the Qotile can fire its own missiles that players must dodge either by moving out of their way or by hiding in the safe zone in the middle of the screen. I thought that these mechanics from *Yar's Revenge* provided some promising suggestions of things that Lissitzky's graphics could do in-game. The white circle could shoot out the Cyrillic words "beat" and "red" at the player, signifying that they were trying to

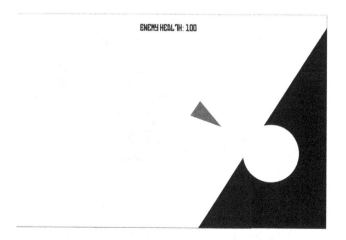

FIGURE 16.6 The first prototype for *Lissitzky's Revenge*, a very simple translation of the original work.

defeat you. While the words were simply copy on the poster, their positioning made them feel as though they were part of the image's constant motion, so I felt that a projectile fit this interpretation. Since I was making two words, I decided to have one be a regularly shot bullet while the other would be a homing missile that fired in long intervals. Likewise, the gray squares, actually fields of closely packed black dots, could be the force fields that let players hide from enemy bullets as they felt much less solid in the poster than the other shapes. The placement of these objects became an important element of level design, as staying in them to reach switches or other mechanisms while the circle fired on players could create a variety of interesting gameplay scenes.

I liked the idea of making players use a special attack to finish the enemy, but rather than having players charge and fire a separate object, I thought it would better fit the poster if the wedge delivered the final blow itself, physically, with a charged-up attack. For this, I made the gray squares double as both safe zone and charging station: players would have to stay in the gray squares for several seconds until they saw a particle effect showing they were charged. The gameplay flow now had players either starting the level with some combination of charging and destroying the barrier (it could happen in either order), then ramming the white circle, all while avoiding the circle's Cyrillic missiles (Figure 16.7).

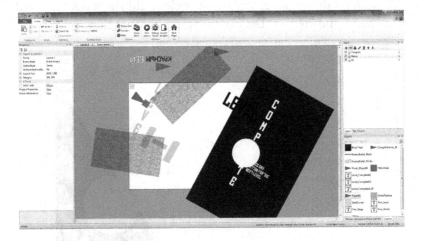

FIGURE 16.7 An in-engine screenshot of a prototype level of *Lissitzky's Revenge* with all the game objects in place. Note the game objects for the particles and bullets outside of the main gameplay area (with a white background) and the magenta box on the tip of the wedge that acts as the attack collider for the player character.

New Levels and Establishing Meaning in Game Symbols

Once I was happy with how the first levels played and looked, I thought to add more content to the game to both extend the number of symbols players interacted with during gameplay and find opportunities to explore propaganda with the game. I decided to have several game worlds, with each representing a different work by Lissitzky or one of his contemporaries. The first world, which teaches players the game itself, would be *Beat the Whites with the Red Wedge*. The second would be based on pages from Lissitzky's children's book, *A Suprematist Tale of Two Squares*, in which two squares try to rebuild the world (Figure 16.8) (Lissitzky 2015). The third would be based on a Bauhaus exhibition poster design by Joost Schmidt, who was a student at the Bauhaus when Lissitzky was working with faculty there. The fourth would be *Proun G7*, one of Lissitzky's experiments with shape and form that he called "prouns" (Figure 16.9). The final world would be based on a preliminary sketch for one of Lissitzky's poster designs from 1920 (Figure 16.10).

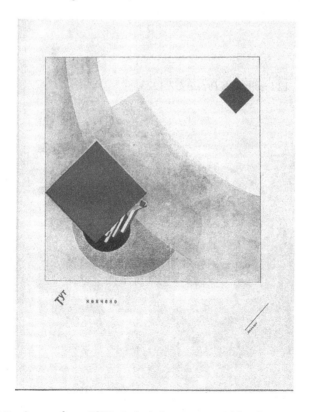

FIGURE 16.8   A page from El Lissitzky's *Suprematist Tale of Two Squares*, 1922.

FIGURE 16.9   El Lissitzky's *Proun G7*, 1923.

FIGURE 16.10   *Preliminary sketch for a Poster* by El Lissitzky, 1920.

As with *Beat the Whites with the Red Wedge*, I derived game mechanics from interpretations of the original artwork. These new mechanics also had to support those derived from *Wedge* and *Yars' Revenge*, as those were the original mechanics of the game. The key to this process was to find places to insert the game's characters into each scene and find some rationale for that scene to exist in the game's world. Some were simple, as they contained elements of *Wedge*, such as the white circle enclosing the Bauhaus logo in Schmidt's poster. For that level, I decided that the shapes in Schmidt's poster, where geometric shapes and lines of several types are assembled into a neat patchwork, should be assembled into their final orientation by players (Figure 16.11). Doing so uncovers the white circle and allows the player to defeat it as they did in the levels based on *Beat the Whites with the Red Wedge* (Figure 16.12).

Other levels required some creative license. In the levels based on the *Suprematist Tale of Two Squares*, the squares became passive characters that had to be moved by the player, where in the original work, they were active in the action of the story (Figure 16.13). Finding interesting interactions between game objects helped this process: the red square in the *Suprematist Tale* levels exploded when it hit the gray safe zones that are beneficial to players. Several portions of this world were modeled after the game *Frogger* (Konami 1981), utilizing the gray squares as the cars that had to be avoided by players carrying the red square (Figure 16.14). Another interesting combination was made with the yellow L-shaped levers in the Schmidt levels which could carry other objects, including the wheels in the *Proun G7* levels to create gear puzzles (Figure 16.15).

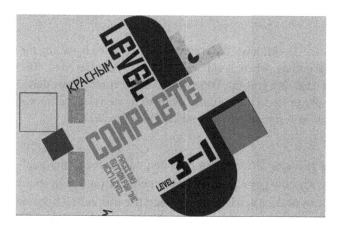

FIGURE 16.11 Moving shapes to create constructions like that in Schmidt's poster is a core element of completing levels in the third world of the game.

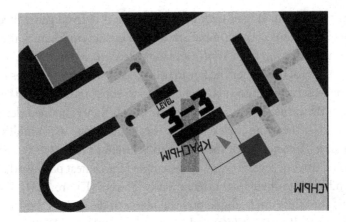

FIGURE 16.12 Moving shapes, as seen in Figure 16.11, uncovers the white circle, which is placed similarly to the white circle in Schmidt's original poster.

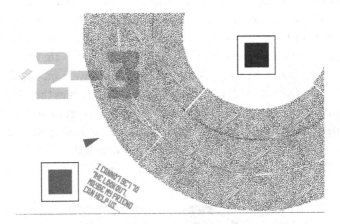

FIGURE 16.13 In this level, the white circle is exposed by taking the red square to the black outline, where it will expand and expose the circle. The red square explodes if it touches gray safe zones, and the darker red square destroys the gray zones. The player has to use the dark square to create a clear path without making it impossible to eventually charge and kill the white circle.

Adding these additional symbols helped me reach my goal of experimenting with how gameplay could create meaning for in-game symbols. If players can make associations between the individual behaviors of each object and an in-game action, then they can make educated guesses of how each works other objects (Totten 2014). From a gameplay standpoint, I had to see if these associations were even discernible by players or if I had

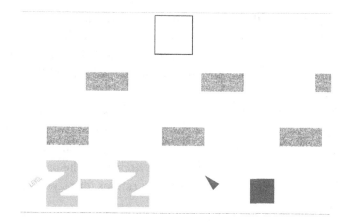

FIGURE 16.14 When carrying the red square, players must avoid the typically safe gray zones or the square will be destroyed, ending the level. This duality allowed me to create a level as an homage to *Frogger*, where players must first avoid the gray zones then utilize them once they've delivered the square to its destination.

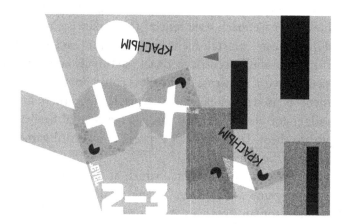

FIGURE 16.15 To extend the functionality of level objects, I designed relationships between objects, such as having yellow L-shaped levers control the position of other objects and having spinning wheels activate one another like gears.

just created a weird abstract art game. To answer these questions, I turned to playtesting.

PLAYTESTING PROCESSES FOR *LISSITZKY'S REVENGE*

The goals of game development that we established earlier in this chapter are evaluated primarily through playtesting. For technical goals, playtesting and quality assurance testing finds glitches that stop the game program from working and other errors that decrease the sense that the game is polished. Likewise, playtesting helps confirm whether the designer's work is both understandable by players and if players find the design enjoyable.

Wishing to balance the game and art goals outlined previously in this chapter, I utilized a targeted playtesting process; taking the game to events that would provide the types of feedback (art-focused or gameplay-focused) I wanted at various stages of development. The process of doing so involved two key elements: preparing questions for playtesters and targeting specific types of playtesters.

Preparing Questions for Playtesters

A frustration for many developers of expressive games is how players at public exhibitions lead conversations toward gameplay-related feedback rather than artistic discussion. To some, this is seen as unfair judgment on their games when they are not asking for it. As stated earlier in the chapter, consumers are used to the gaming magazine method of game discussion, so their feedback style reflects this. Likewise, many independent developers create entertainment-focused games and are looking for entertainment or usability-centric feedback, so this also molds the type of feedback people give at showcase events. It is common, however, for these entertainment-focused developers to go to playtesting situations with prepared questions for players so they can get the type of feedback that is most helpful to them. Developers of expressive or artful games may be well served doing the same.

For *Lissitzky's Revenge* exhibitions, which at the time of this writing have occurred at game developer gatherings, Baltimore's Artscape festival, and the Smithsonian American Art Museum Innovation in Art event, I expected a spectrum of discussions ranging from purely art-driven to purely game-driven and mixes in between. The questions I prepared were based on the goals outlined earlier in the chapter: things designers might want answered by observing players interact with their games. When I playtest, I collect any and all notes I can get from testers, but I also try to go in with a series of questions so I can direct my conversations with players toward the information I want at a specific stage of development. Standard questions for many of the playtests I conduct include some version of "Does my game work?" "Are there places where players get confused when they play?" "Are my players having fun?" "Is the interface clear?" "How is the game's pacing?" and "How much would you pay for this game?" (less applicable here because *Lissitzky's Revenge* is free).

Since *Lissitzky's Revenge* has artistic goals as well, it would be appropriate to implement the same question-asking process, but with questions designed to evaluate these artistic goals. Doing so brings the artistic aspects of art game creation closer to the field of design, which regularly integrates presentation and feedback into the generative process. Gathering feedback for artistic aspects of game creation also helps align artistic goals with the iterative game development process. Based on the artistic goals of the game outlined earlier in the chapter, the questions I prepared for playtests included "Do the graphics of the game create a playable version of Lissitzky's work that captures themes from the original designs?" and "Does gameplay transform the shapes into symbols that players can understand?" After several playtests where I discovered new art goals for the game, I added "Does the game make players think about the commands they are being given by the game?"

Varying Types of Playtesters

For a game with varying types of goals, I determined that targeting playtester groups who could provide the best feedback for each type of goal would be more productive than showing the game randomly.

Game-Centric Feedback

I focused early playtests on gathering game-centric feedback, so I targeted game developer meetups and some of my own game development classes. I've already stated that usability is an important goal for games, but in the case of *Lissitzky's Revenge*, I specifically wished to test each level's solutions for their clarity and the ability of players to find their way through challenges. The mechanics of *Yar's Revenge*, despite being a well-regarded classic arcade game, and therefore, *Lissitzky's Revenge*, are not as direct as the mechanics of many modern games. Likewise, while the abstract artwork of the game lends itself to symbol-making, I wanted to test my process for communicating those symbols to players through game-feel elements.

I also wanted gamer and game developer feedback on the difficulty of the game. I have found that when designing levels of a game, the developer will create something that they feel has a reasonable difficulty and continue adjusting levels to their own standards. When they have others play the game, however, what they thought were easy levels are actually very

FIGURE 16.16 The first several levels teach the player how to play the game by integrating text tutorial information into the graphic design of the level.

difficult for playtesters. I have in other games taken the level I thought would be the first level and moved it to the third or fourth level after finding that it was too difficult for new players. Many level designers fall into this trap, especially ones just starting out.

Showing the game at events with gamers or game developers is ideal for solving these types of issues, as playtesters are articulate in giving feedback on gameplay. For a typical interaction with these testers, I told players the controls of the game, but was otherwise quiet as they played. The game provides text integrated into the graphic design of the courses as a tutorial (Figure 16.16). If I saw them take a long time to solve a course or saw them falter in how to play, I would ask some of the questions I had prepared beforehand. Likewise, if I saw behaviors from players that indicated that they were confused by a symbol, not using a vital game object, or having a difficult time, I would take note of it.

Art-Centric Feedback

I had focused early playtests on game-centric feedback because the issues outlined by game goals are much more foundational to the game as a functional experience. Many art goals can be accomplished with little external input by artists who do proper research to accomplish the work they are attempting—in this case historical research and design analyses of works by and influenced by Lissitzky. However, switching to playtests that targeted art-centric feedback toward the end of development helped hone how the game accomplished its artistic goals. For these tests, I showed the game at art festivals and museum events. Testers at these events were arts patrons and museum administrators. Likewise, I showed the game to colleagues who themselves walked the line between game development and art.

The process of working with these testers was far more conversational than the process I adopted for the gamers. While gathering game-centric playtest information, it is most appropriate to observe how someone naturally uses your game, but for art-centric goals, they are best evaluated by seeing how meaningful the conversation that occurs because of the game is. This is one of the primary differences between games and art and is a sticking point for game makers who consider themselves artists more than developers. The typical goals of games revolve around gaining the approval of audiences through reviews and sales, while many of the goals of contemporary art are centered on making the art a relevant part of a broader conversation. To fail in the game's artistic goals would be having a conversation that ended at, "but this is not like Lissitzky at all because..." or other brick-wall statements that delegitimize the entire work. Someone may not like the individual work, but if there are no brick-wall statements or major gaps in how the developer researched the project, there is still room for meaningful conversation.

By adopting these methods and mind-sets, I was able to get meaningful feedback for *Lissitzky's Revenge*'s design in both the game-centric and art-centric arenas. The next section will outline some of the trends I found while testing with multiple players and how I adjusted the design of *Lissitzky's Revenge*'s levels to solve game issues while maintaining the game's artistic mission.

Findings from Playtests and Adjustments

When filtering feedback from playtests, I look for trends: if you hear something from one playtester it may be just that person's opinion, but if you see trends across multiple playtests you should pay attention. This section will discuss the trends I found during the playtests of *Lissitzky's Revenge*, the adjustments I made to the game while maintaining the game's artistic mission, and what this process says about balancing art and gameplay goals in art games.

Fixing Information Design

Perhaps the biggest challenge during the design of *Lissitzky's Revenge* was communicating the procedure for beating each level to players. Many were initially confused by the need to charge before being able to defeat the white circle and that the gray squares were where they gained their charge. The elements that I had added to signify this process in my first versions were

- Textual directions in the background of tutorial levels in gray lettering
- The player would flash red and orange when charging
- Another particle effect that emitted when players' attack was charged
- The player had a particle effect follow them when they were charged

Upon playtesting, it was discovered that few players read the directions in the background either because they did not stand out very well or because the player admitted to not reading text in video games. Likewise, the signifiers for the charging process were unclear to players. Some even suggested that they would like to see a particle effect play while the wedge was charging when one already was! Among the changes they suggested were changing the shape of the wedge into something else when they were charged and using more particles to show charging.

These suggestions are important as they demonstrate the difficulty of balancing art and gameplay goals. What players may find clear, such as changing the shape of the wedge into something else, could destroy the game's artistic mission of preserving the iconography and violence of the red wedge, so I had to ignore the suggestion of changing its shape. However, some other state changes applied to the wedge were not out of the question. The elements that I originally utilized to signify the charging process were flashing, then a particle, then another, different particle. I reshuffled some of these effects so they could be better indicators based on tester feedback. The list of signifiers in the final version is

- Textual directions in the background of tutorial levels in black lettering
- The player would emit a particle effect when charging
- Another, larger particle effect that emitted when players' attack was charged
- A sound effect when the attack was charged

- The player had a particle effect follow them when they were charged

- The player would flash red and orange when they were charged

I wanted tutorial information to be subtle, so I shied away from creating a sequence that stopped gameplay. To make the existing tutorial text more prominent, I made it black. While this did not solve all problems of people ignoring the text, significantly more players saw the text and understood the game. Likewise, the remixing of the indicating particles and the flashing wedge to this order communicated much better to players. The flashing wedge communicated power to players without needing a form change. Likewise, the flash could be programmed so that when the game action stopped at the end of levels, the resulting image resembled a constructivist artwork.

Information Design in Level Design

As I was conducting these playtests, I was still building later levels of the game. I took some of the lessons from studying player reactions to the game's information design and integrated them into the designs of more complex puzzles later in the game. In addition to how players learn the game with game-feel building elements, such as particle effects and sound effects, level design was another important component of controlling how players learned game mechanics. An important element for levels that taught new mechanics were skill gates—areas that would not allow players to pass unless they completed a specific gameplay action. These gates are not gates in the literal closed-door sense, but in the sense that they are an obstacle that players must overcome using one of their avatar's abilities. This is a great element for teaching players mechanics, as a player must enact new mechanics to move forward, and the gate itself can be an object that the player comes to associate with the mechanic (Figure 16.17).

Another important element of information design in level design is the order in which levels are presented to players. The order outlined earlier in the chapter, while making some stylistic sense—earlier levels use a black/white/red palette while later levels use other colors—resulted in a very uneven difficulty curve. Mechanically, the player encountered basic gameplay elements in the first level, character escort in the second, escorting and mechanism manipulation in the third, then a much simpler level fourth, and then the finale of the game. Wanting a much smoother transition and to lower the sense that the fourth world was a throwaway level mechanically, I changed the order in which players reached each level.

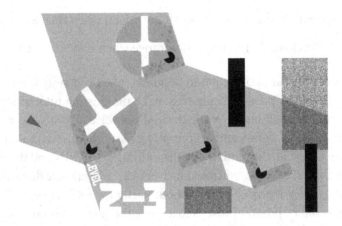

FIGURE 16.17 This screenshot shows the level in which players learn about yellow levers. When players hit one, it activates another in the level. This level begins with a lever blocking the player from progressing, so they must learn to activate the lever to move onward.

Here, playtesting was important for understanding which worlds players found easy and which they had difficulty with, resulting in an educated level order that guided players through the game's mechanics properly. The final order was the *Beat the Whites with the Red Wedge* world (featuring basic gameplay introductions) first, *Proun G7* (spinning wheels and levers) second, *Suprematist Tale of Two Squares* (character escort) third, Schmidt's Bauhaus poster (character escort and levers) fourth, and Lissitzky's blue poster design fifth.

These methods are key to one of the artistic goals of *Lissitzky's Revenge*: exploring how abstract symbols can be assigned meaning through gameplay. Elements such as particles and sound effects give feedback to players as they interact with a game. Likewise, the way symbolic game objects are arranged in a scene affects how and when players encounter these objects. The order that a player interacts with symbolic objects can greatly impact their understanding of these objects' functions. Based on playtests, this goal was a success. However, the goal of exploring a game's propagandistic effects had not fully been explored.

BREAKING THE RULES OF YOUR OWN DESIGN SYSTEMS FOR ART

One playtester commented that the tone of the tutorial text in the first several levels of the game was authoritarian, as though the red wedge was taking orders. Earlier, I had referred to several of the game objects—the wedge, circle, and squares—as characters. I had never thought of the textual instructions as similarly anthropomorphized, but decided to pursue the text in levels as competing voices vying for the allegiance of the wedge. Throughout the game's levels, I put black blocks as obstacles. If players attacked these blocks as they attacked the black blocks in the first world, they would move. I saw this as an opportunity to introduce the dissenting voice of the game. In several levels, I placed text that was the same color as the background. If players pushed the black boxes into the right place, this text would reveal itself and deliver messages contradicting the antiwhite-circle tutorial text (Figure 16.18). As the player approaches the final world, these messages become more frequent.

The final world is where the propaganda topic of the game comes to a head and allows the player to question the morality of the game's prescribed mechanics. To represent this, I created designs with combinations of objects familiar to players, but changed the outcomes of these interactions. For example, I had levels where the red square could be placed into its usual goal, but instead of revealing the white circle, a yellow wedge is fired at the red square, destroying it. The game essentially makes the player execute their comrade (emphasized by text placed next to the square that says "for the cause") (Figure 16.19). This implementation of the red square puzzle provides a twist ending to its usual outcome where the square helps the player find solutions to puzzles. It is also repeated twice: the first time is a surprise, while the second time the player must do the deed with knowledge of their act.

FIGURE 16.18   In this shot, the player has uncovered some dissenting text by pushing the black square into the proper place in a level. This quote uses the nature of the in-game tutorial from the first world, in which the white circle does not attack the player in the first level so players can learn the game's basics, to accuse the player of attacking first.

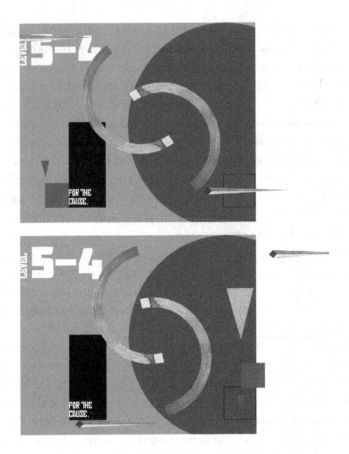

FIGURE 16.19 These shots show a subversion of the player's typical interactions with the red square character. The level design is intended to tell the story of the player executing the red circle and the circle wishing it for the betterment of their cause (shown through text placed next to the square itself.)

These interactions lead to a recreation of the first level where the player can either kill the white circle or walk away (Figure 16.20). Many of the game's core symbols are subverted here, including having the black square only move when players throws themselves into the lethal yellow square. Throughout the final world, subverting the system set up in previous levels became a way to create shocking experiences that forced players to think about the meaning of the symbols and commands that the game was giving them. As an artistic goal, this was evaluated by the quality of discussion that players had about the topic as they experienced the propaganda elements. However, a weakness of this system was that it

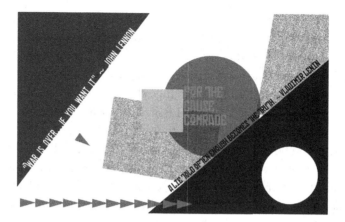

FIGURE 16.20 The truth is revealed in the game's final level. The player cannot uncover the white circle the normal way, but must instead throw their character into the yellow square (yellow was previously revealed as lethal) multiple times to do so. Each time the wedge is replaced by another from the lineup of extra troops below. The player can alternatively walk away from the scene and defy their superior's orders.

took several levels to set up, and few players at public events where there were other things to do and play stayed long enough to reach the final world.

CONCLUSION

This chapter described a process for finding balance between gameplay goals and artistic goals when making artistically motivated games. It described several goals of both media then described the development and playtesting processes utilized for the game *Lissitzky's Revenge*, which was trying to both be a fun video game and fulfill artistic goals of exploring a famous artist's work, playing with how games use gameplay to assign meaning to in-game symbols and make players question the propagandistic nature of game mechanics and tutorials.

To balance the often dissonant goals of gameplay and art, it is best for game developers to prepare a series of questions for their testers so they may direct discussion of the game toward getting helpful feedback. Likewise, targeting specific audiences for answering either art or gameplay-centered questions is beneficial. Game players will focus on things they either approve or disapprove of in a game prototype, while art viewers will pause to have intense conversations about a piece.

Through this process during the development of *Lissitzky's Revenge*, it was observed that feedback from these groups must be carefully balanced, as they are often contradictory: what may be good for gameplay may be harmful to artistic goals and vice versa. In the case of *Lissitzky's Revenge*, players wanted the red wedge to change shape while art patrons enjoyed the ability to play as the hero of Lissitzky's poster unaltered. The best course of action was to utilize other tools in the game maker's visual communication toolbox to create a compromise. While less direct, additional signifiers and creative introductions to gameplay mechanics allowed players to learn how to play while keeping the artistic elements intact.

While playtesting is often a process of testing and confirmation for level and game designs, here it demonstrated its power to be a powerful tool for ideation. Through playtesting, discussions of the art led to new narrative ideas for the game that strengthened the game's artistic goals. The goal of creating a game that makes players think about propaganda motivated me to think more deeply about how I communicated the meanings of in-game symbols to players. Likewise, confirming that the system I had set up for communicating these symbols through playtesting allowed me to master the system in such a way that I could confidently subvert it later on. Playtesting, then, becames a process by which designers can master their own designs and create exciting new implementations of them.

Fully embracing the iterative process of playtesting for a work that had artistic motivations was potentially counterproductive, but with proper preparation of the method and proper analysis of outcomes, it became an invaluable tool. Playtesting not only confirmed the value of the art, but also helped me find further depth to my work that I would not have found on my own. For *Lissitzky's Revenge*, this resulted in attention from not only museums and art festivals, but also publications such as *Kill Screen* and the New York online art magazine *Hyperallergic*. I am looking forward to using this style of playtesting in future games within the Atelier Games series and future level designs.

REFERENCES

Atari. 1981. *Yars' Revenge*. Atari 2600 game.

Beat the Whites with the Red Wedge. 2016. *WikiArt*. Accessed January 5. http://www.wikiart.org/en/el-lissitzky/beat-the-whites-with-the-red-wedge-1920.

Bogost, Ian. 2007. *Persuasive Games: The Expressive Power of Videogames*. Cambridge, MA: MIT Press.

Braun, Alexander, and Winsor McCay. 2014. *Winsor McCay: The Complete Little Nemo*. Los Angeles: Taschen America.

Campbell, Colin. 2013. How to tackle gaming's lack of racial diversity. *Polygon*. http://www.polygon.com/2013/9/16/4728320/how-to-tackle-gamings-lack -of-racial-diversity.

Decherney, Peter. 2012. *Hollywood and the Culture Elite: How the Movies Became American*. New York: Columbia University Press.

Donovan, Tristan. 2010. *Replay: The History of Video Games*. East Sussex, UK: Yellow Ant.

Duro, Paul. 2007. Imitation and authority: The creation of the academic canon in French art, 1648–1870. In *Partisan Canons*, edited by Anna Brzyski. Durham, NC: Duke University Press.

Ebert, Roger. 2010. Okay, kids, play on my lawn. *Roger Ebert's Journal*. http://www .rogerebert.com/rogers-journal/okay-kids-play-on-my-lawn.

El Lissitzky. 2015. *About Two Squares: A Suprematist Tale of Two Squares in Six Constructions*. Mustang, OK: Tate Publishing.

Holmes, Tiffany. 2003. Arcade classics spawn art? Current trends in the art game genre. In Melbourne DAC2003, 46–52. http://hypertext.rmit.edu.au/dac /papers/Holmes.pdf.

Konami. 1981. *Frogger*. Arcade game.

Manchel, Frank. 1990. *Film Study: An Analytical Bibliography*, Volume 1. Madison, NJ: Fairleigh Dickinson University Press.

Meggs, Phillip B., and Alston W. Purvis, eds. 2011. *Meggs' History of Graphic Design*, Fifth Edition. San Francisco: Wiley.

Murray, Christopher John, ed. 2013. *Encyclopedia of the Romantic Era, 1760–1850*. New York: Fitzroy Dearborn.

Nintendo. 2000. *The Legend of Zelda: Majora's Mask*. Nintendo 64 game.

Norman, Donald. 2013. *The Design of Everyday Things: Revised and Expanded Edition*. New York: Basic Books.

Ormiston, Rosamund. 2014. *50 Art Styles You Should Know*. New York: Prestel.

Papathanasis, Andreas. 2015. The tech arms race in AAA—And why I'm aban- doning it. *Gamasutra*. http://gamasutra.com/blogs/AndreasPapathanasis /20150601/244768/The_tech_arms_race_in_AAA__and_why_Im_abandon ing_it.php.

Pie for Breakfast Studios. 2015. Atelier Games—About. http://ateliergames.tumblr .com/about.

Rogers, Scott. 2010. *Level Up! The Guide To Great Game Design*. San Francisco: Wiley.

Ryan, Simon. 2015. Auteur theory. Australian Catholic University Academic Staff Pages. Accessed December 31. http://dlibrary.acu.edu.au/staffhome/siryan /screen/auteur theory.htm.

Sharp, John. 2015. *Works of Game: On the Aesthetics of Games and Art*. Cambridge, MA: MIT Press.

Swink, Steve. 2008. *Game Feel*. Amsterdam: Morgan Kaufman Game Design.

Totten, Christopher W. 2011. Games aren't art, they're architecture. *Video Game Writers*. http://videogamewriters.com/games-arent-art-theyre-architecture-7752.

Totten, Christopher W. 2014. *An Architectural Approach to Level Design*. Boca Raton, FL: CRC Press.

Totten, Christopher W. 2015. *Lissitzky's Revenge*. Web and PC game.

Conclusion

Throughout the text, we have seen writers who are game players or for whom their gameplaying and work with level design have made a significant impact in their lives or careers. Likewise, we have seen designers who bring a particular viewpoint and builders who use approaches both cerebral and practical for their work. Lastly, we saw some of these designers come full circle, showing their work to new players who may find their own inspirations in today's gamespaces.

When I teach, I like to tell students that the game industry is a house with a very well locked front door but all the windows open. The reasons I say this is to show them that while there are some direct paths into the industry with hurdles to overcome (getting a job in a studio, joining academia, etc.), we are also in a state where significant contributions are being made to games by people—both professional and independent—armed with their passion for the medium. One of my goals of this project was to provide a candid look at how people involved with games at multiple levels view the worlds of games. I did not think that would come from a book of only industry writings or only academic writings. Instead, I looked for the gamer, the big industry vet, the indie, the academic, and other voices that could provide a snapshot of what people in games today think about game worlds.

As stated in the introduction, we have gotten ourselves into the habit of writing about the games themselves and not the things that make up games. Alternatively, there are whole communities who break games into parts—game music cover bands, artists, cosplayers, designers, developers, and so on—and have a great understanding of what makes gamespaces and worlds memorable, who are not having their voices counted. We have not yet "figured out games," whatever that means, and cannot rest on the laurels of previous dissections of the medium or methods of analysis. We have to find knowledge both outside of games and within the communities that explore them on a daily basis—professional, hobbyist, or otherwise.

The voices in this volume have, through their diverse perspectives, shown us that there are still many possibilities for new knowledge in level design. Likewise, other possibilities exist in taking deeper dives into the games themselves to delineate how their individual components can inspire their own bodies of analytical work. These multiple views have shown us, above other things, that there is no one way to create game levels. As I highlighted at the beginning of this volume, it is beyond one author to give an accurate picture of what happens within a designer's mind as they work. Instead, this collection of authors has shown that there are many tools and many, many approaches available to level designers. In many cases, they have also shown that while a deep knowledge of games is not necessary for great level design, it certainly helps, or at least makes level design less daunting. Throughout every section are citations of games that have inspired designers and made them think deeply about how to create meaningful gamespaces. Hopefully, these writings and the games you make and play will provide your own inspirations to help you create the next "great game worlds."

Index

Page numbers followed by f indicate figures.

Printed in the United States
by Baker & Taylor Publisher Services